PASTEL
INNOVATIONS

60+ TECHNIQUES AND EXERCISES FOR PAINTING WITH PASTELS

dawn emerson

NORTH LIGHT BOOKS

CONTENTS

MATERIALS

Don't feel like you need to have all of these products in order to start painting and creating. Begin with the techniques that require materials you already have or the basic necessities: Pastels, paper and ink. Then ,as you progress through the book, add a few new tools and materials as they strike your fancy. Pretty soon you will know what suits you and where your passions lie, and you'll have the tools and materials you need to follow your pastel painting dreams.

- General's Jumbo Compressed Charcoal, 2B, 4B, 6B
- pastel sticks
- PanPastel
- pencils
- wax crayons
- sumi ink
- Akua blending medium
- Akua Intaglio ink
- water-miscible oil paint
- watercolors
- paintbrushes
- fan brush
- brayer
- palette knife
- kneaded eraser
- hard plastic eraser
- cosmetic wedge
- paper towels
- newsprint pad, 18" × 24" (41CM × 61CM)
- drawing paper
- Stonehenge paper
- Rives BFK paper
- freezer paper
- colored cardstock
- standing easel
- plastic plates, 9" × 12" (23CM × 30CM)
- digital camera
- photo editing software
- pin press
- glass surface
- timer
- masking tape
- scissors
- knitting needle
- comb
- textured objects
- cotton swabs
- baby wipes
- plastic card (like credit card)
- razor blade
- color wheel
- liquid dish soap
- spoon
- small bowl
- leaves
- reference photos

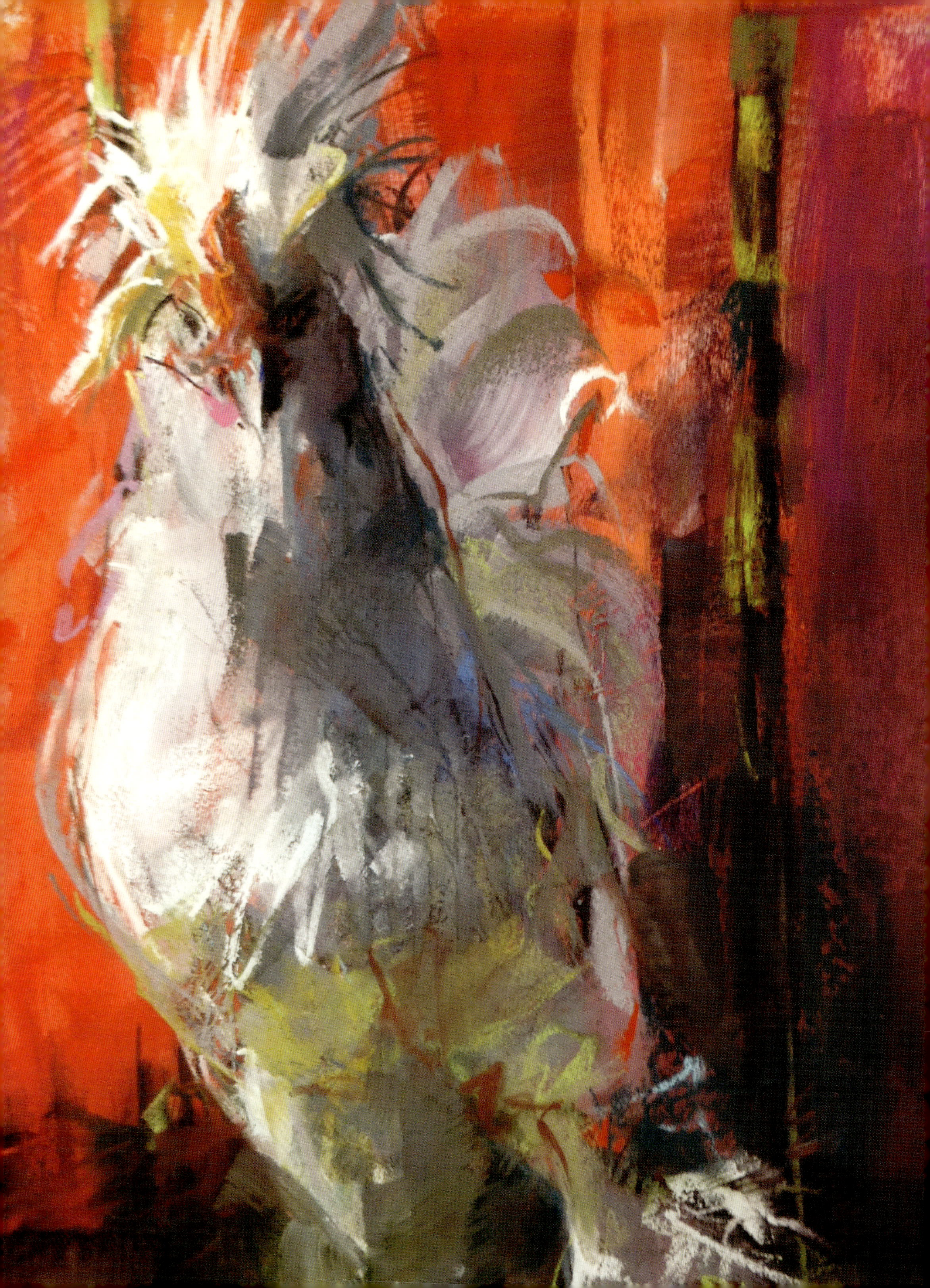

INTRODUCTION

This book is about learning to experience art-making rather than reproducing images. My belief is that it doesn't matter what subject you paint—or even what you paint with—but how you see what you paint and how you express it. I've spent countless hours playing in the studio experimenting with tools and materials just for the joy of exploring. Honestly, if I had only one image to paint for the rest of my life, my goal would be to make it a new experience each time I painted it, and I would try to find as many ways as I could to make each one unique and beautiful.

This book is designed to present the language of art—the elements and principles—in a more inviting and poetic way that will encourage you to rethink everything you do with respect to painting with pastel and mixed media. I'd like to challenge you to question what a drawing is or could be. I'd like you to go back to using simple, inexpensive materials and tools and do a lot of everything rather than one precious piece. Each time you do so, you'll find you can let go of expectations, relax and enjoy the process of making art.

The worst things you can do to yourself are:
- use a support that is very expensive and that you only have one of
- use your most precious colors and materials
- use a picture reference that is perfectly cropped
- keep noodling away at something that should have been thrown out an hour ago
- ask your significant other his or her opinion

The best things you can do for yourself are:
- use humble materials like newsprint and drawing paper so you can PLAY
- use all the materials you've been collecting for decades
- take photographs that give you lots of options for design
- do many versions of a painting, stop often, and stop early
- explore and judge for yourself

My approach to painting has dramatically changed over the years because of the influence printmaking has had on me over the last decade. I have reconsidered everything I thought I knew about drawing in order to free myself of negative judgement and expectations, and it has been a transformative experience. I now feel more excited to paint than ever, and I can't wait to see what will happen in the studio! I truly hope this book helps you feel the same way.

~ DAWN

SATURDAY NIGHT FEVER / 22" × 15" (56CM × 38CM) / OIL PAINT, PASTEL, CHARCOAL, COLOR PENCIL ON MIXED-MEDIA PAPER

MATERIALS

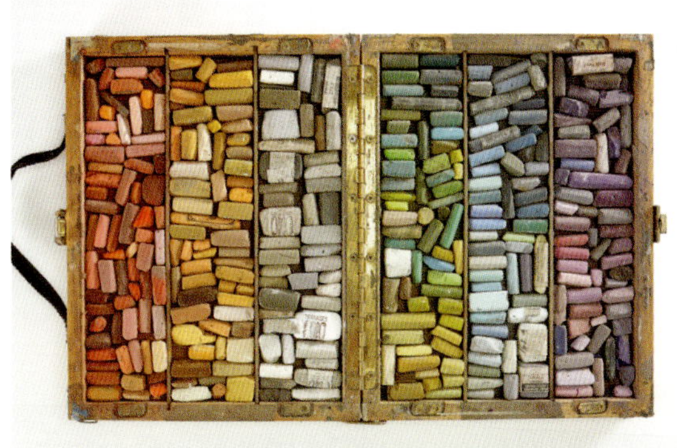

STICK PASTELS

I use many different brands of pastels sticks, both hard and soft. Among my favorites are Great American, Diane Townsend Terrages and Blue Earth. Because I draw most often with the side of the pastel, I remove all wrapping, break them in half, and arrange them in a carrying box by color and value.

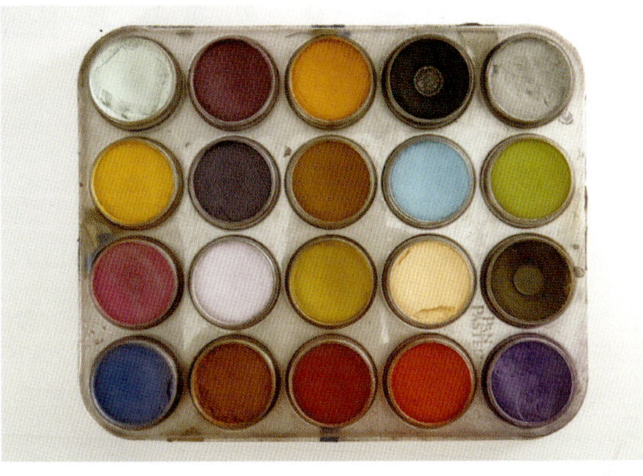

PANPASTELS

These highly pigmented pastels are wonderful for using in conjunction with stick pastels. I find them to be useful for adding transparent color over monotypes, for using with stencils, and for layering imagery and color. They are less powdery than most stick pastels, are erasable, and are easy to transport.

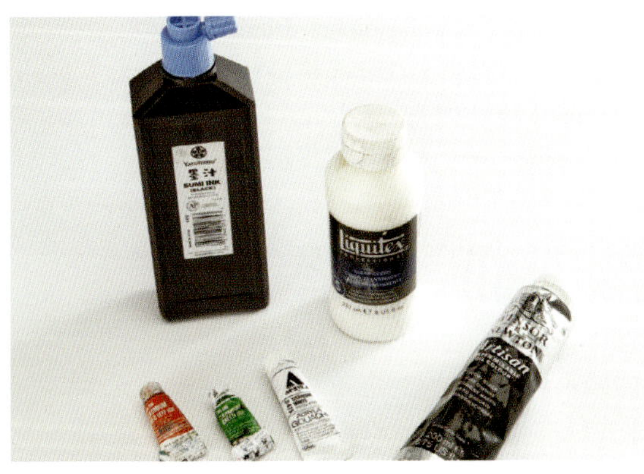

WET MEDIA

Sumi ink, water-based oil paints, watercolor, gouache and clear gesso are all media I use with pastel, because they dry with the same matte finish as pastel. Water-miscible oil can be rolled with a brayer for monotypes, trace monotypes and brayer drawing.

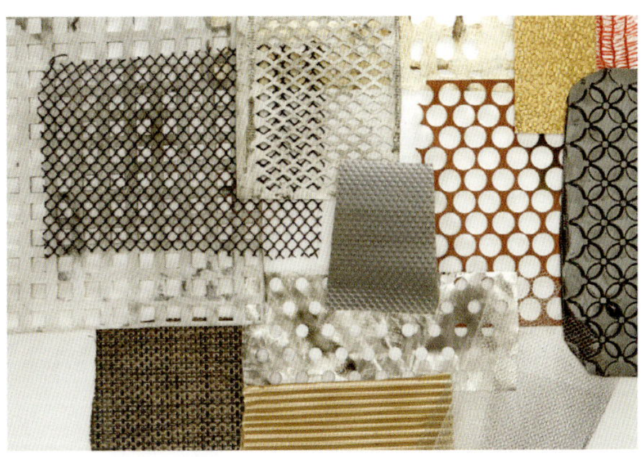

TEXTURES AND STENCILS

A personal collection of textures and stencils is essential for incorporating frottage, stamping, offsetting, stamping, rollography and printmaking into your work. Textures can become important signature elements in your work and can inspire your creativity in ways you never imagined.

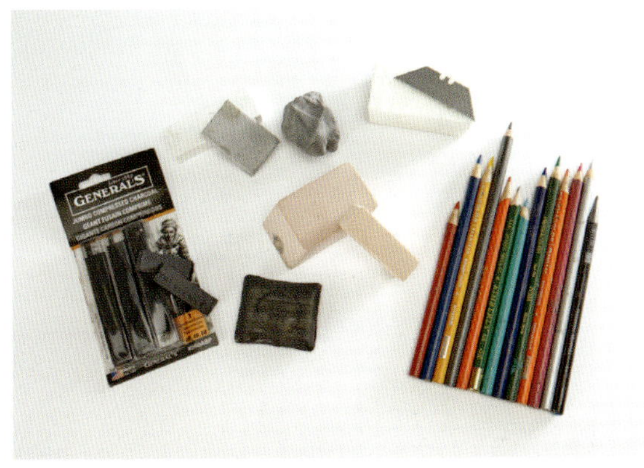

DRY MEDIA AND ERASURE MATERIALS TO USE WITH PASTEL

Virtually any dry medium can be used with pastel. I use General's Jumbo compressed charcoal for the bulk of my drawing and sketching because it comes in three hardnesses and isn't messy like other compressed charcoals. It has a wide surface for easy gripping, and flat, sharp edges for making calligraphic marks. Colored pencils and ink crayons both work with pastel.

For erasure and mark-making, both a soft, kneaded eraser and hard plastic one are necessary. A flat razor blade is great for scratching through pastel. Sofft sponge applicators are shown, as well as a "smoosher," a piece of compressed foam I use to smear dry materials.

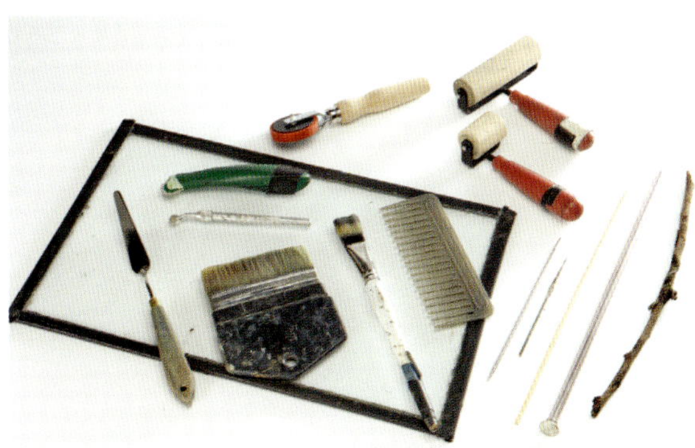

INK APPLICATION AND REMOVAL TOOLS

You will need a glass surface or flat plate to roll out ink and paint, an assortment of soft rubber brayers, a collection of brushes, sticks, baby wipes, rags, netting, credit cards, cotton swabs, foam, sponge, combs and anything else you can think of for applying and removing ink or paint.

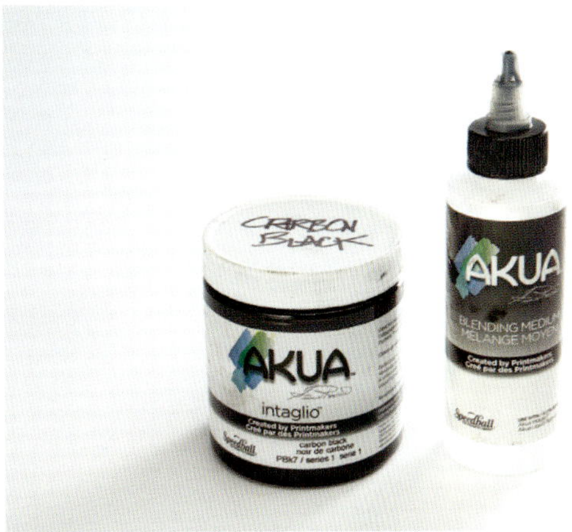

AKUA INTAGLIO PRINTMAKING INK AND BLENDING MEDIUM

Speedball's Akua Intaglio ink is perfect for making monotypes on or off the press. Because the ink will not dry on a nonporous surface, you have plenty of time to create! It cleans up with dish soap and water or hand wipes, and it dries to a matte finish. Instead of water, use blending medium to make the Intaglio ink more brushable. Blending medium is thinner and less viscous than Intaglio ink and will resist it as a result.

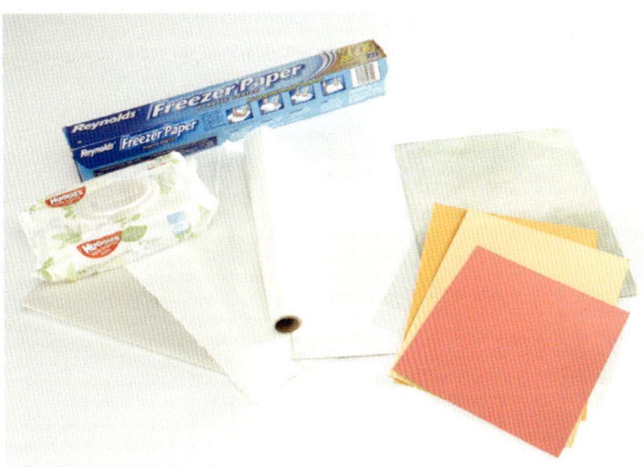

TRANSFER PAPERS, PRINTING PLATES, PRINTMAKING PAPERS

Nonporous papers like freezer paper, wax paper, parchment paper, cellophane, glass, acrylic and polycarbonate can be used as "plates" or ink carriers for handprinting and transfer processes. When using a press, glass is not advisable. Even absorbent papers like newsprint, cardboard, glossy papers, and color bookmaking papers can be used as printing or transfer plates. For printmaking and embossing, inexpensive papers like Stonehenge and Rives BFK work well. Baby wipes are perfect for quick clean-up and ink or paint removal.

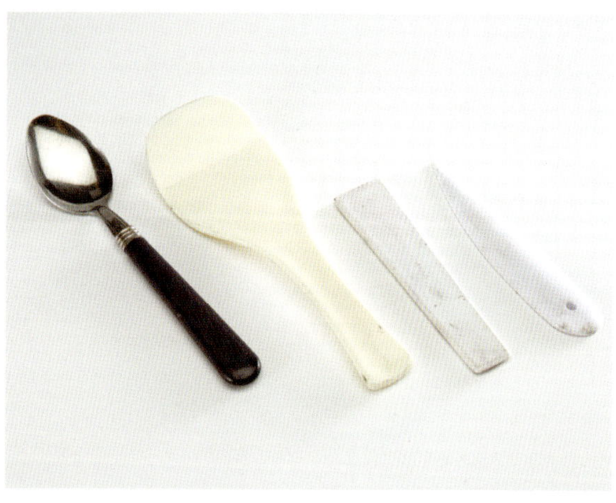

TOOLS FOR PRINTING BY HAND

Rubbing with the back of a spoon, a plastic spatula
or plastic or Teflon paper-folders can all be used to
transfer an inked image to a paper surface. Depending
on the size of your work, find a tool that feels
comfortable in your hand and does not cause fatigue.

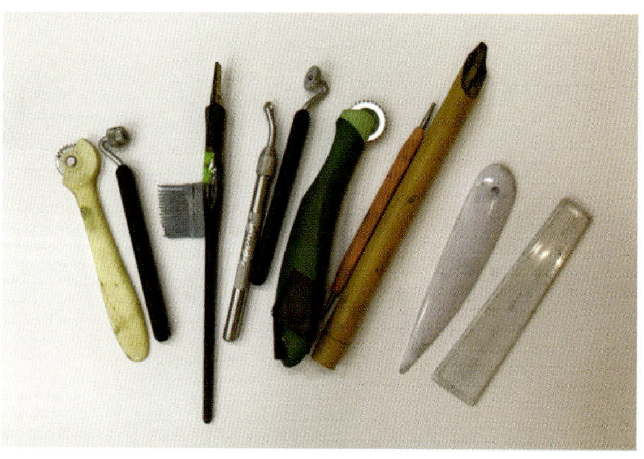

MARK-MAKING TOOLS

Almost anything can be used to make marks
including tracing wheels, combs, pens and clay
tools. Thrift stores are wonderful places to scrounge
for new tools.

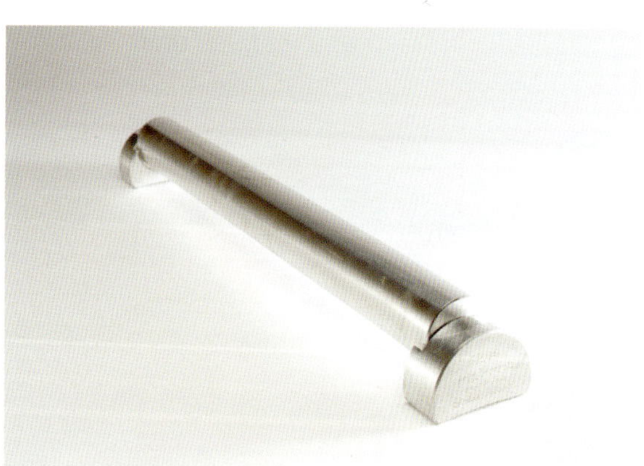

AKUA PIN PRESS

Ergonomically designed and portable for printing
off press with Akua Inks, this economical and hefty
rolling pin is a great alternative to rubbing by hand
or purchasing a press.

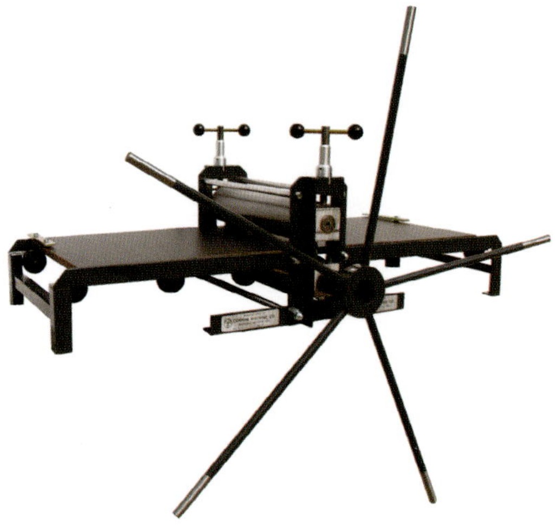

PRINTING PRESS

A press like this table top Conrad monotype printing
press is perfect for doing monotypes. (Image provided
by Conrad Machine Company.)

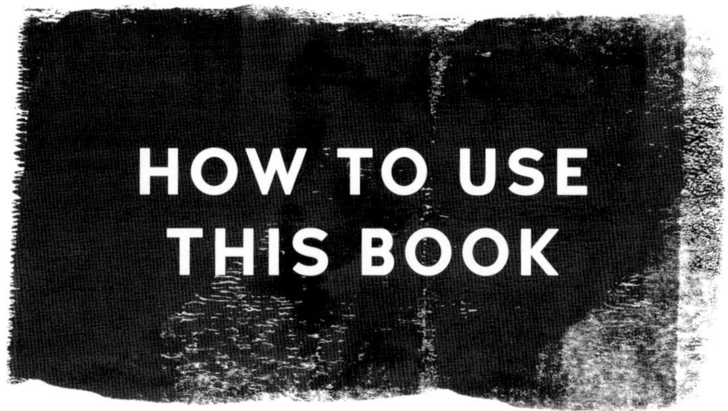

This book is about learning to engage in the process of painting with pastel
and mixed media in a way that will help you be more creative and happy with
your work. To use this book, I would suggest going through the book from
beginning to end. Each chapter builds on the one before it, and exercises at
the end of chapters 1–5 offer hands-on practice for material presented in
the chapter. You will see that each topic is discussed in a two-page spread to
allow you to open the book flat and try what you see. I hope you'll mess up the
book and get your hands dirty.

chapter 1

A FRESH LOOK AT THE VOCABULARY OF ART

If you've ever watched young children draw, you've probably seen them become totally absorbed as they develop their imagery. Their entire body seems to move the crayon as the tool records their energy and movement like a seismograph. Their subjects are alive to them, and even the crayons seem to take on character. This is the "getting lost in our art" that we all strive for.

In this chapter I ask you to imagine you are a child again as you explore the seven elements and seven principles of composition and design as though you were learning about them for the very first time. In this exploration of the language of art you will find new ways to engage your imagination and express your emotions. No matter what your level of experience with drawing or with the pastel medium, this is an opportunity to experience the magic and joy of making marks again.

At the end of this chapter you will be guided through exercises that explore the seven elements and seven principles of composition and design a little more. Included with these exercises is my approach to self-critique which I use to help me keep growing as an artist. This begins a process that will be repeated throughout the book as you dig into the tools and techniques presented here and work to integrate them into your own growth as an artist.

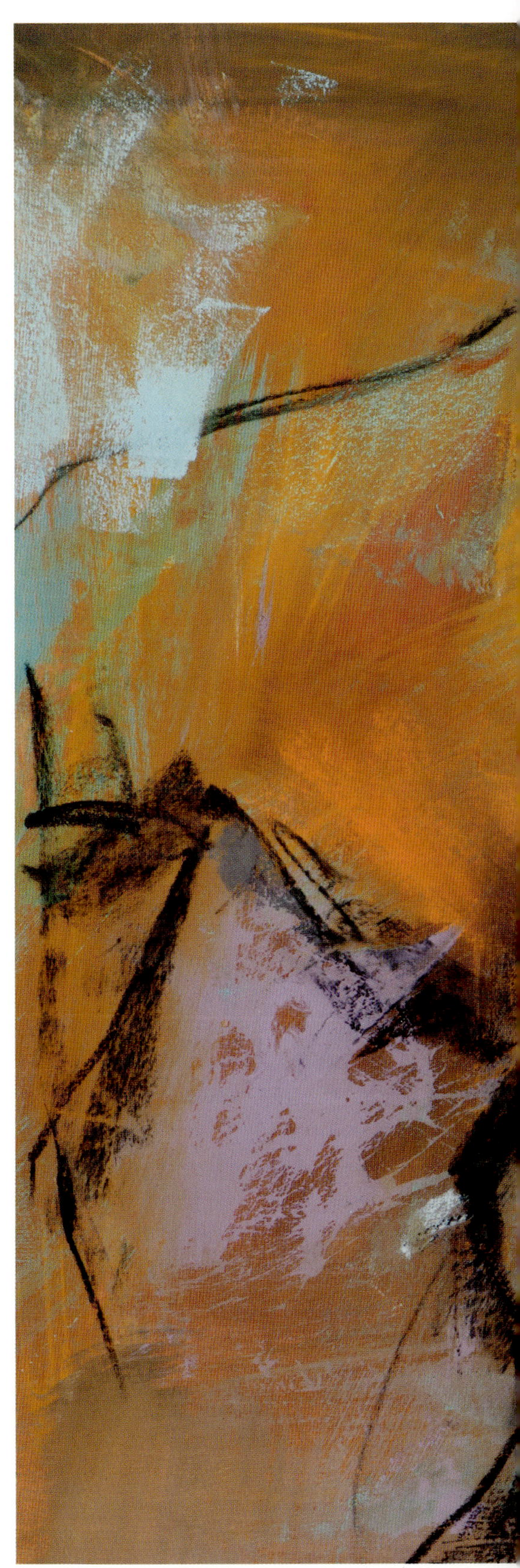

CAVE BUFFALO / 22" × 30"(56CM × 76CM) / MIXED MEDIA (ACRYLIC, PASTEL, CHARCOAL) ON BOARD

This image expresses the love I have for pastel, and the power of simple line and beautiful color.

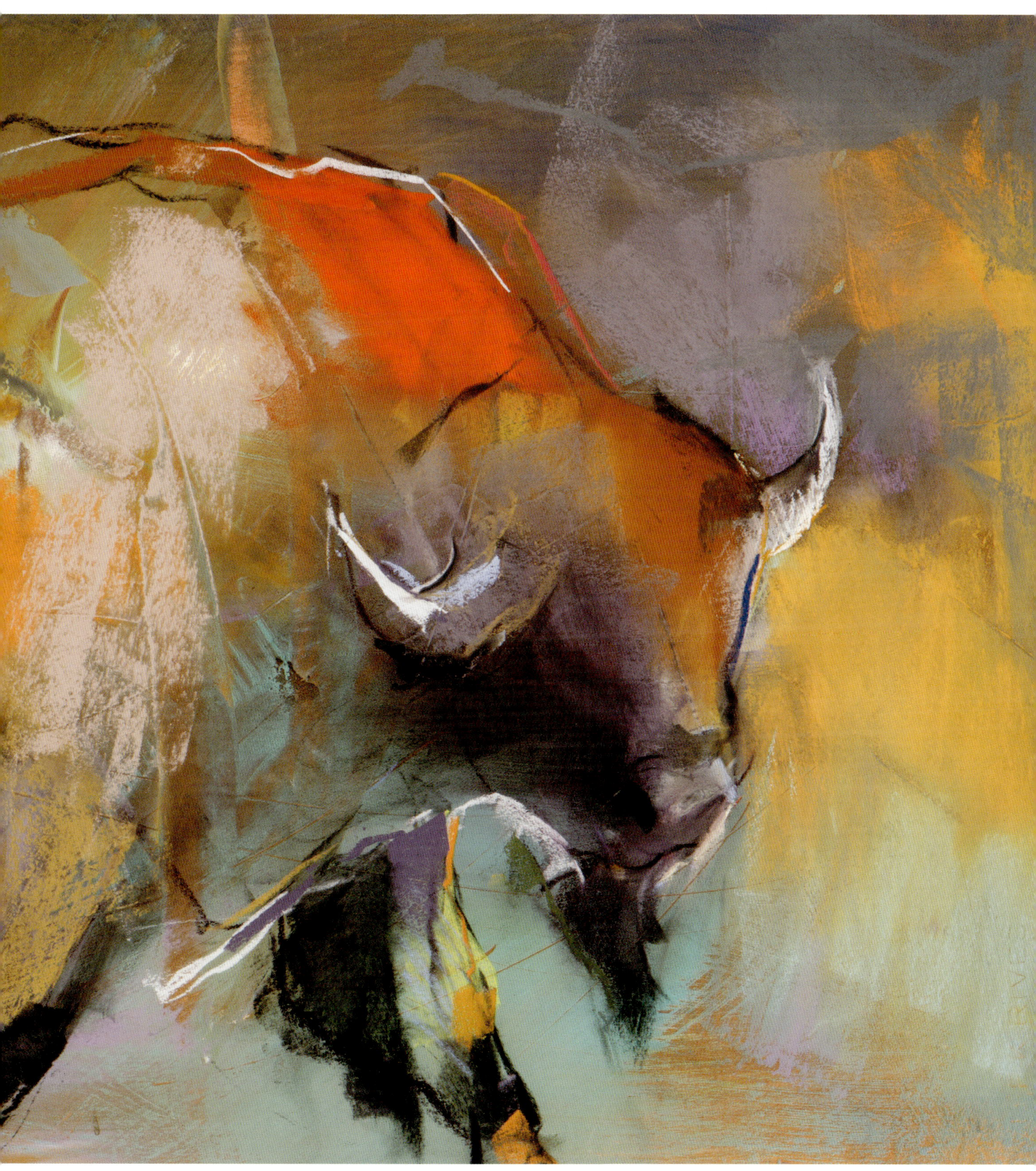

THE SEVEN ELEMENTS OF ART

The seven elements of art are what the artist uses to describe their imagery. You may have learned some version of this list but may not have deeply studied the role each element plays in creating imagery. As you read, note that each element is presented individually, but it is the interaction among and the relationships between them that create the story the artist wishes to tell. Each element conveys a distinct character and records the energy of the mark-maker in the process. It is important to know that any of the elements can describe or even be the subject of your painting.

The seven elements are defined below, first in the traditional manner you may have already learned and then in a more poetic way. This alternative interpretation will hopefully inspire new ways of thinking about each element and the way they can contribute to the overall work.

LINE

Traditional: Line is the path of a point moving through space that may be two- or three-dimensional, implied or abstract.

Innovative: Line is the seismographic record of a mark that conveys its speed, emotion, weight and shape.

SHAPE

Traditional: Shape is created when a line crosses itself or intersects with other lines to enclose a space. Shapes can be geometric or organic.

Innovative: Shape is a gang of marks that hang out together as a unit.

TEXTURE

Traditional: Texture refers to the tactile qualities of a surface or to the visual representation of surface qualities.

Innovative: Texture makes your eyes remember what your hand and heart felt when it touched something.

EDGES

Traditional: An edge is the boundary of a shape or the intersection of two or more shapes.

Innovative: Edges are the different contours the eye detects as it surveys the visual landscape of an image.

VALUE

Traditional: Degrees of lightness and darkness that are used to describe an image.

Innovative: Value is the architect that builds structure with light and shadow.

COLOR

Traditional: Color comprises hue, saturation and intensity.

Innovative: Color is the harmony the artist adds to their mark-making melody.

SPACE

Traditional: Artistic space refers to the boundaries of the surface a work of art is made on, the way the surface is divided, and the kind of dimensional illusion a work creates for the viewer.

Innovative: Space is the stage where the elements dance together to perform their magic.

THE SEVEN PRINCIPLES OF ART

The principles of design and composition are used to organize the elements. Identifying problems with an artwork, or evaluating when your work is finished ,is made easier when you use these principles as a guide for objectively looking at your work. The seven principles I find most useful are listed below.

Rather than try to define the principle, I have provided a set of questions that I ask myself that help me assess how this principle is expressed in a particular image. When I have a problem with an artwork, my process of evaluation is to take inventory of each of the elements of art, and then to see how they are working to achieve each of the principles. I'll use this process over and over until the piece feels finished. This process of evaluating your work will be discussed later in the chapter.

UNITY AND HARMONY

- Does the work seem complete? Do the elements seem to be working well together to support the main "character," or are they fighting with each other or vying for attention?
- Does the work feel like the same person made it, or do some parts seem out of character?
- Do certain areas seem unresolved or tentative?

VARIETY AND CONTRAST

- Is there enough (or too much) variation among the elements to keep the viewer's attention? Or does there seem to be an overall sameness that makes things boring?
- Do elements relate to each other in a way that makes things too even or predictable?
- Do I have enough variation of sizes—small, medium and large?
- Does any element stand out by being unique or different from those around it?

DOMINANCE AND EMPHASIS

- What grabs my attention first, and why? Is that where I want the viewer's eye to go?
- Is there a visual hierarchy that makes it clear when one thing is more important than something else?
- Is there an element which is the star of the show and which is being supported by the other elements?

MOVEMENT AND DIRECTION

- How is the viewer's eye led through the composition?
- Where or why does our eye leave the image?
- Is there anything that impedes or distracts eye movement, and if so, is it intentional?
- Are there angles, curves, arrows or implied movements or undercurrents that prevent the viewer from exploring the entire piece?

SCALE AND PROPORTION

- Is there a way to tell how large or small, distant or close the image is?
- What is the eye level of the viewer and how does this affect the response we have to the image?
- Do we feel a relationship of the parts of the image to the whole? How does the format of the work help or hinder the image?

REPETITION, RHYTHM AND PATTERN

- Is there a visual beat that helps or hinders the viewing of the image, and if so, what role does it play in creating movement, mood or structure?
- Is the use of pattern decorative or supportive? How is pattern being used to create scale or space?
- Is there a visual echo or repetition of elements that supports the theme of the piece?

BALANCE

- Is there a sense of visual weight that makes the composition feel lopsided?
- Is there any element that can be eliminated without affecting the composition?
- Do any areas seem unnecessarily cluttered? Do other areas feel empty?
- Do any areas seem to cause tension because of proximity to an edge of the overall shape of the work?

LINE

. . . the seismographic record of a mark that conveys its speed, emotion, weight and shape.

Just as the musician varies the sound of their instrument, so does the artist choose from a broad menu of marks to connect with their viewer. Strength, weight, attention, intent, mood and speed can all be felt through the artist's line. Lines can swoon, swell, hop, twist or slog across a page. A line can be the wake a fish leaves behind it in the water, or it can be the edge between the sea and the sand. A line can be the expansion crack in the sidewalk, or the worm track in tree bark. Deer tracks in the snow, or lines recorded in the sand by the dune grass—each line is different in character and quality. When the artist makes marks or lines, they are recording their feelings and intention, as well as connecting with the energy of the object or image they are making. A line is like a breath, and when you put all of your attention into feeling each breath, each line becomes unique and fascinating.

PEARS EMPHASIZING LINE

As you view this image, focus on how line is used to:

- suggest character
- define shapes
- describe contours and edges
- suggest mass and volume, weight and size
- create groups of lines that blend together to make a value
- make an area or edge stand out

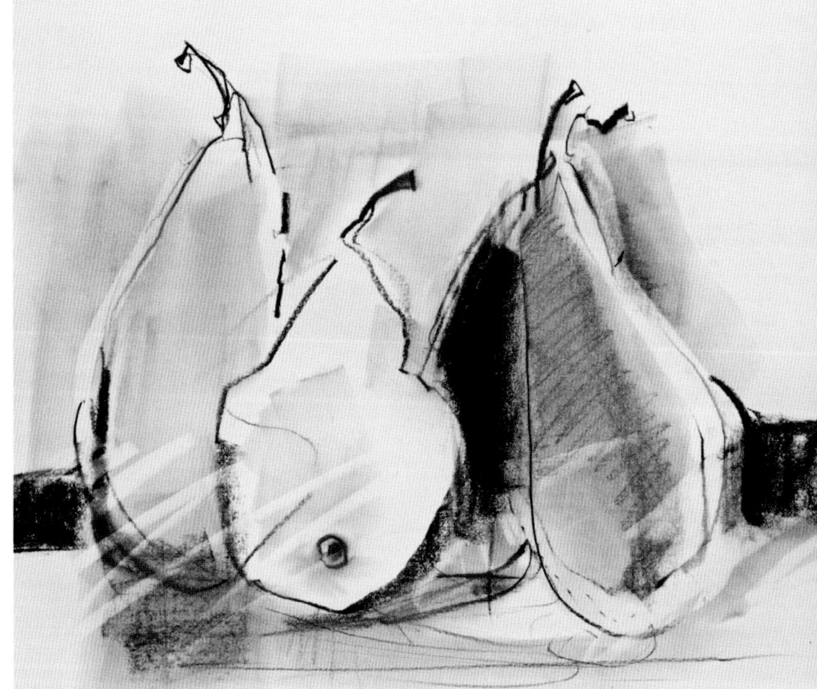

LINE / 12" × 16" (30CM × 41CM) / CHARCOAL ON DRAWING PAPER

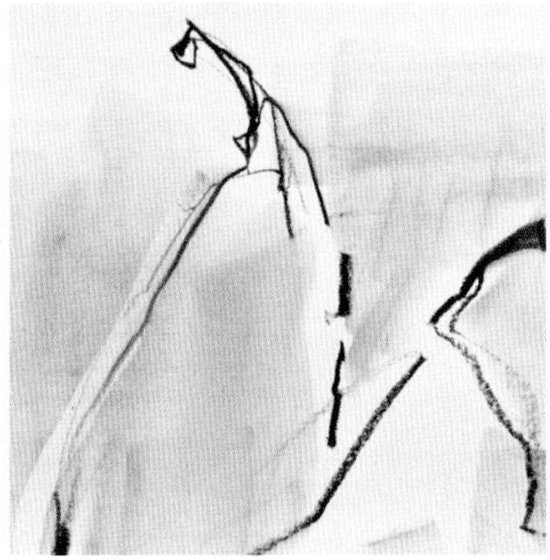

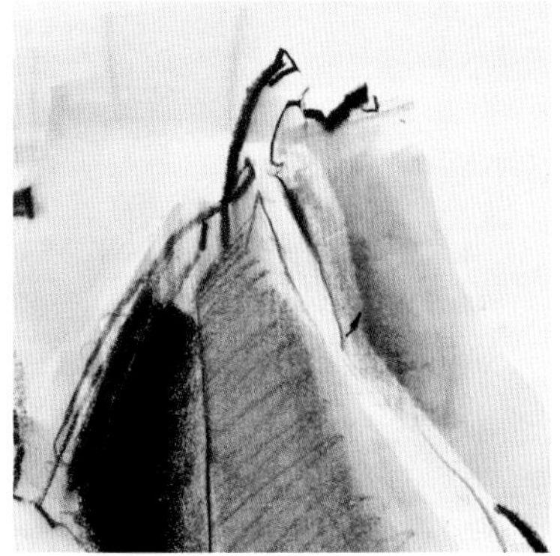

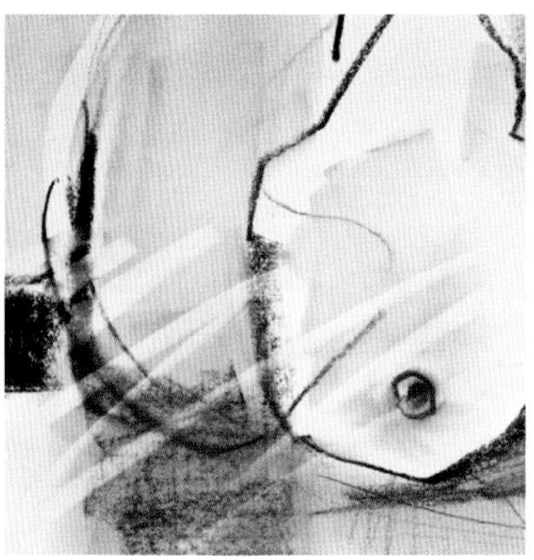

Notice how the line is broken and varied in weight and width. Our eye fills in the gaps and completes the line.

A zigzag line is used to give added value to the shaded area of the pear. The stems are each differently described with calligraphic marks created by twisting the charcoal while changing the pressure. Each stem has a slightly different character.

Eraser marks add texture to the surface, and echo the zigzag marks in the previous image but on a larger scale. The eraser crosses over the edges of the pears to defy realistic spatial description.

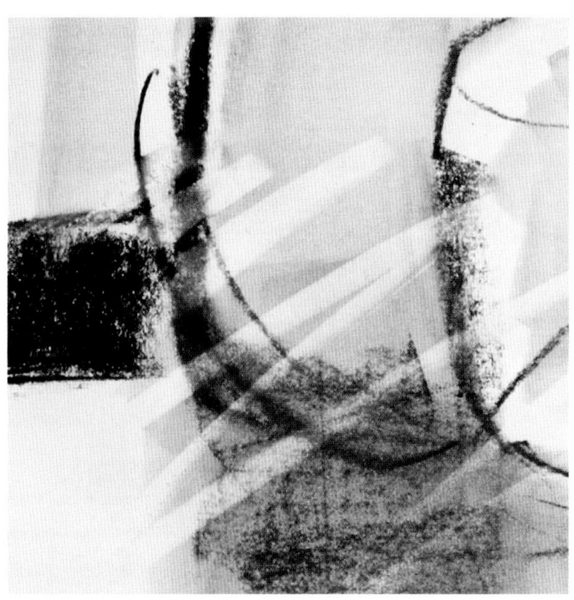

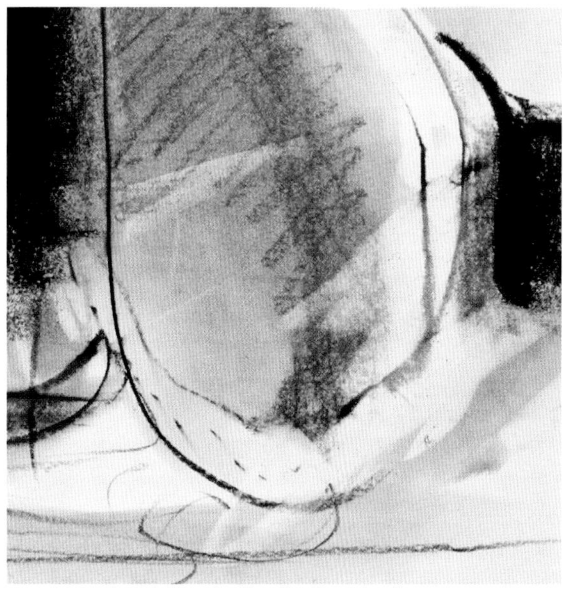

Notice the way some of the lines are blurry and some are hard-edged. Every line can express a unique quality by the way it is created and the surface it is applied to.

Notice how the dots and dashes imply a line, like a sewing thread in fabric. This variation of line is barely visible but adds nuance to the mark-making within this image.

SHAPE

. . . any gang of marks that hang out together as a unit.

Shapes do not have to be enclosed within a line. A chevron of geese flying together makes a shape, and so does a murmuration of birds flying around a pasture in a constantly changing form. One shape may seem to be flat or outlined, and the other more round or dimensional. In drawing, this translates to creating shapes with different kinds of edges. The chevron is like a dotted line, and our eyes close the triangle and connect the dots into a line, even though it isn't closed or connected. The murmuration of birds looks dimensional because it holds together as a value or a texture. At times the shape or the shape's edge looks dark or light because the density of birds keeps changing. More birds, like more overlapping marks, make for denser texture, darker value. If we think of making shapes that are intriguing to look at, we can make art that will be new, different and exciting. In other words, the artist can feel free to recreate their subjects in new ways, with new shapes, that are not closed off from the environment or background but move in and out, forward and back.

PEARS EMPHASIZING SHAPE

Line and color are at work here, but focus on how shape is used in this image:

- to create a kind of implied horizon line
- to break up space into small, medium and large shapes
- to connect and link areas together
- to create edges (on the pears, for example) without using line
- to create visual rhythm through the repetition of small shapes
- represent a flat or graphic space rather than a volumetric or realistic one
- to connect three edges of the composition with shape
- to create depth by overlapping

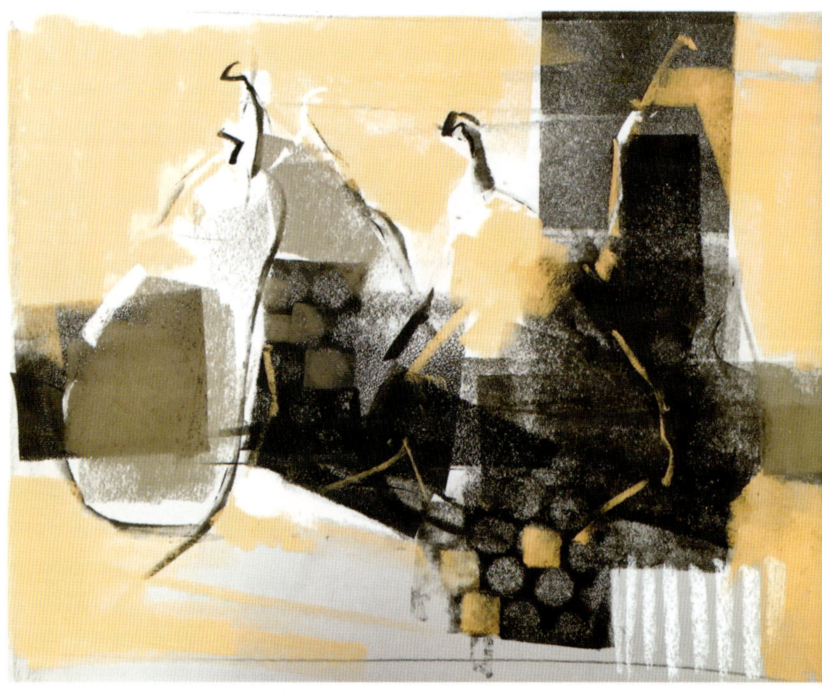

SHAPE / 12" × 16" (30CM × 41CM) / CHARCOAL, PASTEL AND OIL PAINT ON DRAWING PAPER

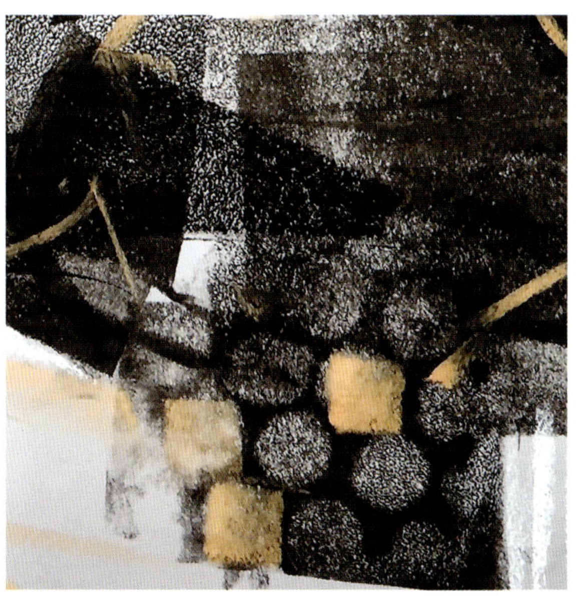

Small shapes create a pattern that merges into a larger one. That dark shape appears to be in front of and behind the pears at the same time. This kind of space becomes imaginary rather than purely representational.

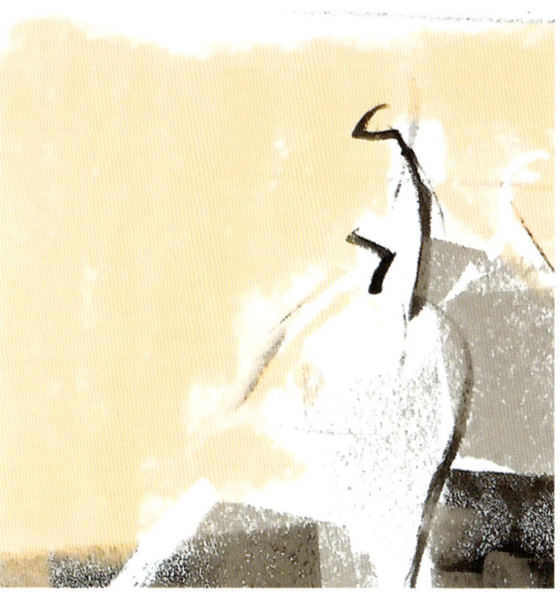

Notice how the shape of the background enters into the shape of the pear. The shape of the interior of the pear defines the edge and helps to avoid looking "colored in."

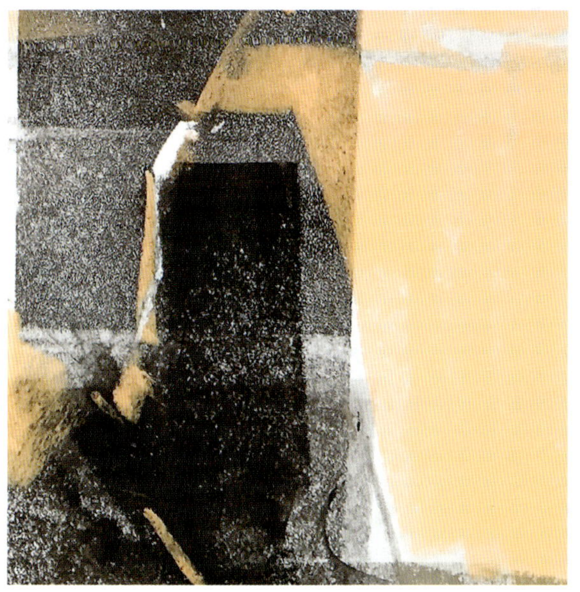

Strong rectangular shapes seem to flow in front of and behind the pears. A few lines that minimally describe the edges of the pear stand in contrast to more geometric shapes. The pear is described with flat color shapes placed next to each other rather than with blended or layered color.

Repetition of vertical lines creates a visual boundary that defines the front of the space or the picture plane, making the pears appear to sit behind this "fence." The lines group together to form a shape and help direct the eye upward to the stems.

TEXTURE

. . . makes your eyes remember what your hand and heart felt when it touched something.

I enlist texture to make visual connections that are unexpected and unique using both drawing and non-drawing techniques. Because texture has the power to evoke memory of touch, our eyes can make visual connections that are metaphoric and poetic rather than predictable. For me, the building up of visual textures, whether bold or subtle, and the weaving together of the imagery that results is where the fun of drawing really begins!

It may be tempting to think of texture as arising from either the physical surface of the substrate or from the illusions I can create with my medium as I paint.

Working with the printing process and mixed media has enlarged my sense of what texture can be until it is perhaps the richest of all the elements. Texture can arise from objects placed beneath my substrate, from digging through the layers with various tools, or from physical additives in my medium. I can manipulate and combine any of the other elements to create textures that might elicit a nearly unlimited range of reactions from my viewer. While all the elements are important, I am particularly fascinated and excited by the visual opportunities that explorations of texture provide me.

PEAR IMAGE EMPHASIZING TEXTURE

While line, shape and color are at work here, the dominant element in this image is texture. Texture on a drawing or painting can be visual or physical. In these images there is no relief from the paper surface—everything is a visual depiction of texture. Notice how texture is used in this drawing to:

- help move the eye through the image and create space

- merge the grouping of pears together as one shape by going through the boundary of each individual pear

- evoke the memory of unrelated subjects that may share this diamond texture (patio table, basket, etc.)

- jolt the eye because the texture is unexpected

- break up the space in new ways that enable the use of line and shape to have different roles

- create darker and lighter values by overlapping textures and using textures that are different in scale

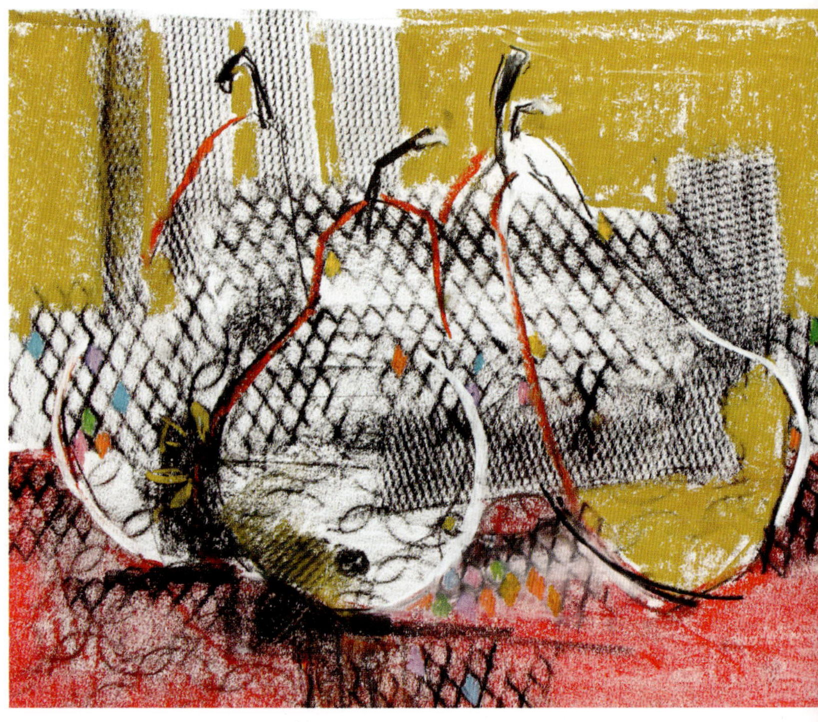

TEXTURE / 12" × 16" (30CM ×41CM) / CHARCOAL, PASTEL, COLORED PENCIL ON DRAWING PAPER

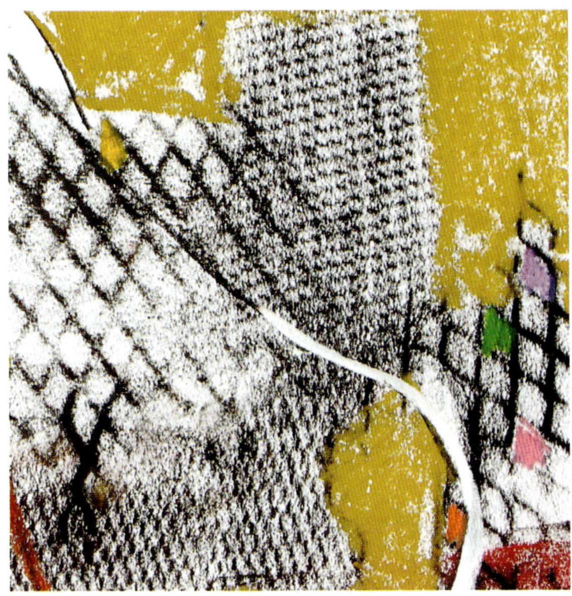

A white line is used to separate the form of the pear from the background; it also links it to the white spaces within the texture. Texture makes it fun to play with space in new ways.

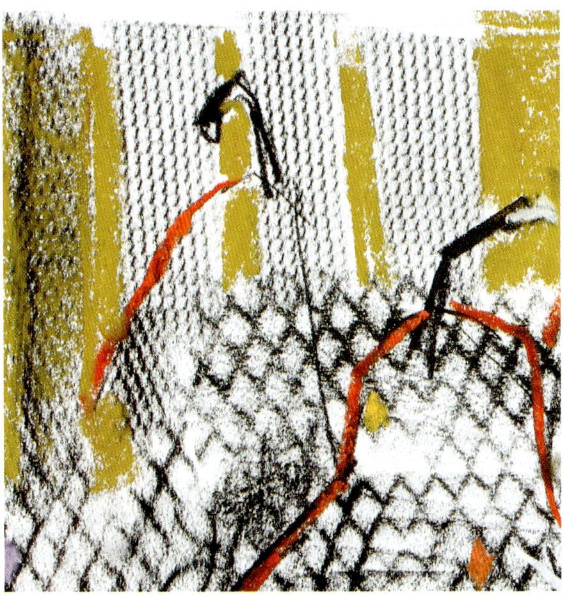

Texture is used to describe both the background and the pears. Line acts in contrast to find the pears' edges.

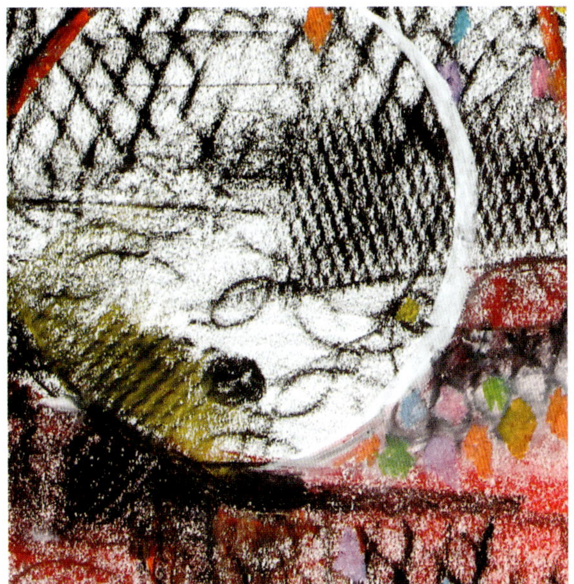

A mixture of textures, line and color creates a kind of imaginary landscape within the circle. Even though there is no light source depicted, our brain still interprets the darkness under the bottom of the pear as a cast shadow.

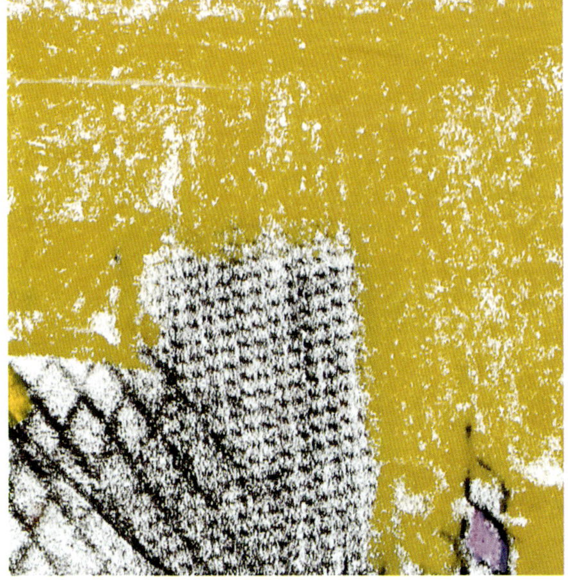

Textures are overlapped to merge into background shapes that could be interpreted as buildings or structures. This encourages the imagination to participate in the storytelling of the image.

EDGES

Imagine driving off a highway onto a dirt road filled with potholes. The transition is dramatic to say the least. Now think of moving your hand across the surface of one person's arm to another's, which is a much more subtle kind of transition. When drawing, the artist gives just as much attention to every nuance of the quality of the edge. Edges can be much more than hard or soft. An edge can be mysterious, unpredictable, irregular and changing in character as it continues on. Torn, crisp edges are radically different from wet, soggy edges emotionally, physically and intellectually.

My personal artistic challenge has been learning to not define every edge! Allowing edges to disappear means letting go of crisply describing every transition.

Addressing this challenge has meant inventing new ways to think about edges. This includes the exploration of layering, pulling the background textures through to the foreground, ignoring lines as visual boundaries, and dragging marks and tools over the edges of items that invite unpredictable and unique shapeshifting to occur. I still have to remind myself not to turn everything into a hard edge and to let the gravel mix in with the grass! Knowing how to use your tools and mediums to create a wide variety of edge qualities is critical to managing and manipulating space in your images.

PEAR IMAGE WITH CIRCLES, YELLOW, PINK AND BLACK

The elements of shape, line, texture, color and value are all at work in this image, but the way edges are used is most interesting. Notice how edges:

- appear and disappear as you look around the image

- share more than one specific space by describing two things at once

- create variation and interest that is unexpected

- separate some shapes while blurring the edges of other shapes

- seem to have a quality of movement

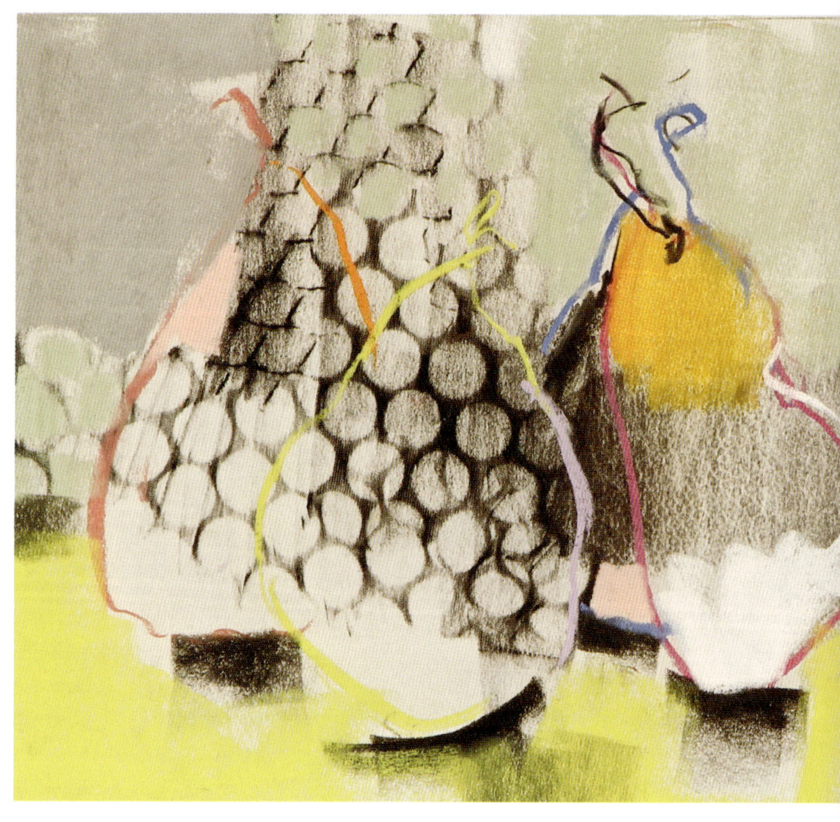

EDGES / 12" × 16" (30CM ×41CM) / CHARCOAL AND PASTEL ON DRAWING PAPER

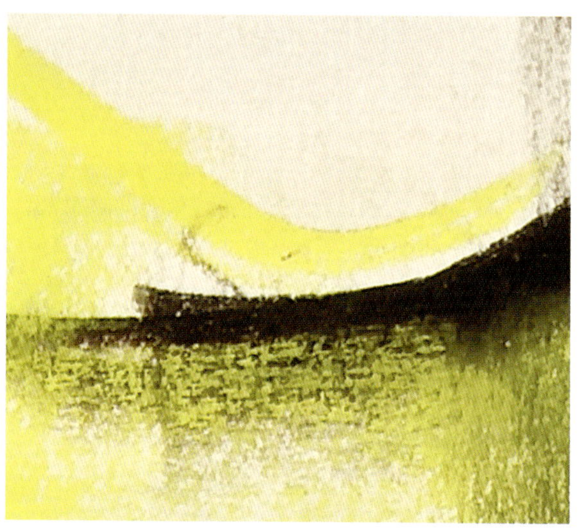

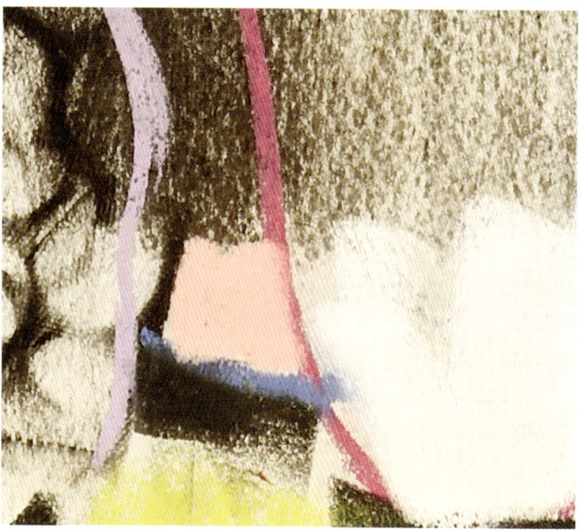

This line creates a hard edge that is dark on one side and starkly light on the other. This approach is used on each of the pears to give visual weight, lend a graphic quality to the image, and create a visual "beat" across the image.

The edges here are a conglomeration of line, texture, shape and value. The space is ambiguous as a result, and conveys a light, floaty feeling that contrasts with the hard, weighted edge.

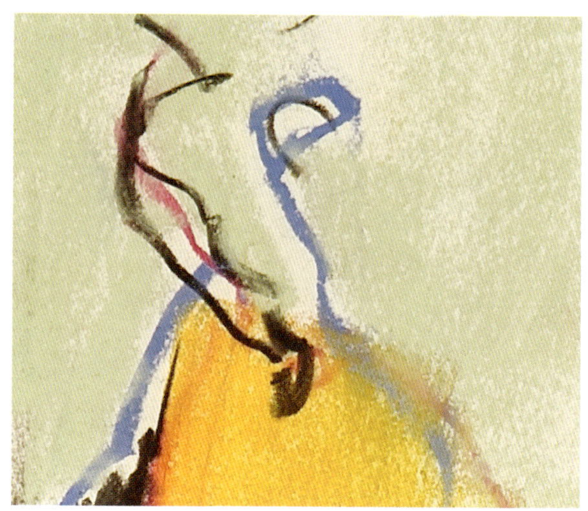

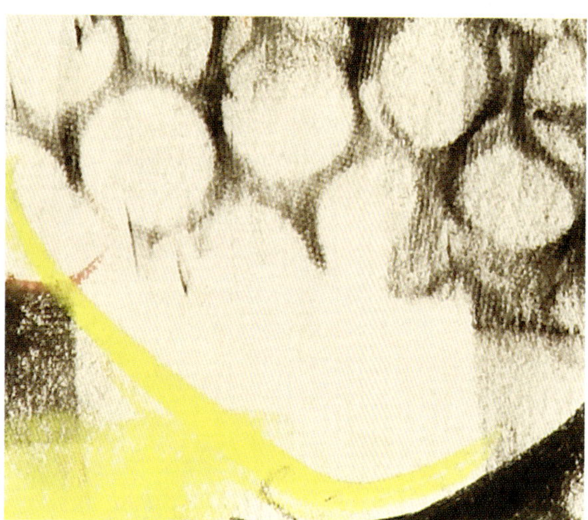

Stem lines seem to float upward like tails of kites, while the edge of the pears are mostly soft and blurred. Because of the contrast of edges, the overall image has a feeling of pears taking off, almost turning into smoke.

Very subtle edge shifts can be created with color that almost disappears, as you see here between the yellow line, white pastel and the whiteness of the paper.

VALUE

. . . is the architect that builds structure with light and shadow.

Like many people, I learned to draw using pencil, and like most people, I focused on line, details and contour. While this approach helped me develop a sensitive line and good eye-hand coordination, it didn't help me learn to perceive the underlying structure of my subjects. Without that understanding it was impossible to really see shape and understand value. To improve my skills, I forced myself to draw with mass drawing only, using no line. I used only the side of the charcoal stick rather than the tip, and squinted to see the big shapes first, not the details. In order to develop a deeper understanding of how light moved across forms, I worded from the center of the forms to the outside, rather than from the edges inward. I worked additively, building value from light to dark like a sculptor adds bits of clay to an armature. I also worked subtractively by toning the surface and removing the darks to reveal the light areas, which is like carving away at stone.

Exploring in this way allowed me to see things differently and feel more secure with my rendering. When I returned to using line a few years later, my lines were more deliberate, expressive and powerful. Mass drawing with value taught me to develop the figure and ground together rather than separately. I learned that to make something darker in value I needed to lighten the space next to it, and vice versa. In the end, I finally understood that color is just value with pigment added, and that changed everything.

PEARS WITH VALUE

This image was drawn with a mass approach, using the side of a charcoal stick to create strokes of value rather than line. I began by toning the paper to a light mid value, and then I added and subtracted charcoal. Occasionally I used the tip of the charcoal to "feather" a value with a lot of lines right next to each other. (This can be done with an eraser also.) The pressure one uses in both of these methods affects the darkness or lightness of the value created. Notice how value is used to:

- imply a mood, time and environment through the quality of lighting and the proportion of lightness to darkness

- create a visual rhythm of light against dark

- create a focal point (or not)

- make subjects seem to have volume, depth and weight

- make edges stand out or disappear

- stop or redirect the viewer's eye

- create a sense of directional movement

- create emotional emphasis through the way value is placed on the page

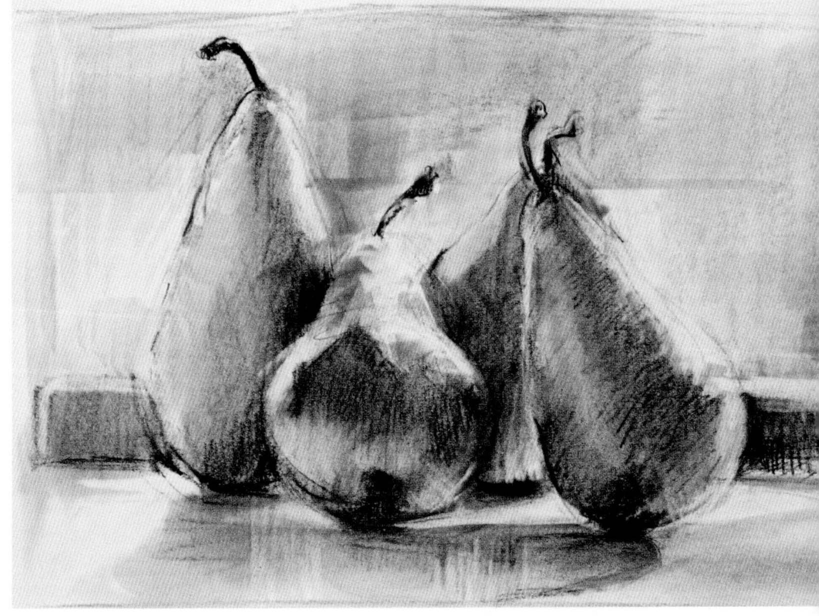

VALUE / 12"× 16" (30CM × 41CM) / CHARCOAL ON DRAWING PAPER

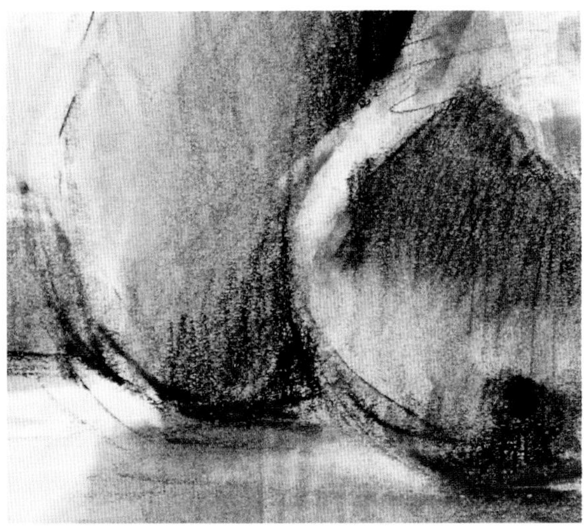

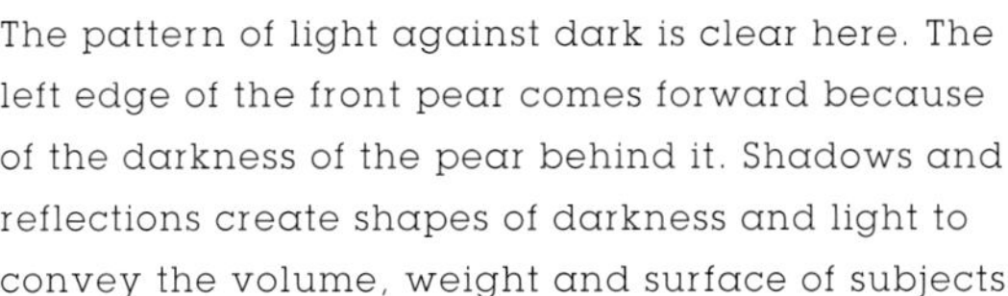

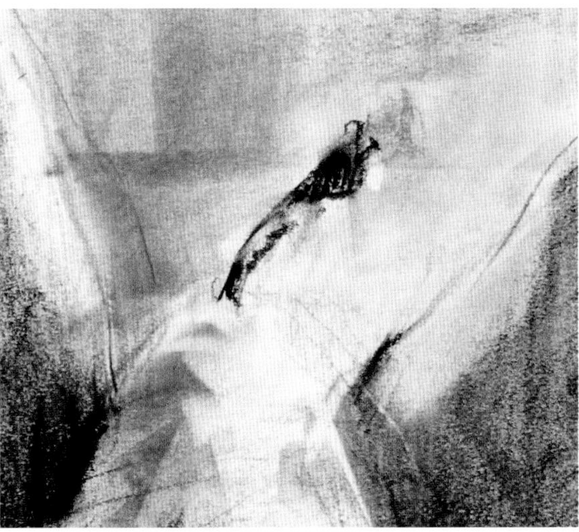

The pattern of light against dark is clear here. The left edge of the front pear comes forward because of the darkness of the pear behind it. Shadows and reflections create shapes of darkness and light to convey the volume, weight and surface of subjects.

The edge of the center pear is a lost edge because it is the same light value as the area around it. Similarly, the edge of the left pear is lost because it is the same dark value as the background. Sharp contrast of value causes the stem to get the attention.

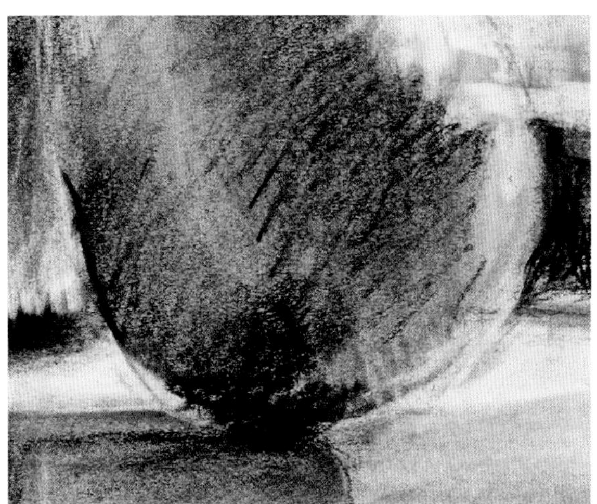

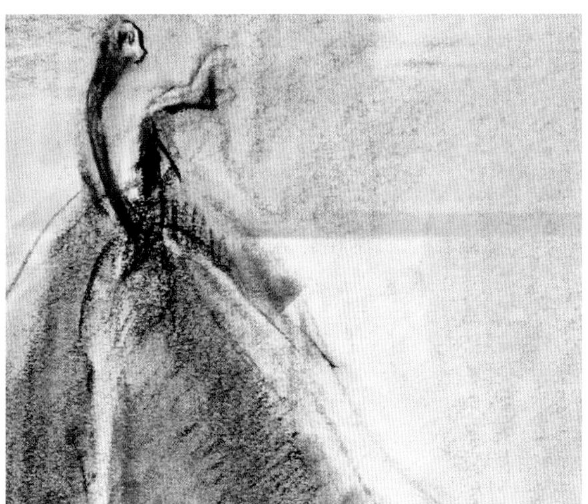

There are many ways to create value: with line, with line over value, with texture, etc. In this example, you can see how the lines within the darkest value in the pear help describe the roundness of the object.

The placement of values in a space or shape greatly affects the emotional power of a composition. In this example, the dark values are huddled in the left corner and look overpowered by the mid and light tones.

COLOR

. . . is the harmony the artist adds to their mark-making melody.

There was an experienced pastel student at one of the workshops I taught who had never drawn from a black and white reference. He had always used a color photo reference. When he finished an exercise exploring color as value he literally cried for joy after discovering the freedom of that experience. Color is by far the most subjective of the elements, and pastelists love color! But so often many beautiful colors lay unused in their box because the landscape around them or the references artists use don't include those colors. The realization that you can use any color in your box as long as it has the right value is incredibly freeing. This is my mantra when I teach, and I can't emphasize enough the importance of drawing and painting in black and white over and over, until color simply becomes a way of adding visual harmony to the marks and values that are already there.

In graphic design color is often used to group information or to make associations between elements. Shape and color can work together to group elements and to make things more or less important. This book won't delve into color theory, but I do suggest that you take color images you see in this book and turn them into black and white images so you will understand the value behind the color choices.

PEARS AND COLOR

The image you see here is very similar to the charcoal image illustrating value but uses color to convey the quality of light and the character of the subject. Notice how color:

- can create mood and environment

- can evoke a sense of temperature and space

- can create a visual rhythm or movement

- can create a sense of visual harmony or dissonance

- can be used to connect shapes or subjects by association with similar color

- can be used to emphasize an area or element

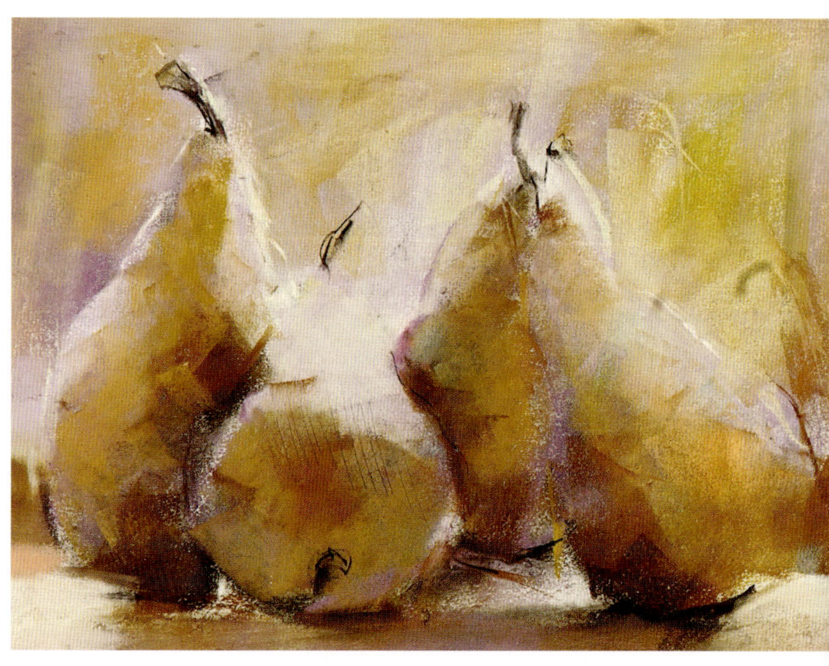

COLOR / 12"× 16" (30CM × 41CM) / PASTEL ON DRAWING PAPER

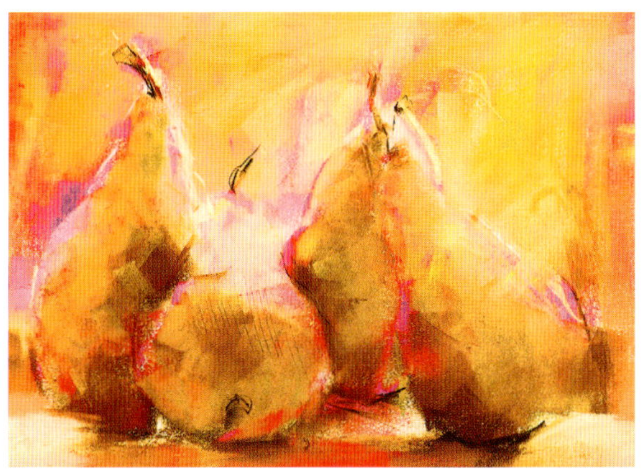

Intensifying the saturation increases the temperature and changes the entire mood of the image.

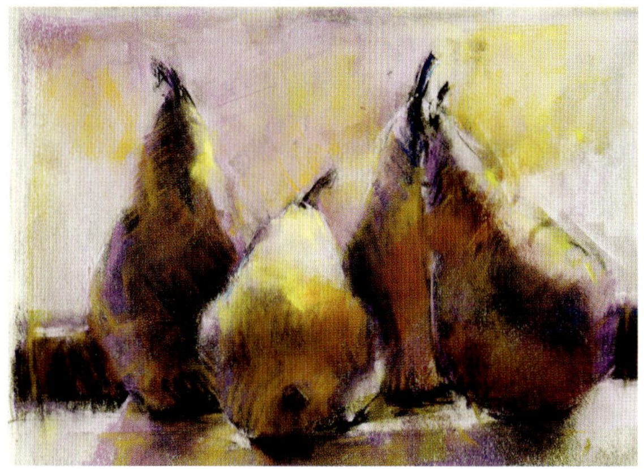

Increasing the value contrast of the color changes the emotional impact of the image.

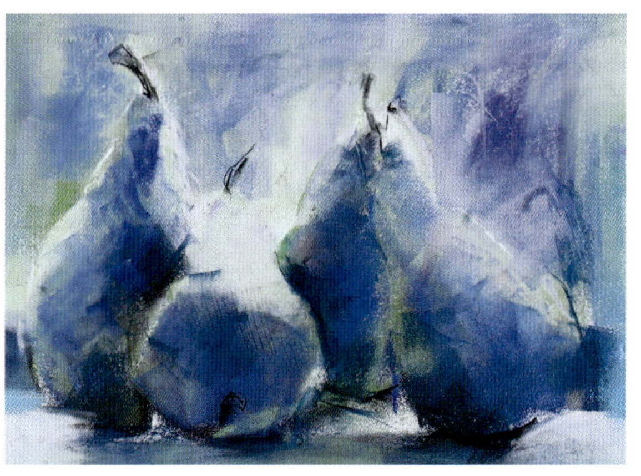

Altering the hue of the image changes the temperature and conveys a different mood.

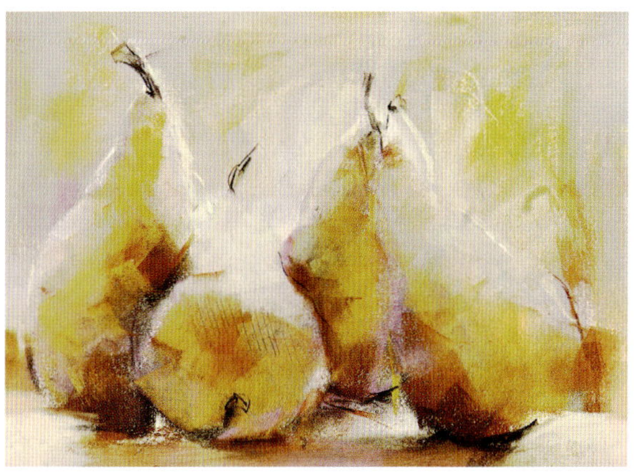

Changing the key from low to high increases the lost edges and changes the overall feeling of visual weight in the image.

SPACE

. . . is the stage where the elements dance together to perform their magic.

It could be said that each of the elements of art acts independently and in relationship with each other to create space. Space can be manipulated by the artist to look shallow, deep, twisted, compressed, flat, warped, fractured, realistic, imaginary, multi-dimensional or contrived. The artist can choose the placement of elements on the drawing surface to create tension or balance. The artist can fill areas of a drawing or painting with stillness or activity, vastness or intimacy. How the artist layers information in terms of opacity and transparency can affect the way a viewer perceives the imagery and story. What is emphasized in terms of edges, value, color, shape, line, texture—as well as what is not emphasized—becomes critical to the story the viewer creates in their mind. The artist sets the stage to tell their story, and on that stage is where the elements dance together to perform their magic. The artist is the director of that stage, the creator of the world and story they want to express.

PEARS EMPHASIZING SPACE

Note how the feeling of the "space" in this image is completely different from the previous image. Line is used to describe the contour of the pears. There are basically two shapes—the pear grouping and the negative space. Value is limited to light, middle and dark. Texture creates a visual pathway through the image and breaks up shape. Edges are mostly hard or nonexistent. Color is used to create a connected shape. Space feels compressed and flattened because of the overlapping cutout shapes and because the entire image has been pushed to the left of the page and allowed to run off the edge. In this image, space—rather than the pears— is the subject. Notice how space can:

- look flat, shallow, deep, imaginary, implied, layered or fractured

- convey emotions by being made to appear calm, crowded, active, agitated, mysterious, etc.

- seem to have a visual weight or tension because of placement and size of subjects

- be altered by manipulating distal cues to contradict our expectations

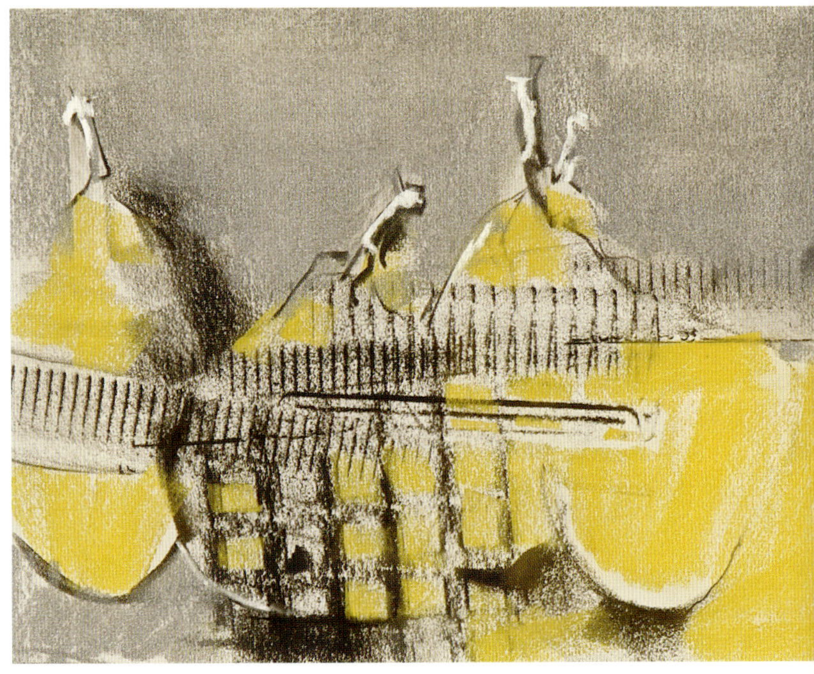

SPACE / 12" × 16" (30CM ×41CM)/ CHARCOAL, PASTEL, COLOR PENCIL ON DRAWING PAPER

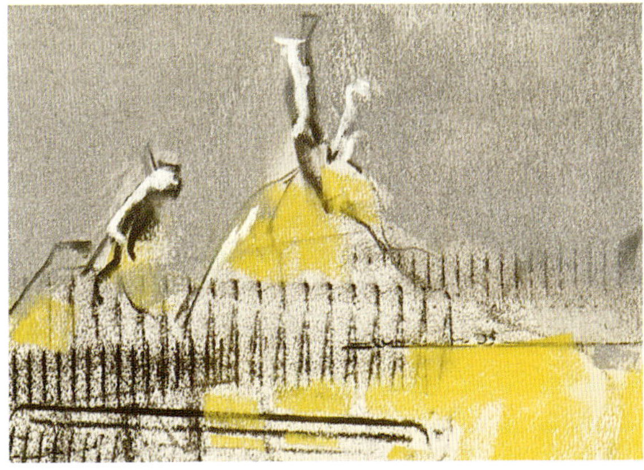

The only spatial cue comes from the overlapping edges of the pears. A feeling of a cast shadow on a wall behind the pears is implied.

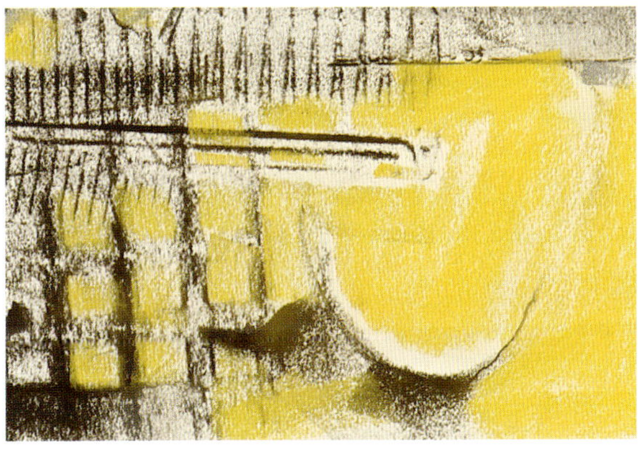

The only feeling of space in this example comes from the drop shadow of the right pear, which looks like it is simultaneously separating from and blending with the foreground.

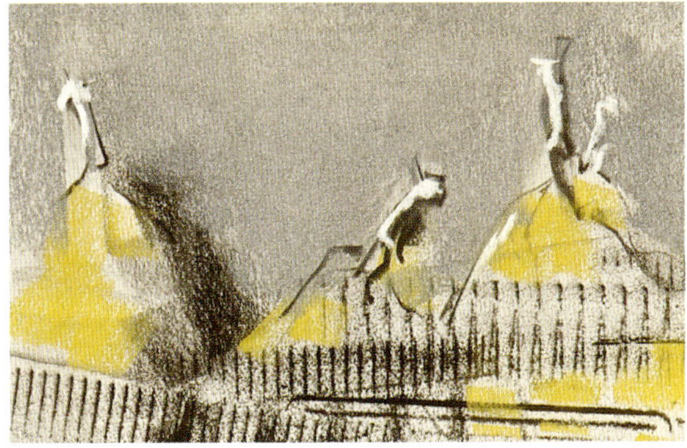

The tooth pattern creates visual movement and a kind of atmospheric perspective as it dissolves into the background.

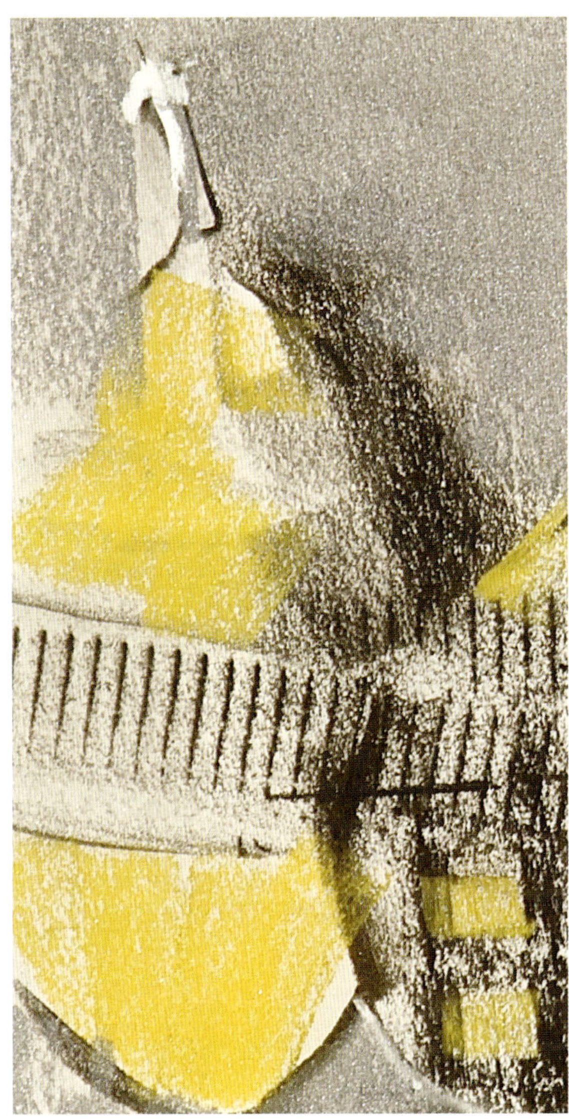

Parts of the pear seem to emerge from the background while other parts sink into the background. The waffle-like texture creates visual cuts into the surface of the pear, while the tooth texture connects the pears like a zipper.

FOUNDATIONS OF THE PRINCIPLES OF DESIGN

As human beings our brains are hard-wired to use our eyes to respond to the world. We group things by shape and size to assess them; we notice movement and direction so we can respond accordingly; we notice similarities and differences to discern what is familiar and what is not; and we sense when things are lopsided or unsteady to maintain balance and survival. We automatically go to the place of greatest contrast or to the sweet spot in a rectangle because of a built-in sense of proportion and space. We use the horizon line and distal cues to determine distance and space. We respond to repetition, and have a need to make order out of visual chaos. Our visual perception is reflected in the principles of design. When I realized how and why my eyes order information the way they do, the principles of design made sense in a whole new way. As you paint, imagine yourself the director and choreographer of the elements of art on a stage. They are at your service!

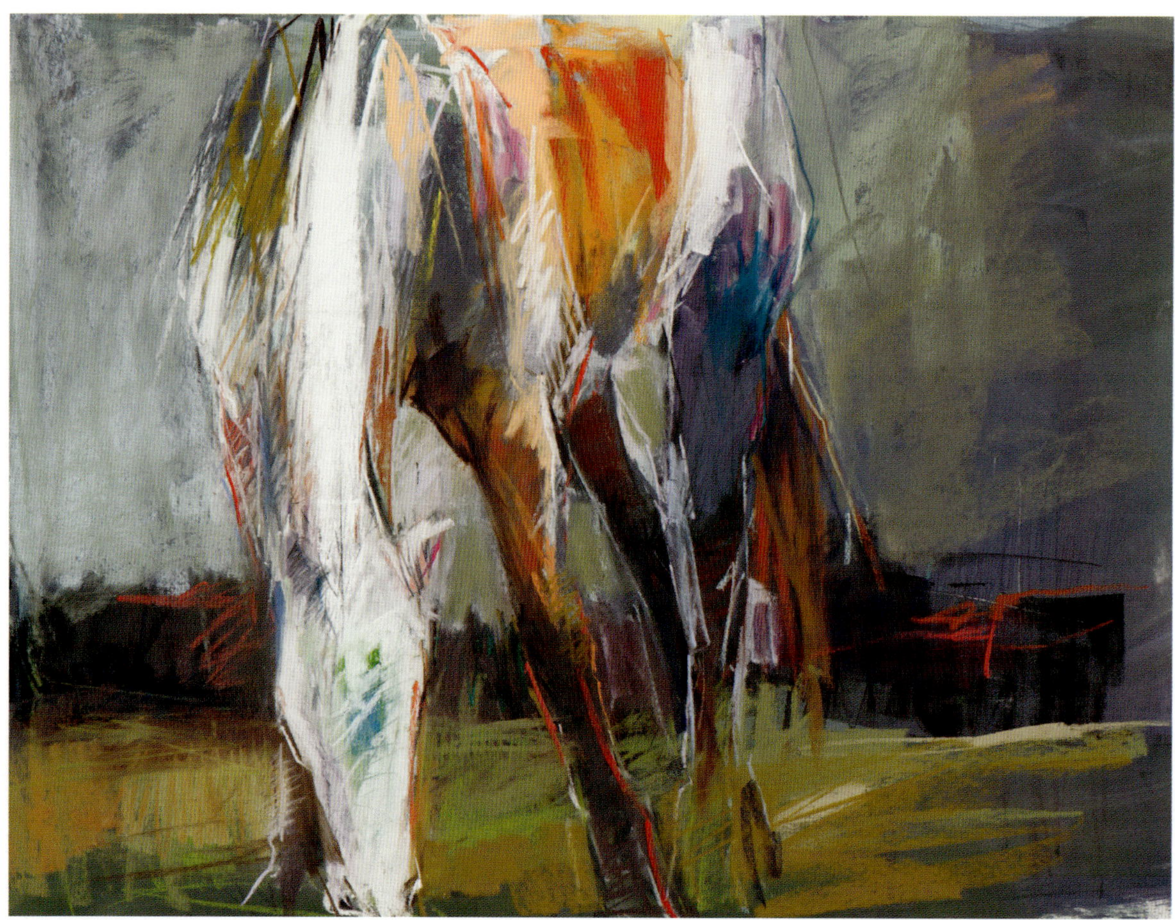

TALKING TO THE GRASS PEOPLE / 22" × 30" (56CM × 76CM) / PASTEL AND OIL ON RIVES BFK PAPER

LOW HORIZON
I began this painting by establishing a low horizon line to feature a big sky. The gradation of the sky from dark to light creates visual movement from right to left that is stopped by the white curve of the neck. The use of neutral gray intensifies the color in the horse to create a balance between movement and stillness. (I used the same reference for each of these three paintings but organized them differently to create a different mood and story.)

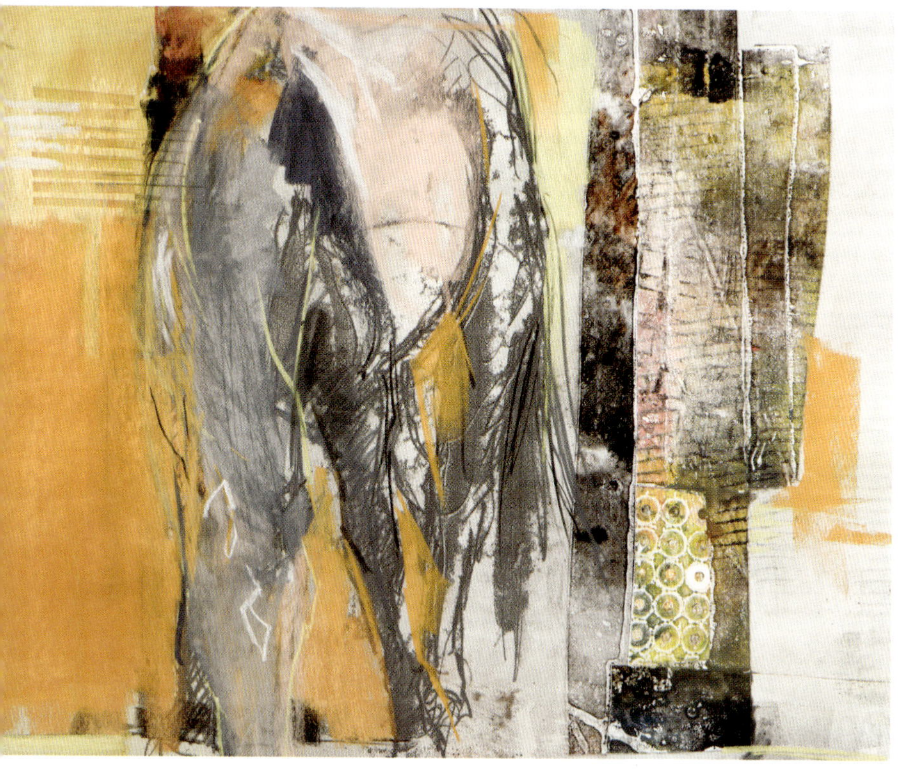

FOOD FOR THOUGHT / 22" × 30" (56CM × 76CM) / PASTEL OVER MONOTYPE AND TRACE MONOTYPE ON STONEHENGE PAPER

ABSTRACTION

I started with a monotype ground that was composed of abstract color and textures. Later, I did a trace monotype of the horse onto the abstract monotype. Then I used pastel to integrate the horse with the background. This process of responsive image making is like jazz improvisation in that the image evolves.

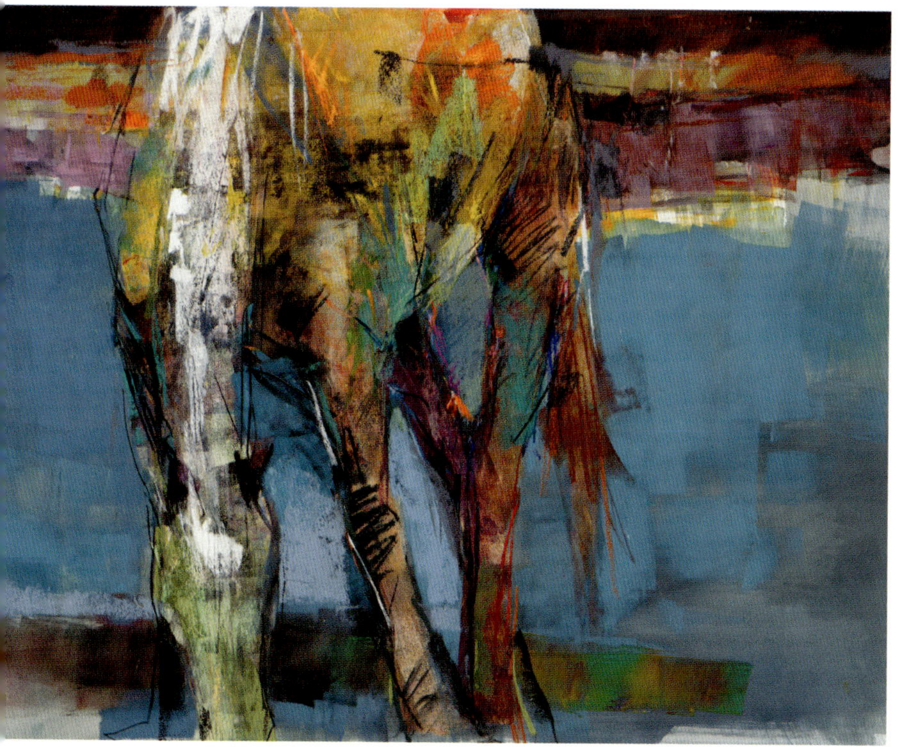

GRAZING THE BLUES / 22" × 30" (56CM × 76CM) / PASTEL, GOUACHE AND ACRYLIC ON STONEHENGE PAPER

HIGH HORIZON

This composition shows a high horizon line with a wide middle ground of blue. I wanted each passage of color to feel like a different riff of notes, my interpretation of the blues. This painting evolved as I responded to each nuance until the painting felt complete.

SEVEN STEPS TO SELF-CRITIQUE YOUR WORK

The main purpose of a critique is to help you resolve issues that are causing problems in a work of art and to help you decide if something is "done." The goal for both is to identify problem areas and to then determine options to resolve it. For example, if the issue is where or how the eye is being led through a painting, the solution might be to add more or less contrast, sharpen or soften an edge, recombine shapes, change a color, or subdue a texture. Often the problem doesn't lie where you think it is. The problem is often somewhere else in the painting. That's when another pair of eyes or a system of evaluation can prove helpful.

The evaluation process needs to take into account how the elements are working individually and collectively to convey the artist's story. Changes that you make to one area ripple through the rest of the elements and may require other adjustments to be made. As each change is implemented, your understanding of the entire image evolves until you converge on a solution that seems to satisfy all the seven principles of design.

Here are the seven steps I find useful to critique my work:

1. Take a photo of your image, so you are forced to objectify the work.
2. Inventory how each element is working.
3. Identify what the problems are.
4. Consider the options for changes.
5. Make one change at a time.
6. Evaluate how the principles are working.
7. Repeat the process until you feel you have arrived at a good solution.

PERFECT HARMONY
(UNFINISHED) / 22"× 30" (56CM × 76CM) / PASTEL AND MIXED MEDIA ON RIVES BFK PAPER

EVALUATE AND CRITIQUE
This is the place I stopped to evaluate whether the painting felt finished.

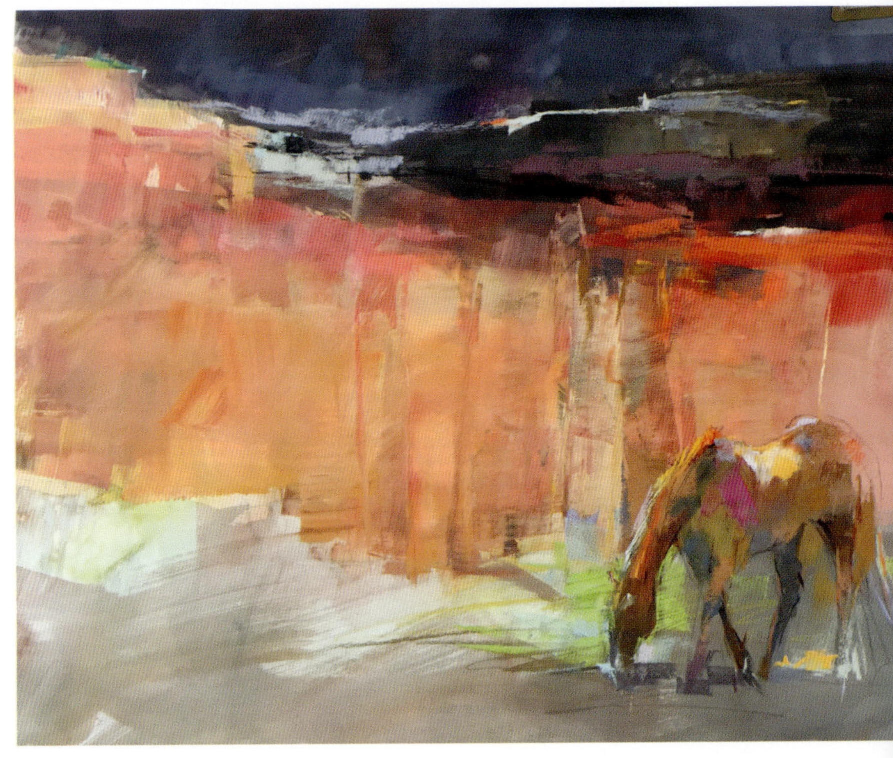

INVENTORY THE ELEMENTS

Below is my analysis of how each of the seven elements was working.

LINE: Generally I like the way the vertical lines of the rock wall give a rhythm to the piece. The line that seems to catch my eye too much is the white line in the farthest cliff. The white edge pulls me to it because it is in great contrast with the dark sky. I know that I don't want that to be a focal point, so I need to tone it down.

SHAPE: I see basically four shapes: the dark cliff and sky, the rock wall, the ground the horse is standing on, and the horse. The shapes in the horse are getting too broken up, especially on the back and neck. I would like to make the horse feel more a part of the landscape than the feeling of separation from the background I'm getting now. Maybe there are too many shapes in the horse. How can I simplify this?

TEXTURE: Texture is not a major player in this painting. The rocks read as rocks without a lot of description, so I can move on to edges.

EDGES: There seem to be rough transitions between edges of the rocks and the sky, from one rock to another right behind the horse, and with the edges of the colors along the horse's neck. I need to address how to tend to these edges.

VALUE: The distant cliff looks too dark in value and blends into the sky too much. The value of the foreground seems too dark and contrasting and so does the horse's neck. What can I do to integrate the horse, the foreground and the background to make this a more interesting painting? How can I add mystery or an element of discovery?

COLOR: I like the color of the red wall of rock and the mood the color is creating. What isn't working is the green in the foreground and in the upper cliff in the background. I know that green is the complement of red, but here it seems to distract my eye. That splotch of color on the horse's back creates a small shape of color that is too distinctly different from everything else around it.

SPACE: The horse seems closer to me than I want it to be, and it feels like I'm trying too hard to describe layering back into space. I don't want the foreground to be so different from the background. I want them to merge better.

EXPERIENCE AND MISTAKES

experience is that marvelous thing that enables you to recognize a mistake when you make it again.

—franklin p. jones

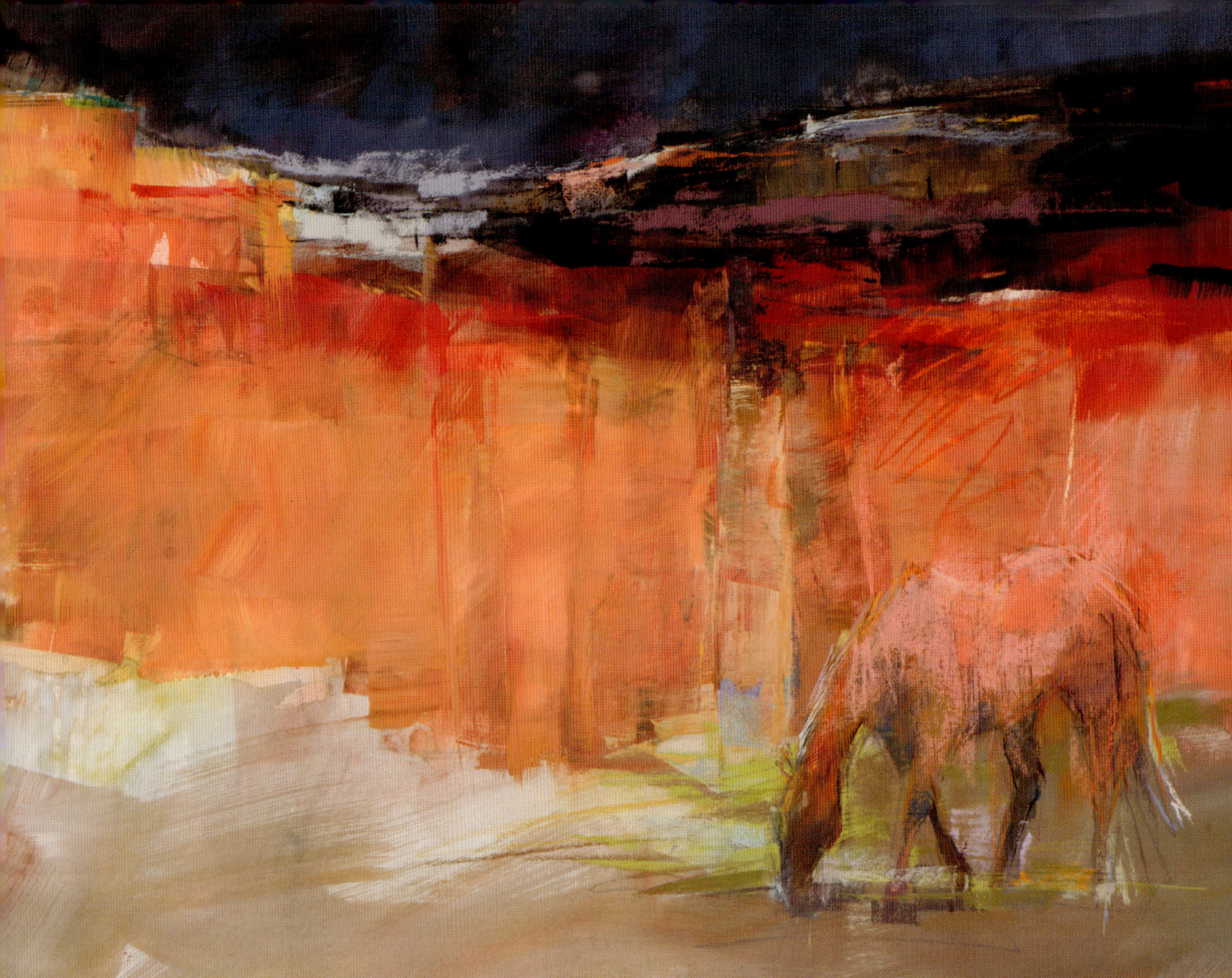

PERFECT HARMONY / 22" × 30" (56CM × 76CM) /
PASTEL AND MIXED MEDIA ON RIVES BFK PAPER

This is the finished image with changes implemented.

WHAT I DID:

- Subdued the ridge line.
- Lightened the distant rocks a bit.
- Lightened the foreground.
- Changed the cool mint green color to be warmer.
- Lightened the values in the ground and rock in the area behind the horse to make it feel calmer.

- Merged values to lose some edges.
- Unified the top of the rock line with more red.
- Simplified the shapes in the horse by letting the red of the rock move right into the horse.

PRINCIPLES

UNITY AND HARMONY: The colors feel like they are working well together to describe a mood. The horse, rock and foreground all feel unified now. The horse doesn't feel disconnected from the background but part of it. It feels like now the viewer can discover the horse and everything is better integrated.

VARIETY AND CONTRAST: The area of greatest contrast is between sky and rock. That is where I want it to be. There is enough variety of the elements, so I don't feel anything is too empty or boring.

DOMINANCE AND EMPHASIS: The color red of the wall is dominant and is where I want the emphasis to be.

MOVEMENT AND DIRECTION: There is a sense of horizontal movement from left to right, and the eye moves back to the horse when it is discovered.

SCALE AND PROPORTION: The horse establishes a nice scale for the rock; the relationship and proportion of sky to rock and horse all seem to work.

REPETITION, RHYTHM AND PATTERN: The repetition of vertical intervals within the rock seems to make a nice rhythm, and the angles of the horse's legs are a nice counterpoint to the verticals.

BALANCE: Yes, there is a feeling of calm and balance. Nothing feels out of whack. It's done!

SELF CRITIQUE

1. Take a photo of your image, so you are forced to objectify the work.
2. Inventory how the elements are working.
3. Identify what the problems are.
4. Consider the options.
5. Make one change at a time.
6. Evaluate how the principles are working.
7. Repeat the process until you feel you have arrived at a good solution.

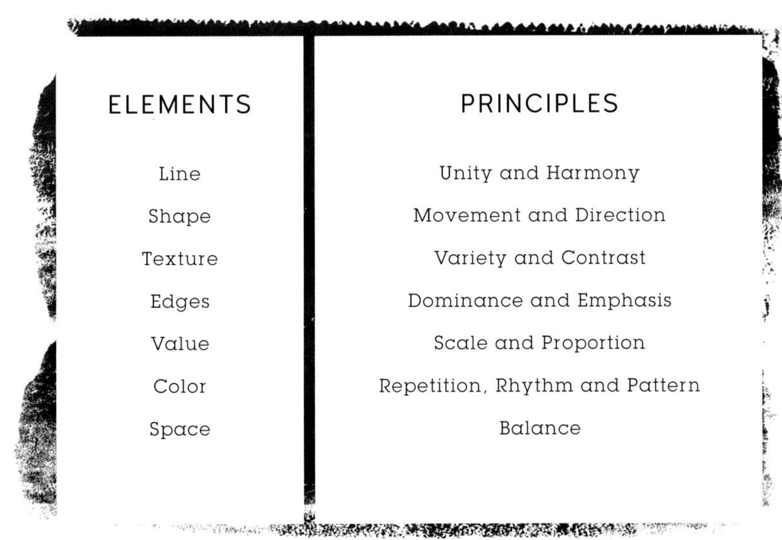

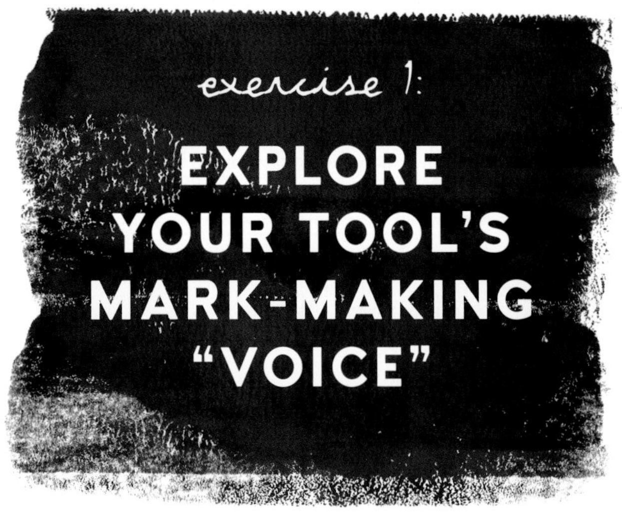

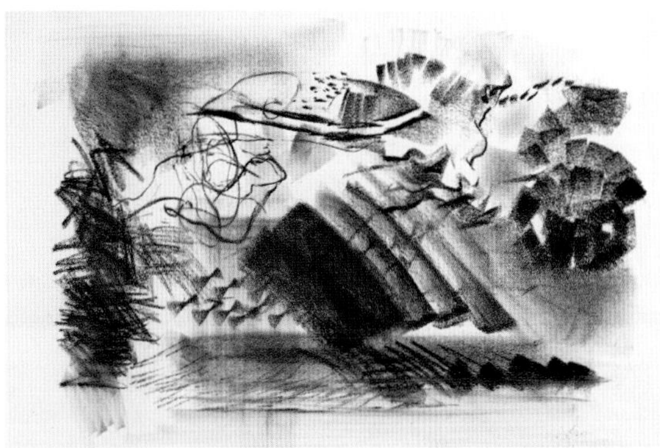

CHARCOAL SAMPLER / 18" × 24" (46CM × 61CM) /
CHARCOAL ON NEWSPRINT

MATERIALS

- 1 pack General's Jumbo Compressed Charcoal
  (2B, 4B, 6B)

- eraser: hard plastic eraser, flat razor blade,
  kneaded eraser, a cosmetic wedge or piece of soft
  paper towel for smooshing or smearing

- pad of 18" × 24" (46CM × 61CM) newsprint (Note:
  make sure when you draw with a dry medium
  like pastel or charcoal that you have several
  other pages below the piece you are working on
  to cushion your work)

- standing easel or smooth wall

- timer

DIRECTIONS

STEP 1

Break each of the charcoal sticks in half.

STEP 2

Stand at arm's length at the easel with your
nondrawing hand at your side. As you draw, rotate
your wrist and engage your whole arm. Let your
arm move loosely, and try not to clutch the easel
with your non-drawing hand. If your easel feels
unsteady, you might tape your paper to a smooth
wall instead.

STEP 3

Explore each of the sticks of charcoal by making
different kind of marks that give you lines, shapes,
textures, values and edges. The goal is to make
marks, not a picture of anything. Pretend you have
never held a piece of charcoal in your fingertips
before, and see what it can do. Overlap elements,
smear areas together, and use the erasers to make
marks. Step back at least 4 feet to view your drawing
every 30 seconds. Fill the entire page with a
composition of marks.

CRITIQUE

- What differences did you notice among each of
  the three sticks of charcoal with respect to value,
  erasability and smearing?

- Do you see a quality of space in your drawing
  of marks?

- Which element is most dominant? Which elements
  did you not include?

- How does your eye move through the image?

- When you rotate your image, how do you feel
  movement, space, visual weight and dominance
  change?

TAKEAWAY

Any time you are trying a new material, take the
time to find out the full range of what it can do on
various surfaces.

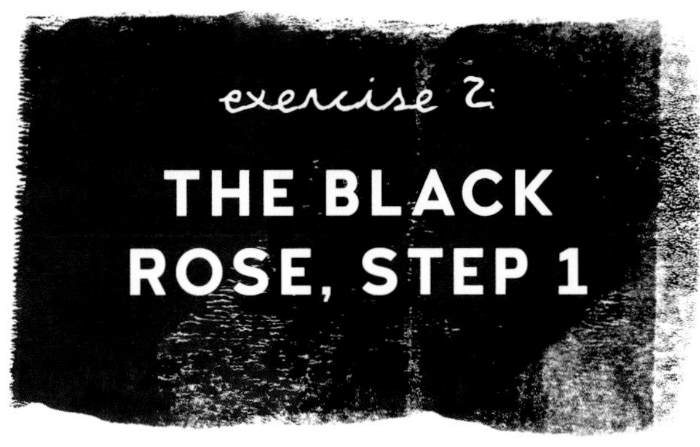

STEP 1

Refer to *The Black Rose* by Georges Braque (left). On newsprint, sketch a rectangle to frame the dimensions of the drawing. Copy the reference image using light lines. Draw the largest shapes first, then move onto the smaller shapes. Compare the relationships of various parts as you draw, seeing what elements line up vertically and horizontally within the image. Spend no more than 15 minutes on this. When done, take a photo.

STEP 2

Using the side of the 4B charcoal, vary the visual weight and width of some of the lines. Each time you change something, step back from the easel and assess the piece as a whole in terms of its visual weight and balance. The goal is not to copy the reference exactly, but to explore the power of line. When you are pleased with the placement and rhythm of the light and dark lines, take a photograph. Spend no more than 10 minutes on this.

STEP 3

Add values to shapes and line by smearing or erasing. Create variation in edges. Squint to see pathways of dark, light and middle values. When you are finished, take a photo. Spend no more than 10 minutes on this.

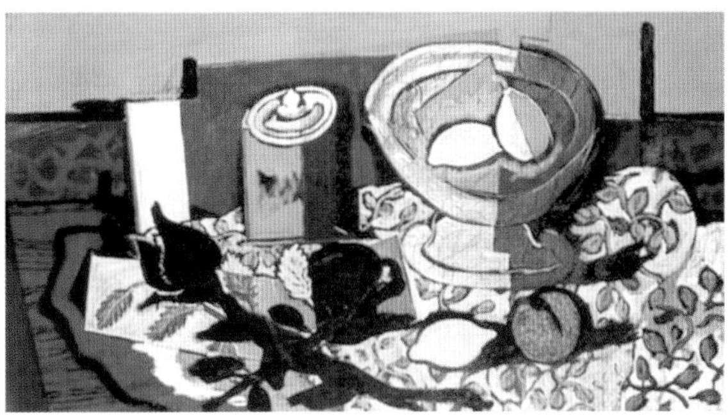

THE BLACK ROSE / GEORGES BRAQUE (1927) / 20" × 37" (51CM × 94CM) / OIL AND SAND ON CANVAS

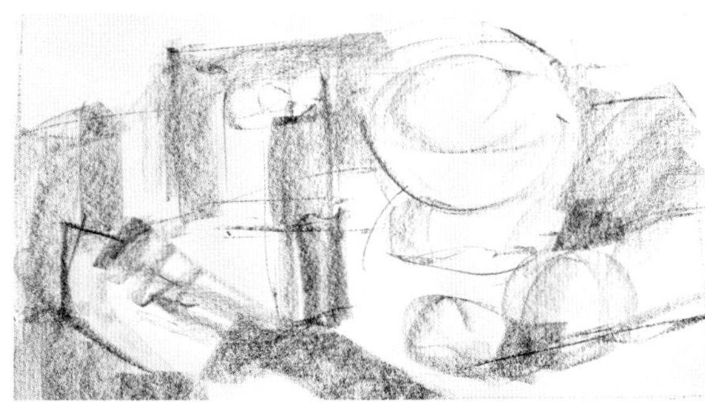

Example of line drawing with charcoal by Denali Brooke.

CRITIQUE

- Analyze the variety of lines, shapes, edges, values and spatial quality of your drawing.

- What do you see first? Second? How does your eye move around the drawing?

- Does it feel balanced?

TAKEAWAY

Training yourself to appreciate the power of each mark means taking the time to assess each mark and its placement in relationship to the whole piece.

MATERIALS

- General's Jumbo Compressed Charcoal

- erasure materials

- 18" × 24" (46CM × 61CM) newsprint pad

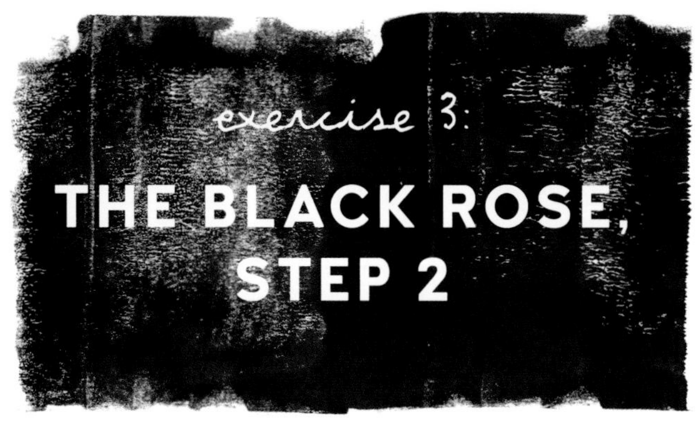

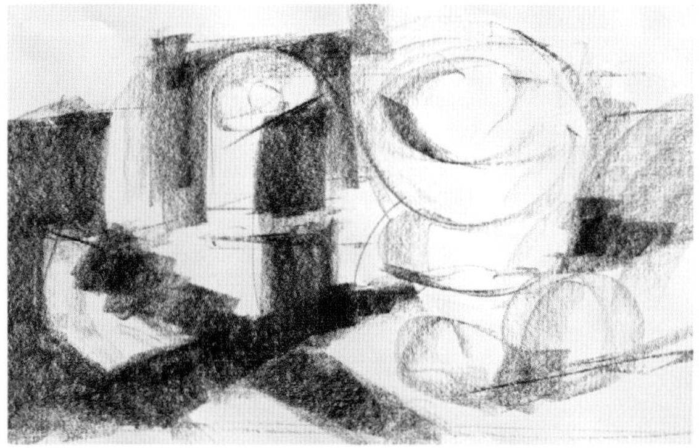

Example of enhanced line with charcoal by Denali Brooke.

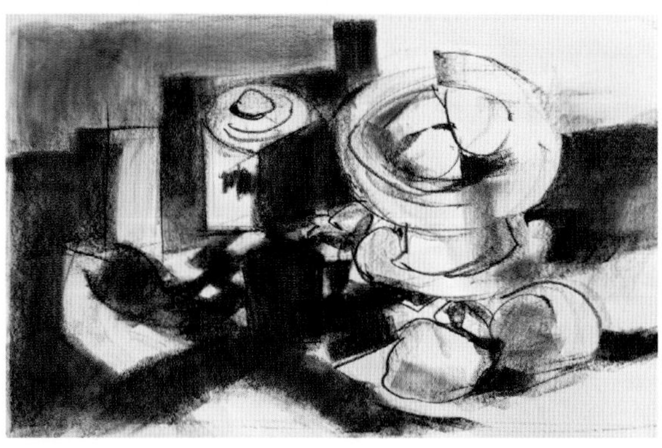

Example of value added by Denali Brooke.

MATERIALS

- same as exercise 2
- white pastel

DIRECTIONS

STEP 1

Continue with the drawing from exercise 2. Use white pastel to highlight a few areas you want to be the lightest value. Do not rub the white with your fingers or blend with the smoosher, as this will make the black look chalky. Step back to evaluate the visual balance, and take a photo.

STEP 2

Re-establish the darkest areas with 6B charcoal. Consider how your eyes link together the dark shapes, mid tones and light shapes. Thicken lines and alter values as desired. Step back from the easel to evaluate, and take a photo.

STEP 3

Find a textured surface that you can use to add texture to your drawing with frottage (rubbing). Place this texture under your drawing paper and rub across the paper and over the texture with the side of the 2B charcoal to transfer the pattern. Add texture where it will add interest to the drawing. Check to see how the texture weaves through the drawing in a connected way. Take a photo.

CRITIQUE

- How does your eye travel through the image now that you have broadened the value range?
- What did adding the texture do to the overall design?

TAKEAWAY

Everything you add to a drawing affects everything else around it.

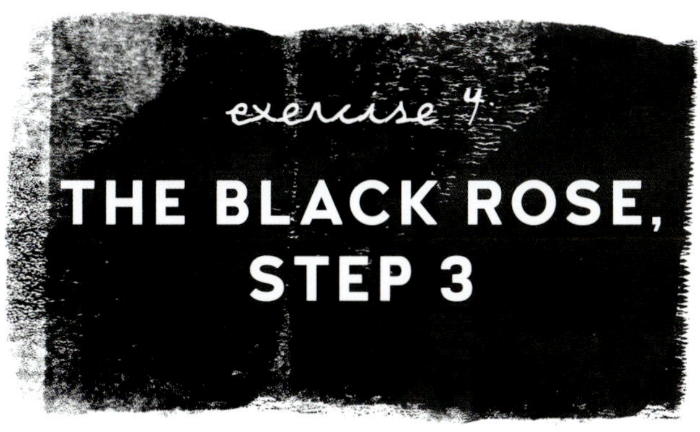

THE BLACK ROSE, STEP 3

DIRECTIONS

STEP 1

Add the lightest yellow pastel to just a few light areas of the image. Step back from the easel and assess the visual balance. Notice how adding a single color brings attention to that area. Take a photo.

STEP 2

Add some of the mid and dark yellow pastel over a few dark shapes. Step back and assess. Continue adding color according to value. When satisfied, take a photo. Add some mid and dark yellow pastel over some areas to create a monochromatic image. Step back and assess, and photograph when satisfied.

STEP 3

Add the complementary purple values to the yellow areas. Step back, assess and photograph.

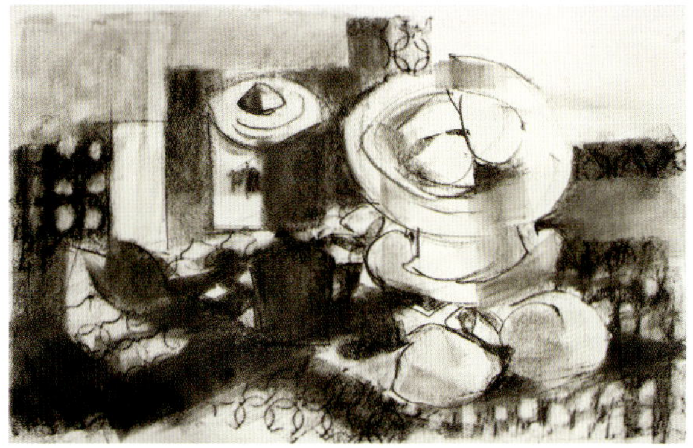

Example of texture added by Denali Brooke.

CRITIQUE

- As you drew this image, you were asked to focus on one element at a time—line, shape, edges, value, texture and color. You have created an illusion of space that is typical of Cubism, but hopefully you have imposed your own version of space.

- How would you describe the different ways you have created space in your drawing?

- How is it different from Braque's?

- What effect did color have on the image?

TAKEAWAY

Isolating each element step by step allows you to observe the impact of each in relationship to the whole.

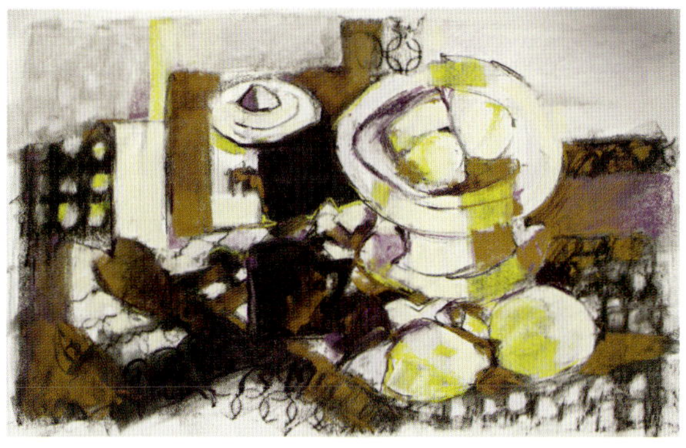

Example of pastel color added by Denali Brooke.

MATERIALS

- same as exercise 3
- a light, middle and dark lemon yellow pastel
- a light, middle and dark magenta/purple pastel

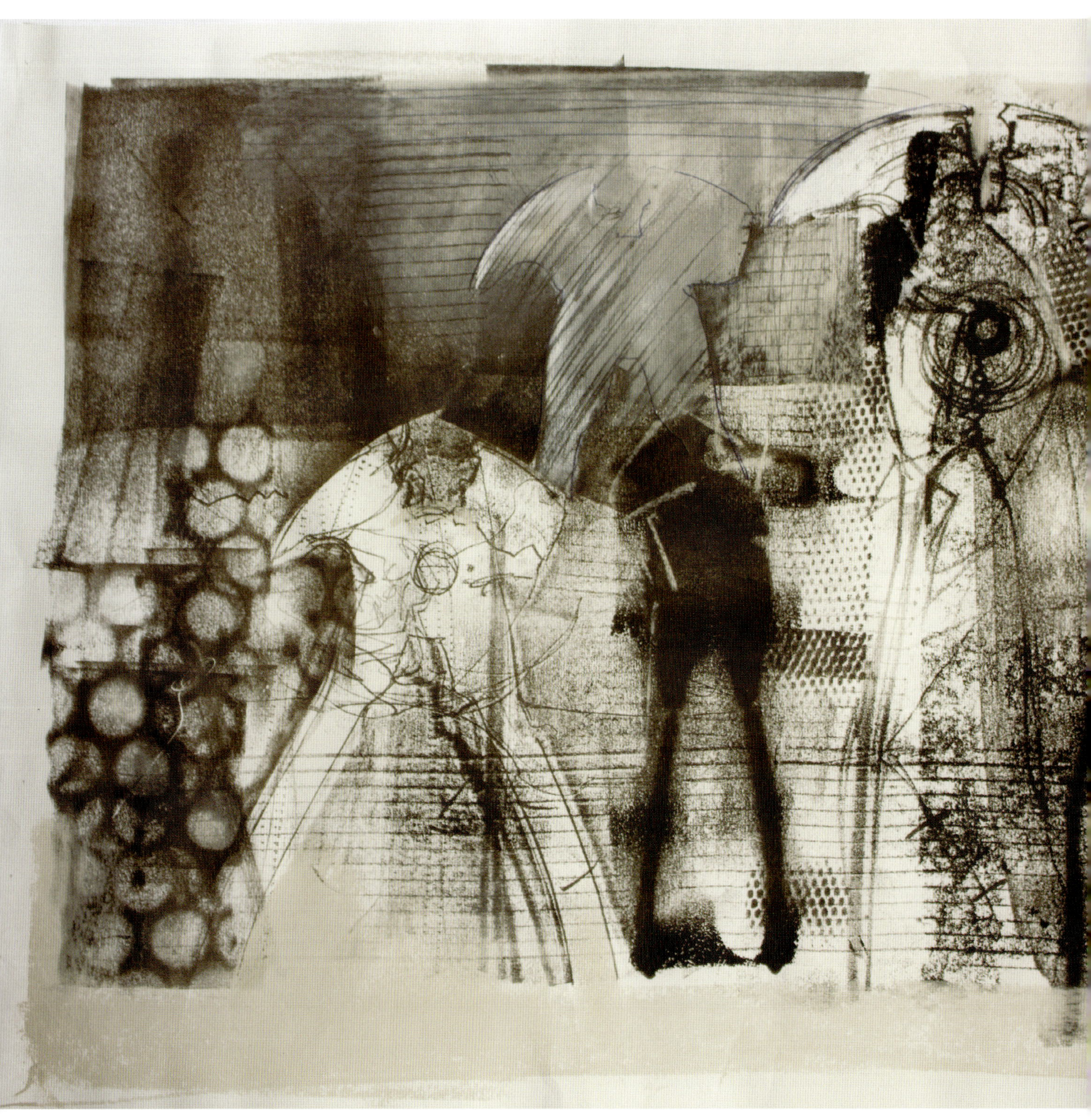

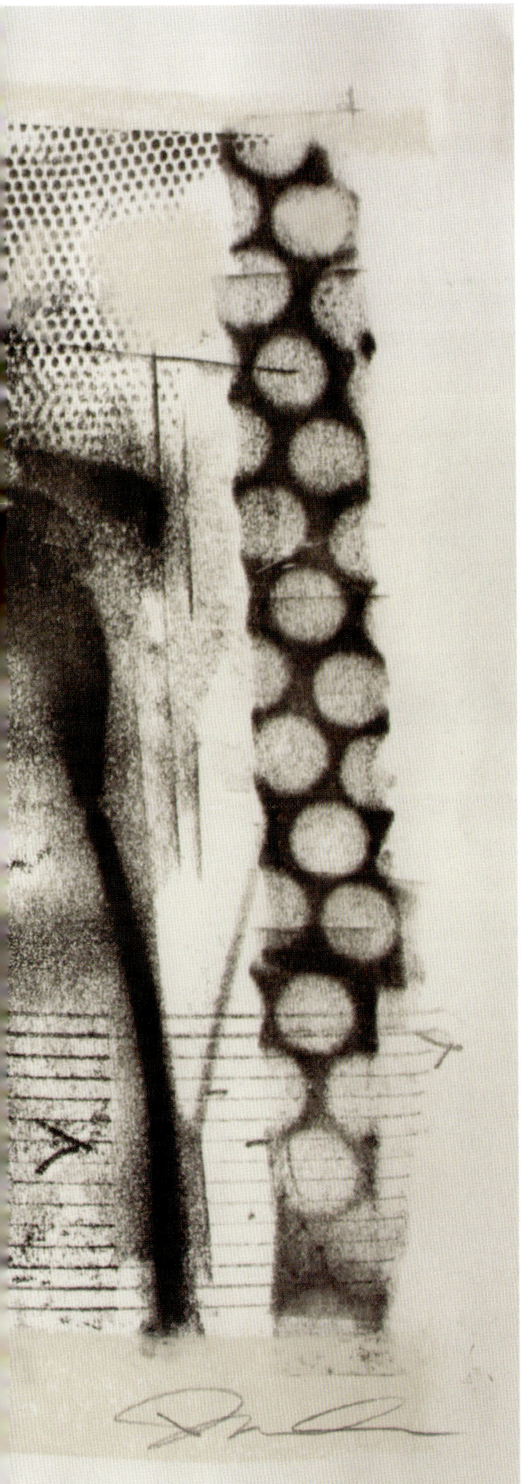

MARK-MAKING MAGIC

In chapter 1 you were introduced to the seven elements and seven principles of design from a new perspective. I shared with you the types of questions I ask myself about my own painting as I try to understand what I might change to improve a painting. I encourage you to create your own questions for self-critique that help you evaluate your work through the lens of the elements and principles.

Chapter 2 will introduce you to a range of techniques to make drawn and undrawn marks that can help expand your vocabulary of the elements. These techniques may challenge your ideas of what drawing is as they offer a pathway to creating innovative and original imagery. Whether your new favorite drawing tool becomes a comb, an eraser or a brayer, the goal is to explore and engage your unique personal perspective on creating images.

The brayer is one of my favorite tools introduced in this chapter. My own experience learning to use the brayer as a drawing tool has been very important in being able to simplify and link shapes together. Each tool will teach you new ways to respond to your surface and encourage the development of new techniques and approaches. I, like so many of my students, had to go through the process of distancing myself from controlling the tool to letting the tool teach me to do expressive mark-making.

FENCING TOOL / 18" × 24" (46CM × 61CM) /
CHARCOAL, OIL PAINT, PASTEL AND GRAPHITE ON PAPER

This artwork utilizes most of the techniques described in this chapter.

ADDITIVE & SUBTRACTIVE MARKS

Drawing is often thought of as a process that begins at one place and ends at another. This assumes that the artist knows what they want to draw and how they want to communicate it. For me drawing is a back and forth process of adding and subtracting marks with various tools and mediums. The activity of drawing is like digging for treasure—you draw here and there, cover up, reveal, until finally you have something that speaks to you. The process itself reveals what you are looking for, as opposed to you knowing exactly what you want to represent. The development of the image below demonstrates how I think about adding and subtracting as I work.

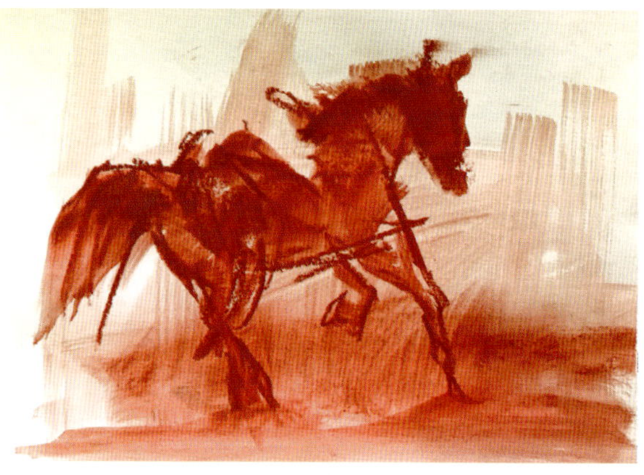

STEP 1: ADD

The light tones in this image were done first by drawing with pastel on dry paper, then adding water on a brush to spread it. The same red pastel is used to draw the body of the horse directly into the wet surface.

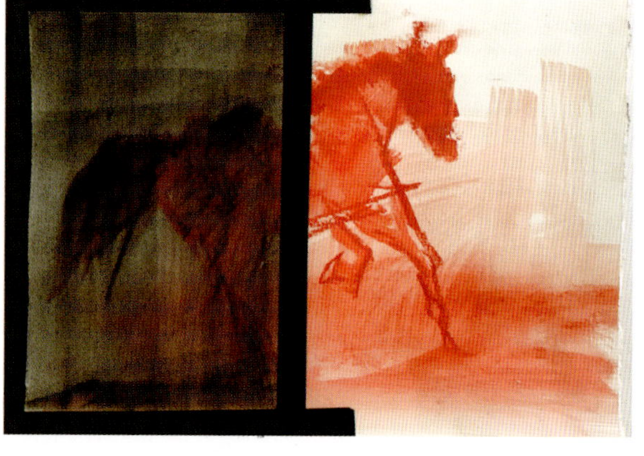

STEP 2: ADD

I tape off a rectangle and apply black pan pastel with a large sponge applicator. I use the pan pastel because it is somewhat transparent, and easy to erase. The tape is to create a clean edge.

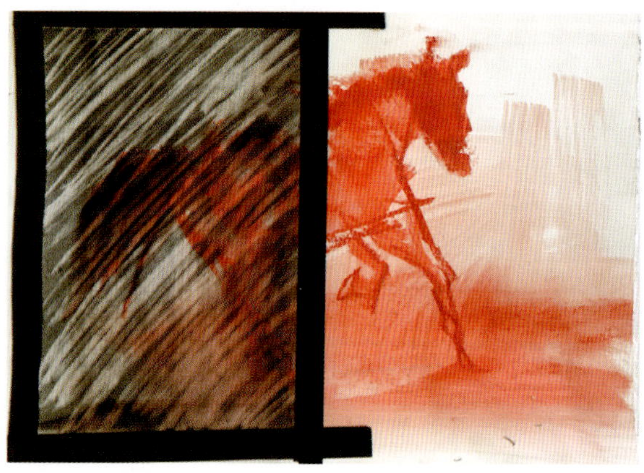

STEP 3: SUBTRACT

I use a sharp edge of a Mars eraser to remove black pastel, which leaves the resulting marks you see here.

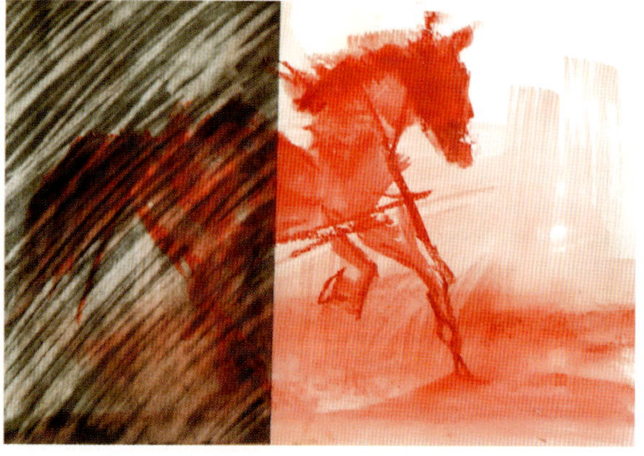

STEP 4: REMOVE TAPE

The lines made with the eraser create a sense of movement and direction. The right edge of the black rectangle cuts through the center of the horse, and is too harsh.

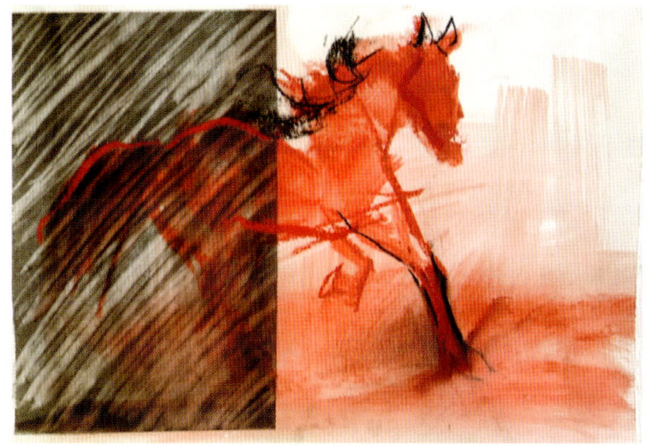

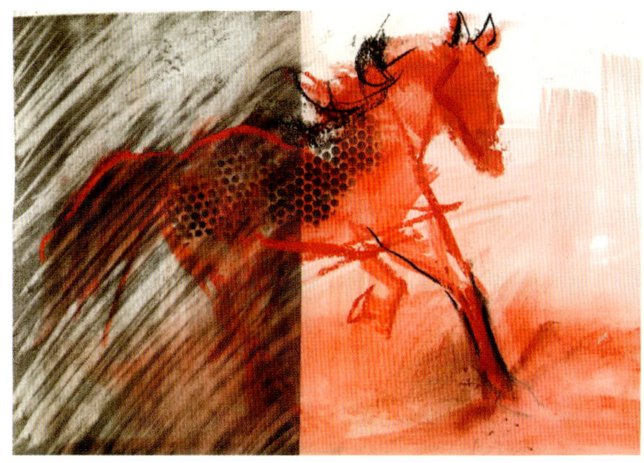

STEP 5: ADD LINE

I go into the drawing with red pastel and black charcoal to try to distract the eye from the harsh vertical edge in the center of the horse. I decide to pull the eye away by adding black line to the mane, ears and leg to counterbalance the black.

STEP 6: ADD TEXTURE

I use a piece of sequin waste as a stencil. I do this by applying black pan pastel with an applicator through the stencil. This seems to help bring the back end of the horse together with the front end.

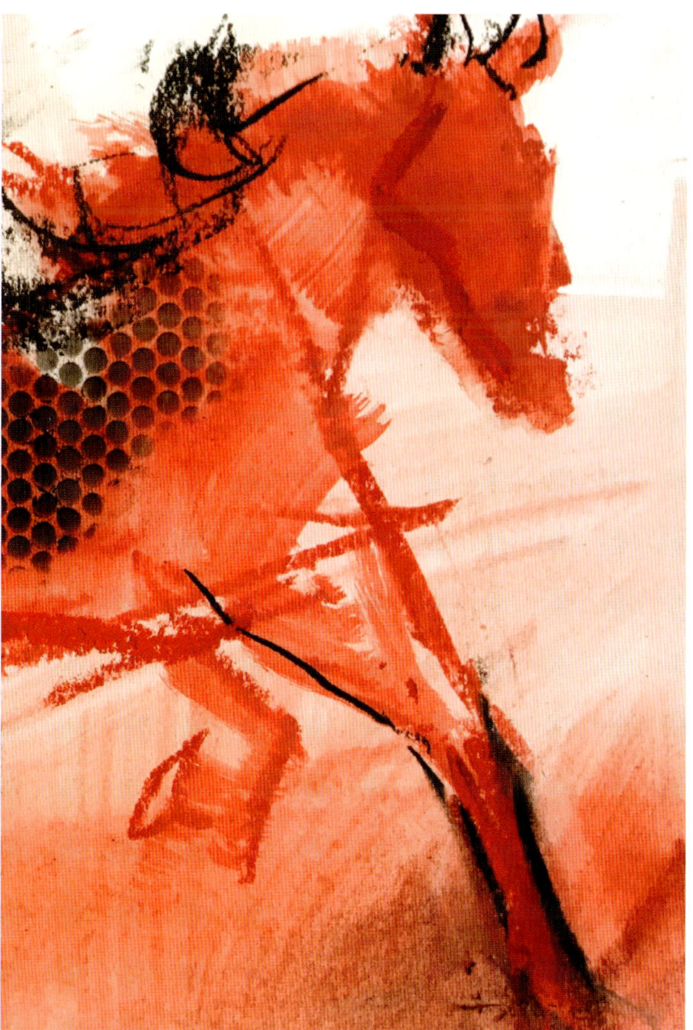

STEP 7: CROP

Here is how I cropped the image in the end. The addition of black rectangle didn't work, so cropping was the next option. Notice how the quality of space has changed because of the cropping. Risking failure is a big part of trying new things, and not being too precious with my work is required in order to do that.

FROTTAGE AND DRUBBING

Frottage means "to rub against something." If you ever transferred an engraved image from a tombstone onto paper with a wax crayon or rubbed over leaves, you were doing frottage. Non-drawn marks like these can be incorporated with drawn marks as textures, images or words as long as the paper is thin enough to record the rubbing. I've coined the word "drubbing" to describe an entire drawing that is done with this process. You can use stencils, textures, cutouts, found objects and surfaces from your environment. Wax crayons, lithography crayons, graphite, charcoal or hard pastels can all be used to rub with. I have found that the process of frottage awakens an awareness of texture in a way that is like rediscovering our tactile sense.

The process of frottage is direct and simple, but using this technique to create a story can be very exciting. When I rediscovered the process of frottage I literally spent hundreds of hours making rubbings. Some ended up as dark messes with no variation in value, but after a while I learned to control the pressure. As I explored further I started making my own stencils with textured surfaces. The search for the right line, pattern, edge, shape or texture will enrich your vocabulary and bring new awareness to your environment. This is a way of drawing that is liberating, and the remarkable marks you create can lead your imagination to pictures and stories you never knew existed.

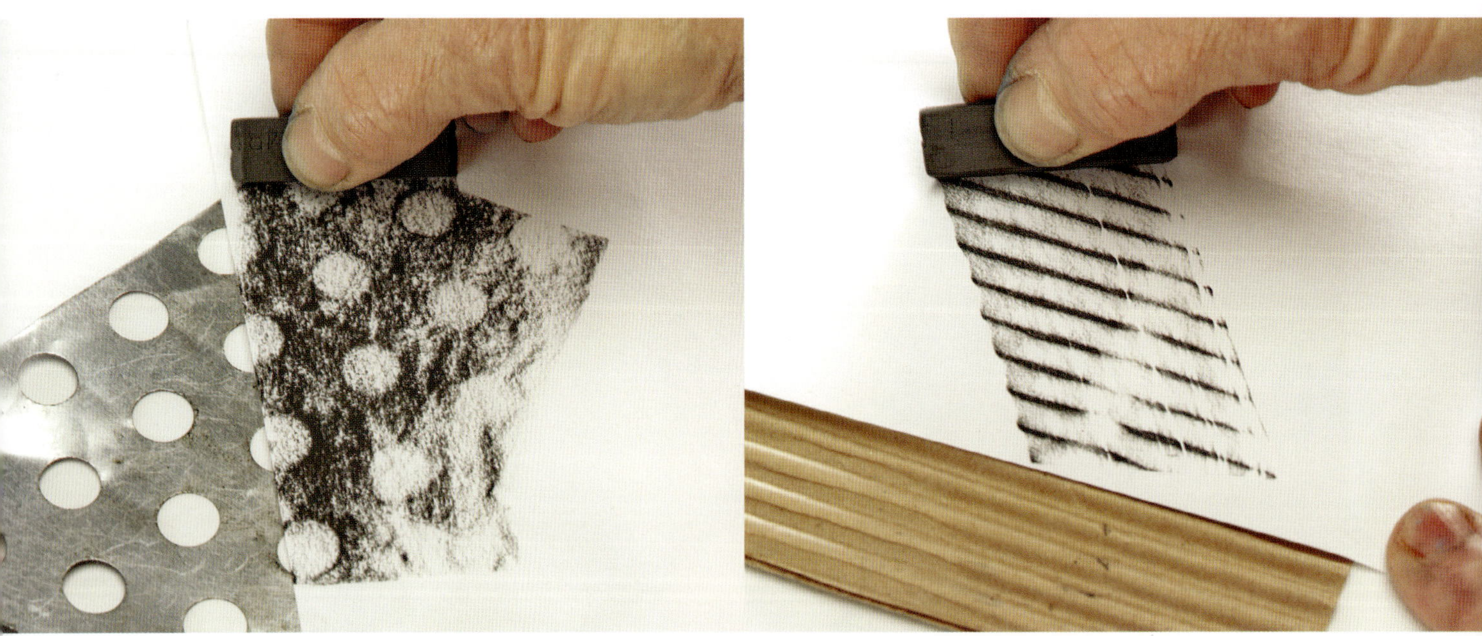

FROTTAGE

Textured material is placed under my paper, then rubbed over with charcoal to transfer the image. The amount of pressure used, the thickness of the paper and the character of the material being rubbed all contribute to the quality of the resulting image. Generally speaking, the harder the medium used to rub with, the sharper the image will be.

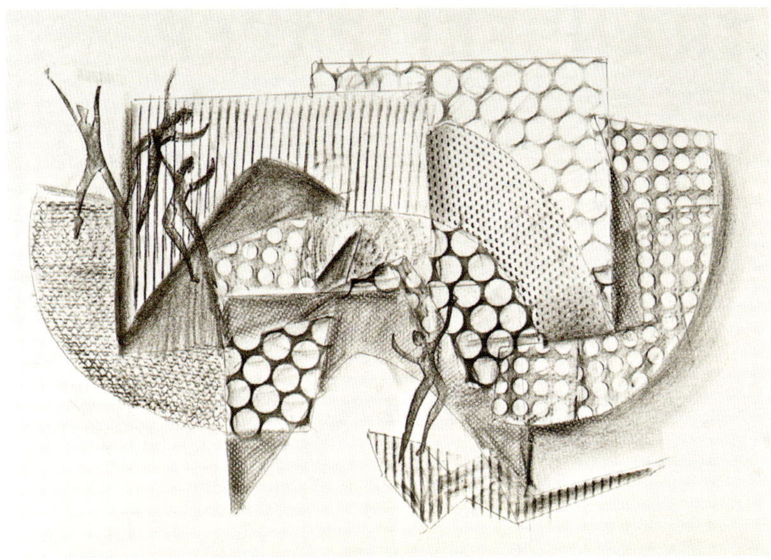

The entire image was created by rubbing different textures. Notice the change in scale from one texture to another. The figures were cut out of cardboard and also rubbed. Notice the playful sense of space and movement that can come from this approach.

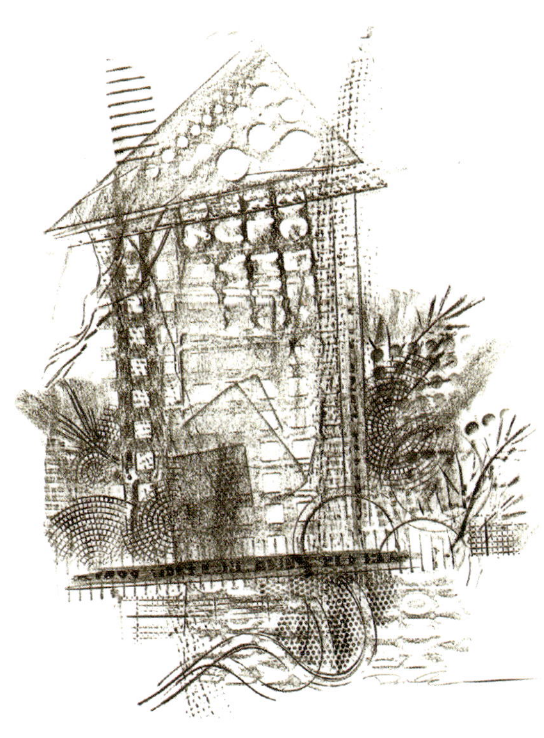

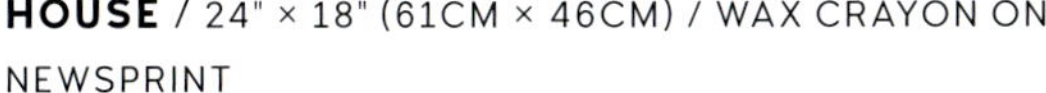

HOUSE / 24" × 18" (61CM × 46CM) / WAX CRAYON ON NEWSPRINT

I rubbed drafting stencils and needlepoint matrixes to create this drubbing of a house. This approach is perfect for freeing your imagination.

FOOD / 16" × 20" (46CM × 51CM) / CHARCOAL AND CUT PAPER COLLAGE

I wanted to make a statement about the industrialized way we think of our food. Simple, old techniques such as rubbing can be used to portray very complex, contemporary issues.

PASTEL TRANSFER PAPER

Creating extremely fine lines can be difficult when drawing or painting directly with a chunky pastel stick. The pastel transfer method is very effective for producing such fine lines. This method can also be used when you wish to trace around an object or transfer the same image repeatedly onto your final surface. Fine lines can be traced through stencils to get perfect letters or repeated patterns.

Nontraditional drawing tools like fingernails, sticks, combs, credit cards and pattern wheels can make wonderful marks when used as scribing tools. When used in combination with other media, pastel transfer can open the doorway to layering imagery in novel and interesting ways.

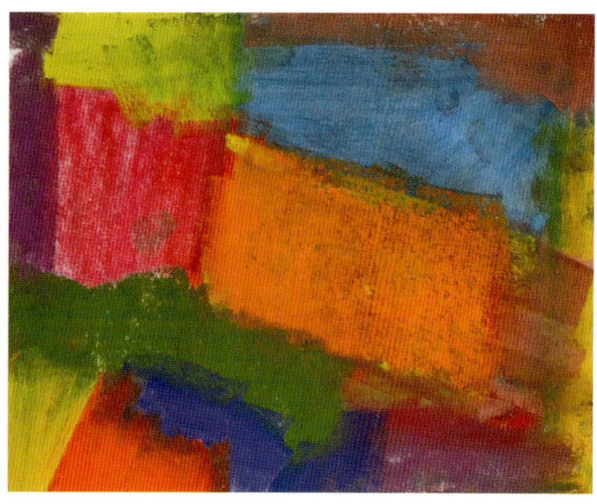

PASTEL TRANSFER PAPER
I've colored one side of a piece of vellum, applying the pastel fairly thickly.

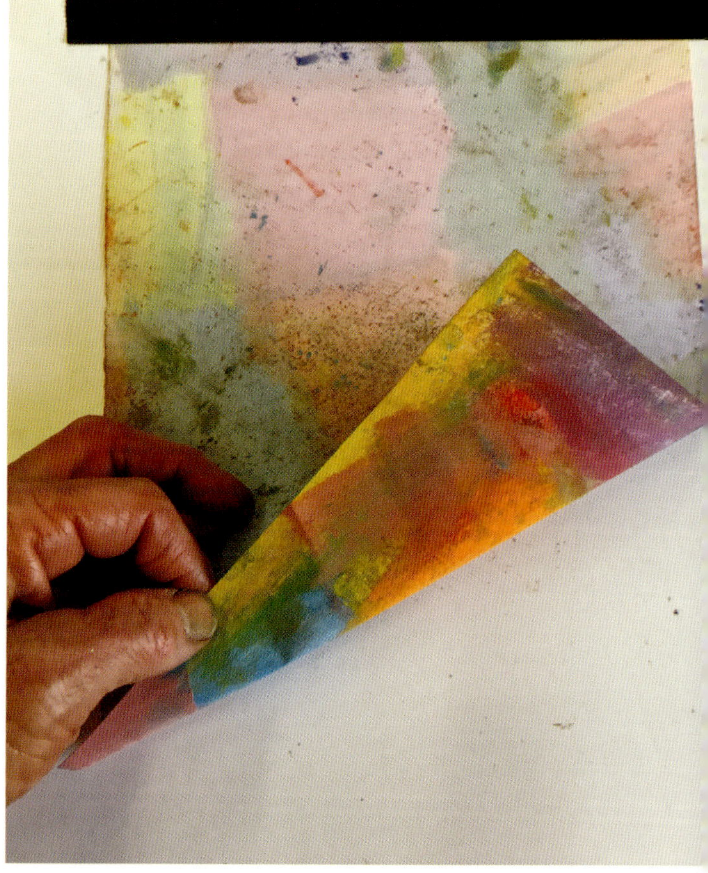

HINGE THE PAPER
I carefully place the vellum pastel side down onto a piece of paper I want to transfer to and hinge it at the top with masking tape.

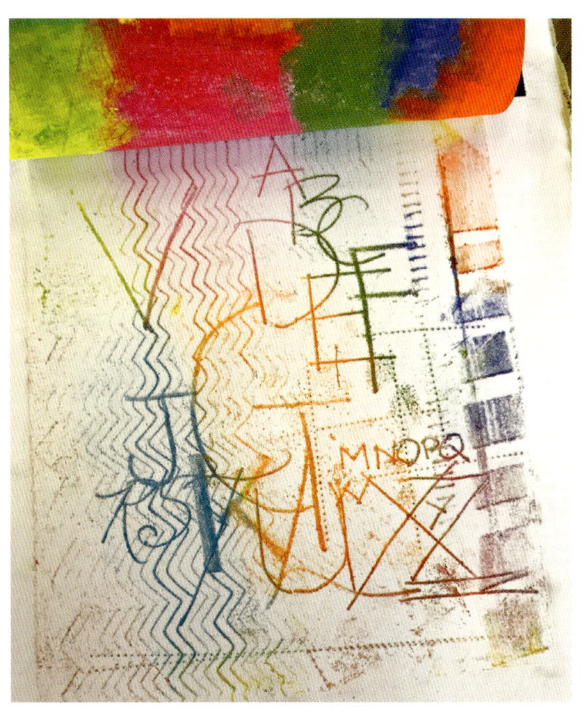

OVERLAPPING

I make marks on the non colored side of the vellum to transfer the pastel to the paper below. Notice how the overlapping of letters and marks creates an illusion of depth.

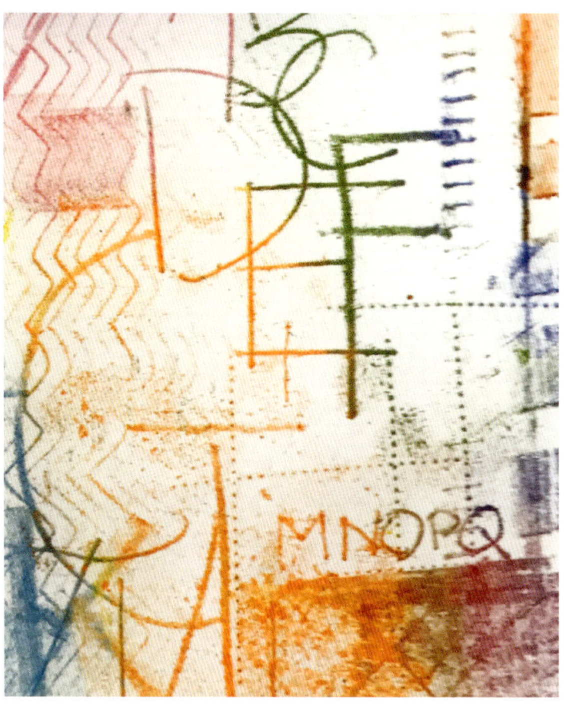

CLOSE UP

You can see how color and size affect the feeling of space that is created by the various tools.

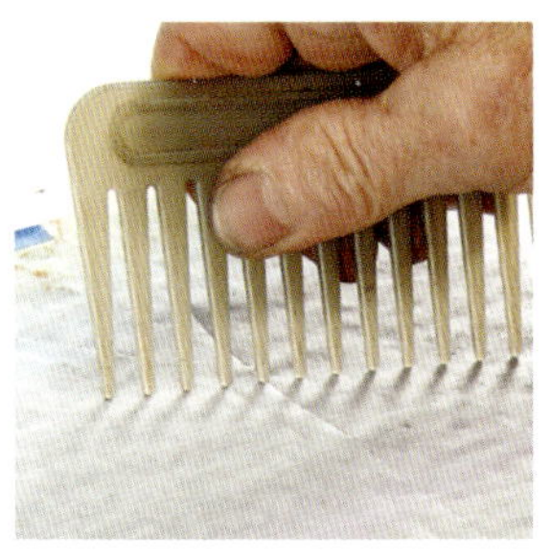

HAIR COMB

The teeth of a comb make parallel lines.

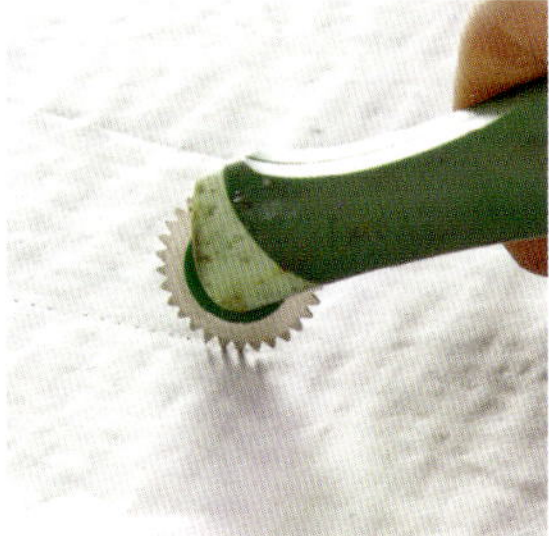

DRESSMAKER'S WHEEL

Dotted lines are fun to incorporate into your vocabulary of marks.

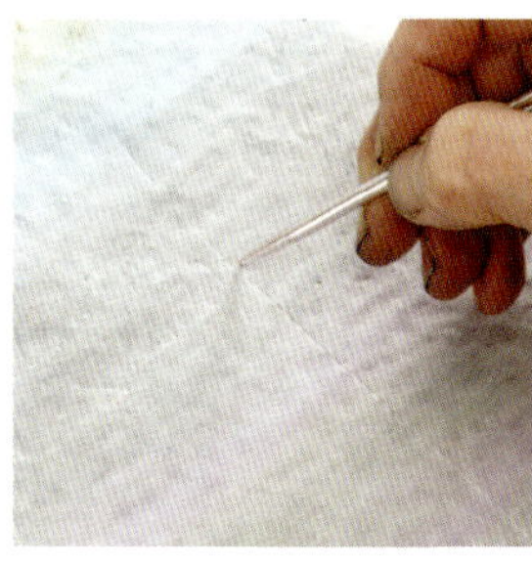

KNITTING NEEDLE

Think of the variety of line weights you can develop with various needle sizes.

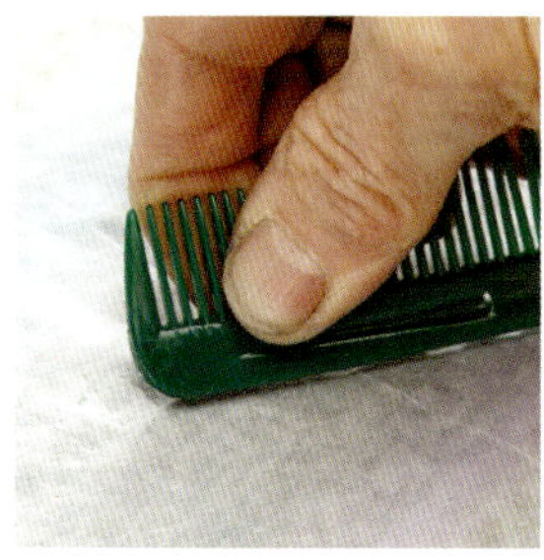

BACK OF COMB

The back of the comb will make softer, wider lines.

STENCILS, STAMPING AND EMBOSSING WITH PASTEL

Stencils, stamps, and embossing are all ways to create beautiful marks without actually drawing. These non-drawn marks can stand alone as beautiful finished pieces or be included with other drawn and painted imagery. Pan pastel is perfect for getting into those small areas of a stencil where chunky stick pastels simply cannot go. A straight or torn piece of paper can make a wonderful edge with either stick or pan pastel, and both can be used effectively with stamps. Blind embossing is another way to create patterns and layering in your work.

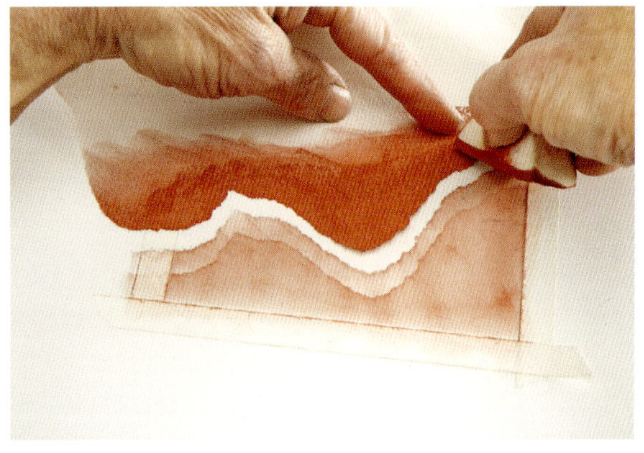

CREATING UNIQUE STENCILS

This is a great technique for creating mountain ranges, clouds, and waves without actually draw-

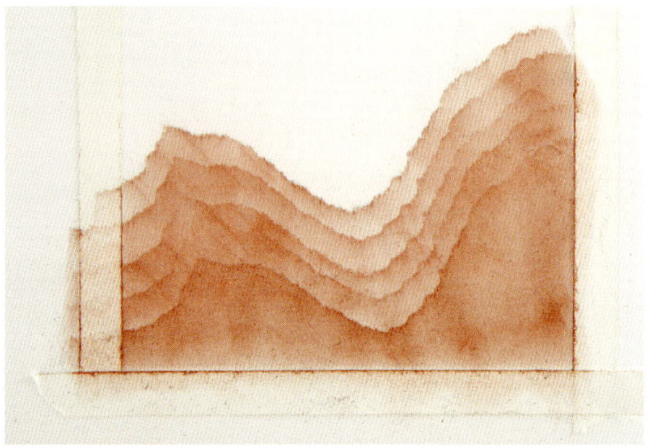

ing. Rip a piece of paper, deposit pastel on it, and rub pastel off the torn edge and onto the drawing paper. Repeat as you move the stencil.

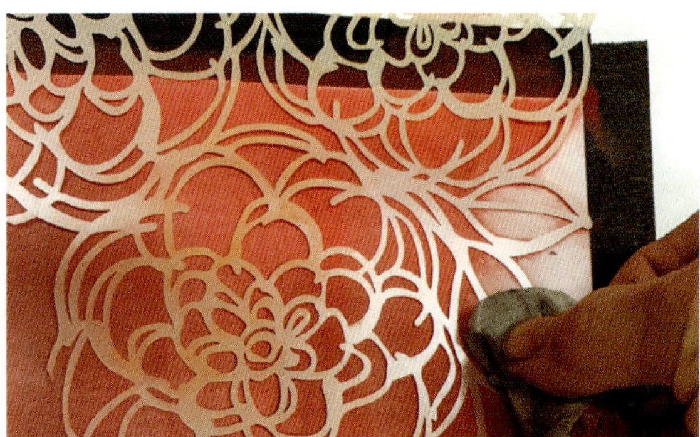

MULTICOLOR STENCILING

PanPastels are wonderful to use with stencils to get into small negative spaces that a stick pastel just can't fit into. I used cosmetic wedges as applicators and four pan pastel colors to make this design. The plastic stencil shown above can be easily cleaned with soap and water.

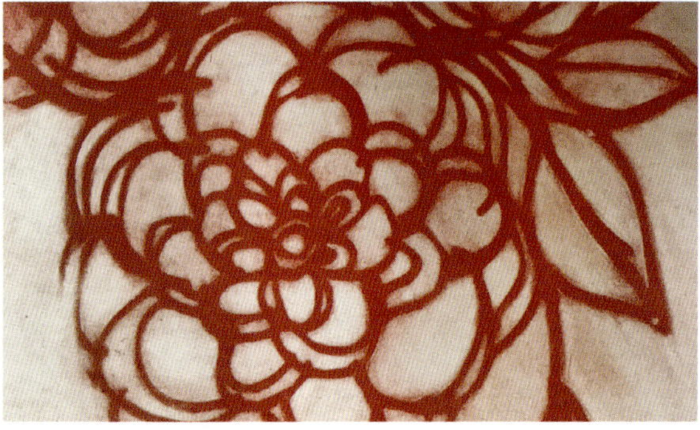

COLORED PAPER

I created the illusion of having drawn the outlines of the stencil by using a light color of PanPastel on a dark red paper. The negative spaces are the pastel, and the red lines are the color of the paper.

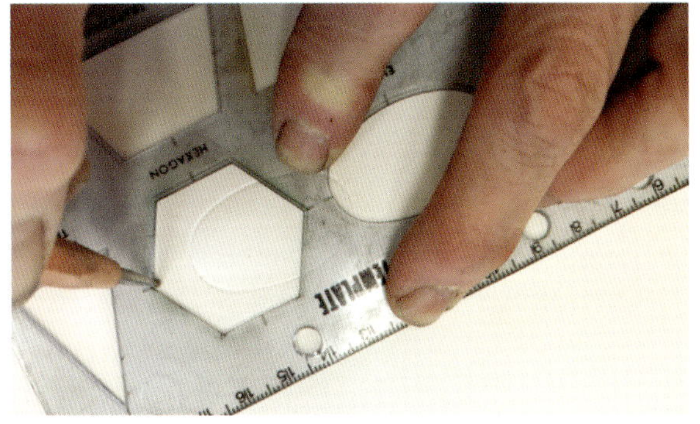
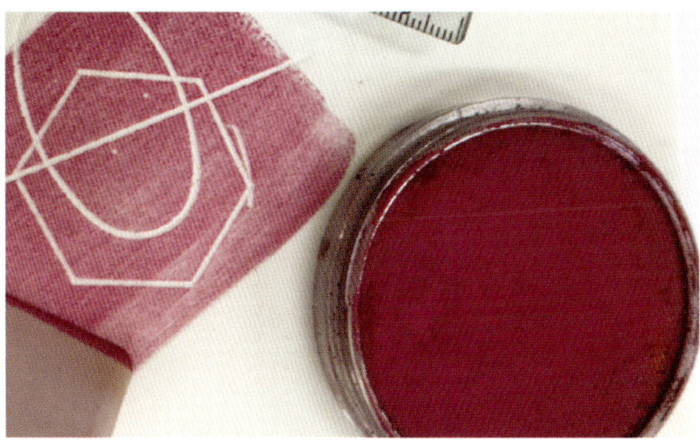

BLIND EMBOSSING

Take a knitting needle or embossing tool and trace around a stencil. Run the side of a pastel stick or flat edged applicator loaded with Pan Pastel over the embossed area. The marks are revealed because the pastel doesn't go down into depressed areas.

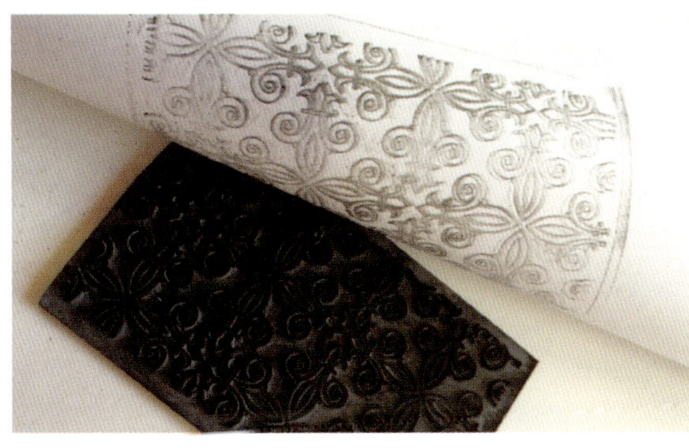
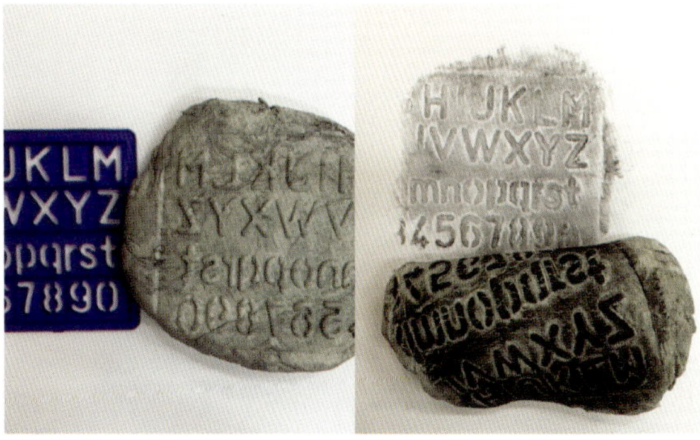

RUBBER AS STAMP FOR PASTEL

Rub a rubber stamp with pastel and stamp with it to make words or patterns.

MODELING CLAY AS STAMP FOR PASTEL

Take an impression of a texture or stencil with modeling clay. Rub with pastel use as a stamp.

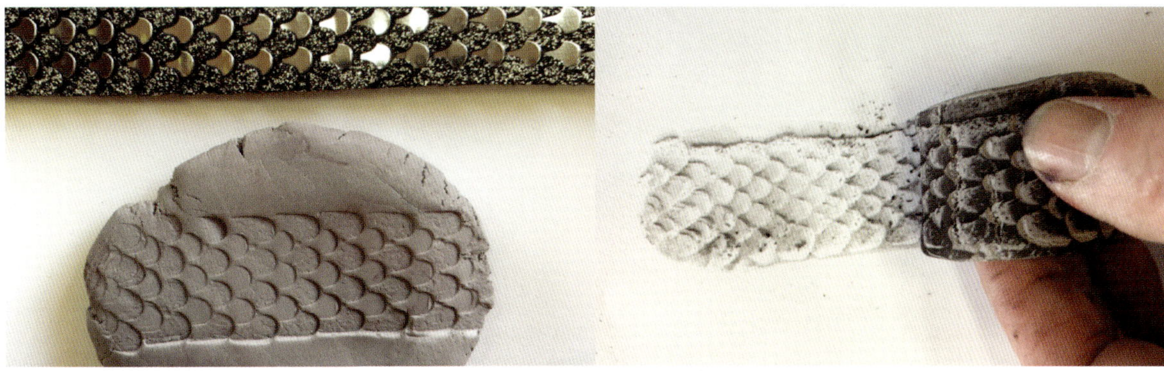

KNEADED ERASER AS STAMP FOR PASTEL

Make an impression of a texture with an eraser, apply pastel to the surface, and you have a stamp!

TRACE MONOTYPE

You can think of a trace monotype as a kind of handmade carbon paper, but instead of carbon the medium is printmaking ink or paint. The lines that are transferred will have a unique quality that a regular drawing implement can't make. Follow the steps below to see how to apply the ink to freezer paper, and experiment using different tools and materials to draw with. This method enables you to make multiple tracings of an image and to make unique marks.

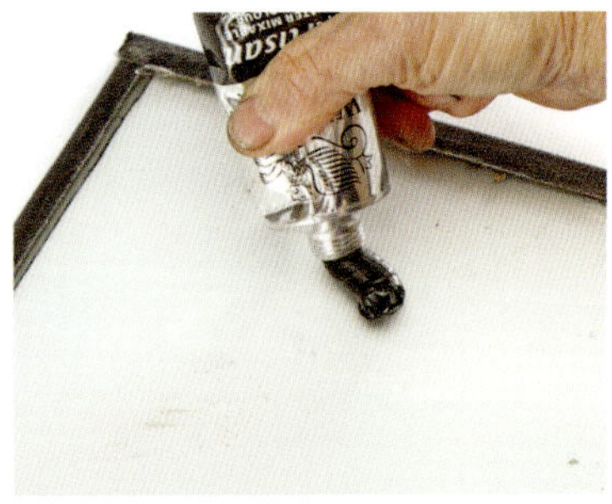

STEP 1
Squeeze out a one-inch (25mm) line of water-miscible oil paint onto a glass surface. This method can also be done with slow drying acrylic or printing ink.

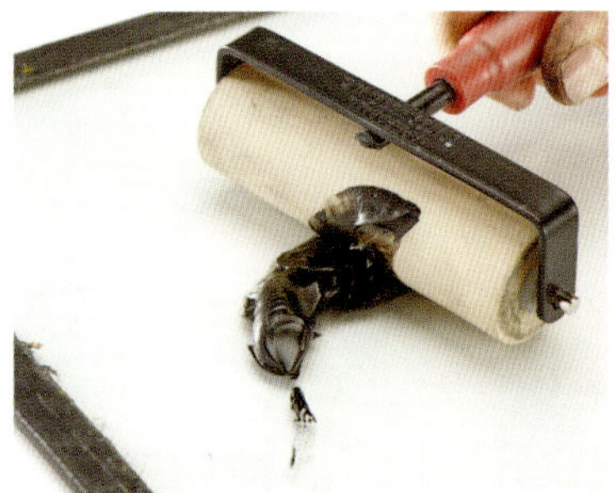

STEP 2
Charge the brayer with the paint by touching the brayer to a bit of the paint, and then pull it toward you to draw down the paint.

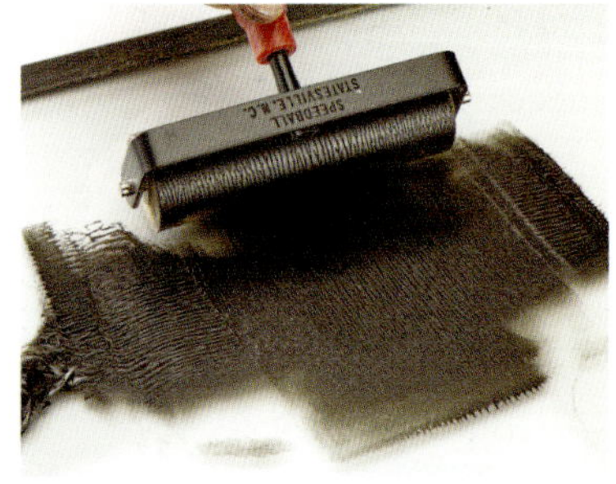

STEP 3
Roll the brayer back and forth in different directions, lifting the brayer at the end of each stroke to coat it evenly.

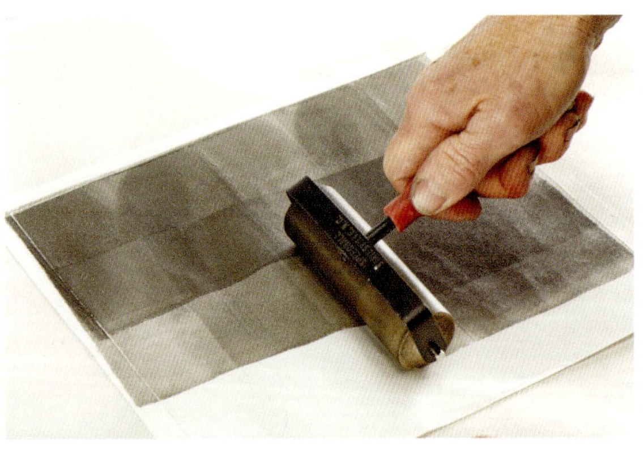

STEP 4
Roll out the paint onto the slick side of a piece of freezer paper or parchment paper. Be careful not to roll the ink out too thickly.

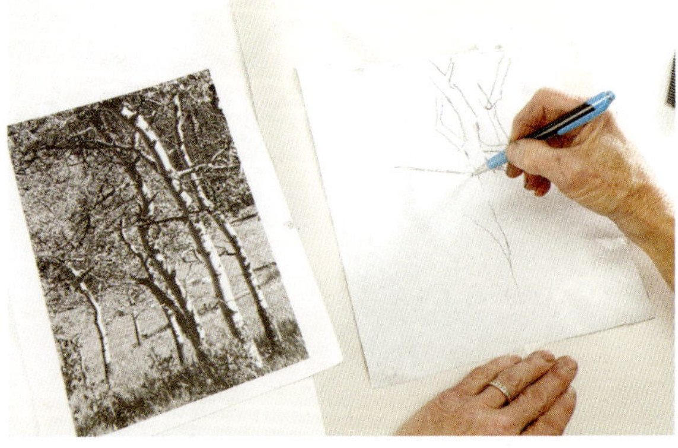

STEP 5
Place ink side down to a clean piece of drawing paper, and hinge at the top. Begin drawing or tracing over another image.

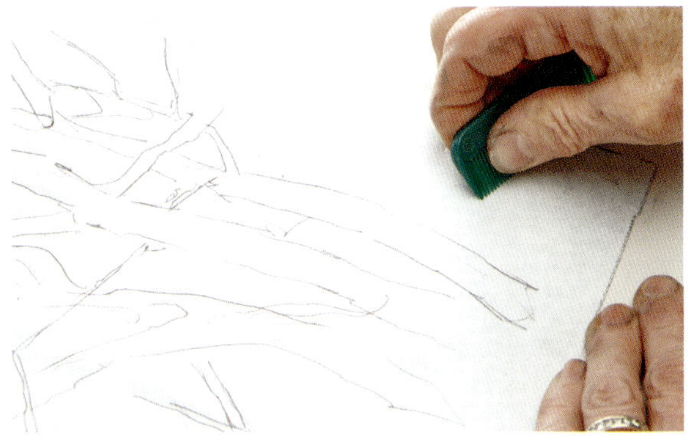

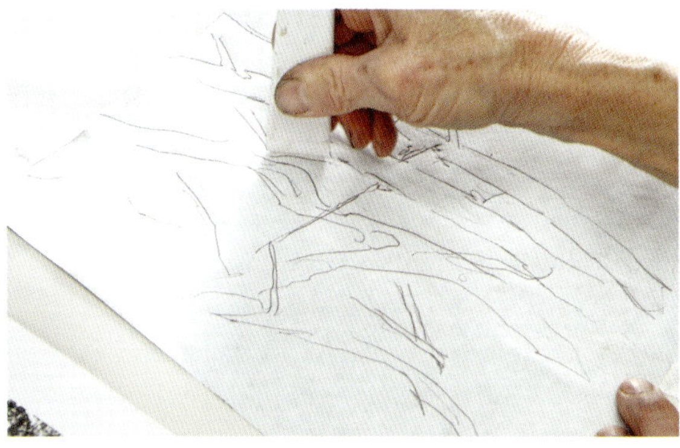

STEP 6

Draw with different tools and vary your pressure to create novel marks. Here I am using a comb to imply grass.

STEP 7

The flat edge of a plastic handle will make a wide line, while the corner will make a thin line. I can get a varied line by twisting.

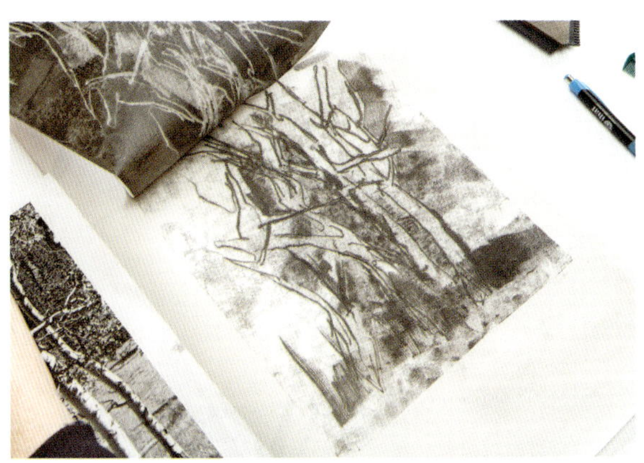

STEP 8

Check your work as you go. Notice that the ink side of the transfer paper is a reverse image of your drawing. You can re-ink the freezer paper and use it multiple times to create more than one drawing.

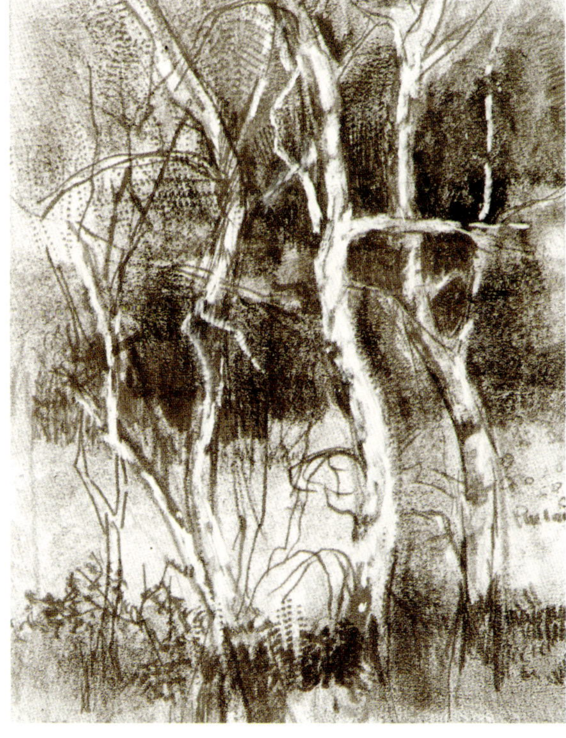

THE FINAL IMAGE

Here is the final image using the trace monotype process. Notice the variety of marks and values I was able to achieve using various tools. The drawing can stand as it is or be added to with pastel.

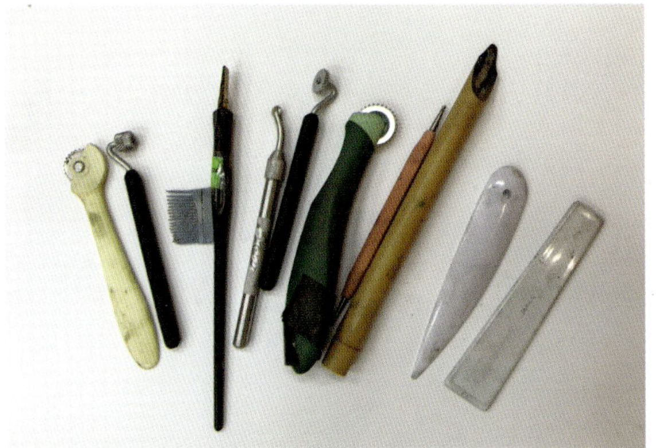

ANYTHING CAN BECOME A DRAWING TOOL

Here is the assortment of tools I used to create the trace monotype.

DRAWING WITH A BRAYER

I credit my practice of using the brayer as a drawing tool for helping me broaden my vocabulary of marks. It has become one of my favorite drawing tools, not just because of the variety of ways it can be used, but because it has forced me to simplify shapes and learn more about abstraction. Using a brayer allows me to actually draw with textures, with a process called "offsetting." The brayer eliminates the urge to outline because it is so difficult to make precise lines, thereby forcing me to think in terms of shape, rather than line and detail. The brayer requires you to use your whole arm and to rotate your wrist as you draw to get a broad range of marks. The size of the marks can easily be increased with a wider brayer. A brayer can make a rolled line or a segmented line, and is as expressive as any other painting tool.

Working with the brayer helps me organize elements and makes me much more aware of placement and overall design. I use the brayer in four different ways:

- to create abstract backgrounds
- to transfer textures and patterns to my surface
- to create high contrast pathways in my work
- to make unique marks.

I've found gouache, acrylics, water-miscible oil paint and various printmaking inks all work well with the brayer in combination with pastel, printmaking and oil work. Depending on the viscosity of the medium, anything that sticks to the brayer in an even manner can be used, as long it doesn't dry too quickly.

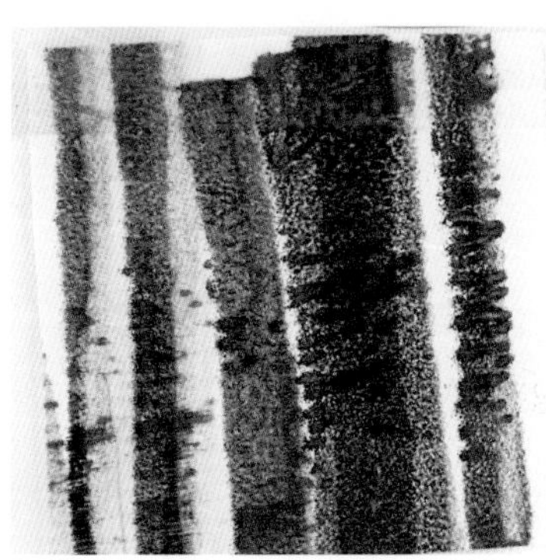

BRAYER MARKS
The brayer is inked evenly and pressed onto the paper without rolling to create lines that are the width of the brayer.

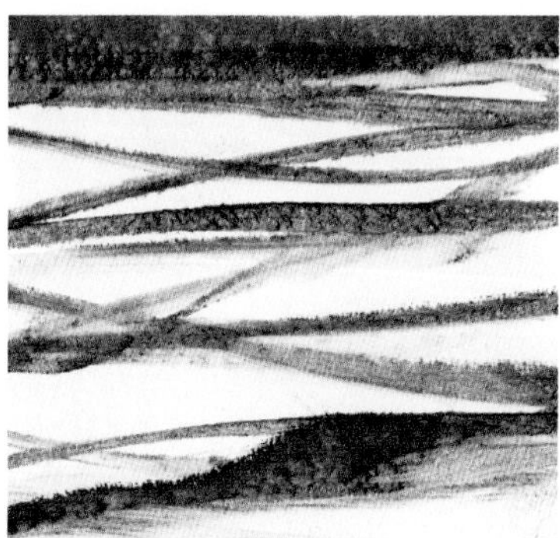

BRAYER LINES
The brayer is inked and tipped on its edge, and then the brayer is rolled, leaving behind thin lines.

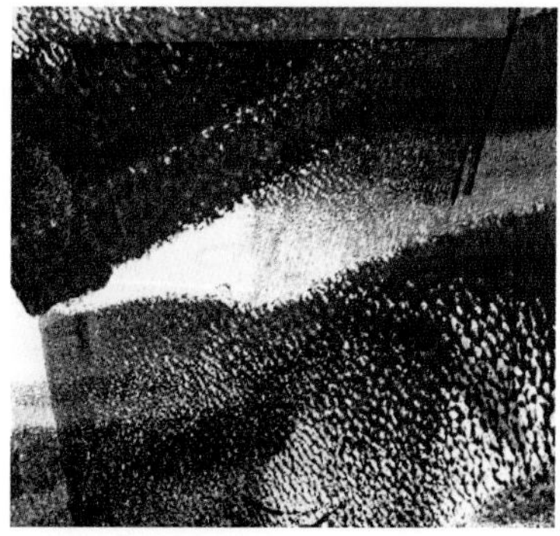

BRAYER TEXTURE
The brayer is inked unevenly, then rocked back and forth as it is rolled.

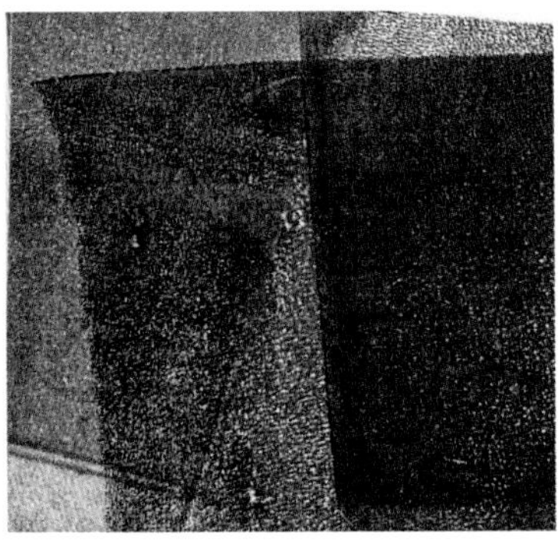

OVERLAPPING STROKES

Overlapping strokes create layering of depth and variation in the opacity of the color.

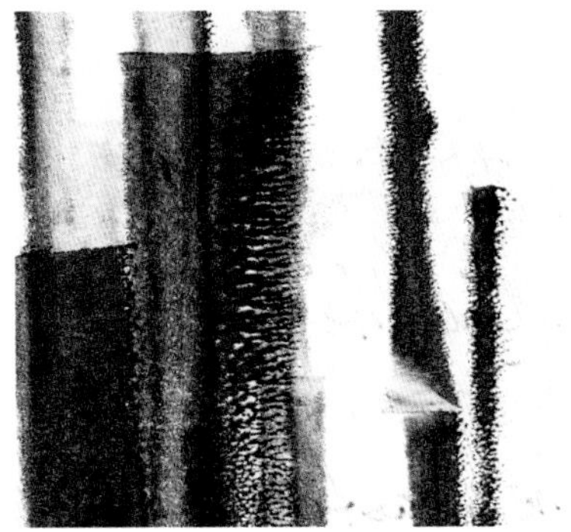

COMBINING MARKS

Mix and match brayer techniques for interesting effects. In this example, lines are combined with rolled strokes.

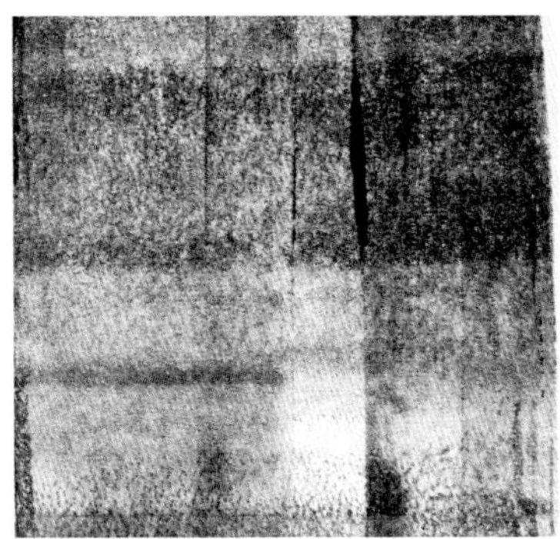

LAP LINES

The brayer's diameter will determine how long a roll you can go before running low on ink. Each revolution will print lighter and lighter. The term for these overlapping lines is "lap lines." If your goal is to achieve a perfectly smooth surface, lap lines may not be desirable. The more you practice using the brayer, the easier controlling the brayer becomes.

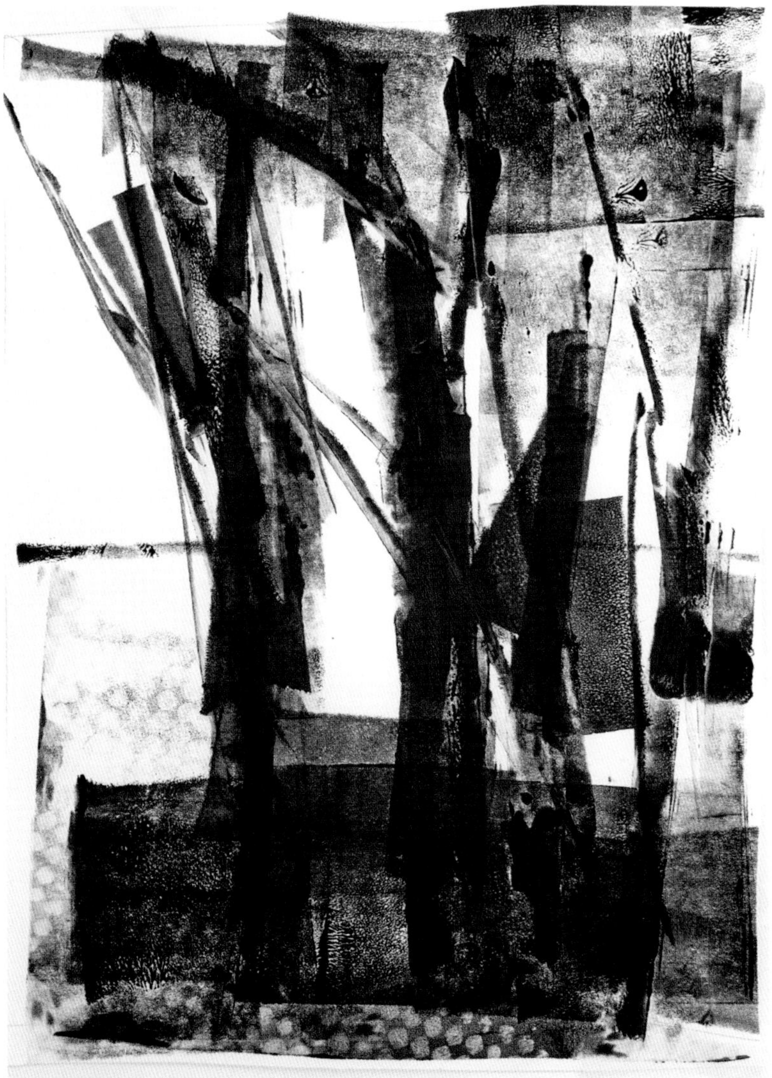

TREES / 14" × 10" (36CM × 25CM) / WATER-MISCIBLE OIL PAINT ON DRAWING PAPER

This image was drawn directly onto paper with the brayer and water-miscible oil paint. The places you see texture and pattern are the result of a process called "offsetting," which will be described in the coming pages. The image is strong because of the quality and variety of marks that are linked together to create shapes. This image can stand alone or be used as an underpainting for pastel.

ROLLOGRAPHY AND OFFSETTING WITH THE BRAYER

The processes described below will allow you to literally roll out textures to incorporate into your drawings. Rollography is my made-up word for the process of rolling over an object placed under your paper with an inked brayer to print a frottaged image of the object onto the paper. This process is best suited for lighter weight paper because the brayer needs to "feel" the object through the paper.

Offsetting is the process of transferring a pattern or visual texture onto the brayer and then rolling that image onto your paper. This process is suitable for any weight paper.

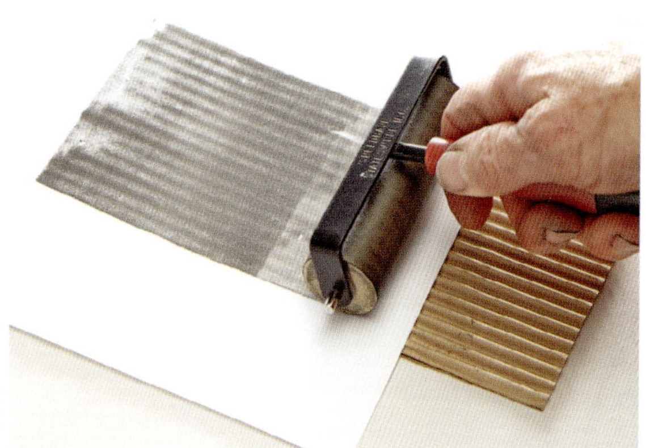

ROLLOGRAPHY

An inked brayer rolls over an uninked piece of ridged corrugated cardboard. The texture transfers onto the paper. This process works best with thinner papers.

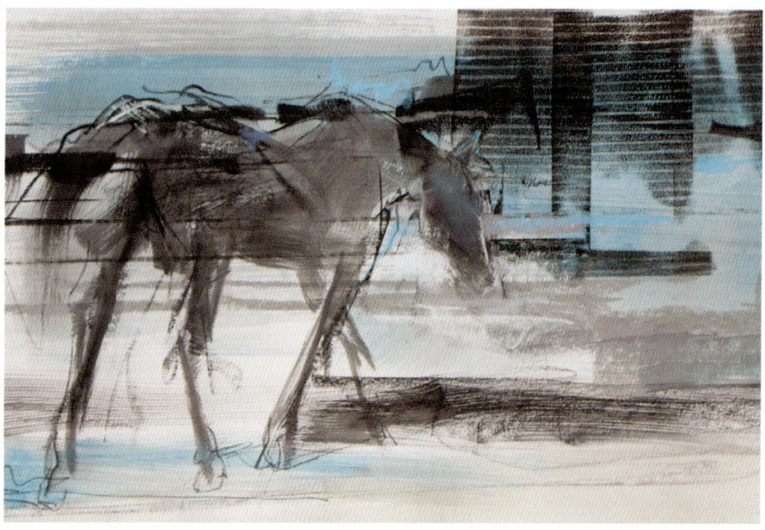

PASSING THROUGH / 15" × 22" (38CM × 56CM) / WATERCOLOR, CHARCOAL, PASTEL, SUMI INK AND OIL PAINT ON STONEHENGE PAPER

Notice the use of offsetting to imply—rather than describe—a fence or building in the top right quadrant. The repeated horizontal lines and broken imagery create a strong feeling of movement, as though the horse is just "passing through."

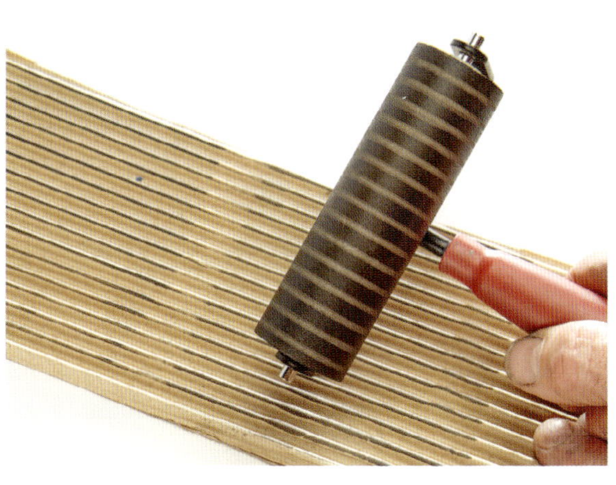 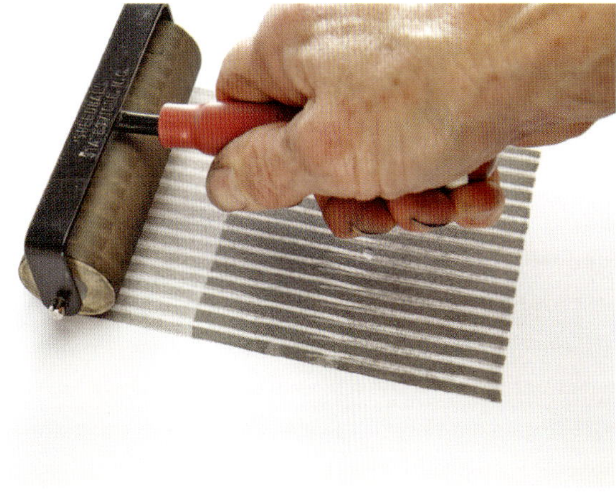

OFFSETTING STEP 1

An inked brayer is rolled over an uninked piece of corrugated cardboard. The ink is deposited on the areas that come into contact with the cardboard, which creates a line pattern on the brayer. This is known as offsetting onto the brayer.

OFFSETTING STEP 2

The offset image is rolled onto a paper surface to transfer the image. This method can be used to transfer patterns and texture to any thickness of paper.

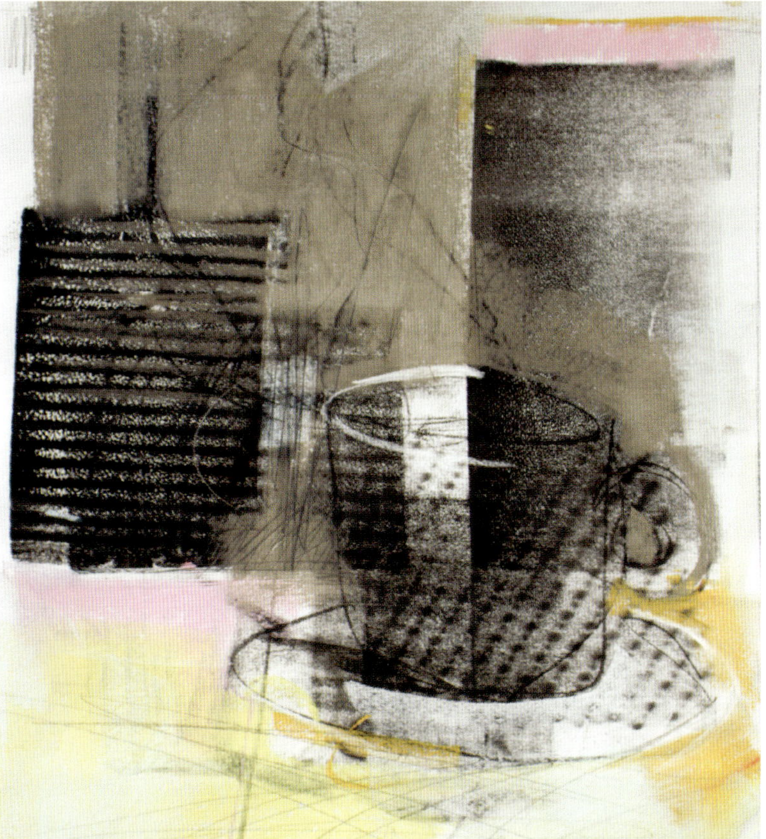

CUP O' JOE / 20" × 18" (51CM × 46CM) / OIL PAINT, PASTEL AND CHARCOAL ON DRAWING PAPER

This image utilizes both offsetting and direct drawing with the brayer. Pastel was added afterwards.

ALTERING THE BRAYER

When a brayer is altered, it can be used as a rolling stamp. Each brayer has a set repeat, based on its diameter and width. As the ink is rolled off the brayer onto the paper, lap lines occur after each revolution as well as at both ends of the brayer. The lap lines add a plaid-like quality to the image. To counteract this you may want to re-ink the brayer after each revolution to maintain continuous value or to make an area more opaque. Instead of throwing away old or damaged brayers, you can alter them by wrapping materials like string around the brayer, or roll over gritty materials that might otherwise damage your brayers. You can create unique surfaces to roll on with found objects or by applying various media to the brayer. Be sure to keep a reference journal of the techniques and results you discover. These special textures can become a personal arsenal of imagery that will be recognizable in your work.

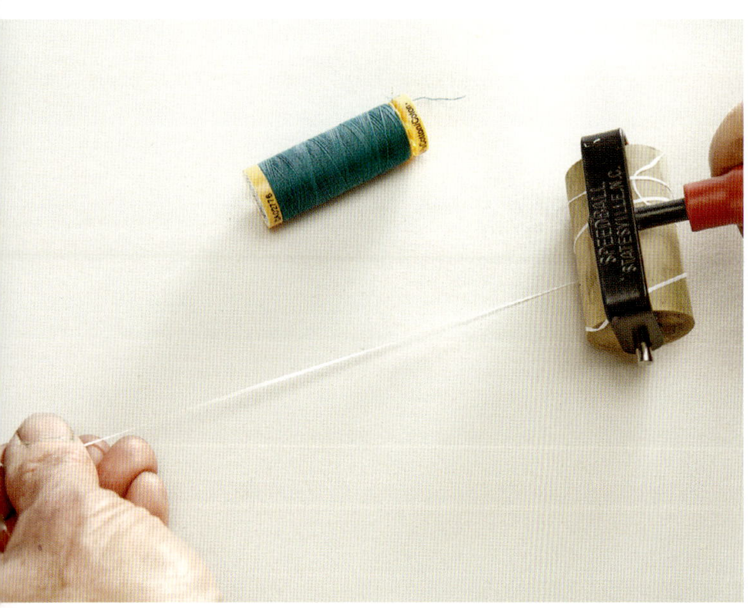
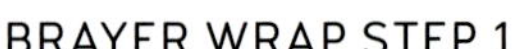

BRAYER WRAP STEP 1
Wrap thread around the brayer and then charge the brayer with ink. Depending on how you ink the brayer, the string will appear as continuous squiggle lines. You can also ink the brayer first, then wrap it with string.

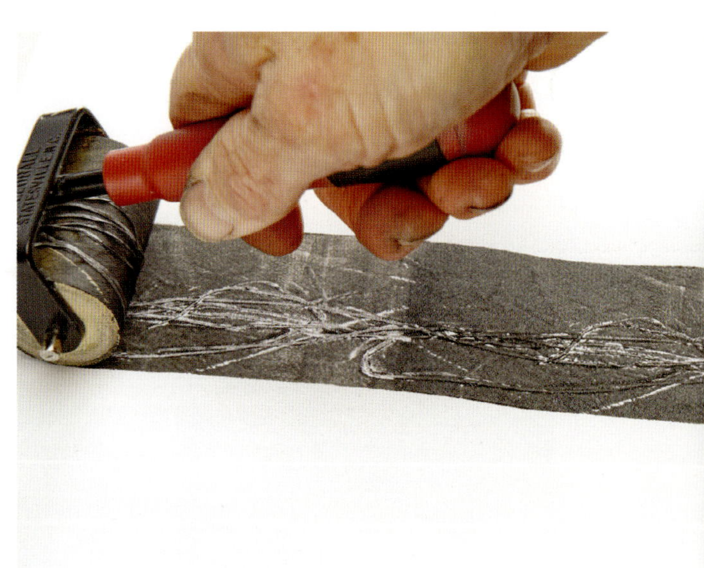

BRAYER WRAP STEP 2
The image and pattern of the string blocks the ink and leaves a continuous pattern of squiggles.

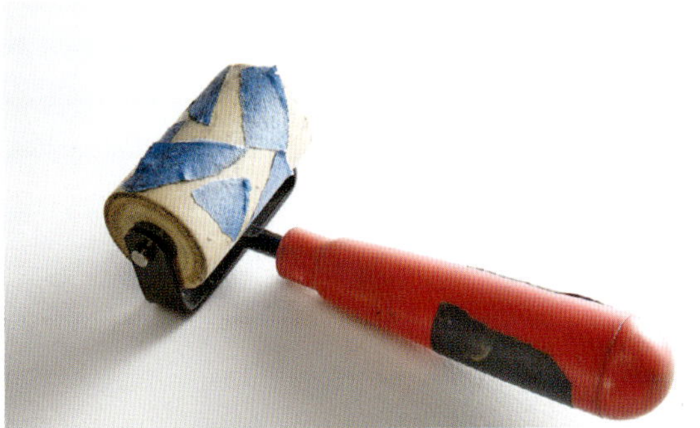

MASKING OUT THE BRAYER STEP 1

Attach pieces of masking tape to the brayer.

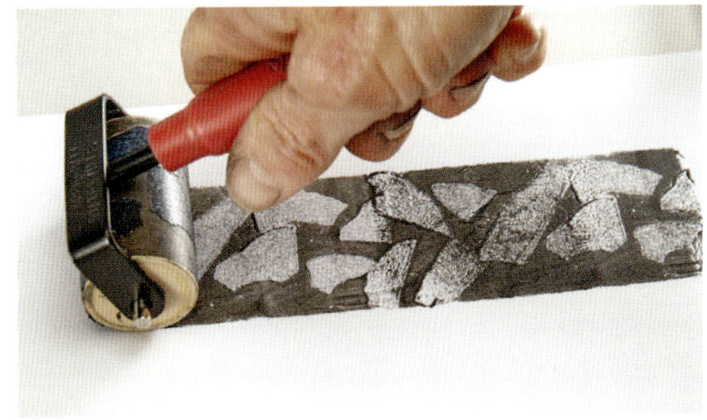

MASKING OUT THE BRAYER STEP 2

Roll the brayer in ink, then roll the brayer over your paper.

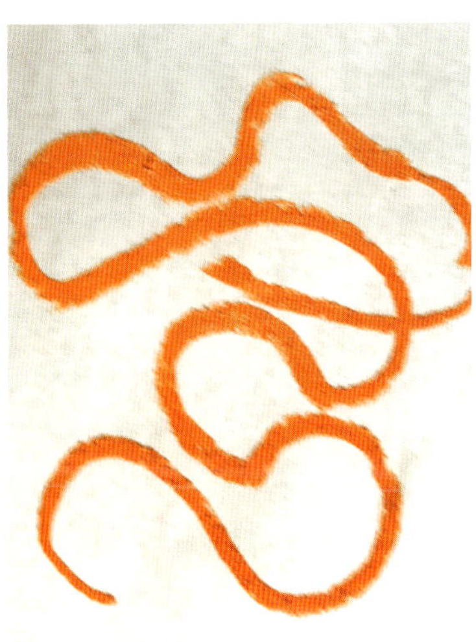

PASTEL AS RESIST STEP 1

Draw with pastel.

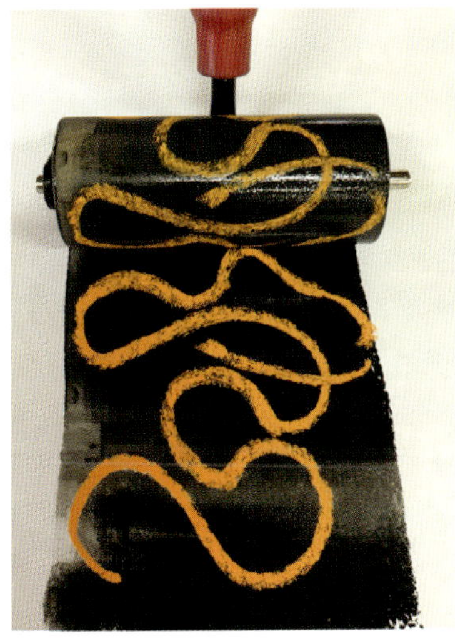

PASTEL AS RESIST STEP 2

When the pastel mark is rolled over with an inked brayer, the pastel resists the ink.

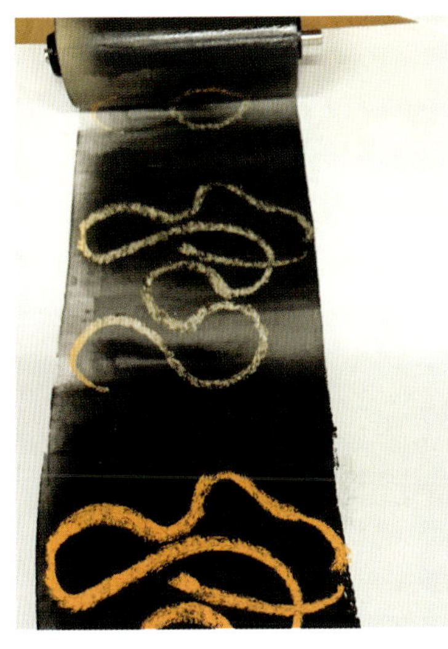

PASTEL AS RESIST STEP 3

As the brayer continues rolling, the pastel continues to block the ink.

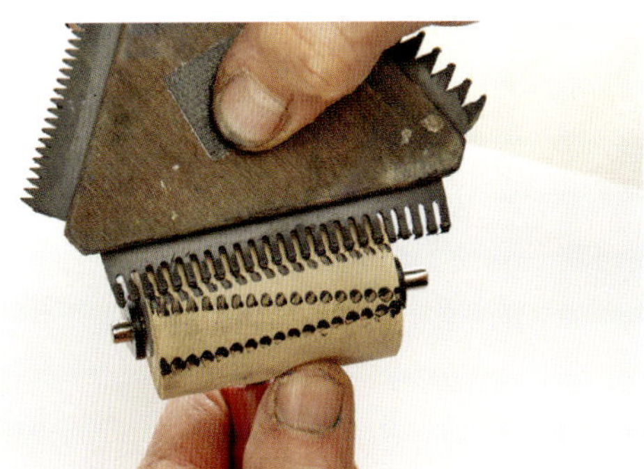

PAINT THE BRAYER STEP 1

Add ink marks to the brayer with any tool you choose.

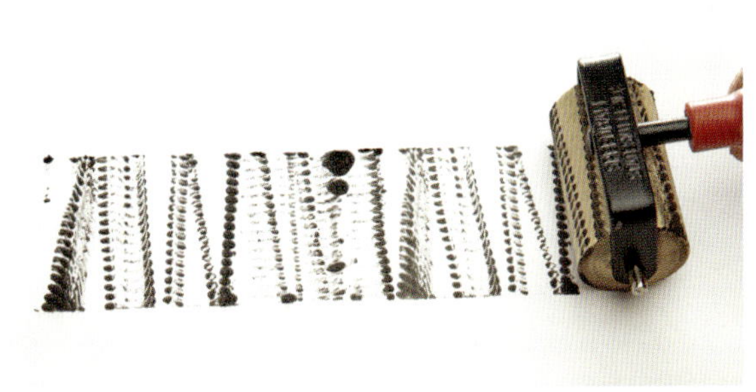

PAINT THE BRAYER STEP 2

Roll the brayer onto your paper to reveal the pattern.

IMPROV DRAWING

Improv drawing will show you how to start with one mark that will lead to the next mark, and then to the next. The idea is to weave unrelated elements together and to make a story out of the marks. This process of improv drawing invites the imagination to participate in the process of creative storytelling and leads you to create drawings you never knew you could do.

The trick is to let your mind float so it's free to respond to ideas as they come up, much like improv actors respond to cues as they perform. You add whatever the drawing tells you it needs as you evaluate and apply the tools of self critique. As you review the sequence presented here, you'll see how the imagery unfolds as a responsive approach to drawing.

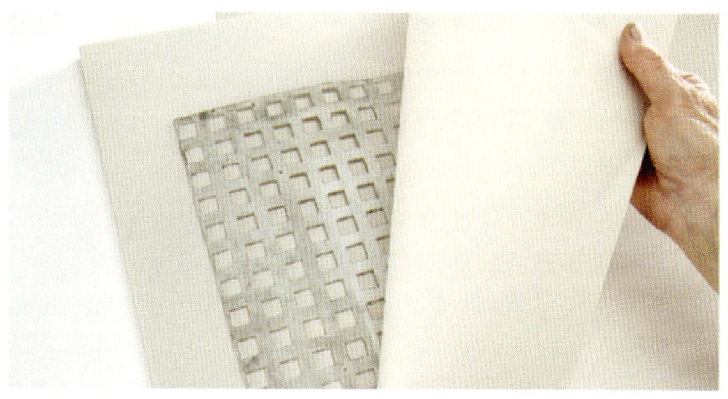

STEP 1

In this demonstration, I begin making an image by choosing my subject and a few simple textures. I do not have a preliminary drawing; I just start creating. I transfer a texture using a trace monotype approach. First, I place a texture of squares below my paper.

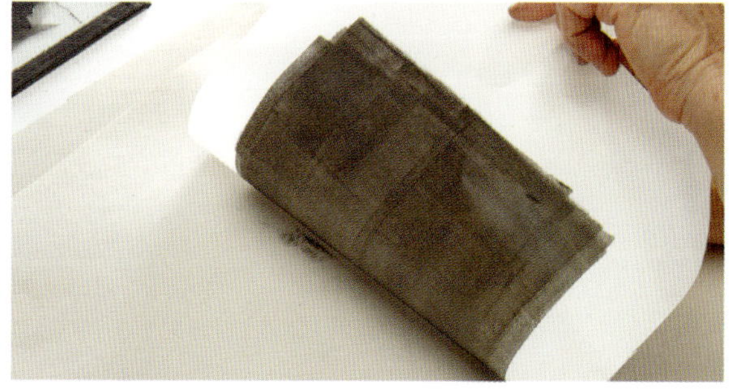

STEP 2

I ink up a piece of freezer paper and put it ink side down on top of my paper.

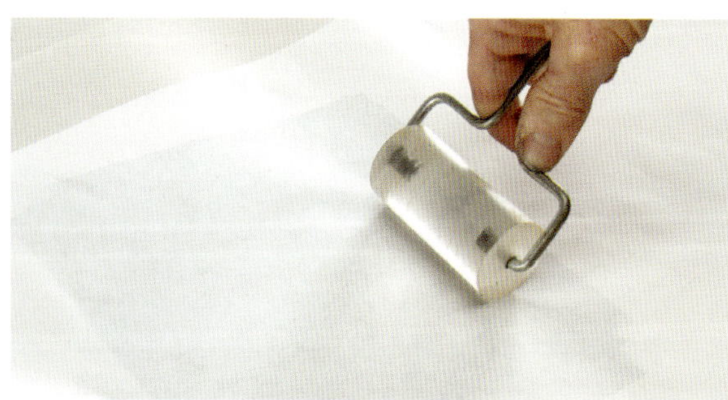

STEP 3

I roll a clear Lucite brayer over the top of the freezer paper to transfer the pattern of ink to my paper.

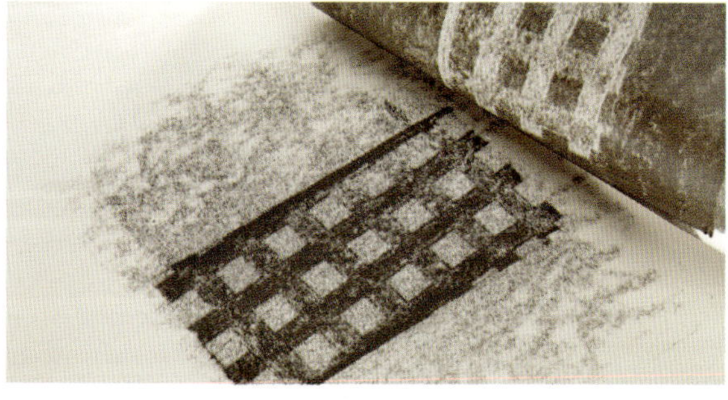

STEP 4

When I lift the freezer paper the impression of the squares is visible, along with some background ink that transferred as well. I will figure out how to integrate the unexpected tone into the piece as I go.

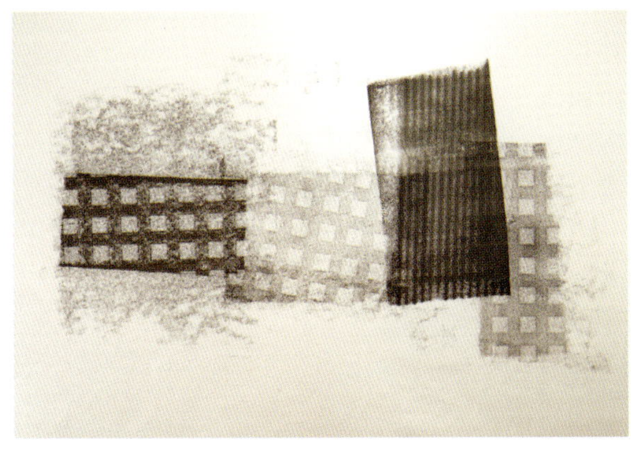

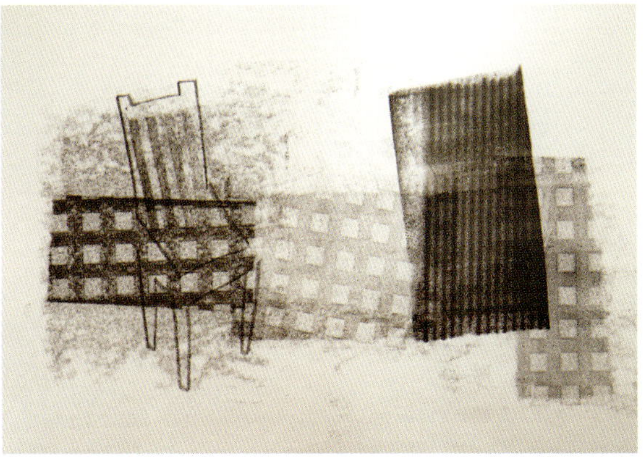

STEP 5

I link together shapes of the same texture to create a continuous shape across the page. I want to make sure that I leave some paper showing and that I vary the values. I add a vertical brayer stroke to the right side to balance the dark horizontal texture on the left.

STEP 6

I draw the chair using the trace monotype paper. I notice that the "stage" is beginning to look like a room.

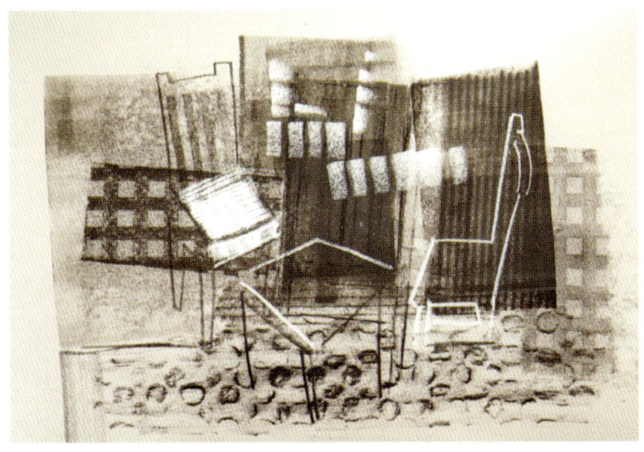

STEP 7

I go with the room idea and rub charcoal over a rough piece of fabric to imply a carpet on a floor. I draw another chair with white pastel, then color in the seat of the left chair. I add a little table with crazy perspective and then frottage a pattern of white rectangles with pastel to link everything together.

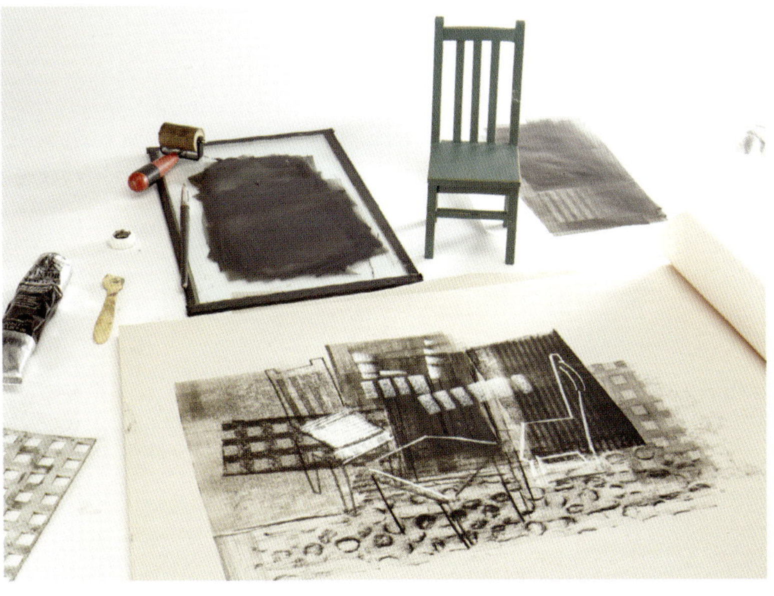

STEP 8

Here is the whole image and the tools I used to make it. This process of creating a drawing is like doing an improv performance. You weave the story in real time, cueing off each thing that gets put down. During this process I constantly check in with the seven elements to see how they are being used in the composition. It is important to explore ideas without judgement and to enjoy the process as you would an adventure.

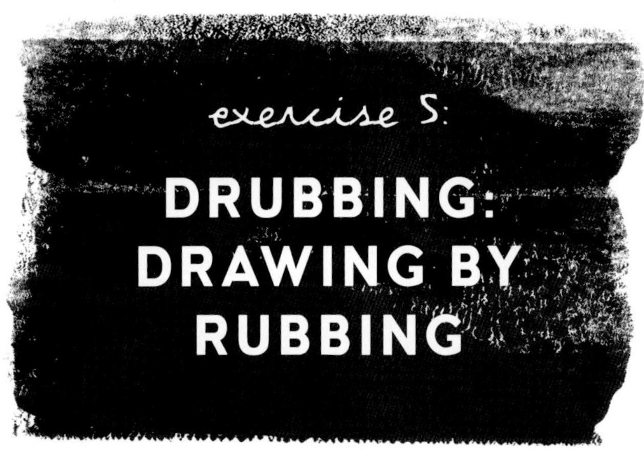

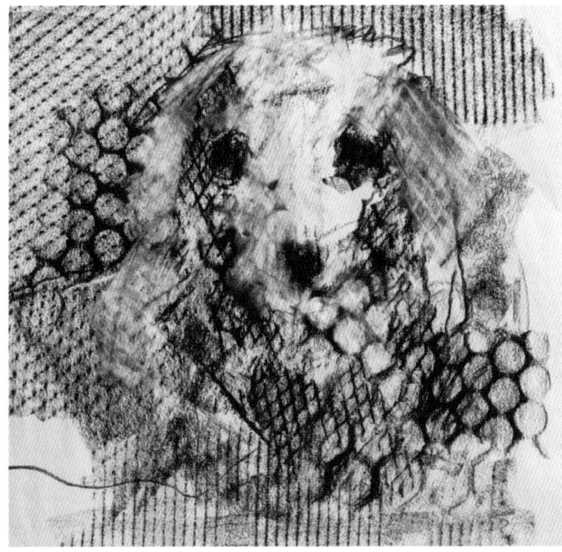

LENA / DENALI BROOKE / 41" × 41" (104CM × 104CM) /
CHARCOAL ON DRAWING PAPER

MATERIALS

- any smooth 18" × 24" (46CM ×61CM) light-weight drawing paper or newsprint
- General's Jumbo Compressed Charcoal 2B, or graphite stick or black wax crayon
- assortment of textured objects or surfaces

DIRECTIONS

STEP 1

Practice rubbing over textures with your drawing tool to see how hard you must press to get detailed rubbings. Rub with the side of your tool, and explore a wide assortment of textures. Overlap the rubbings occasionally, and link some together, one rubbing with the next. Observe the value and scale of each texture.

STEP 2

Using one of your drawing tools, draw an animal, house, tree, truck or other everyday object. Imagine you are doing this for a children's book and have fun with simplifying the image. Enjoy hunting for just the right texture as your "drubbing" unfolds.

CRITIQUE

- How many different textures do you see in the image? Do some of them share a similar pattern but in a different scale?
- Can you begin to see possibilities for creating other images as you were hunting for textures?
- Could you think of a series of these that would be fun to do?
- How do the elements present themselves in this piece?

TAKEAWAY

Drawing with textures helps you learn to simplify information. Repeating the same texture in a drawing helps the viewer associate shapes together.

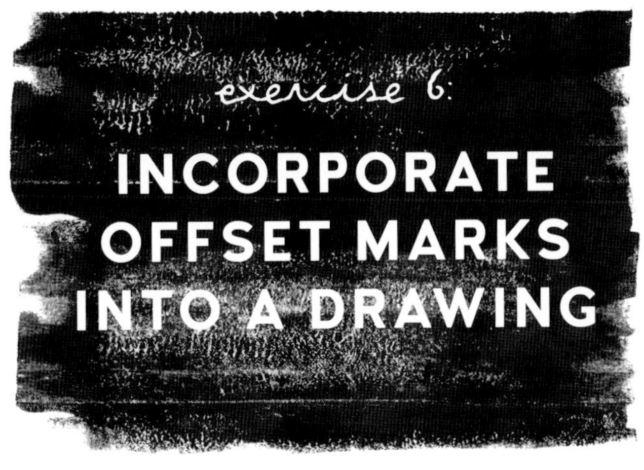

DIRECTIONS

STEP 1

Practice making marks with the brayer, rolling the brayer flat, then tipped on its edge.

STEP 2

Start off with simple subjects, like stick figures, an ice cream cone, a tree or a sailboat. Simplify the subject as a child would, and use only the brayer to draw with. Have fun making the images.

STEP 3

As you develop more finesse with the brayer, try incorporating offset textures into your imagery.

CRITIQUE

- How did drawing with the brayer help you simplify your subject?
- Could you see incorporating brayer work into your artwork?

TAKEAWAY

You can combine nondrawing and drawn imagery together in one image.

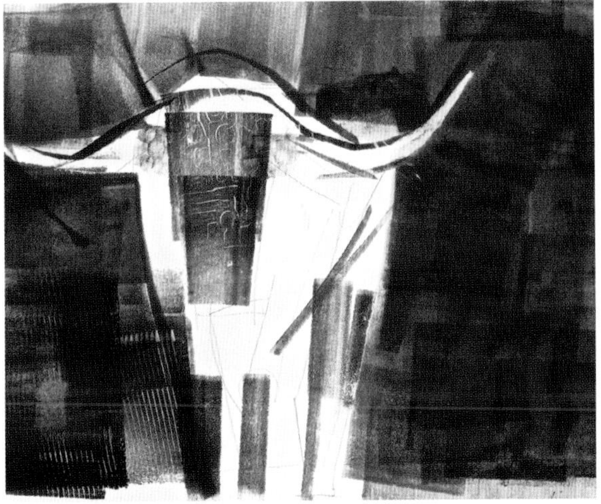

BULL / 12" × 16" (30CM × 41CM) / OIL PAINT ON PAPER

Notice the use of offsetting in the face of the bull.

MATERIALS

- black water-miscible oil paint and surface to roll out the paint
- drawing paper
- General's Jumbo Compressed Charcoal 2B
- brayer

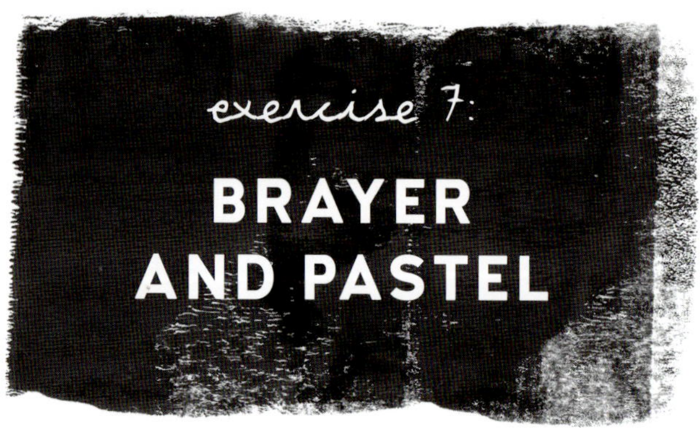

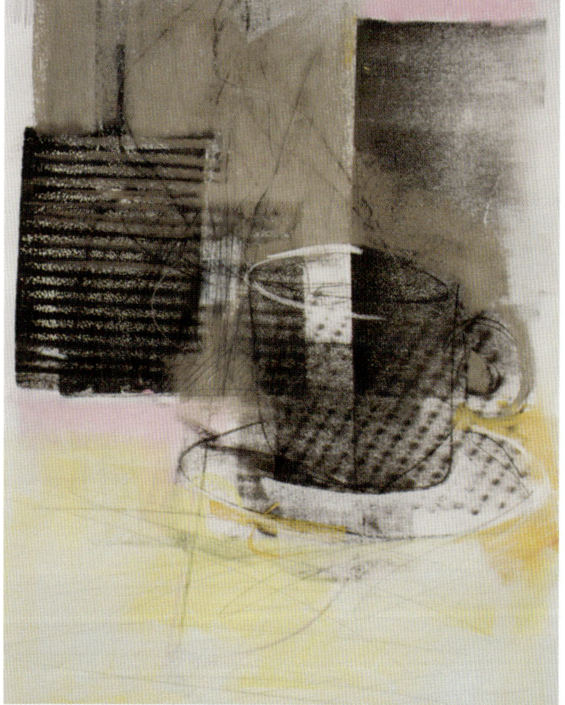

CUP O' JOE / 20" × 18" (51CM × 46CM) / OIL PAINT, PASTEL AND CHARCOAL ON DRAWING PAPER

This image utilizes both offsetting and direct drawing with the brayer. Pastel was added at the end.

MATERIALS

- brayer and inking surface
- black water-miscible oil paint
- half stick General's Jumbo Compressed Charcoal 2B
- 18" × 24" (46CM × 61CM) drawing paper or rough newsprint
- Assortment of textures
- soft pastel sticks or PanPastel

DIRECTIONS

STEP 1

Refer to the image on this page, and study it for shapes, textures and brayer marks. The image includes frottage (rubbing) with charcoal, offsetting with the brayer, direct drawing with the brayer and rollography. The pastel color was added at the end.

STEP 2

Try to reproduce this image, not with the intention of copying, but to understand the process of layering imagery. On the back of your drawing, jot down the steps you took to make your drawing.

STEP 3

Repeat the process to create your own drawing that incorporates some of these techniques.

CRITIQUE

- What did you discover in the process of trying to reconstruct how the coffee cup image was made?
- If you developed a series of images using this technique, what subject would you choose as a theme?
- How might you incorporate brayer techniques into your artwork?

TAKEAWAY

As you explore new approaches, write down the steps of your process so you won't forget what you did.

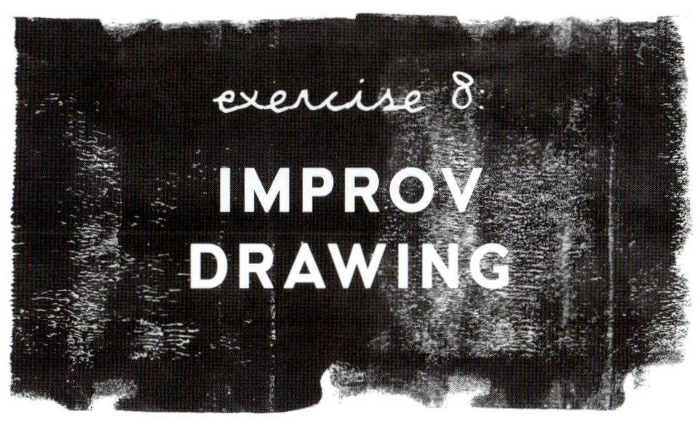

exercise 8:
IMPROV DRAWING

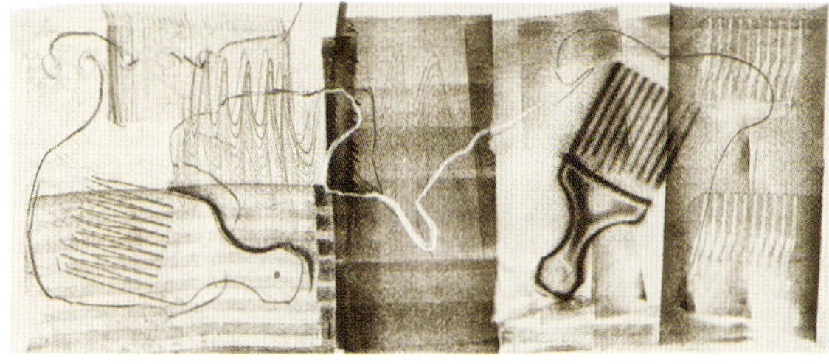

COMB OVER / 10" × 16" (25CM × 41CM) / OIL PAINT
ON NEWSPRINT WITH PASTEL

MATERIALS

- brayer and water-miscible black oil paint or
  Akua ink
- freezer paper to use as trace monotype paper, cut to
  12" × 18" (30CM × 46CM)
- flat tool like scissors
- several soft pastels
- General's Jumbo Compressed Charcoal
- 18" × 24" (46CM × 61CM) drawing paper or newsprint
- smoosher and erasers

DIRECTIONS

STEP 1
Study the chapter 2 opening image and the image
below. Both were created using techniques presented
in this chapter. See if you can identify the techniques.

STEP 2
Begin your drawing by making a horizontal 12" × 18"
(30CM × 46CM) rectangle with a pencil. Ink up your
trace monotype paper, and hinge it to the drawing
paper, ink side down. Create a musical staff-like
symbol with a toothed comb using the trace monotype technique. Add multiple tracings of a tool of your
choice onto the staff as though you were adding musical notes to the staff. Vary the position of the object,
and overlap if you wish.

STEP 3
Add to your image with value, textures and marks to
develop a feeling of space. Follow your imagination
as you let this tool story evolve.

STEP 4
Evaluate the drawing by going through the checklist
of the elements, and add pastel color at the end if
you wish.

CRITIQUE

- Can you imagine doing more images like this?
- If so, what tools or subjects would you focus on?
- Does the subject have special meaning in your life?
- If you added color, how did you decide where to
  put it?

TAKEAWAY

Thinking of your artwork as visual "compositions"
allows you to imagine beyond the subject you
are drawing and invites your imagination into
the process.

BEHIND THE SCENES

In the previous chapter you were introduced to ways to make and transfer drawn and nondrawn marks. You were encouraged to call upon your unique personal perspective as you explore the potential of these tools. Improv drawings were introduced as a way to develop a more responsive (rather than predictable) drawing process.

Chapter 3 will introduce you to novel ways to set the stage for creative image-making. We will incorporate big shapes, new marks and exciting textures with other media—such as sumi ink and watercolor as underpainting. This "stage" is a platform for your responsive drawing skills. In this chapter the language of figure-ground (where the foundation is the ground and your subject is the figure) will be introduced.

I was introduced to sumi ink during my study with a Chinese brush painter. I loved the character of the marks that I could get with sumi ink and large brushes as well as the dramatic massing of values it encouraged. For a time I started nearly every image with a gestural and abstract ink painting as the underpainting. I was fascinated with where this process took the pastel imagery I built on this unpredictable foundation. From this experience came my excitement for exploring the impact of an abstract underpainting on the finished image.

LEADING THE WAY / 22" × 30" (56CM × 76CM) / PASTEL, WATERCOLOR AND SUMI INK ON STONEHENGE PAPER

The background of this image was created with big shapes and gesture marks that set the stage for action.

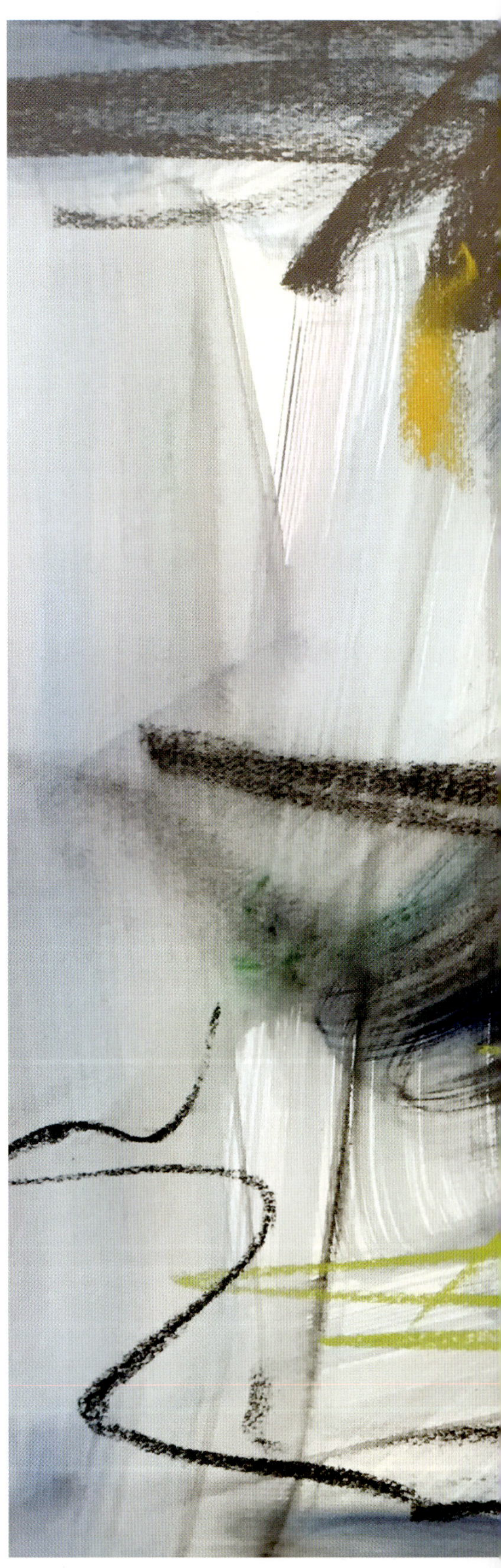

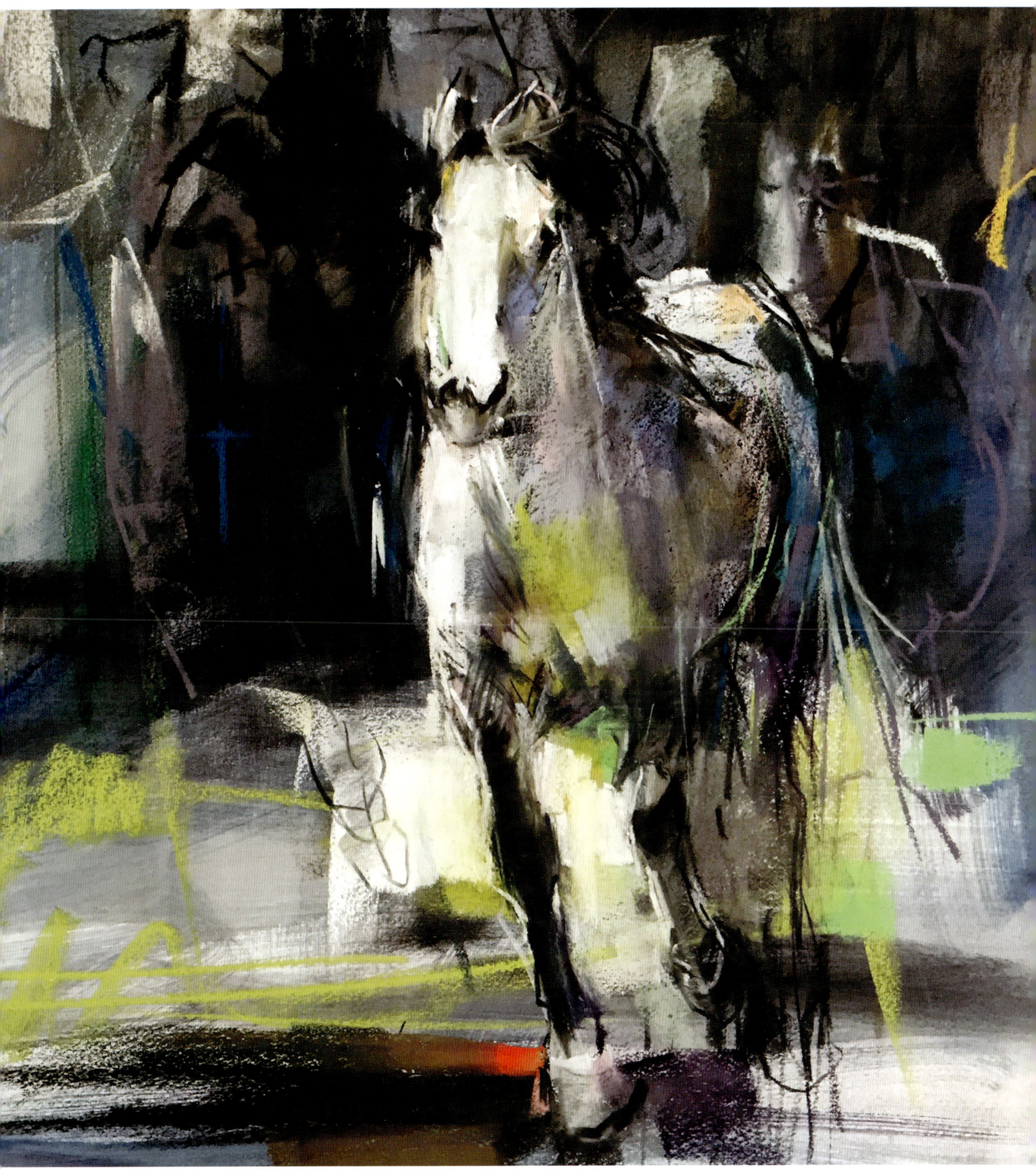

SETTING THE STAGE

For many beginners, starting a painting is where they get stuck. It's right at the beginning they set their expectations for making a finished work they can put into a frame. What I propose is that you set aside time to just have fun, and declare an intention to explore, rather than to produce anything "finished." The first step on this journey is to give yourself permission to play in the studio. One way I've found to set the stage for creativity is demonstrated below. I make several abstract designs that I think of as potential underpaintings for an image that will be added later. I do not begin with a subject in mind. Once I have an underpainting design, I let my mind go as I look at it, and let the image wake up my picture making imagination. Ideas for combining imagery will evolve in ways that I can't predetermine or expect. I have found that play like this is essential to my continued growth as an artist and helps me keep my work fresh, and I hope it will do the same for you.

 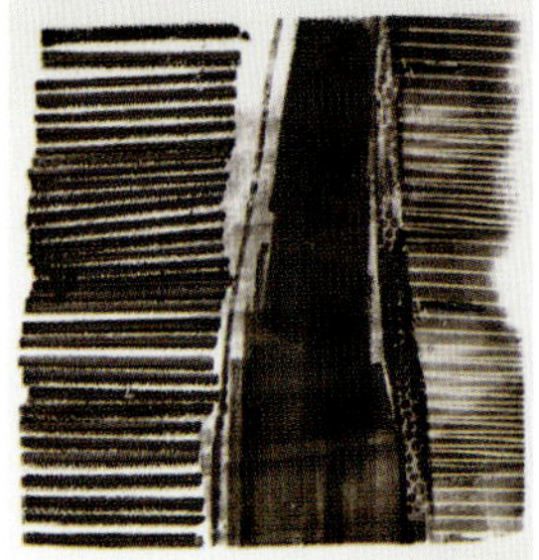 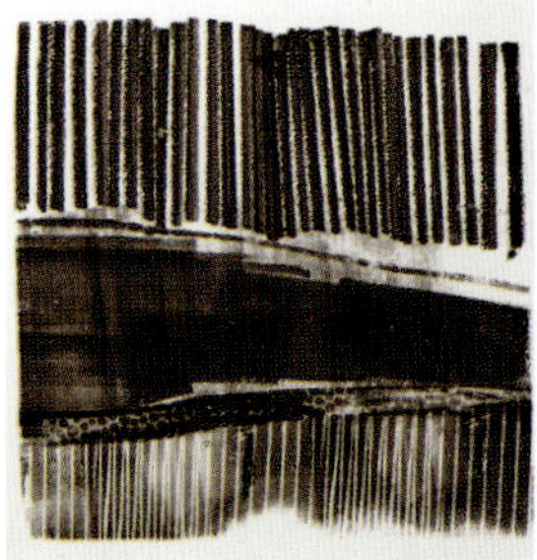 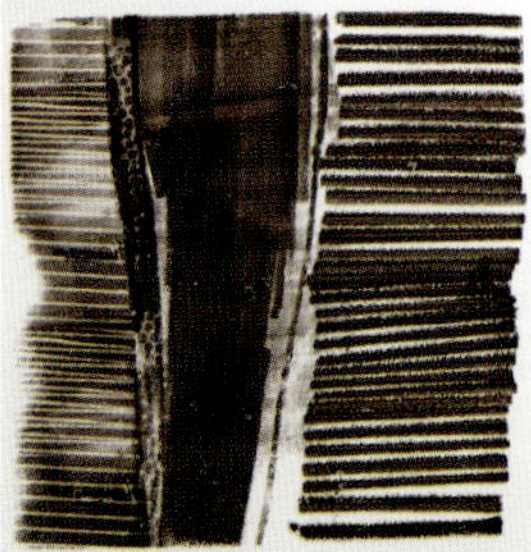

ABOVE: FROM LEFT TO RIGHT

ABSTRACT GROUND #1
I created this square, abstract design using a brayer and water miscible oil paint. I had nothing specific in mind, but as I looked at it, the image evoked a cave-like structure imbedded in a basalt rock wall.

FIRST ROTATION
I rotated the image to the right, and then it evoked a road in perspective.

SECOND ROTATION
After a second rotation the image felt more like a forest of trees at the edge of a river bank.

THIRD ROTATION
This orientation evokes imagery of a deep layer in a river bed, as if looking down through water into a deep hole, and then I thought of fish moving through the river.

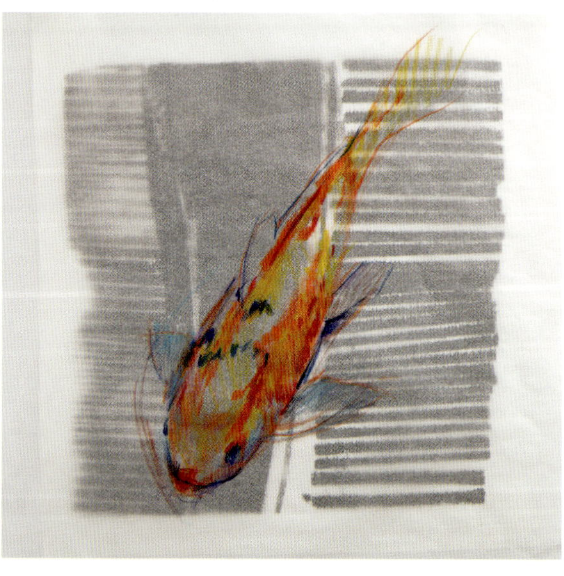

ADDING A SUBJECT
The idea of fish led me to draw a Koi on a piece of tracing paper with color pencil, and I placed the tracing paper over the ground to see how it looked on the design. The abstract ground acted as a springboard for my imagination and helped me discover new possibilities for subjects I would not have thought of any other way.

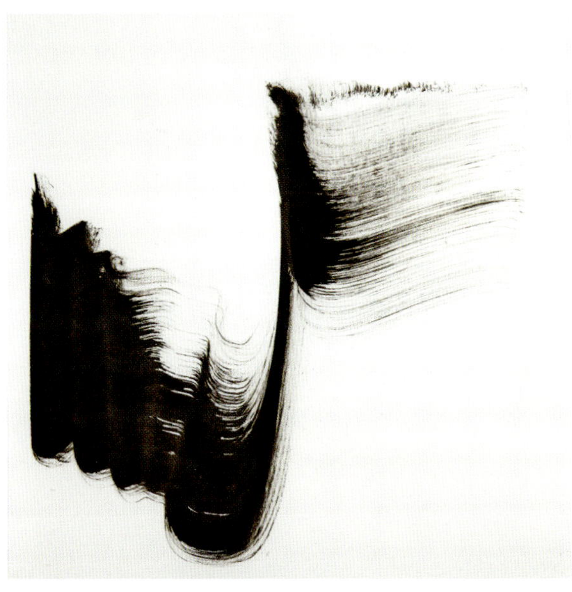

ABSTRACT GROUND #2

I use the same square format, but use a 4" paddle
brush with Sumi ink to create a dramatic brush stroke
as my design. This orientation of the image has a lot
of movement from left to right and evokes a feeling
of wind.

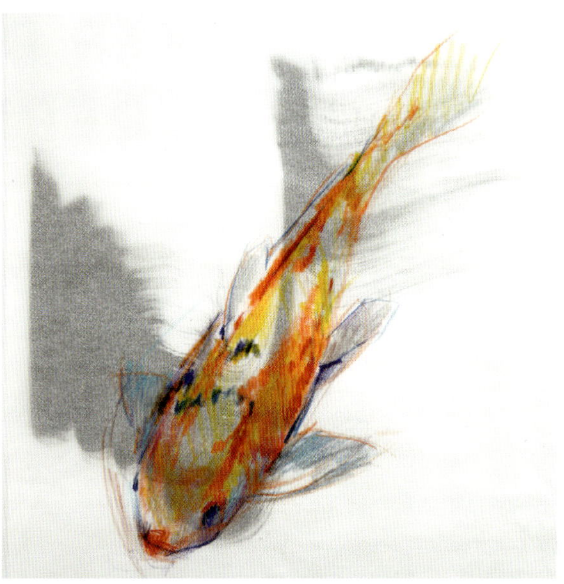

ADD THE SUBJECT

I put the tracing paper with the drawing of the Koi
atop this new abstraction to see how it looks. The
feeling of place, space, and environment is totally
different than in Abstract Ground #1.

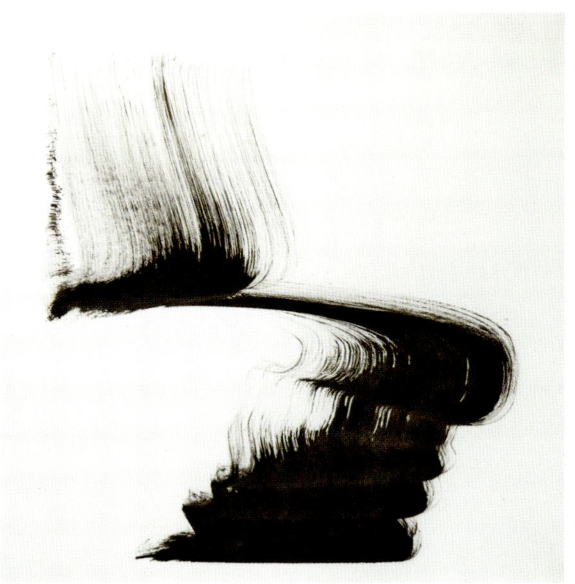

ROTATE THE GROUND

Rotated this way, the movement and weight changes
dramatically. The visual weight is on the bottom, and
the movement is from the bottom to the top left.

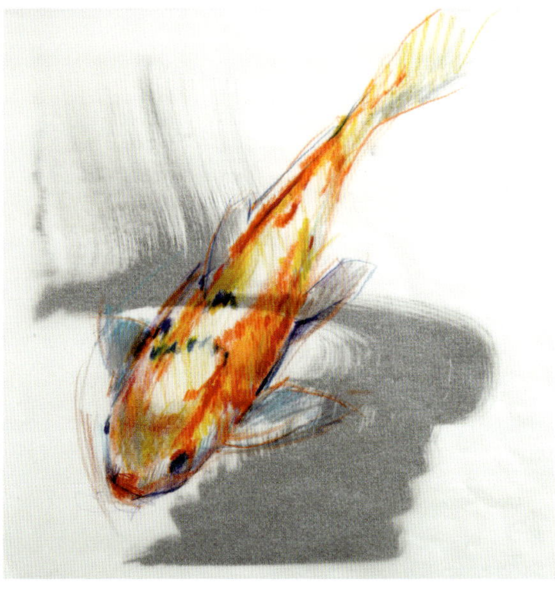

EVALUATE

When the Koi is positioned over this orientation of the
brushstroke the fish seems much closer to the viewer.
Which do you prefer? Why?

BRAYER DRAWING AS UNDERPAINTING

The brayer is a tool of remarkable versatility. It naturally creates high contrast shapes and provides immediate feedback about the structure of your image. The brayer resists your desire to get detailed and encourages you to edit and simplify. Brayer drawing quickly reveals how the space of a painting is divided in terms of dark, middle and light values. It is a great tool for learning to simplify forms, put down big shapes first, and link shapes together. Lines can always be put in later to separate shapes or add detail. Using the brayer to create the underpainting sets the stage by organizing values and shapes. The high contrast foundation provides a background to merge other imagery with.

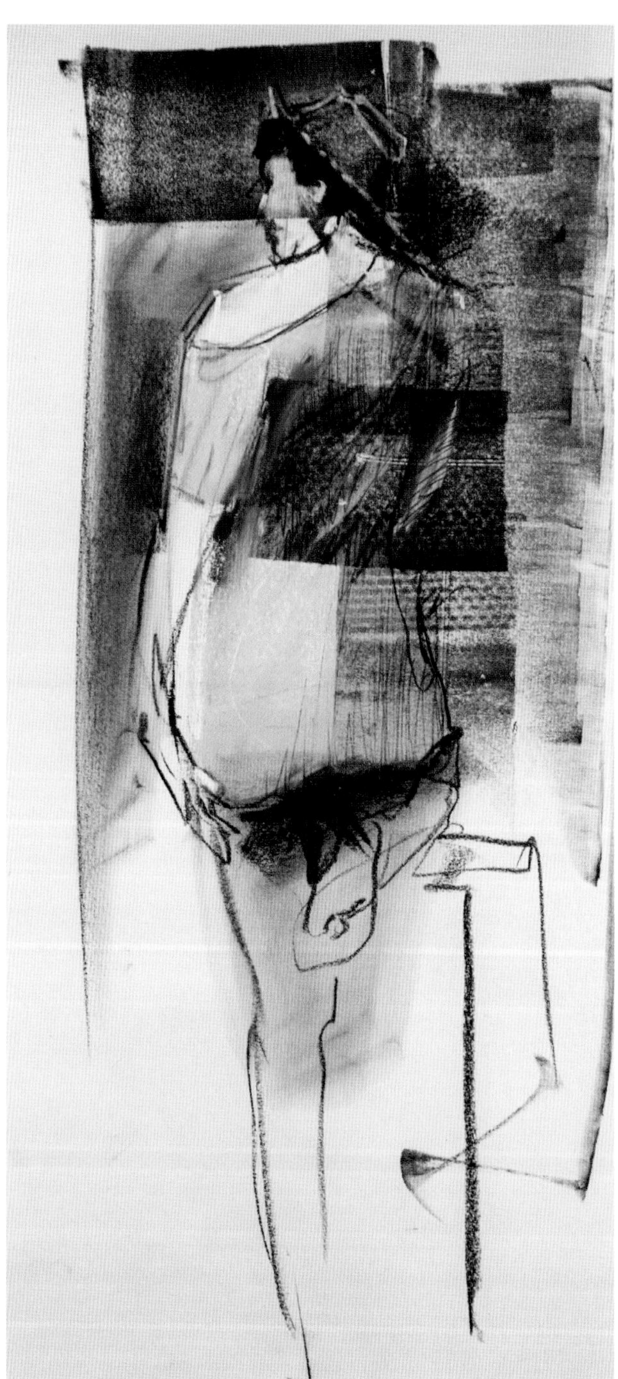

OFF THE SHOULDER / 24" × 14" (61CM × 36CM) / OIL PAINT WITH CHARCOAL AND PASTEL ON PAPER

By incorporating nondrawn marks into the image, the image seems richer and more interesting than just another pretty pose.

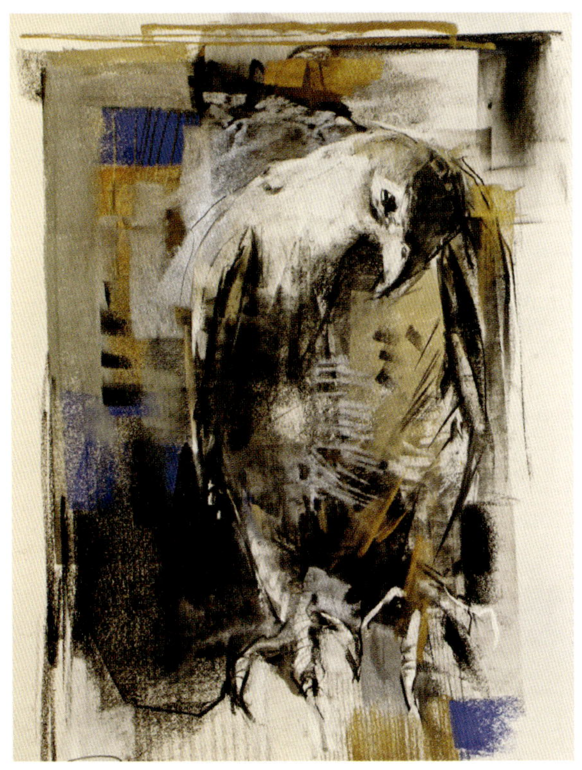

MAGIC / 24" × 18" (61CM × 46CM) / OIL PAINT WITH
CHARCOAL AND PASTEL ON PAPER

The underpainting was created by drawing directly on
the paper with a brayer. I push and pull the image of the
bird out of the abstraction, but I also want to let the
background be seen through the subject in places, as
though it is in the process of emerging.

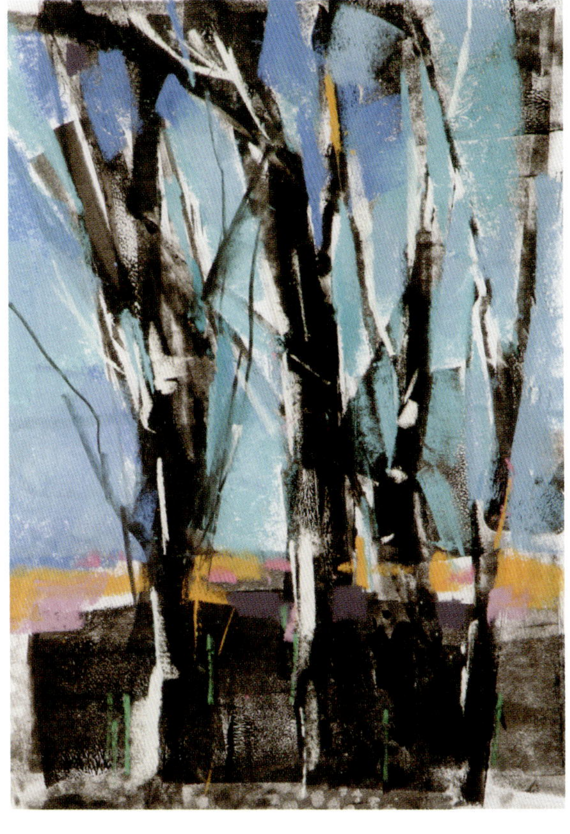

SKY HOLES / 14" × 12" (36CM × 30CM) / OIL PAINT
WITH PASTEL ON PAPER

The beauty of using the brayer is in the way forms are
boldly simplified. The black, irregular marks convey
only what is absolutely necessary, allowing color to be
the star.

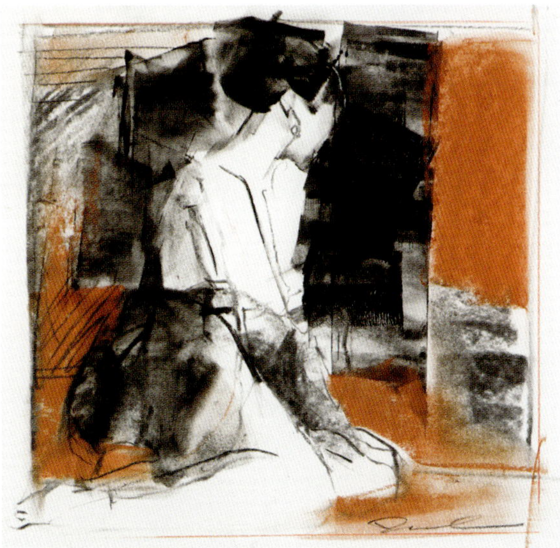

LOOKING BACK / 14" × 14" (36CM × 36CM) / OIL PAINT
WITH CHARCOAL AND PASTEL ON PAPER

I wanted to create the illusion of deep space behind
the model, and the variety of brayer marks helped me
convey that.

SUMI INK
AS UNDERPAINTING

I started using black sumi ink with pastel because of how well the pastel adheres to the satin finish of the ink. It provides a strong value contrast for the pastel colors and allows me to add many layers on top of it. Sumi ink can be used at any point in the painting process, both on top of or under the pastel. When lines are scraped through pastel that's been layered over sumi ink, the ink is revealed as beautiful black lines. Scraping can be done with a razor blade, scribing tool or even a finger

nail. Sumi ink can be watered down for painting as lighter values, or a brush can be dipped into the ink unevenly for a gradated wash. You can even paint one brush with another to create specific value gradations. A dry brush works beautifully with sumi ink to make twisted or broken lines. Natural materials like sticks, vegetables and feathers all make unique drawing tools when dipped in sumi ink.

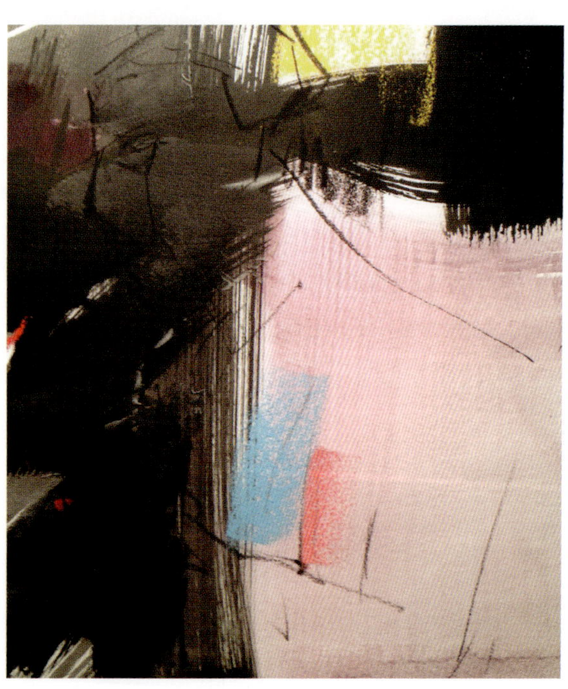

IN THE PINK / 12" × 11" (30CM × 28CM) / SUMI INK AND PASTEL ON STONEHENGE PAPER

I use sumi ink to brush on bold black strokes in the same way I use the brayer to roll on black marks to build texture and shape.

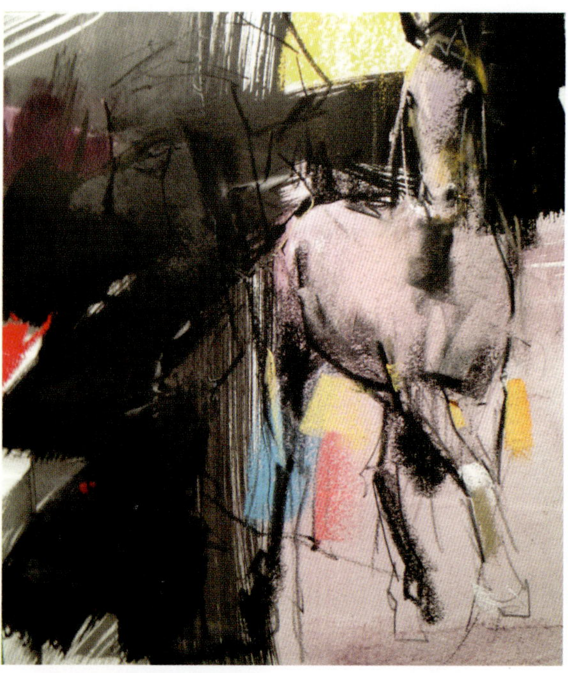

IN THE PINK / 12" × 11" (30CM × 28CM) / SUMI INK AND PASTEL ON STONEHENGE PAPER

Notice how adding the horse to the abstract ground changes the feeling of space, place and scale.

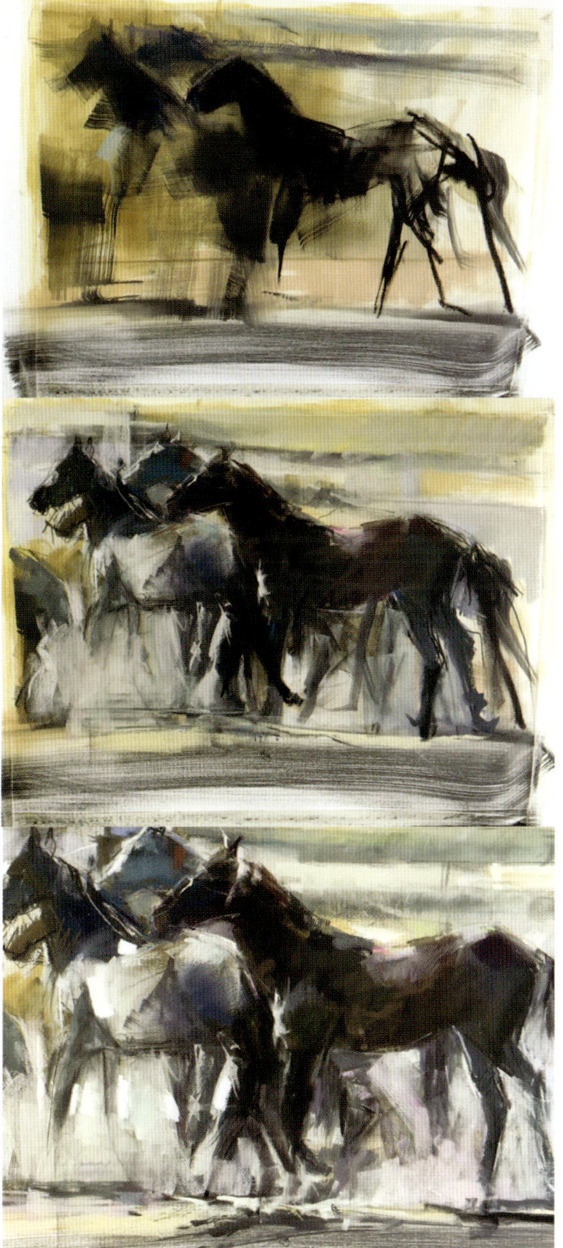

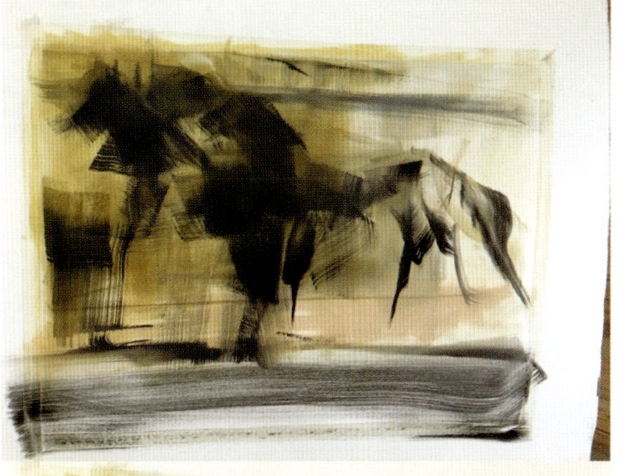

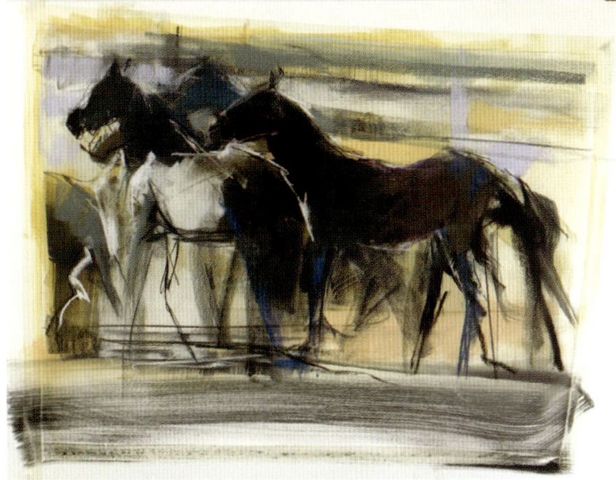

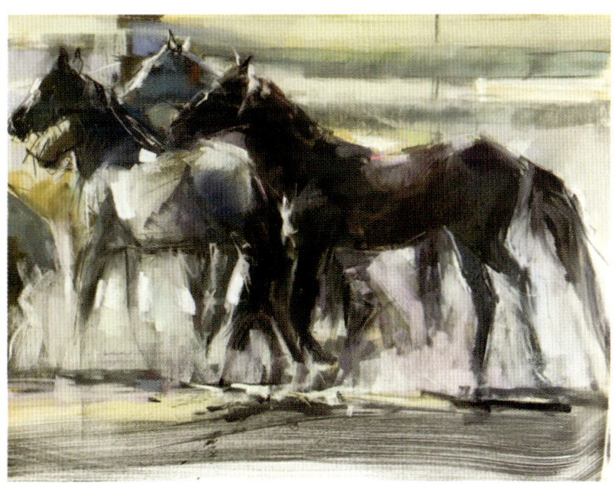

CROWD SOURCING / 22" × 30" (56CM × 76CM) / SUMI
INK AND PASTEL ON STONEHENGE PAPER

In this sequence, you can see how sumi ink is used to
create the gesture and shape of the subject (rather than
an abstracted background). Bold ink marks prevent me
from getting overly detailed, and allow me to easily see
the areas of dark and light.

WATERCOLOR AS UNDERPAINTING

Many artists use watercolor for pastel underpaintings because it shares the same matte finish as pastel and doesn't plug the tooth of the paper surface. I've found that concentrated liquid watercolors require less water, which reduces the risk of warping the paper surface. I love the broken texture that is created using watercolor with a dry, flat paddle brush. I also use watercolor when I want to underpaint with bold gestural brushstrokes to illuminate the paper surface before pastel is added. Pastel itself can be used as a water-based medium by either drawing with pastel onto a wet surface or wet brushing over pastel marks. When pastel is added on top of a watercolor underpainting, you can scrape down through the layer of pastel to reveal the watercolor below.

BARN STORM / 12" × 12" (30CM × 30CM) / WATERCOLOR AND PASTEL ON RIVES BFK PAPER

The underpainting of this painting was done with watercolor.

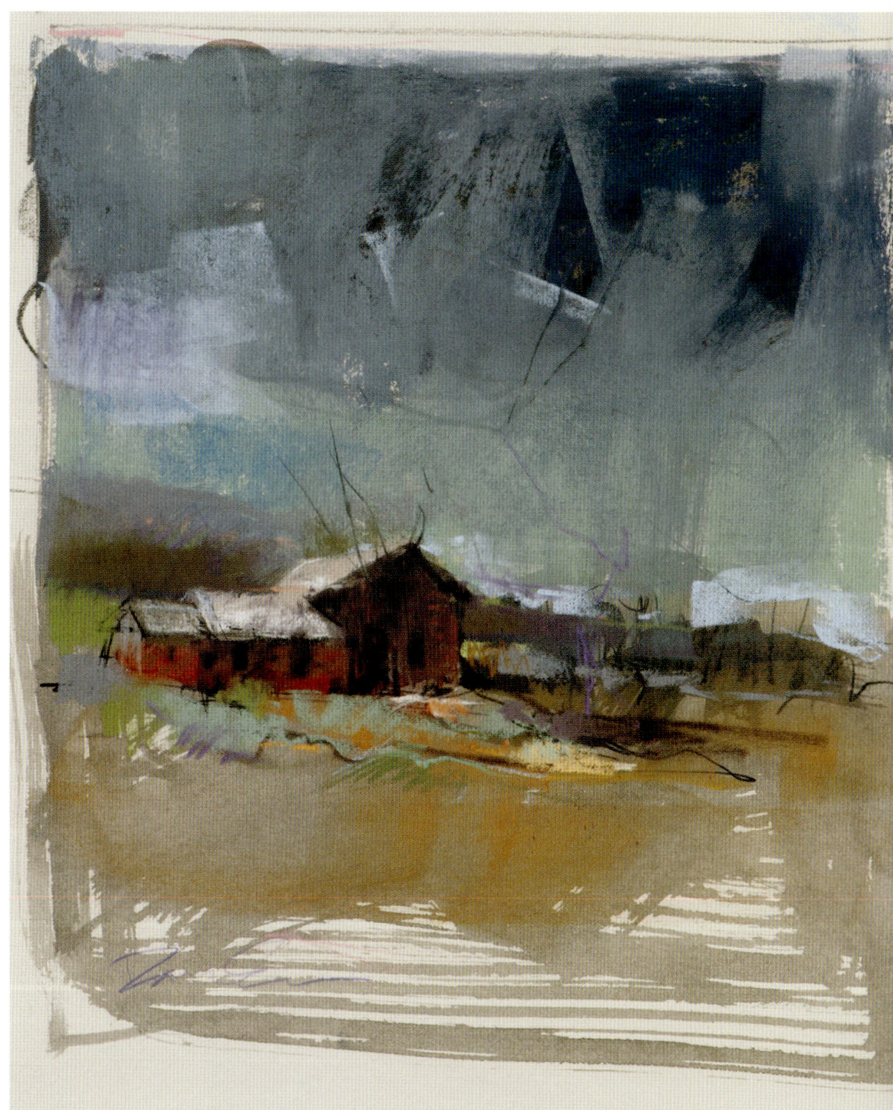

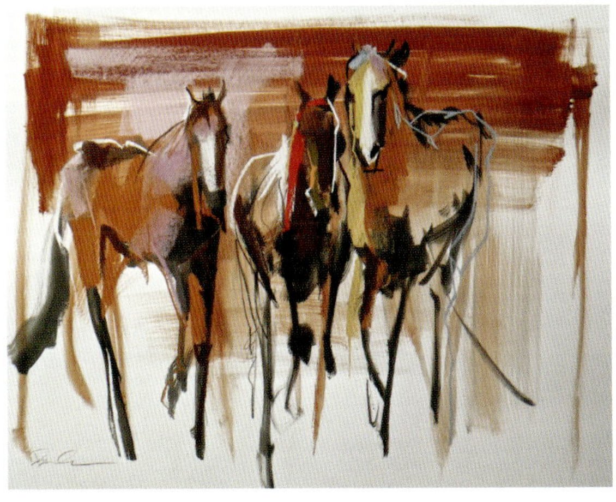

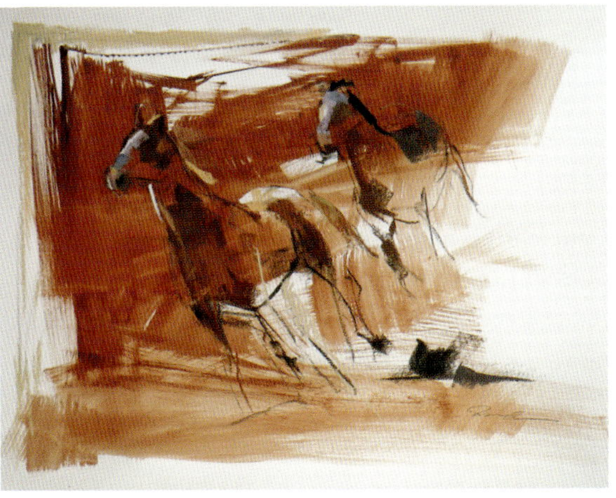

THREE FELLOWS / 22" × 30" (30CM × 28CM) /
WATERCOLOR, PASTEL AND CHARCOAL ON RIVES
BFK PAPER

I brushed on concentrated fluid watercolor with a 4"
(10CM) paddle brush to create the sepia colored sky
ground. I used sumi ink and a smaller brush to paint the
horses. Pastel was added last.

ANCIENT HOOFBEATS / 22" × 30" (56CM × 76CM) /
WATERCOLOR, PASTEL AND CHARCOAL ON RIVES
 BFK PAPER

I dribbled concentrated fluid watercolor to create an
abstraction that looked like a canyon. I described the
horses only minimally to suggest their presence.

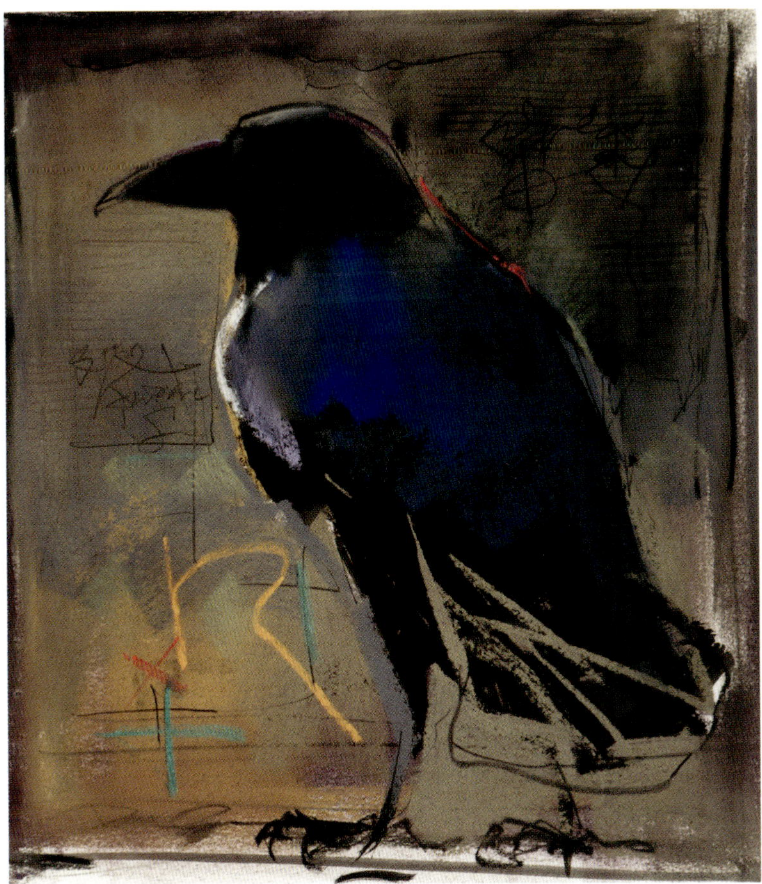

RAVEN / 12" × 12" (30CM × 30CM)
/ WATERCOLOR, SUMI INK, PASTEL
AND WAX ON STONEHENGE PAPER

I flooded the paper with watercolor
and drew lines with clear wax over
it when it dried. When I put the sumi
ink bird on top of the watercolor,
the ink resisted the clear wax,
leaving lines in the background
color. PanPastel was added on the
wing, and stick pastel was used on
some edges.

CHARCOAL AS FULL VALUE UNDERPAINTING

General's Jumbo Compressed Charcoal is a medium that generates a full range of values. The flat shape of this charcoal allows it to be used both like a brayer and a calligraphic tool. Charcoal is a forgiving medium that supports additive and subtractive processes to create drawings or underpaintings to which pastel can be added. In a subtractive approach, the paper is toned by smearing it with an even value of charcoal. Light areas are pulled out by erasing, and areas are made darker by adding charcoal. An additive approach begins with a blank surface to which you add charcoal to create the image. In both approaches the artist goes back and forth adding and removing darkness and light until the resulting image is a full value drawing. The advantage to this kind of drawing is that once the design and composition is worked out as a full value image, color can be added on top of the charcoal by simply matching the value of a color to the value of the underpainting. Any color can be added as long as it is the right value!

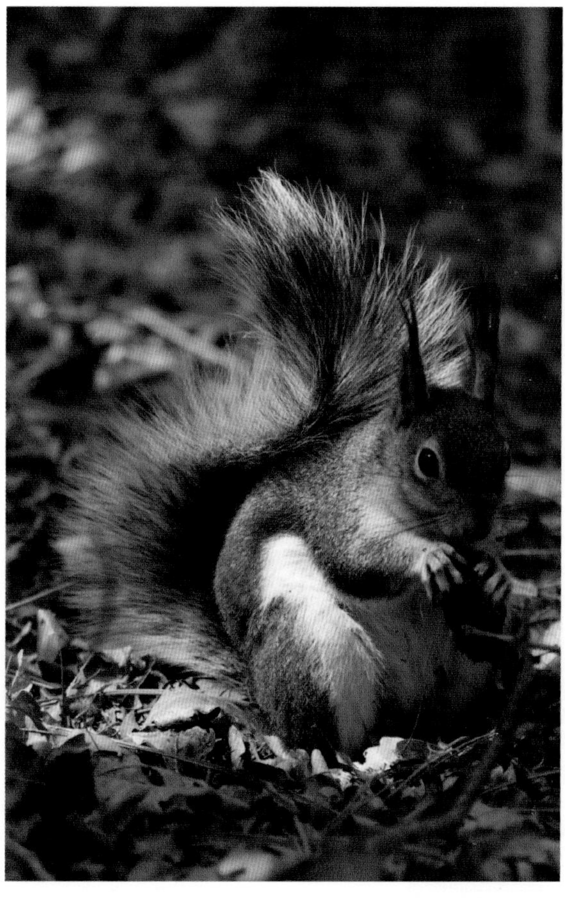

TUFTED EAR SQUIRREL PHOTO
This black-and-white image is the reference for the series that follows. It is helpful to remove color when developing a full value drawing.

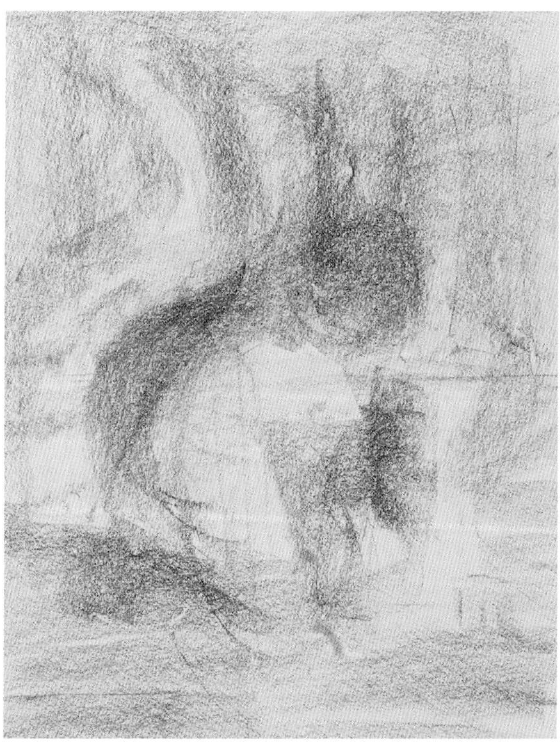

STEP 1: LIGHT MASS DRAWING OF SQUIRREL
Mass your drawing on a toned surface. This approach uses no line, only the side of the charcoal to amass darks by adding layers of charcoal strokes on top of each other.

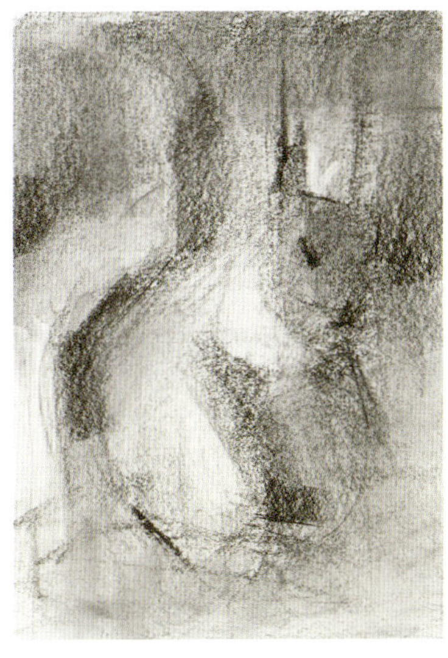

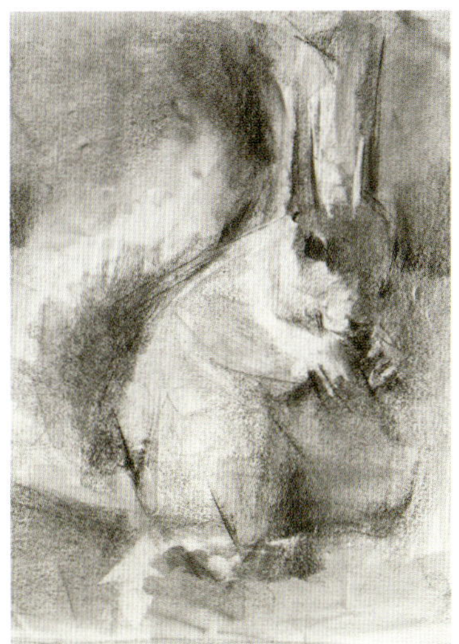

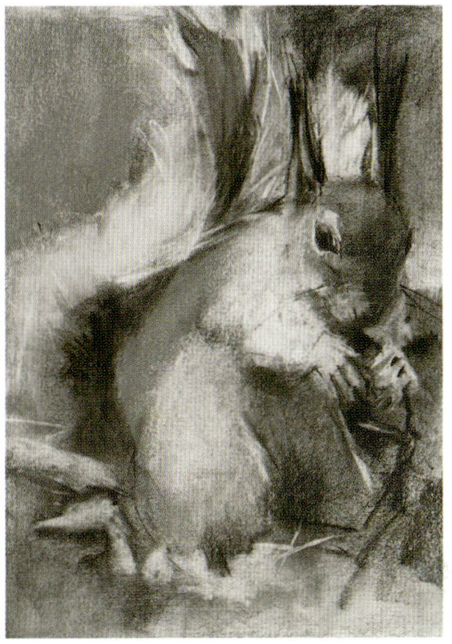

STEP 2: ADD VALUE WITHOUT DETAIL

The entire image evolves simultaneously, figure and ground together.

STEP 3: ADD SMALLER SHAPES, AND SUBTRACT LIGHT AREAS WITH ERASER

There now should be more variety of shape sizes and more distinction between different kinds of edges.

STEP 4: FINE-TUNE ALL THE ELEMENTS

The smoosher is used to increase the value range and contrast smooth with grainy textures. Final highlights are erased with a sharp eraser, and darker darks are added where needed.

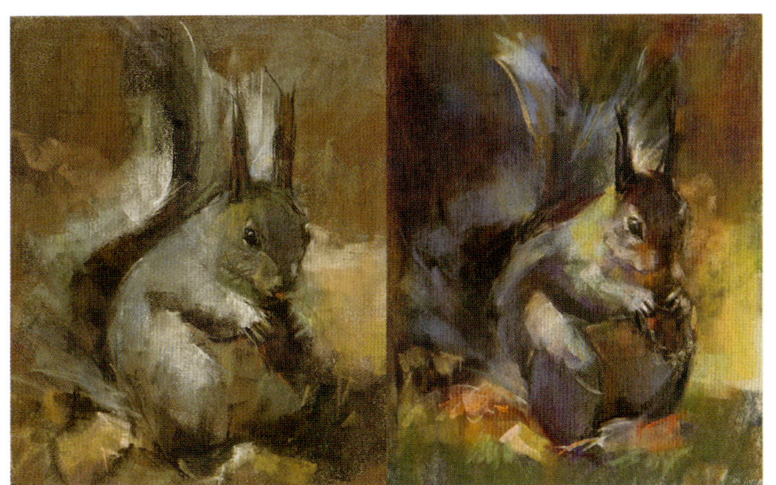

STEP 5: COLOR AS VALUE

Color has been added directly on top of the charcoal in each of these images, matching dark, middle and light values of color for dark, middle and light values of charcoal. The image on the left uses "local color," which are the colors we expect to see, while the image on the right uses unexpected color to create a more playful mood.

TRACED MONOTYPE AS UNDERPAINTING

As you saw in chapter 2, the trace monotype is like carbon paper that can be replenished and made into any color you wish. It can be used to layer different imagery—by tracing or freehand drawing—or to create abstract backgrounds upon which other imagery can be added. The trace monotype can be used on top of any drawing, painting or print, and is a correct-reading image.

As the ink is transferred off the ink side of the trace paper to another paper, you are left with a negative image on the inked surface. In other words, the lines you transferred off the inked paper are now white, or the reverse of the image you transferred. If you take that reverse image and transfer it to another paper, you will get a reverse (negative) trace monotype. Printing of the reverse trace monotype can be done by hand rubbing, using a pin press, or with a printing press.

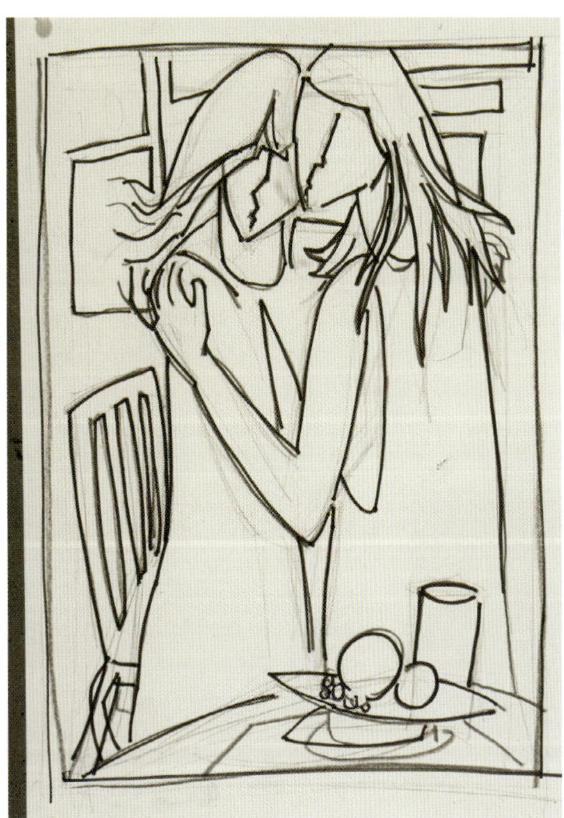

STEP 1: DRAWING

This is my drawing on the non-shiny side of freezer paper. I have inked up the shiny side of the freezer paper with water miscible oil paint. I will trace this drawing onto a clean piece of drawing paper.

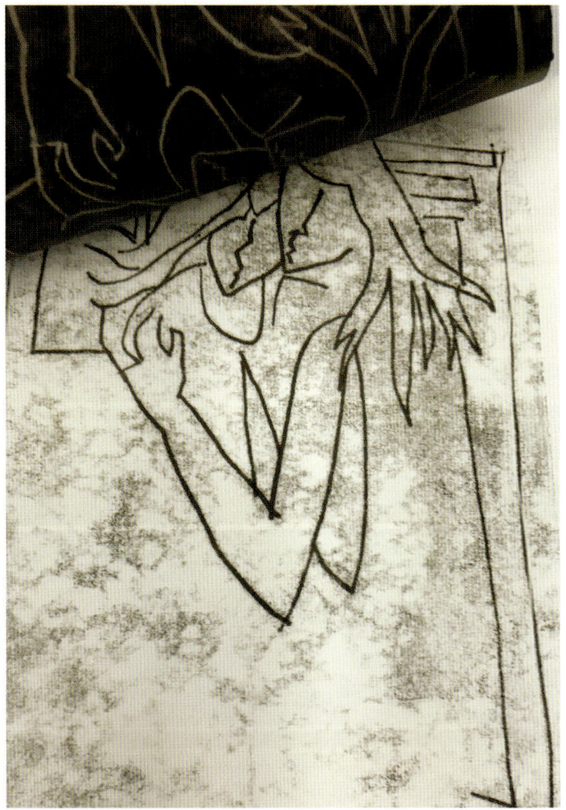

STEP 2: TRACE

I check to see how the lines are being transferred to the drawing paper. The tone you see is offset ink from the transfer sheet. You can see that the ink side of the transfer paper is dark with white lines where the ink has been transferred. This inked side can be printed to make a reverse monotype.

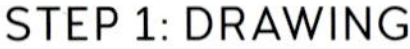

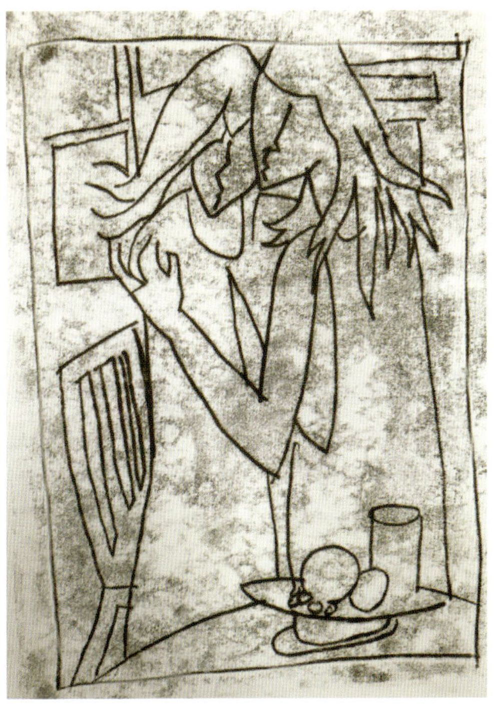

STEP 3: REMOVE TRANSFER PAPER

This is the completed trace monotype to which
I will add pastel.

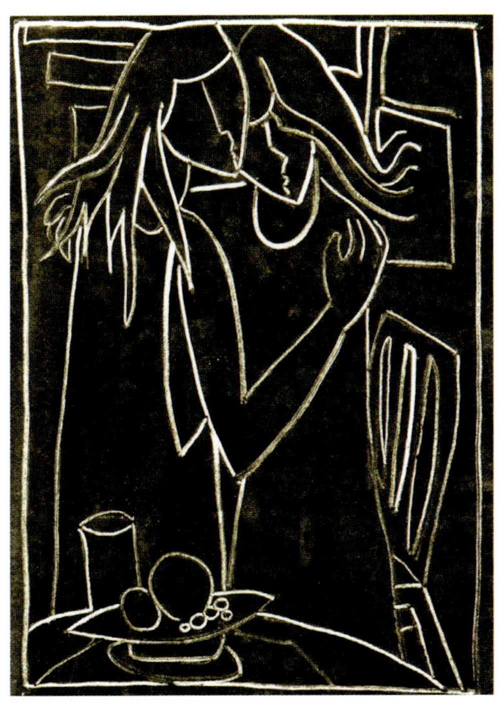

STEP 4: REVERSE TRACE MONOTYPE

This is the image that was printed from the
inked side using a press.

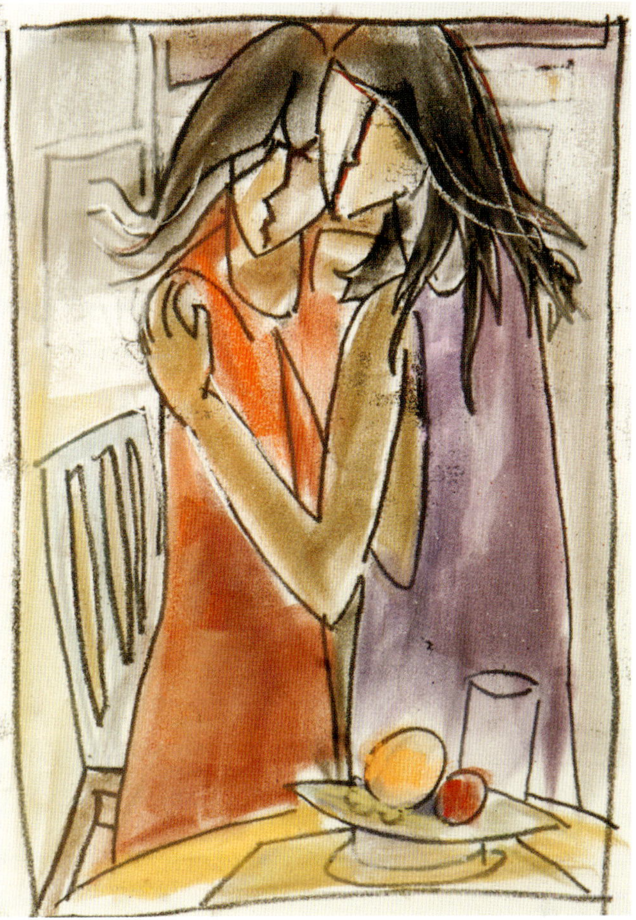

FRIENDSHIP / 15" × 12" (38CM × 30CM) / TRACE MONOTYPE
WITH PANPASTEL ADDED

I applied PanPastel to the trace monotype to color the image.

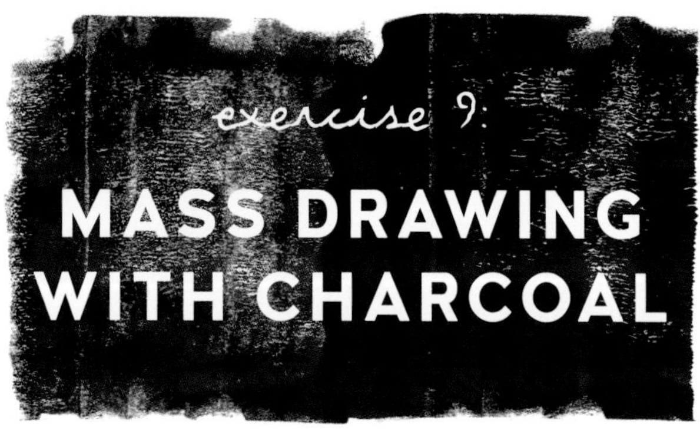

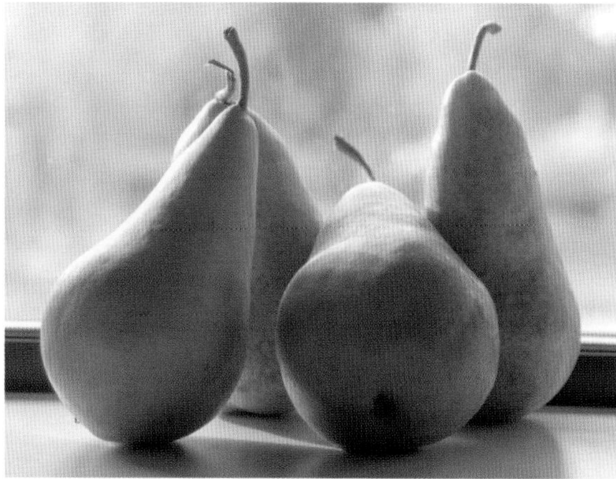

PEAR PHOTO IN BLACK AND WHITE

You might recognize this image of pears from chapter 1.

MATERIALS

- General's Jumbo Compressed Charcoal 2B, 4B, 6B
- rough newsprint pad 18" × 24" (41CM × 61CM) or white drawing paper
- erasers (kneaded and hard plastic)
- smoosher, soft paper towel or cosmetic sponge for smearing the charcoal
- standing easel

DIRECTIONS

STEP 1

Refer to the image of pears below, and lightly outline 2" (5CM) in from the edge of your pad a rectangle that matches the proportions of the image. (A border helps you confine the image to a specific shape.)

STEP 2

Do a mass drawing of the pears using the side of the charcoal. Add stokes as though you were adding bits of clay. Make no lines, only "masses" of values. Develop the background and the pears simultaneously, comparing values as you go. Remove charcoal with the kneaded eraser, and add charcoal as needed, smearing occasionally with the smoosher. Take photos as you work, and step back often from the easel to observe your work from a distance.

STEP 3

Consider the whole image as you work on the parts. Focus on the contrast of values and variation of edges to create the illusion of dark and light, volume and weight. When you are satisfied, take a photo.

STEP 4

Add lines for the stems, making each one unique in character. Check that you've developed a full value drawing including all the values from dark to light except white.

CRITIQUE

- Observe the background. Is there a feeling of space and depth behind the pears?
- Do the pears seem to be part of the background or separate from it?
- Does anything seem to float or be unresolved?
- If you were to add white, where would you put it?
- Observe how the stems stand out because they are the only lines. Consider that the way to emphasize line is to do less, rather than more!

TAKEAWAY

Working the figure and the ground simultaneously helps to create a stronger awareness of the "whole," rather than the "parts."

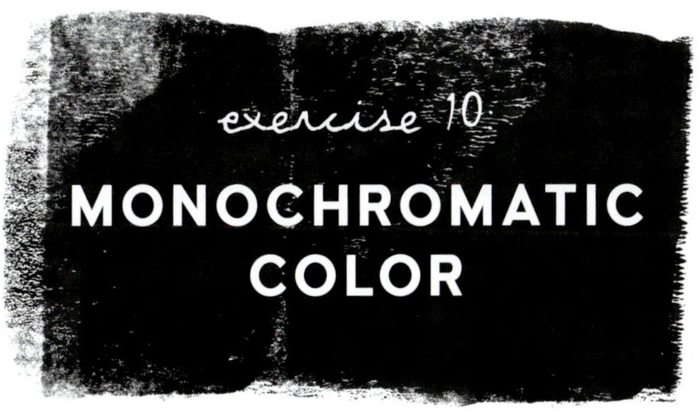

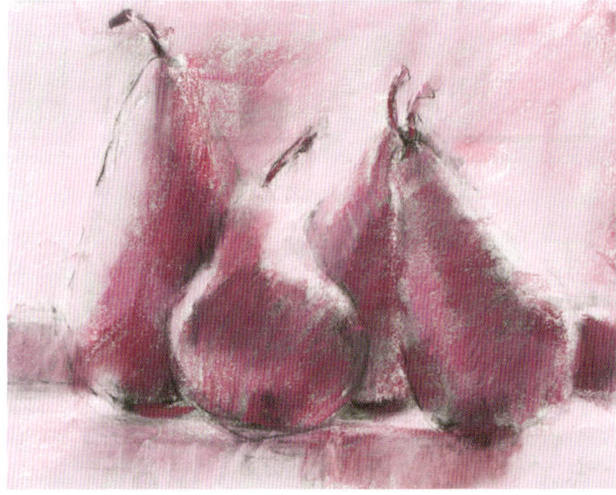

Using three values of a pink, this is an example of one possible result of adding monochromatic color over a full value charcoal drawing.

MATERIALS:

- soft pastels: three values (light, mid, dark) of one color
- charcoal full value mass drawing from exercise 9
- razor blade
- color wheel

DIRECTIONS

STEP 1

Choose light, middle and dark values of one color, such as light pink, pink and dark pink. Using the side of your pastel stick, lightly add the dark pastel over all the dark value areas of the charcoal underpainting you created in exercise 9. Avoid the urge to blend with fingers, erase or smear. Vary the directions of the strokes of pastel as you build up layers of pigment. Use the tip of the pastel to create masses of lines (called "feathering"). Develop the figure and ground simultaneously, and when satisfied, take a photo.

STEP 2

Repeat this process using the midtone color value over the areas that are midtones in the charcoal underpainting. Take a photo.

STEP 3

Repeat for the lightest value using the lightest pastel stick. Take a photo.

CRITIQUE

- Observe the monochromatic image you've created in the camera and compare this to your charcoal photo.
- Turn the photo into a black-and-white version to see how your values are working. If you need to lighten or darken anything, you can go in and remove or add pastel or charcoal.

TAKEAWAY

A monochromatic image can help you understand how color and value relate to each other.

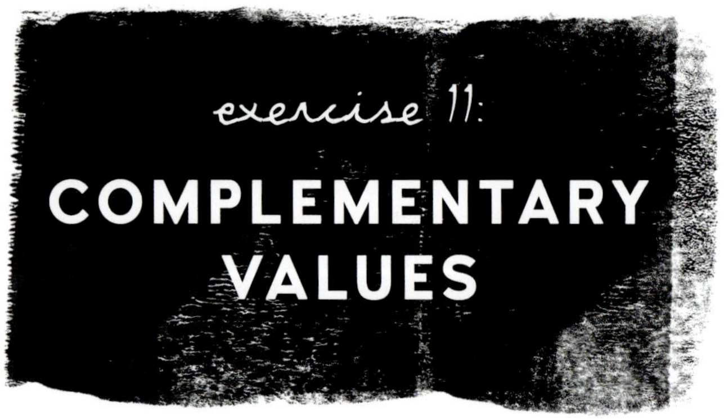

COMPLEMENTARY VALUES

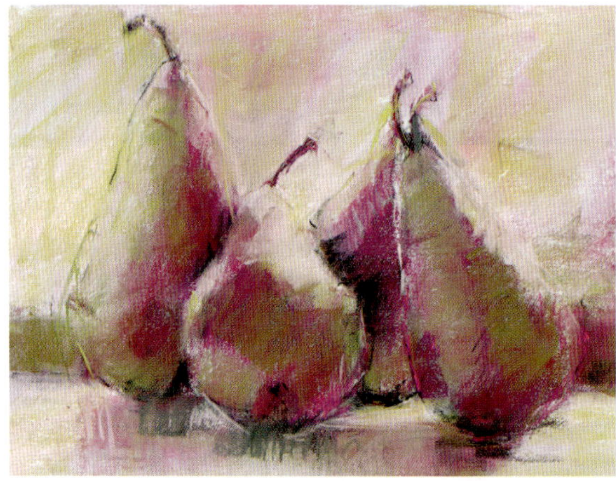

This is one possible result of adding the complementary color values to the monochromatic color of exercise 10.

MATERIALS

- same materials as in exercise 10, plus three additional pastels
- color wheel

DIRECTIONS

STEP 1

Refer to a color wheel to identify the complement of the color you used for exercise 10. (As a reminder, complements are directly opposite each other on the color wheel.) Select three values of that color—a light, middle and dark. For example, if you used pink in exercise 10, you will choose three values of the green, pink's opposite.

STEP 2

Apply the corresponding values over the monochromatic image from exercise 10, working from the darkest to the lightest value. Develop the figure and ground simultaneously. Avoid rubbing or blending the colors together, but work lightly using the side and tip of your pastel. Step back often from your easel to see the work from a distance. Add charcoal to increase contrast, and go back and forth between the complementary colors to tweak the image to your satisfaction. Take a photo.

STEP 3

Observe how the complementary colors have neutralized the image without dulling it. Applying pastels in layers without blending prevents muddy colors.

CRITIQUE

- Study the drawing, and see how the complements are working together.
- Convert your photo to black and white to see if your value distribution has changed.
- Does one of the two colors seem to be more dominant?

TAKEAWAY

Complementary colors mixed together physically will make mud, but applying pastel lightly in layers allows optical mixing to occur.

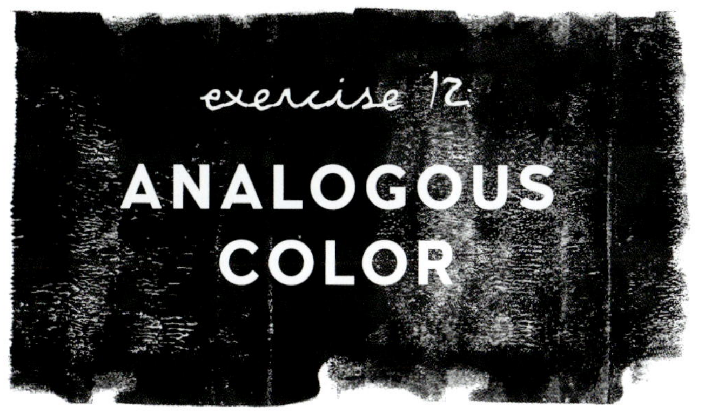

DIRECTIONS

STEP 1

Looking at the color wheel, choose colors that flank both sides of the colors you have used. These are the analogous colors. Each color will have analogous colors that are warmer on one side and cooler on the other. For example, yellow has yellow-orange on one side and yellow-green on the other side.

STEP 2:

Choose analogous colors for both of the colors you've used up to this point, and find light, middle and dark values of those colors. Add these analogous colors into your drawing, again working the figure and the ground simultaneously. Work with a light touch, matching values, weaving lights with lights, mid values with mid values, and darks with dark values.

NOTE: To prevent your work from getting "spotty," add each color into both the figure and the ground. This will help to maintain harmony in the work. Step away from the easel to view your work, and take photos as often as you can.

STEP 3:

Extend your pastel palette beyond the immediate adjacent color on the color wheel to expand the range of the analogous colors.

STEP 4:

Determine which colors have not been included in your work. Add a small amount of those "zinger" colors where you would like to attract special attention. Watch the zinger colors work like little jewels to sparkle up your drawing. Take a photo.

CRITIQUE

- Review the entire process on your camera to see how the image developed. Is there a place that you wish you had stopped?
- Repeat the entire process using other color choices.

TAKEAWAY

You can use any color as long as it is the correct value!

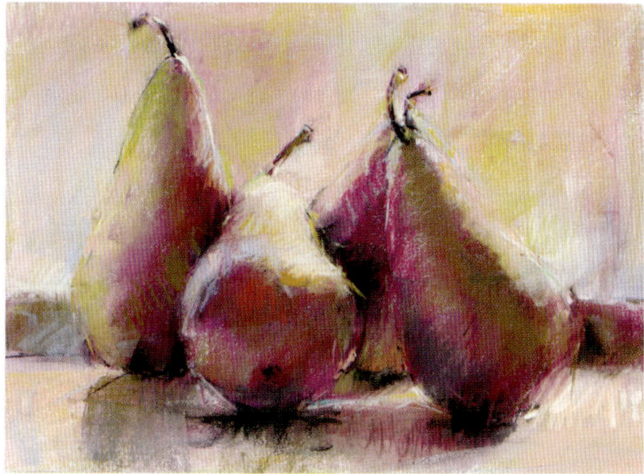

This is one possible result of adding the analogous colors to the image in exercise 11.

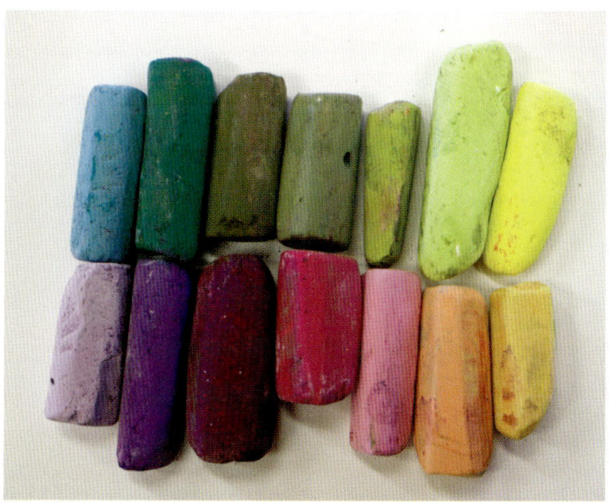

These pastels were used in the chapter 3 exercises.

MATERIALS

- drawing and materials from exercise 11
- pastels

MONOTYPES AND PASTEL

In chapter 3 you were introduced to different approaches to create underpaintings for your images. This foundation influences, rather than describes, the look and feel of all the layers built on top of it.

Chapter 4 will introduce you to several ways to create and use a monotype as a fabulous new tool to produce an underpainting for pastel. You will learn how to print a monotype with and without a press and see how this simple and efficient process can evoke new possibilities for pastel. You'll see how the monotype can become a platform on which you will build your image in a spontaneous way. Allowing the texture and marks of the underpainting to suggest imagery is a responsive and improvisational approach to drawing that can help you quickly lose any fear of the blank surface. The immediacy and versatility of pastel is a perfect partner for this approach with the monotype!

My world of drawing changed when I began printmaking. Though I had drawn all my life, I found myself on totally unfamiliar ground. It forced me to slow down and take a closer look at everything I did. I was instantly intrigued by the freedom and spontaneity the monotype process offered, allowing me to work with the elements of texture in a completely different way than I'd ever experienced or addressed with pastel. The merging of printmaking and pastels has opened a doorway to endless new ways to work as an artist both for me and many of my students.

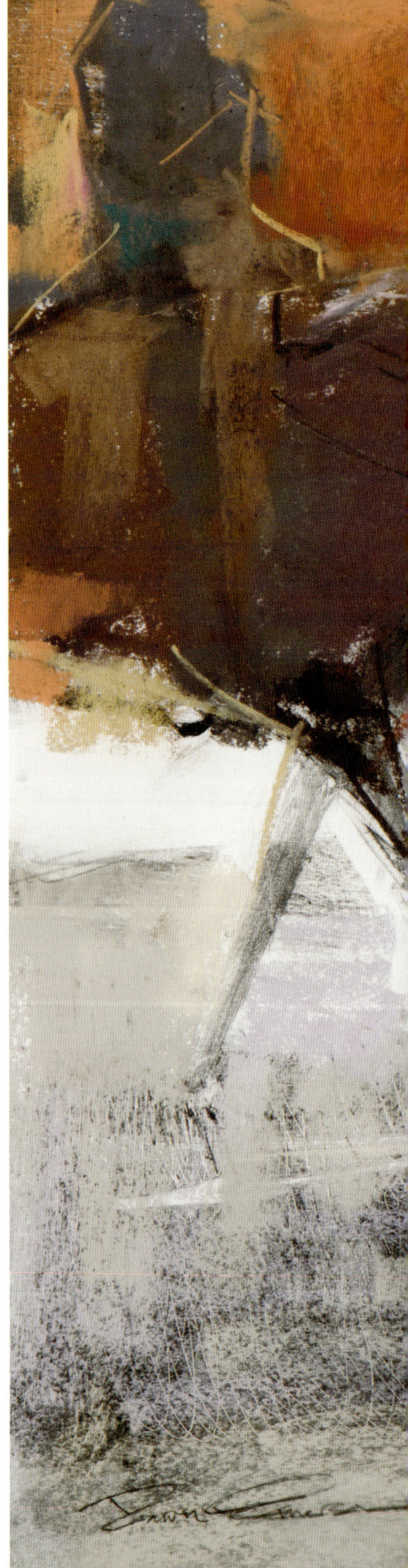

SUNDOWN SKY / 19" × 19" (48CM × 48CM) / DARKFIELD MONOTYPE PRINTED ON STONEHENGE PAPER, DRAWN INTO WITH SOFT PASTEL

This image began as a dark field monotype underpainting. I drew into the printed image with soft pastel, allowing some of the textural underpainting to remain visible. Because the monotype laid out the image and areas of dark and light, I was free to focus on the color palette, shapes and textures.

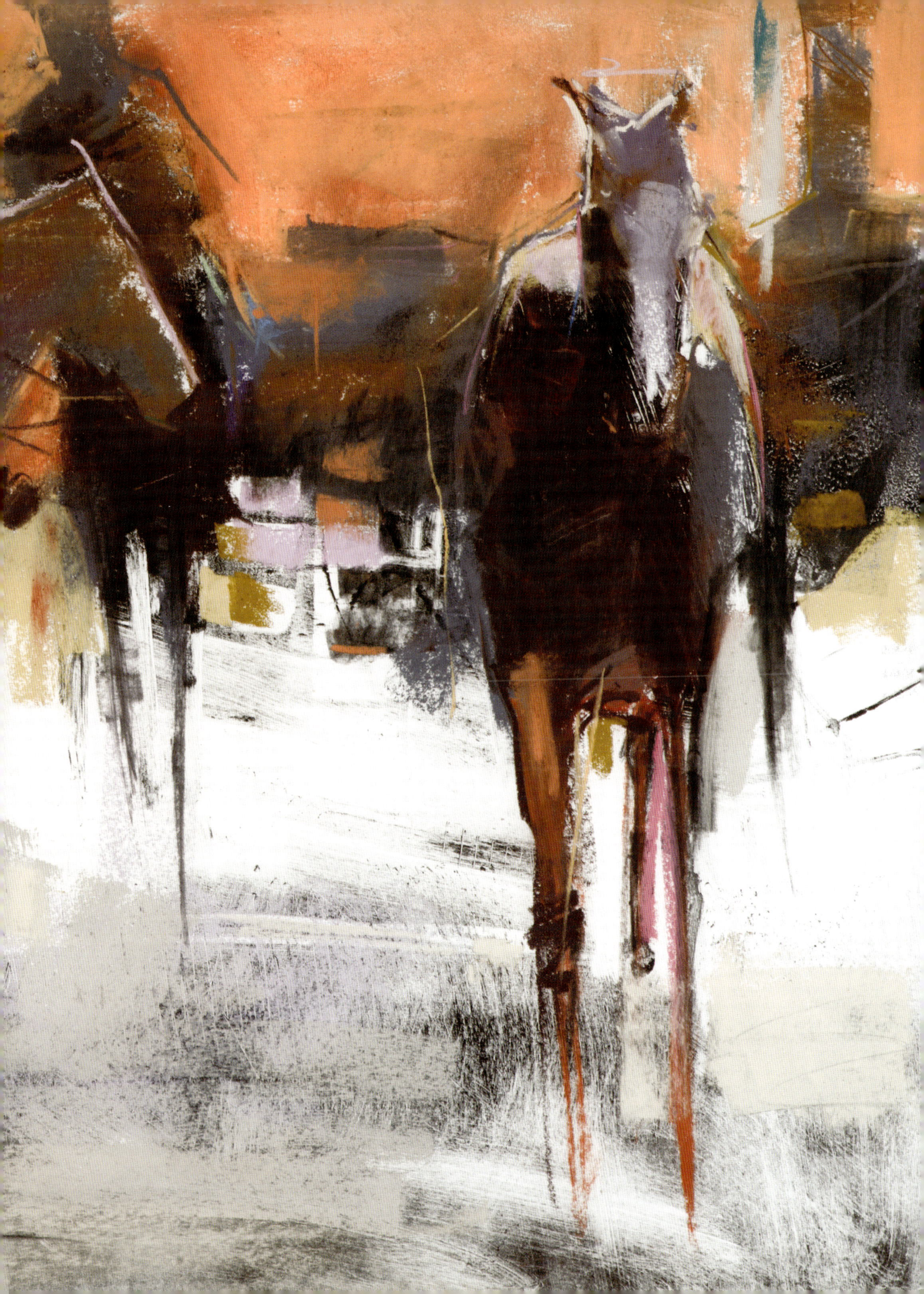

THE DARK FIELD MONOTYPE

A dark field monotype starts by completely inking the plate with a brayer. The artist starts working *subtractively* to remove the areas that will be light, much like drawing in reverse. The ink can be wiped away with towels, scrapers, sticks or sponges. Ink can be added back to the plate with brayers or other tools at any time. Edgar Degas was the first pastelist to explore using the dark field monotype as a way to create an underpainting for his pastels. This process allowed him to quickly modify compositions and textures by manipulating the ink on the plate.

WHAT IS A MONOTYPE?

The monotype is a unique process that crosses boundaries between painting, drawing and printmaking and is often referred to as the "painterly print." A monotype is made by adding or subtracting ink onto a surface called a "plate," and then transferring that image to another surface. The transfer process can be done using hand rubbing or by feeding the plate and paper through a press that creates pressure in the thousands of pounds per square inch. The resulting image is a reversed reading (or a mirror image) of the original image. In a monotype all of the ink is on the surface of the plate, so when the ink is gone, so is the image. Like a painting, a monotype can be a work of art unto itself or it can be combined with other drawing and painting media after it's printed. A monoprint differs from a monotype in that there is some permanent element that is embedded in the plate that is repeatable. In a true monotype every image is unique. Monotypes can be combined with other printmaking techniques or embellished with other media to create limitless possibilities.

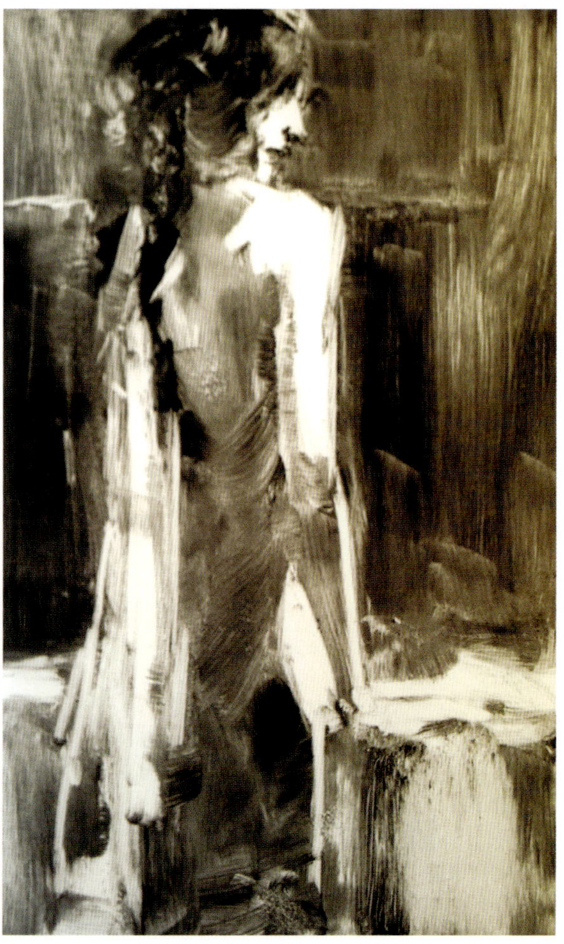

STEPHANIE / 10" × 6" (25CM × 15CM) / MONOTYPE ON STONEHENGE PAPER

This monotype was done during a 20-minute pose at a life-drawing session. I printed the image with the use of a press after the class.

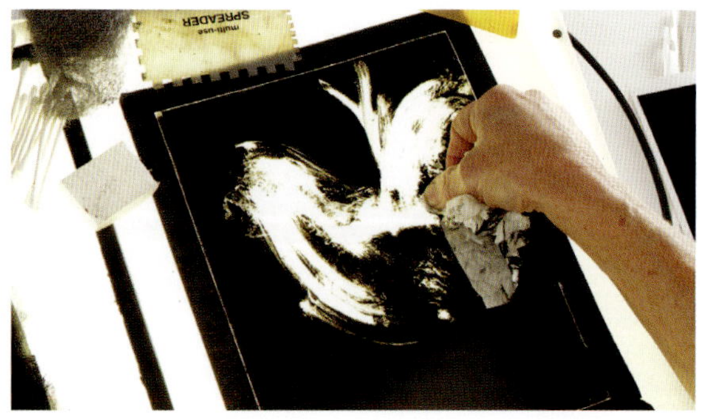

REMOVING INK FROM THE PLATE

I'm using a baby wipe to remove Akua Intaglio ink from the dark field plate. (My plate is a piece of cellophane.) Working on a lighted surface such as a lightbox or near a window makes it easier to see the marks and density of the ink as you work.

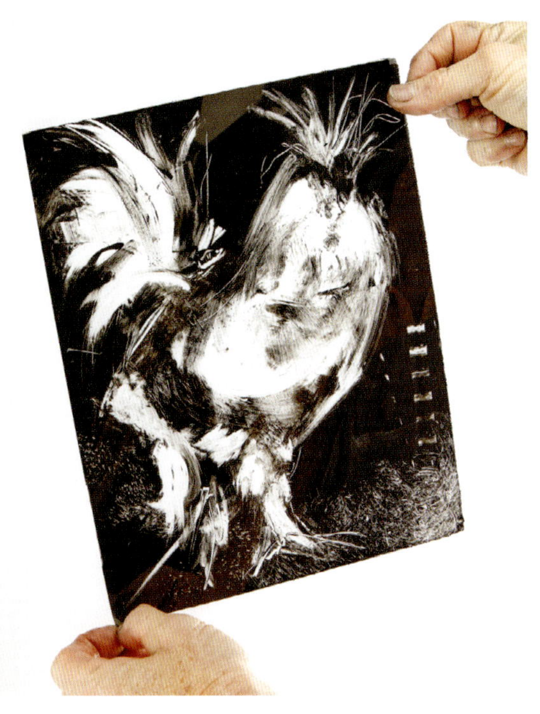

MONOTYPE MARKS

The kind of textures and marks that can be made on the monotype plate are limited only by your imagination. Invent tools that will create unique signature marks.

CHECK THE PLATE BEFORE PRINTING

Hold the plate up to a light source to check for unwanted blobs, fingerprints and foreign objects. Remove the tape and clean edges before printing.

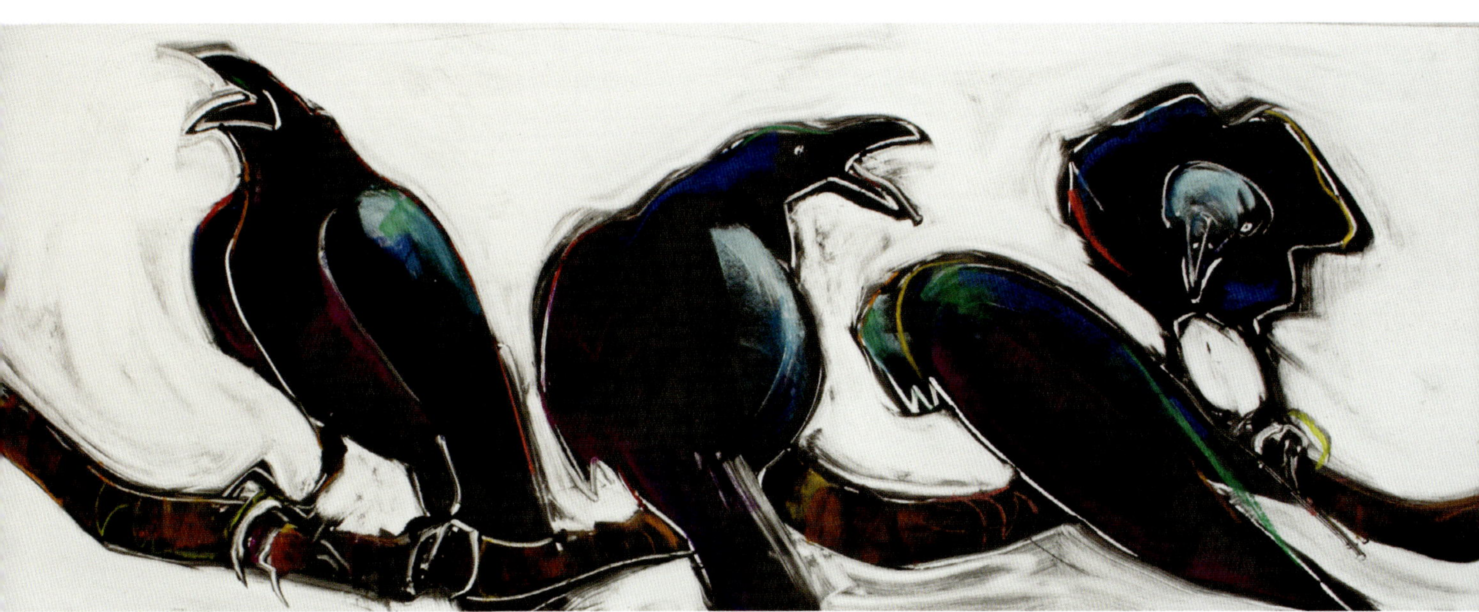

QUARTET / 9" × 23" (23CM × 58CM)/ MONOTYPE ON STONEHENGE PAPER WITH SOFT PASTEL ADDED

I began with a solid dark field of ink, then outlined the birds with cotton swabs. I wiped away the background to show the shape of the birds. The marks remaining in the background activate the space around the birds. I then added soft pastel to the image.

THE LIGHT FIELD MONOTYPE

The light field monotype is exactly like starting with a blank piece of paper or canvas for a painting. In this *additive process*, ink is applied to a blank plate with brayers, stamps, brushes or fingers. Thin objects like leaves, grass, feathers or cut paper can also be placed on the plate. A leaf put down on top of ink on the plate blocks out the ink below, while an inked leaf will print the form of the leaf in color. Once the image is printed, objects and forms can be re-inked, flipped over or rearranged. The new plate can be printed again, creating a unique image each time. The "ghost image" is the second (and sometimes third) image that is pulled from the same plate. These more muted and softer ghost images can be printed on top of other monotypes to create beautiful layering.

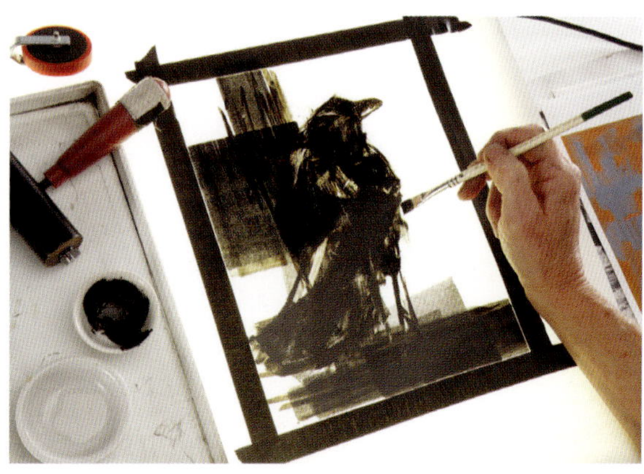

BRUSHING INK ONTO THE PLATE
Mixing Akua blending medium to Intaglio ink makes the ink more transparent and more brushable. Blending medium should be used instead of water.

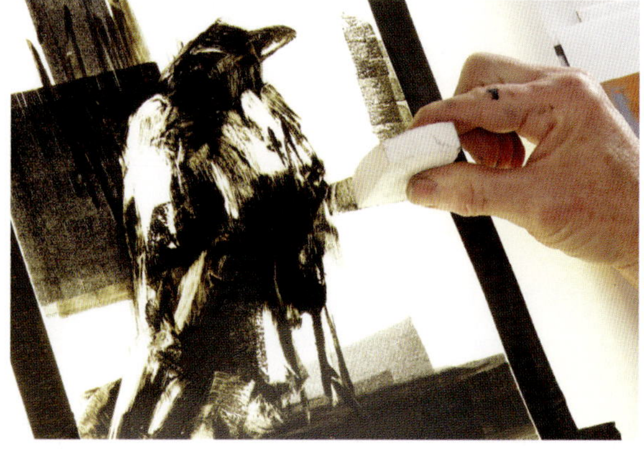

STEP 1
Tools other than brushes can be used to add ink to the plate surface. Here I am using a piece of foam to apply the ink.

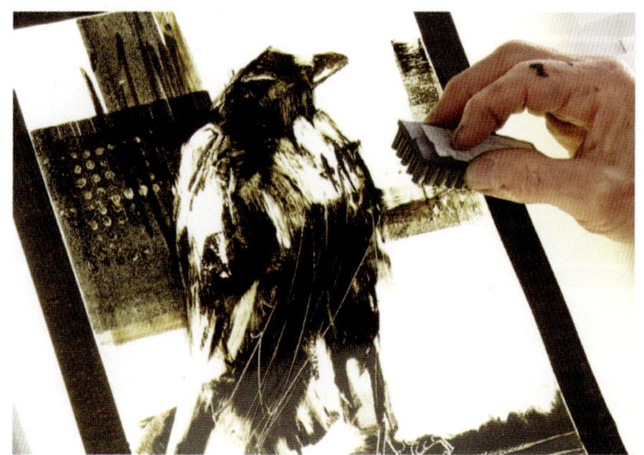

STEP 2
A rubber texture is dipped or painted with ink to apply a pattern of circles to the image. Care should be taken to avoid depositing blobs of ink on the surface, which will spread out when the image is transferred to paper.

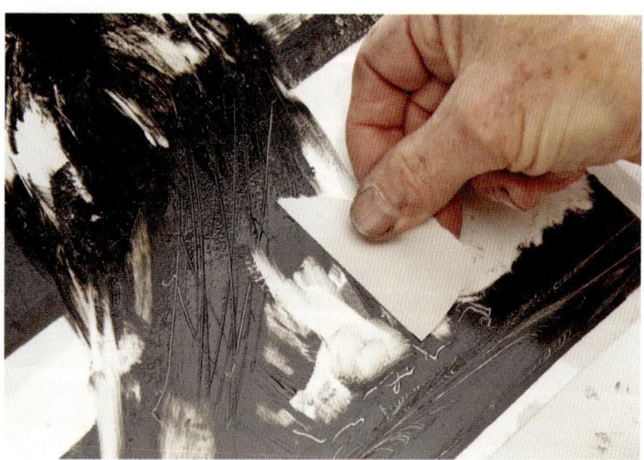

STEP 3
I'm using a piece of razor to remove a straight line of ink from the plate. Care should be taken to avoid making permanent scratches in the plate.

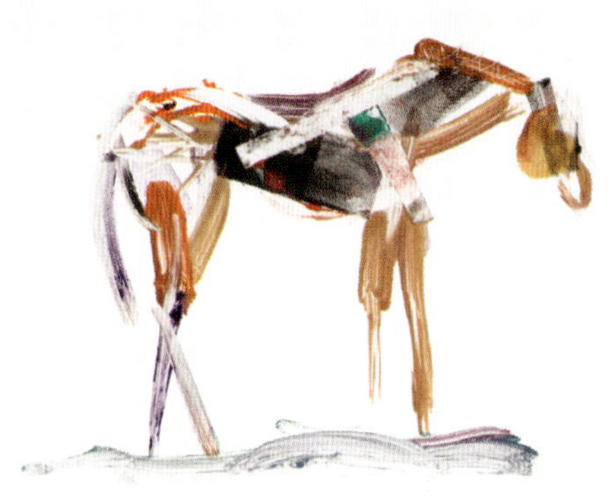

AFTER BUTTERFIELD #1 / 5" × 8" (13CM × 20CM) / MONOTYPE WITH INK

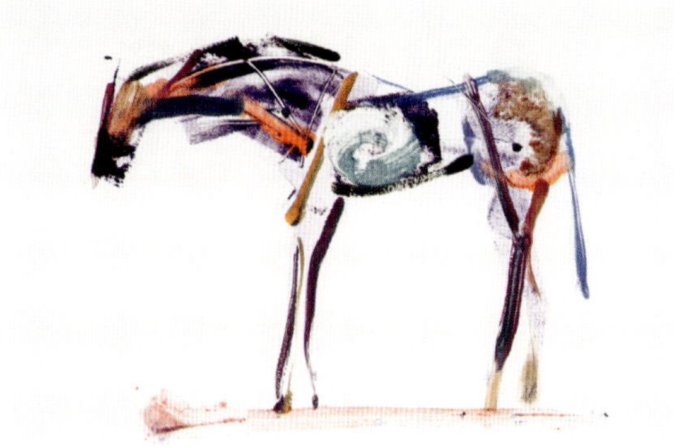

AFTER BUTTERFIELD #2 / 5" × 8" (13CM × 20CM) / MONOTYPE WITH INK

Both these images were painted directly onto the plate with soft brushes. The monotype process captures every nuance of each stroke you make. Though no pastel was added atop these images, pastel could be added to the print at a later time if desired.

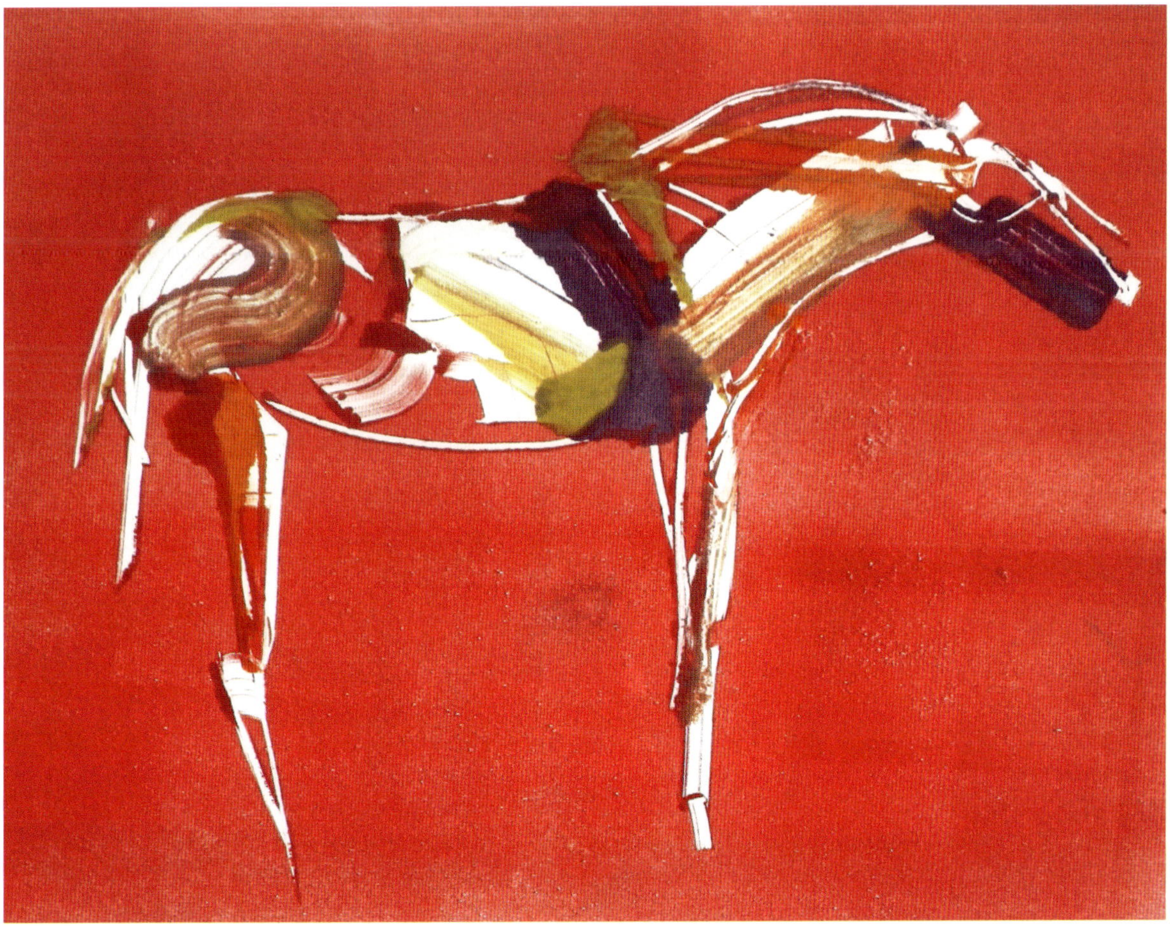

AFTER BUTTERFIELD #3 / 5" × 8" (13CM × 20CM) / MONOTYPE WITH INK

A combination of dark and light field was used to produce this image. Red ink was rolled onto the plate with a brayer, and then various tools removed the ink. Brushes were then used to paint colors back onto the plate. The process of creating a monotype heightens your awareness to the potential of each line, mark and color.

PRINTING THE MONOTYPE ON A PRESS

In this demonstration, a polycarbonate plate was completely inked up with soy-based printing ink, and the image of the horse was created by working subtractively in the dark field method. The "plate" was then put onto the "bed" of the monotype press ink-side up. A dry piece of Stonehenge printing paper was laid on top of the plate, blankets added, and the bed moved beneath a roller to exert the pressure needed to transfer the ink. The first print that came off the press was dark and rich, and picked up every detail of the marks that had been created. A second piece of Stonehenge paper was soaked for several moments in a tray of water and toweled off before it was used to print the second, or ghost image. The ghost image has a softer feeling because there is less ink left on the plate and the paper was moistened first.

With two prints from the same plate, I was able to explore using different color choices on each one.

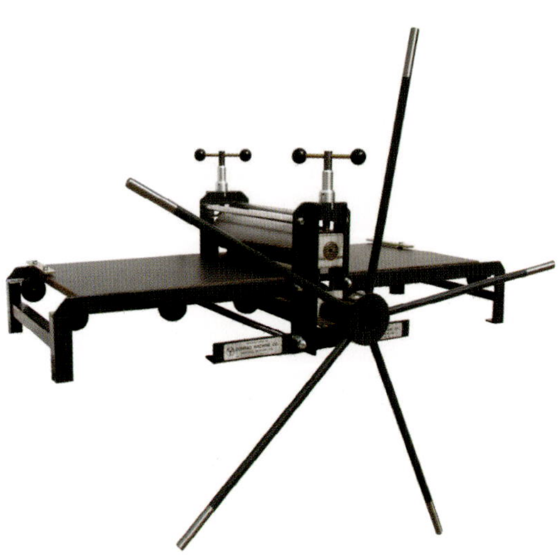

CONRAD MONOTYPE PRESS

An etching press or monotype press exerts 2,000+ pounds psi as opposed to 100–200 psi when you rub an image by hand with the back of a spoon.

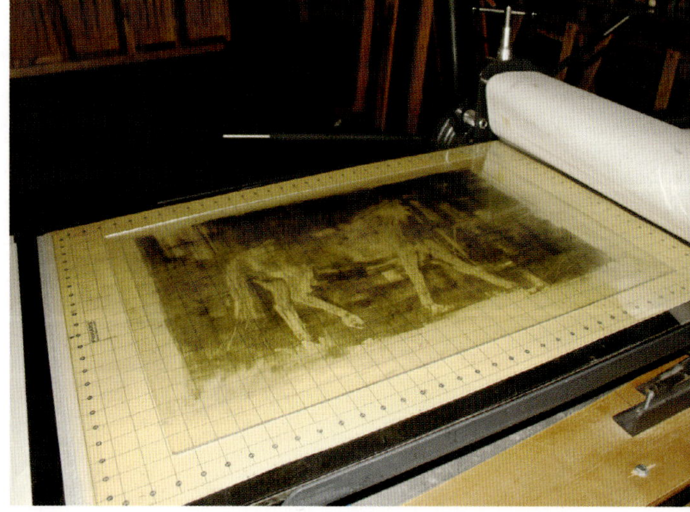

ON THE PRESS

Here is the monotype plate of the horse image you see printed on page 87. The next step is to place paper on top of the plate, pull the press blankets over the paper, and roll it under the drum. This is the monotype press I use in my studio, and its name is Presley.

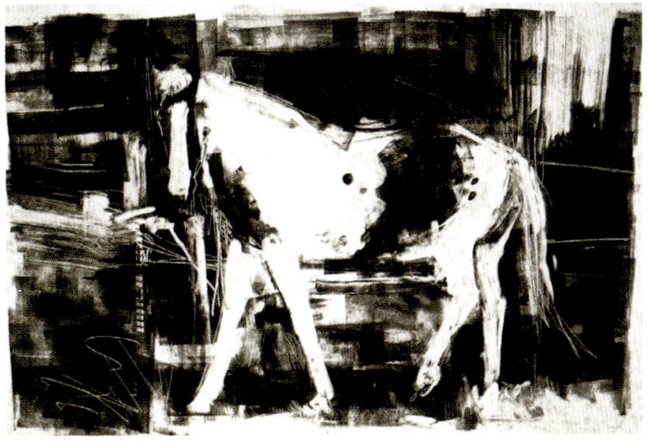

THE FIRST PRINT

This is the first print off the plate, printed onto dry Stonehenge paper. Notice the pattern of light and dark and the textural quality that this process produces.

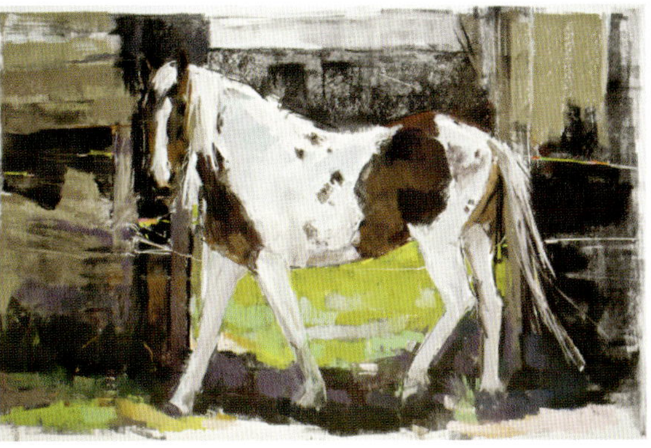

PASTEL IS ADDED TO THE MONOTYPE

I've added pastel to the first print, allowing much of the texture from the dark field monotype underpainting to show through.

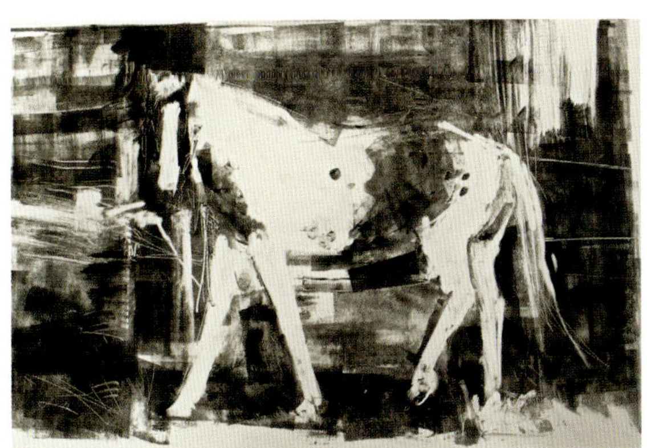

THE GHOST PRINT

This is the second print off the same plate, printed onto moistened Stonehenge paper. There is less contrast, but the image is more evenly toned and has a softer feeling.

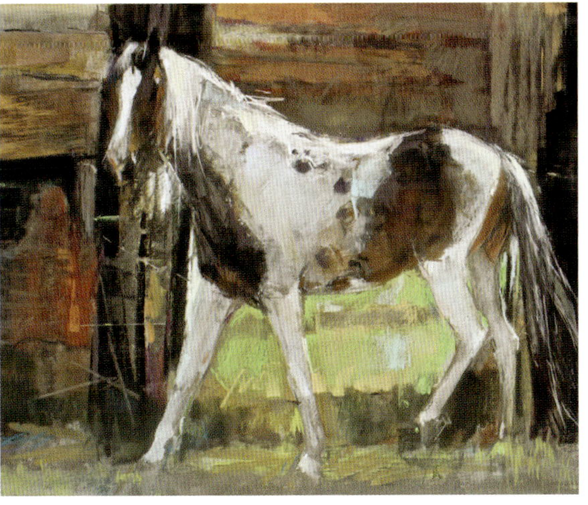

GHOST PRINT WITH PASTEL ADDED

I drew into the ghost print underpainting with different colors of pastel. Notice that less of the monotype underpainting is visible here. How much or how little you cover the underpainting is your choice.

PRINTING THE MONOTYPE BY HAND

Spoons, spatulas, smooth wood and other tools may be used to transfer ink from the printing plate to paper. Take your time when transferring ink to paper by hand, and to use a methodical, consistent approach. Find a tool that feels good in your hand, doesn't damage the paper and won't cause fatigue.

Printing by hand cannot compete with the amount of pressure exerted by a press so you may want to be heavy-handed with the ink to ensure solid coverage. Before you print, take the time to check the plate for ink blobs that could squish under pressure. Remove them by blotting gently with a piece of newsprint. When rubbing, use downward pressure in small back and forth or circular motion. The first print will always be the darkest, and subsequent "ghost" prints will be lighter.

To print a second or third ghost, you can moisten the printing paper to help draw the remaining ink off the plate. Another option when using Akua Intaglio ink or Akua Liquid Pigment is to brayer on a thin layer of Akua Release Agent to the plate after your first print to help release the ink without the need for moistening the paper.

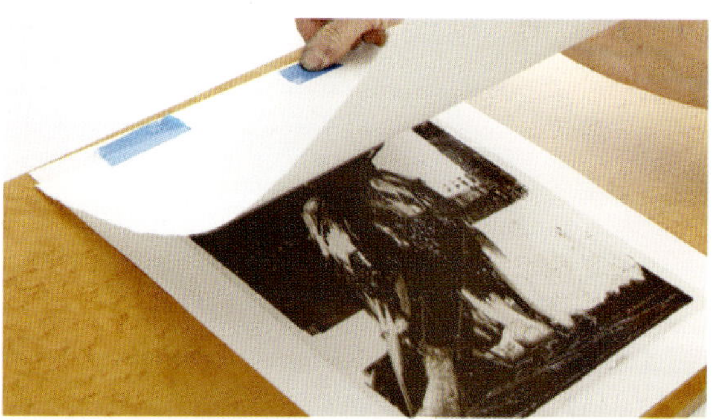

SET UP TO PRINT BY HAND
The plate is placed ink-side up on a smooth flat surface. A piece of white paper below the plate makes it easier to see the plate. Stonehenge paper is placed over the plate and hinged to prevent slipping.

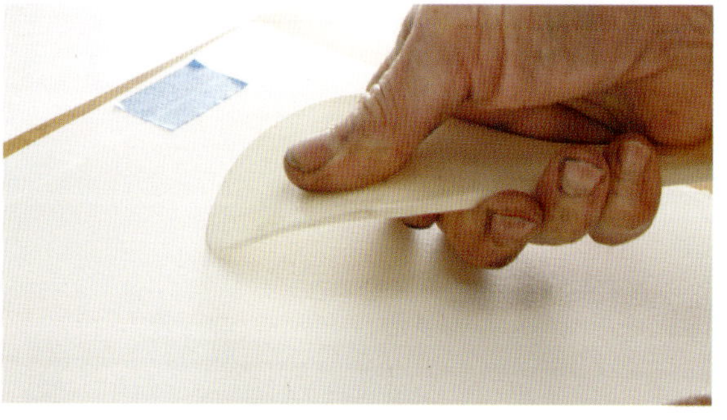

TRANSFER THE IMAGE
A tool is used to rub over the back of the paper to transfer the image. Rub with consistent pressure and check your work frequently for the best results.

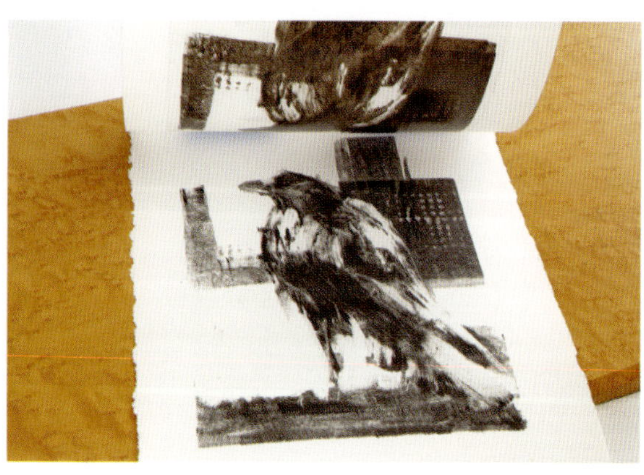

MAKE THE FIRST PRINT
The paper is lifted to check the printed image.

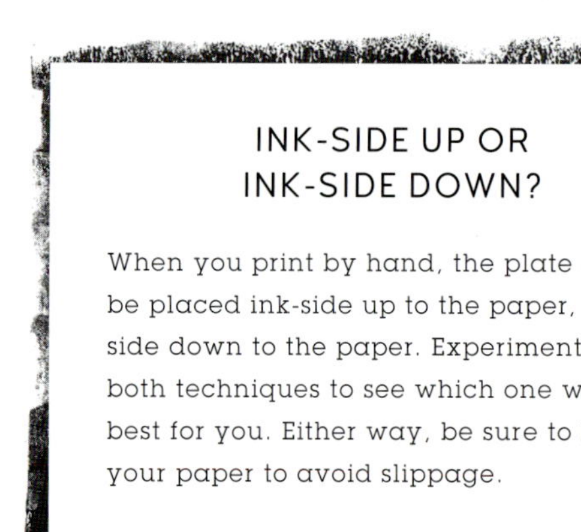

INK-SIDE UP OR INK-SIDE DOWN?

When you print by hand, the plate can be placed ink-side up to the paper, or ink-side down to the paper. Experiment with both techniques to see which one works best for you. Either way, be sure to hinge your paper to avoid slippage.

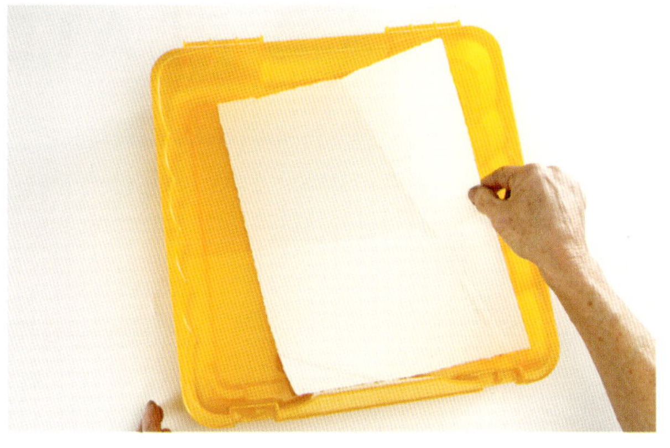

SOAK THE PAPER FOR THE GHOST PRINT

Paper for the ghost image is soaked in water for several minutes.

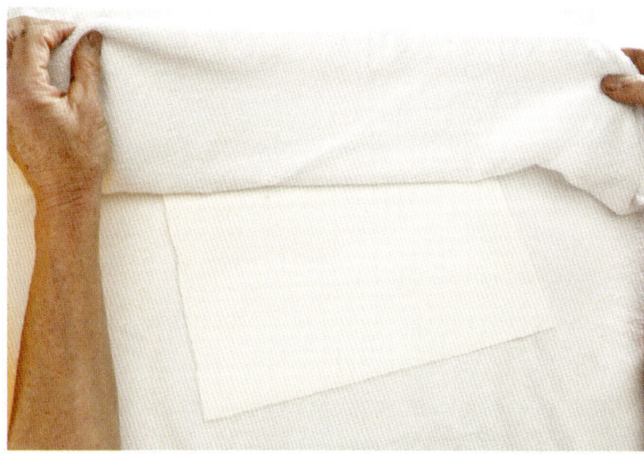

DRY THE PAPER FOR THE GHOST PRINT

Towel off the soaked paper so there are no puddles or wet areas on the surface.

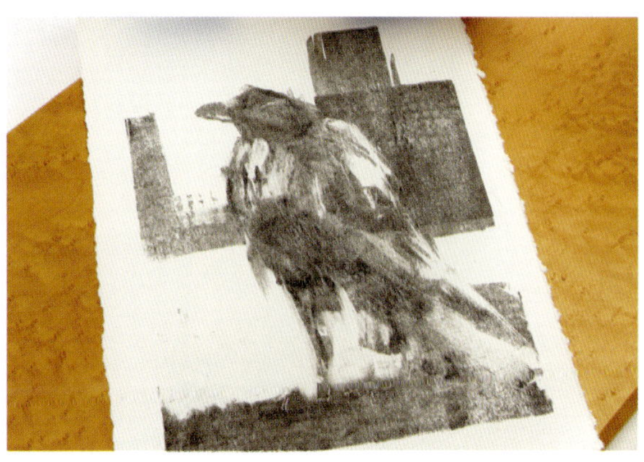

THE GHOST PRINT

The ghost print will be lighter and have less contrast than the first print, but makes a beautiful surface to draw into or print on top of.

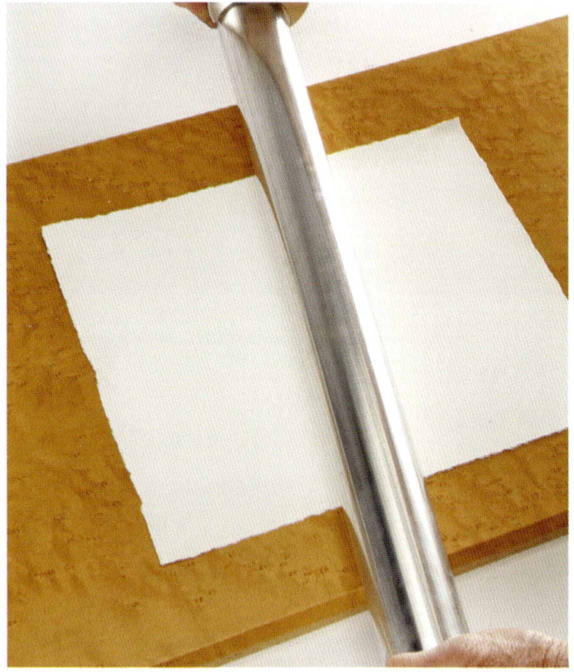

TRANSFERRING WITH THE PIN PRESS

With the pin press, firmly press down in the center of the paper, and roll outward in all directions, being careful not to move the paper. Exert even pressure downward as you roll.

Place one hand on the center of the paper so the paper will not shift, and lift one corner to check the print.

PRINTING WITH PAPER AS A PLATE

Virtually any material can be used a plate for monotype printing: cellophane, polycarbonate, acrylic, glass, tinfoil, metal, parchment, cardboard, paper, fabric, rubber, wood, etc. Paper like cardstock can be easily cut to any size. Each of the images below was printed using paper as a printing plate. I drew with pencil first, then blocked in with brayers, brushes and sponges. After printing, I either refresh the ink and continue printing, or save the plate with whatever ink remains on the surface for future reference. The unexpected marks and colors that come from previous printings enhance the layering and surface of the new prints.

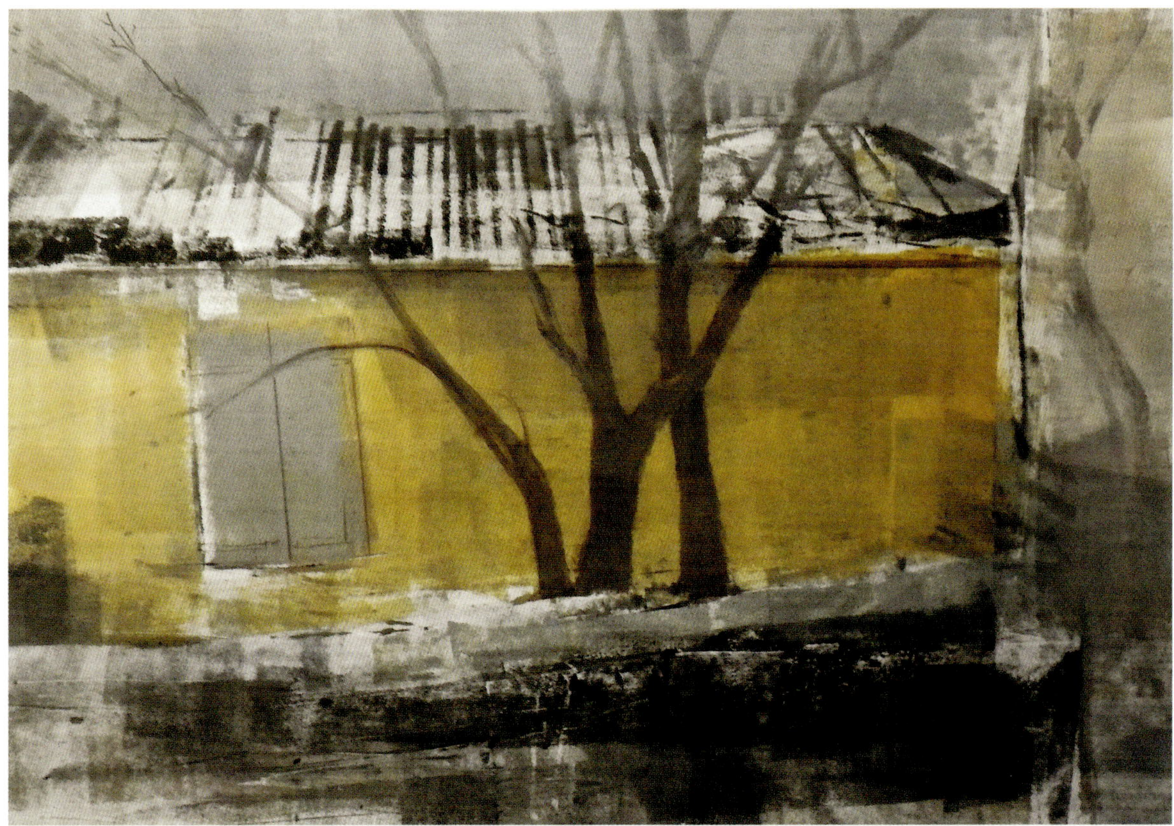

BEHIND THE WALL / 10" × 6" (25CM × 15CM) / MONOTYPE ON STONEHENGE PAPER

The plate used for this print was a piece of Stonehenge paper. I painted directly onto the plate with brayers and other tools, then trimmed the paper to the exact size I wanted the image to be. I mark the paper I will print onto with light pencil marks so I will be able to place the plate exactly where I want it on a clean sheet. No pastel was added to the print here.

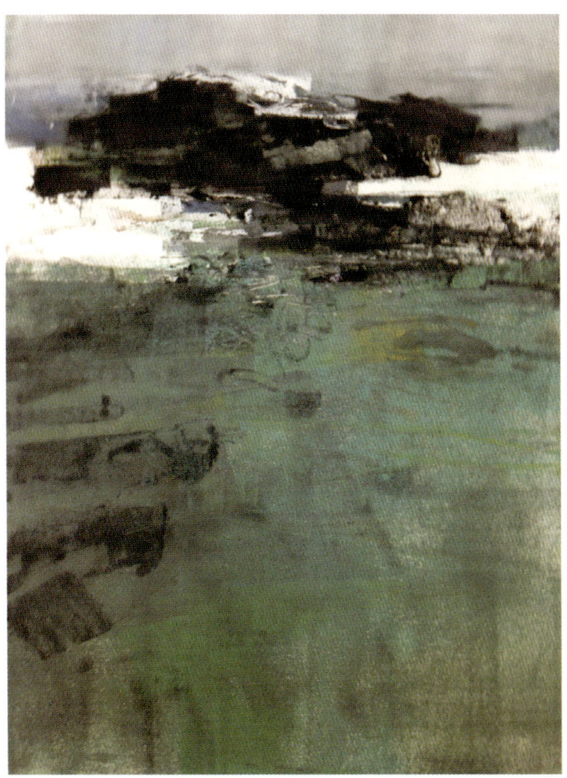

CHANGING RIDE #1 / 16" × 12" (25CM × 15CM) /
MONOTYPE ON STONEHENGE PAPER

CHANGING RIDE #2 / 16" × 12" (25CM × 15CM) /
MONOTYPE ON STONEHENGE PAPER

Both of these images were made from the same paper plate. I applied various colors of Akua Intaglio inks with brayers, re-inking areas on top of the plate each time I printed. Observe the variety of marks made by the brayer, as well as from offsetting. Much of the result is accidental, making the monotype process even more exciting!

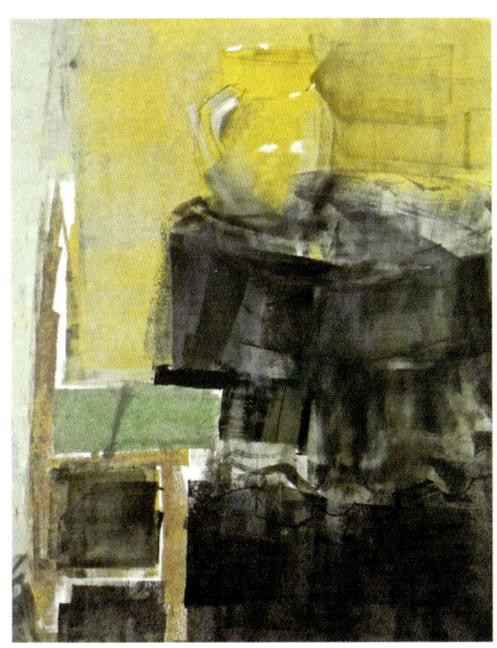

TABLE FOR ONE / 10" × 8" (25CM × 15CM) / MONOTYPE
ON STONEHENGE PAPER

Paper was used as a plate for this print. Notice that the areas of white that remain on the print are places that were not covered by the ink. Leaving places for the paper to show through gives sparkle to the print.

LAUNCHING THE IMAGINATION

In each of these images a monotype was used as a platform to launch my imagination. When I created the underlying monotype I was thinking about how I organized the elements and not what subject might be joined with this print. The key to making a nonobjective (nonrepresentational) ground is to imply rather than describe. Color and value can evoke mood. Shapes and line can imply density, size and weight. Texture can evoke feelings of depth, surface, space and mystery. The way I organize the big shapes of color and texture, with pathways of darks and lights, sets up tensions between forms and spaces. I want the figure (subject) to feel like it has been pulled out of the ground rather than having been forced onto it. I also want to allow the background to "breathe" through the image in places, so there is an exchange between the two. An underpainting that satisfies the seven principles is a foundation from which almost any subject can be pulled. As I work, I respond to the elements in the underpainting and let them take me on a creative journey. I find that this way of working frees my imagination from the constraints it might impose if I began with a specific or more realistic underpainting.

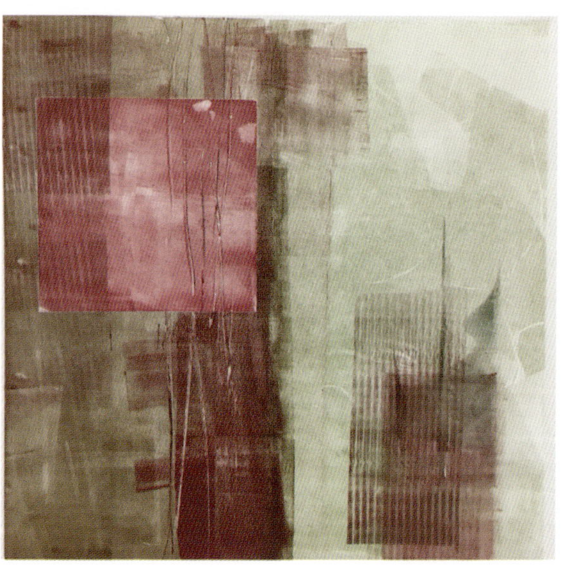

ABSTRACT GROUND / 19" × 19" (48CM × 48CM) / MONOTYPE ON STONEHENGE PAPER

I printed this monotype purely as an abstract ground, with no preconception of adding any particular subject or figure to it.

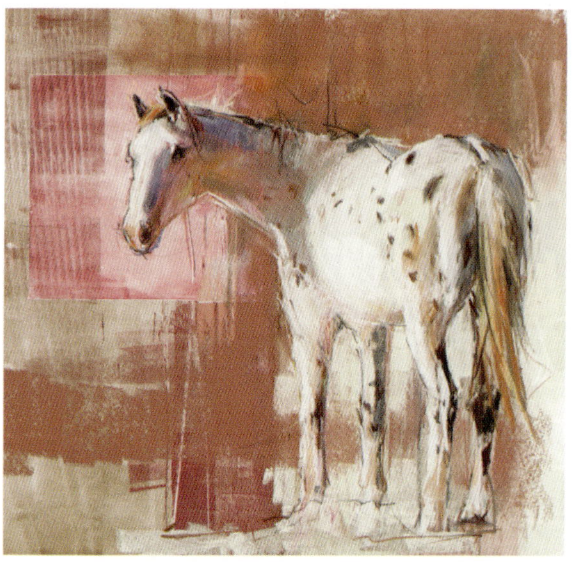

QUARTZITE HORSE / 19" × 19" (48CM × 48CM) / MONOTYPE WITH SOFT PASTEL AND CHARCOAL ON STONEHENGE PAPER

I added the image of the horse to the abstract ground using pastel and charcoal. You can see how beautifully the pastel blends in with the ink, making the transition from figure to ground a seamless one. The idea behind integrating figure and ground is to make the boundaries between media invisible.

ABSTRACTION AND THE IMAGINATION

the abstract grounds you create with the monotype can change the way your imagination engages with the figure/ground relationship and the entire image making process.

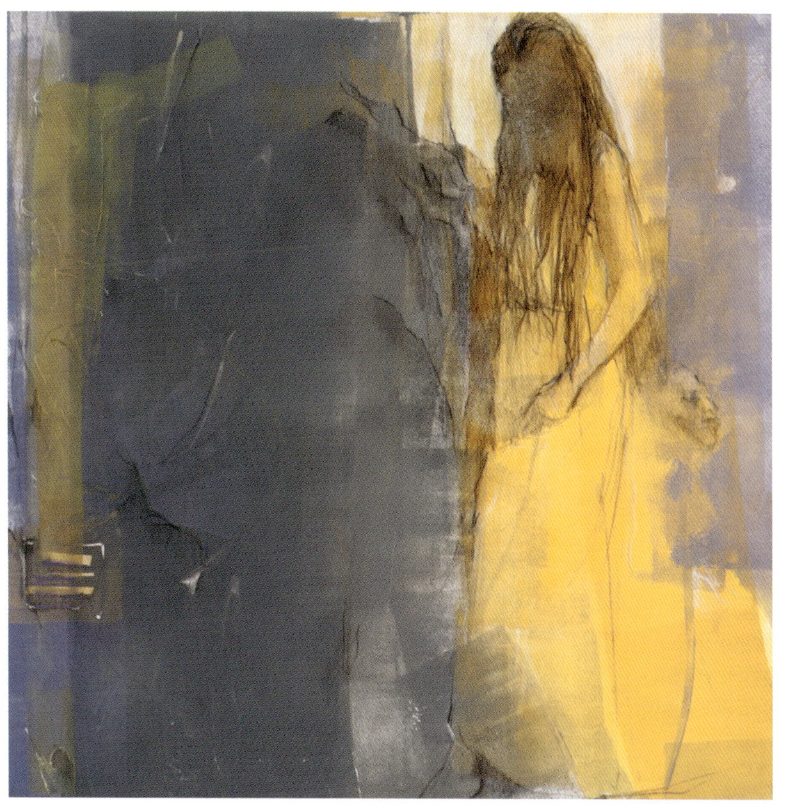

PERSEPHONE / 18" × 18" (46CM × 46CM) / MONOTYPE WITH SOFT PASTEL ON RIVES BFK PAPER

The ground for this image was produced as an abstract monotype on a plastic plate. When I looked at the print some weeks later, my imagination saw the vertical shape as a shaft of light from another world. I thought of the Persephone myth and drew the woman as though she was descending into the darkness.

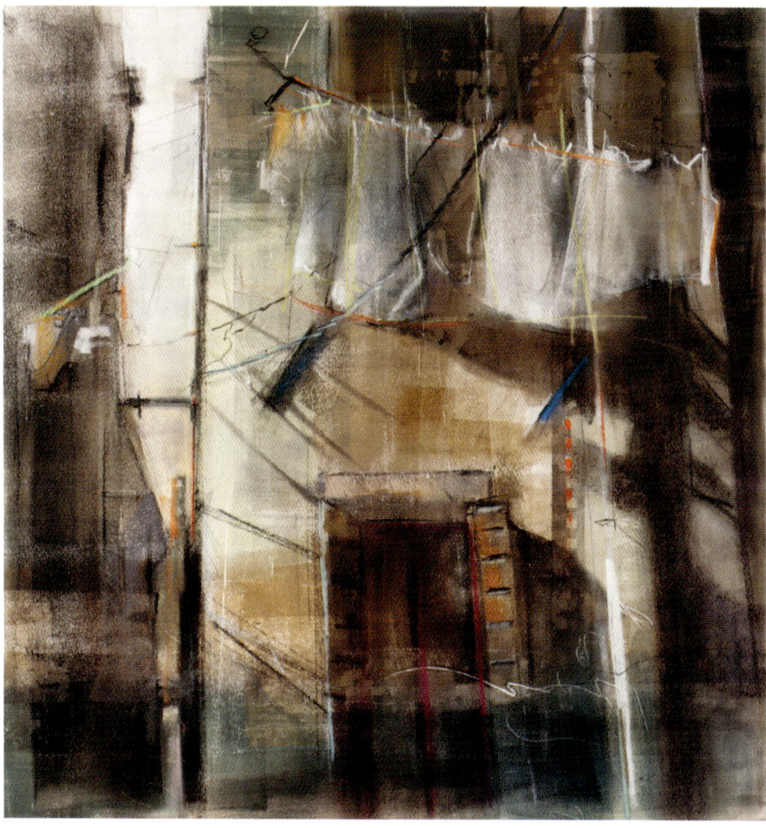

PRAYER FLAGS / 19" × 19" (48CM × 48CM) / MONOTYPE WITH SOFT PASTEL ON RIVES BFK PAPER

The ground for this image was produced as an abstract monotype. The imagery of laundry hanging on a building was developed later as a response to what my imagination invented within the abstraction. I have found that setting up a visual structure with a vertical and horizontal grid helps launch my imagination. From this grid of lines and textures, it is easy to create landscapes and stages on which to impose subjects.

DRAWING INTO THE MONOTYPE WITH PASTEL

The ground for each of these images was a monotype created as a nonobjective design and with no preconception of what image or subject would be drawn into them later. I try to set aside time in the studio to simply play and explore the creation of grounds. At the end of the day I set the grounds aside for a few weeks.

When I revisit them, I check in to see what imagery the surface suggests. I'll rotate the ground to see if it feels better in one direction or another, and often the rotation alone will make an idea pop up. Other times I let my imagination float as I look back and forth between the prints and various photo references I've accumulated. If a particular subject suggests itself, I draw the figure (or subject) onto tracing paper and place it on top of the print to check it out. Drawing onto clear cellophane with a dry erase marker also works well. I'll hear a kind of "click" in my head when it feels right, like a puzzle piece locking into place.

If nothing clicks, I go to the next ground, or the next. If something does click, I'll do several sketches of the subject to familiarize myself with it. This helps me feel more confident when I approach the monotype surface with charcoal and pastel. I begin by choosing colors that are already present in the monotype. That way I can maintain color harmony and reinforce elements without the complication of introducing more colors until I need to. When I do introduce new colors, I will include them both in the ground and the figure to maintain that sense of unity.

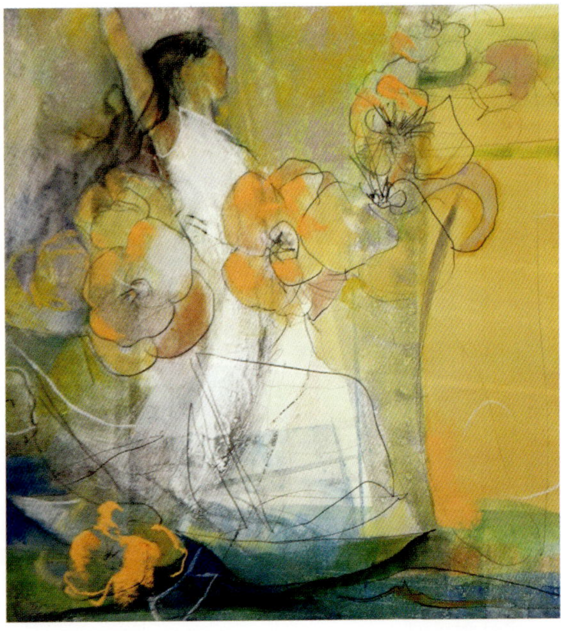

SAILING TO BYZANTIUM / 19" × 19" (48CM × 48CM) / MONOTYPE ON RIVES BFK WITH PASTEL

The figurative imagery you see here was developed as a response to the underlying abstract monotype. Like looking at clouds, the monotype itself suggests the story to my imagination. I set aside time in the studio to create monotype grounds that will prompt my imagination— sometimes hours, weeks or even years later.

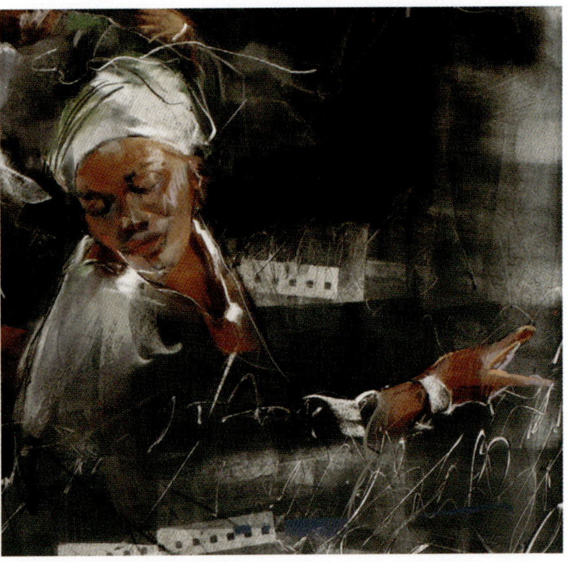

TELLING HER STORY / 19" × 19" (48CM × 48CM) / MONOTYPE ON RIVES BFK WITH PASTEL ADDED

This image is another response to an abstract background. I was intrigued with how the filmstrip images used to create the monotype inspired me to think of time passing, and how stories are told through movement and dance. The dark background behind the woman alludes to space and time gone by. By imposing the figure on this background, I wanted to pull her out of the past literally and figuratively.

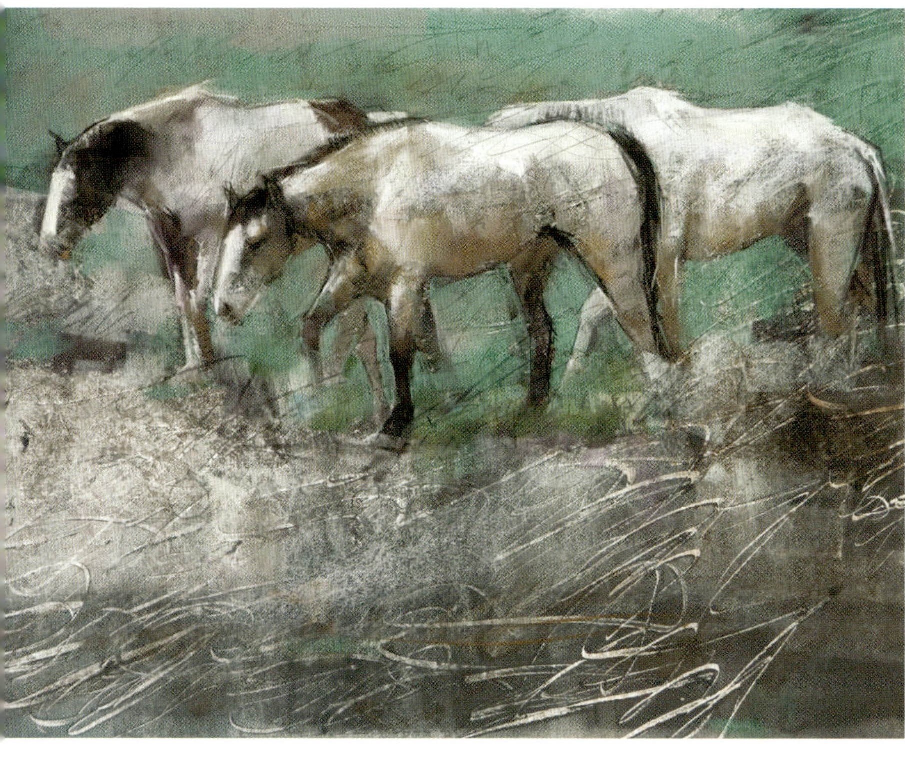

LIVING GREEN / 17" × 23" (43CM × 58CM) / MONOTYPE WITH SOFT PASTEL ON RIVES BFK PAPER

The idea of adding the three horses came about after looking at the abstract ground and seeing that the texture in (what is now) the foreground felt like a grassy pasture. Pastel was used extensively to change the color of the ink and to develop the equine imagery, but the underlying textures of the monotype read clearly and are integrated into the image to make it look as though the horses were always there.

HOWLING AT THE MOON / 18" × 18" (46CM × 46CM)/ MONOTYPE WITH SOFT PASTEL ON RIVES BFK PAPER

This image was a joy to draw. Once I saw the background as a landscape, what a fun challenge it was to integrate the buffalo into it! It is helpful to remember that our eyes will fill in so much information simply with a suggestion of land or rock. A texture can evoke the memory of a place, and a hint of light or shadow can create the feeling of place, time and space.

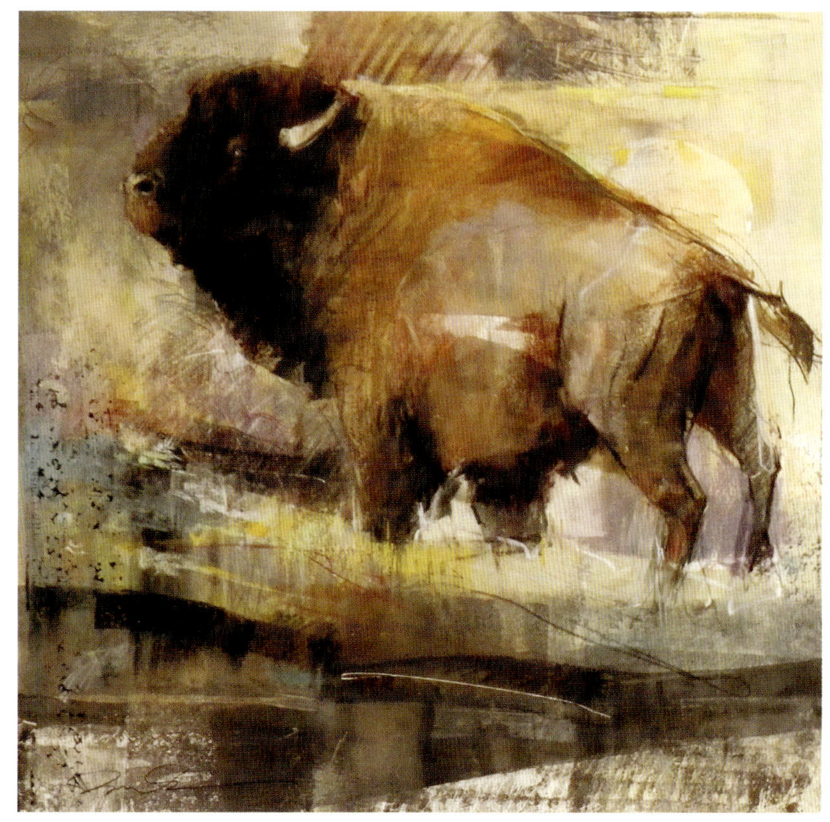

COLOR INSPIRATION

The colors we choose to dress ourselves in, surround ourselves with, or pick from the pastel box often become routine. How can we take our color imagery to the unexpected places shown in these images? When we explore different environments and cultures, we can get out of our established color habits. Visiting Hawaii for the first time, my eyes were transfixed by the unfamiliar variety of colors I encountered. When I returned to the desert, I was excited to use the colors in my pastel box

I'd never tried before. Monotypes are a great tool to explore color. It is straightforward to change colors in the monotype to produce multiple versions of the same design. You can enjoy taking color risks with monotype because the process is fun and doesn't demand a lot of time. When printed, the layers of ink on a monotype are "flattened" together, which often produces unexpected and unusual color results.

THE PASTEL MAGIC ERASER

A trick I have found most helpful when using pastel with a solid color ground is to identify a pastel that is close to the same color as the ink color. This color becomes a "magic eraser" that restores the background color whenever you want it to bring it back.

EXPAND YOUR COLOR HORIZONS

Like learning to play a different musical scale, using unfamiliar colors helps to expand our visual language of art.

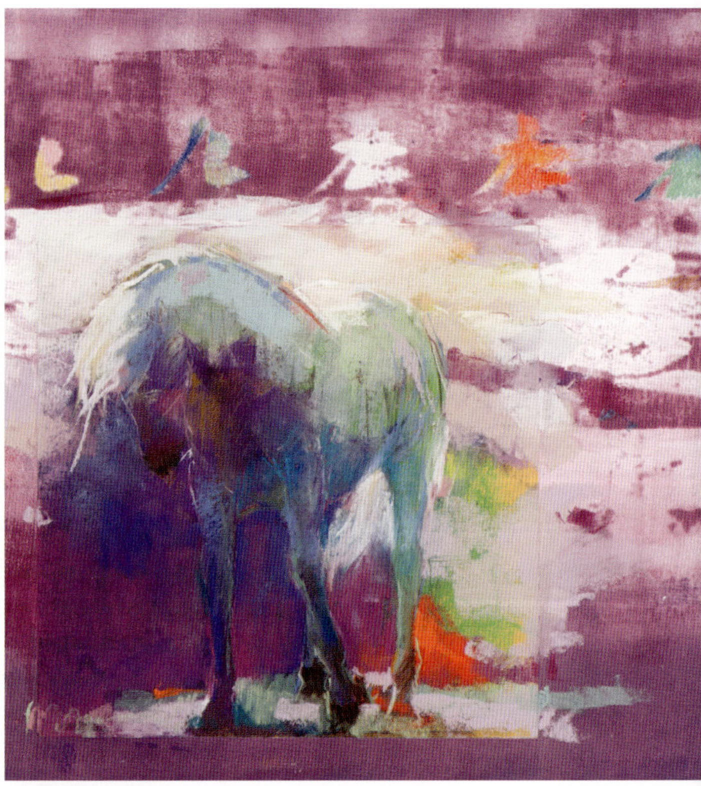

ALOHA HORSE / 18" × 18" (46CM × 46CM) / MONOTYPE WITH SOFT PASTEL ON STONEHENGE PAPER.

Aloha Horse was my artistic response to having visited Hawaii for the first time. The colors of Hawaii inspired me so much that I set out to create abstract monotype grounds that featured the new colors I'd experienced.

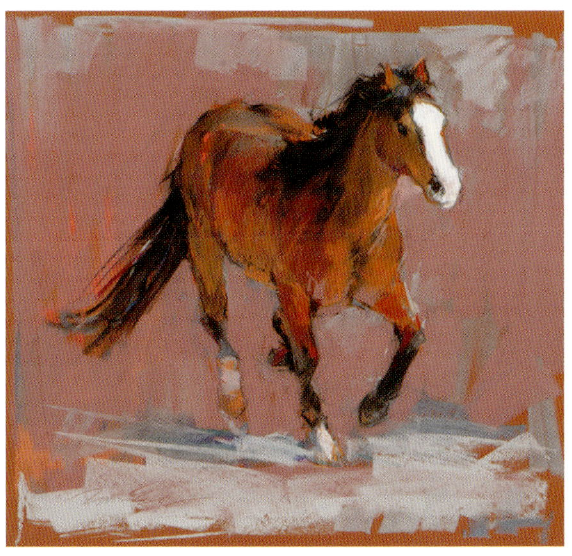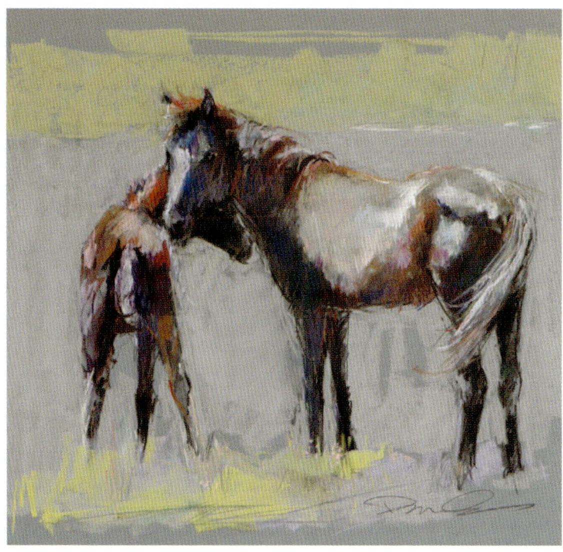

ABLAZE / 17" × 18" (43CM × 48CM) / PASTEL ON MONO-TYPE GROUND PRINTED ONTO TAN STONEHENGE PAPER

The color of the ink printed on tan Stonehenge is visible mainly near the top and bottom edges of the painting, and in some places on the horse. I find the Akua ink to be a lovely, smooth ground that accepts soft pastel readily.

A NEW DAY / 15" × 17" (38CM × 43CM) / PASTEL ON MONO-TYPE GROUND PRINTED ONTO TAN STONEHENGE PAPER

It was a surprise to see how the color of blue-gray ink appeared to look metallic against the tan color of the paper. I used silver pastel in the painting to illuminate this, and the result is an image that seems to capture the intense bright light of a midsummer's day.

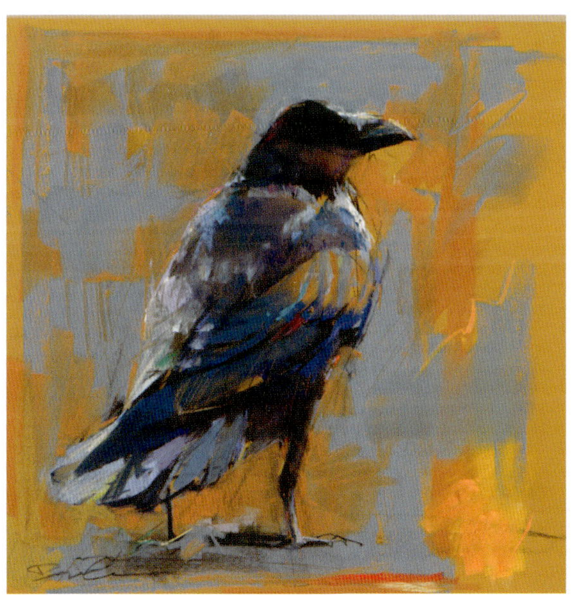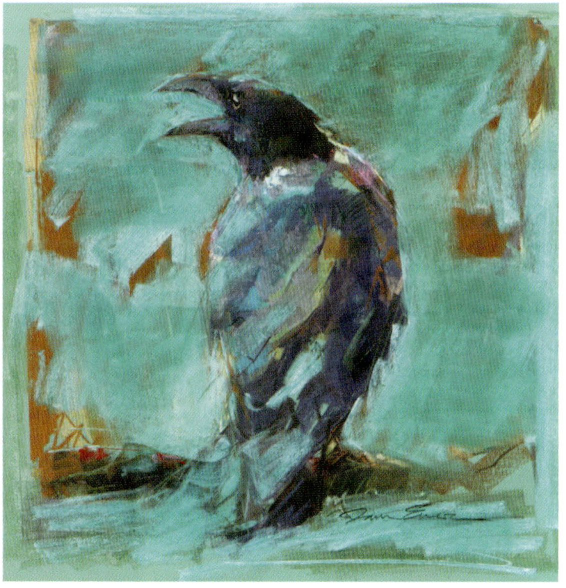

RAVEN GOLD / 17" × 18" (43CM × 46CM) / PASTEL ON MONOTYPE GROUND PRINTED ONTO TAN STONEHENGE PAPER

The ink looked like amber and gold when it was printed onto the tan Stonehenge surface. I used blues and purples in the bird and wove the golden colors into the feathers. The broken gray shapes lend interest to the surface and create a rough texture to contrast with the sleekness of the bird.

EMERALD LIGHT / 18" × 18" (46CM × 46CM)/ PASTEL ON MONOTYPE GROUND PRINTED ONTO TAN STONEHENGE PAPER

I wanted to make the bird look as though it was almost dissolving into its world or materializing out of emerald light. It was helpful to have the exact pastel color to match the background ink color. That color became a "magic eraser" that helped integrate the figure and ground together.

COLLAGED MONOTYPE

Each example below uses an approach to making monotypes that involves creating a plate from various assembled pieces. Thin pieces are individually inked, then cut up and assembled on a stiff support to form a single plate. The stickiness of the ink itself holds the pieces together. The support makes it easier to transport the entire collaged plate to the press or a handprinting table. The paper should be placed on top of the collaged plate to prevent separation or movement of the pieces. If the individual pieces of the collaged plate are thin enough,

the overlapping edges will barely show up when the piece is printed. When using thicker collage materials you will find that the overlapping edges will result in white outlines when printed. Those lines can be fixed later with colored pencil or pastel if you find them undesirable. Piecing together plates can lead to a weaving of imagery that would otherwise be difficult to accomplish on a single plate. Colors and patterns can be separated or literally woven together without muddying the colors.

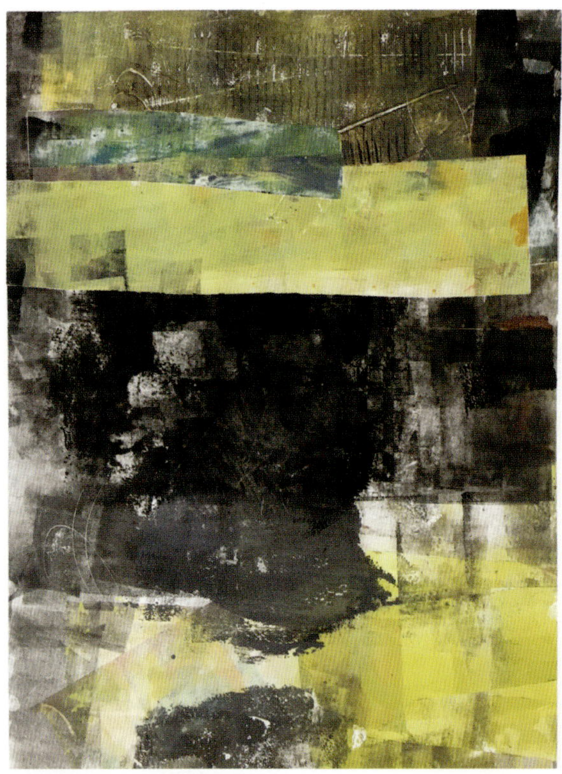

ABSTRACT MONOTYPE FOR *FALL HORSES*
The plate for this image was created by assembling different inked pieces of plastic together to form one plate. What you see here is the base print for the final monotype to the right.

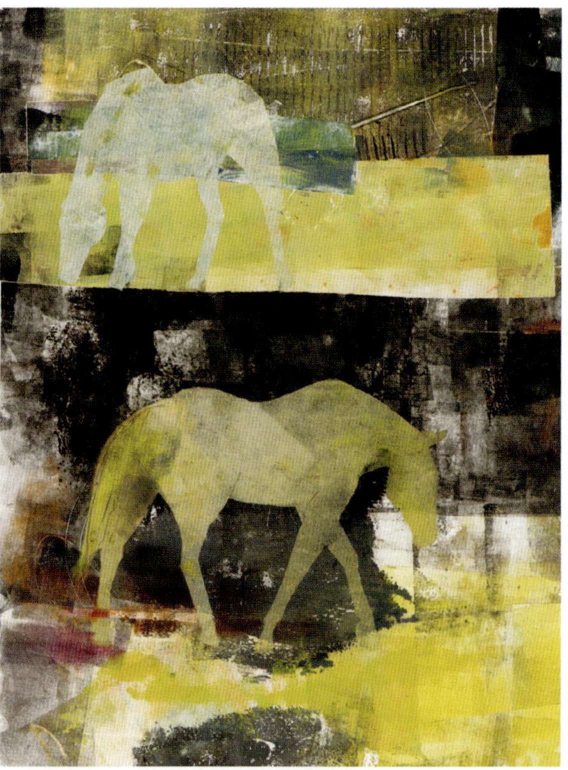

FALL HORSES / 25" × 18" (64CM × 46CM) / MONOTYPE ON STONEHENGE PAPER WITH SOFT PASTEL ADDED

The horses were stencils made with the same plastic material, inked and printed with a pin press onto the print to the left. The horses are moveable and can be used over and over, in either orientation. Some soft pastel was added to the print for color.

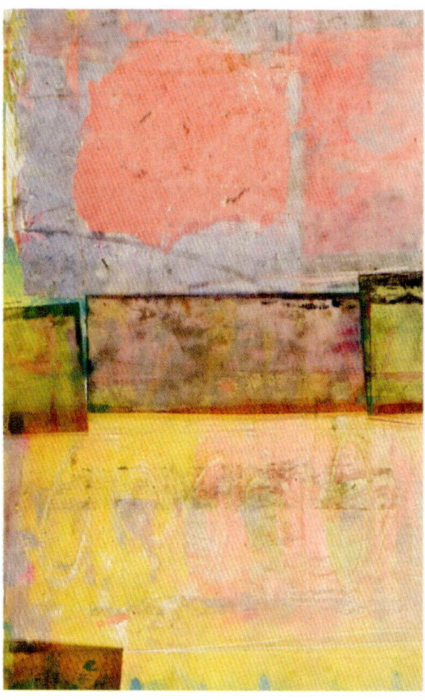

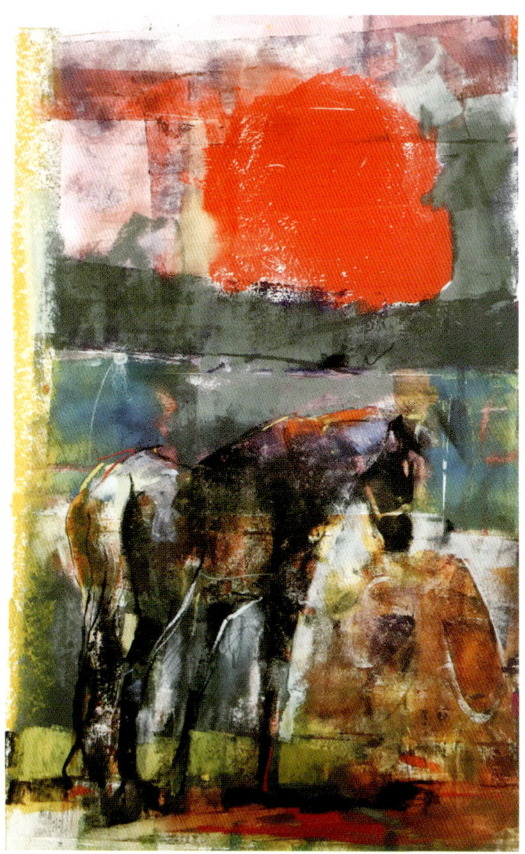

HORSE UNDER RED SUN / 25" × 18" (64CM × 46CM) / MIXED MEDIA MONOTYPE ON STONEHENGE PAPER

This image was produced in three stages. First, the underpainting monotype was printed. Then a trace monotype of the horse was added directly onto the print. Finally, pastel was added to enhance edges and to color the horse.

COLLAGED PLASTIC PLATE

This is the pieced-together plate that was used to create the underpainting for *Horse Under Red Sun*. Most of the ink has been removed from the plate during the printing process, but this clearly shows the edges of the pieces and how they were put together.

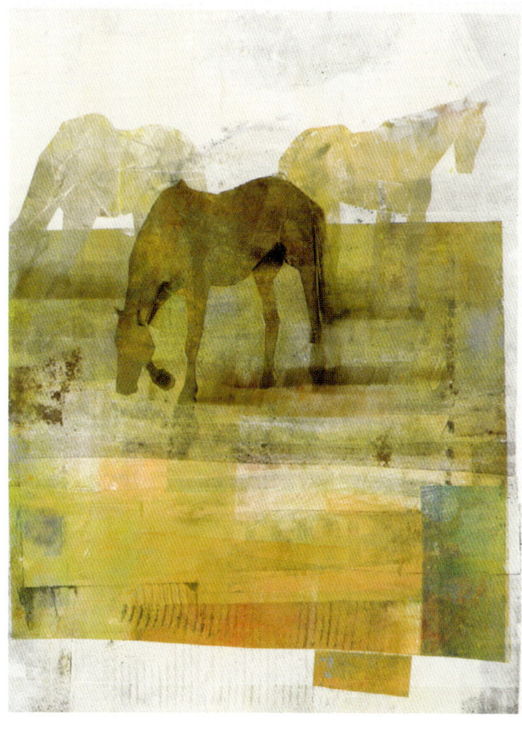

SUMMER GRAZING / 25" × 18" (64CM × 46CM) / MONOTYPE ON STONEHENGE PAPER

The horses were cut out of plastic, inked and printed with a pin press onto the initial monotype. I save the stencils I create to use them again in other work.

MONOTYPE UNDERPAINTING

This image was printed off a collaged plate and is the underpainting for *Summer Grazing*.

DISCOVER NEW IMAGERY

Earlier in the book I discussed creating a monotype ground that implied—rather than described—a specific place, mood or space. In this series, I created a monotype plate simply by inking areas onto a white cardboard plate with a brayer. Notice how the space is divided into small, medium and larger shapes, and how the edges of the plate are considered in the composition. I made three prints from the same paper plate and colored each print differently with mixed media.

In the two landscapes, I added pastel color to give a different mood to each. In the image of the boat, I rotated the print 180 degrees and recombined shapes with color to create a totally different image. The trick is to start with a simple composition that has clear shapes and good divisions of space. This can be thought of as your "design structure," and the more you explore this concept, the easier it is for your imagination to go to work and discover new imagery.

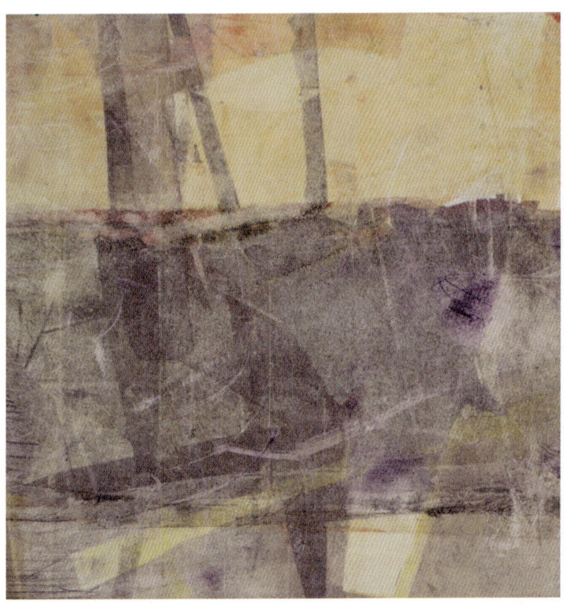

IMAGE REMAINS ON THE PAPER PLATE
A heavy cardstock was used as the plate to make the three images you see on these two pages. There is very little ink remaining on the paper, but you can see the brayered shapes and division of space. I printed the image three times off the same plate and then drew into the prints three different ways.

LEARN TO SEE ABSTRACTLY

new imagery can be discovered by breaking larger shapes into smaller ones or by recombining shapes within an image.

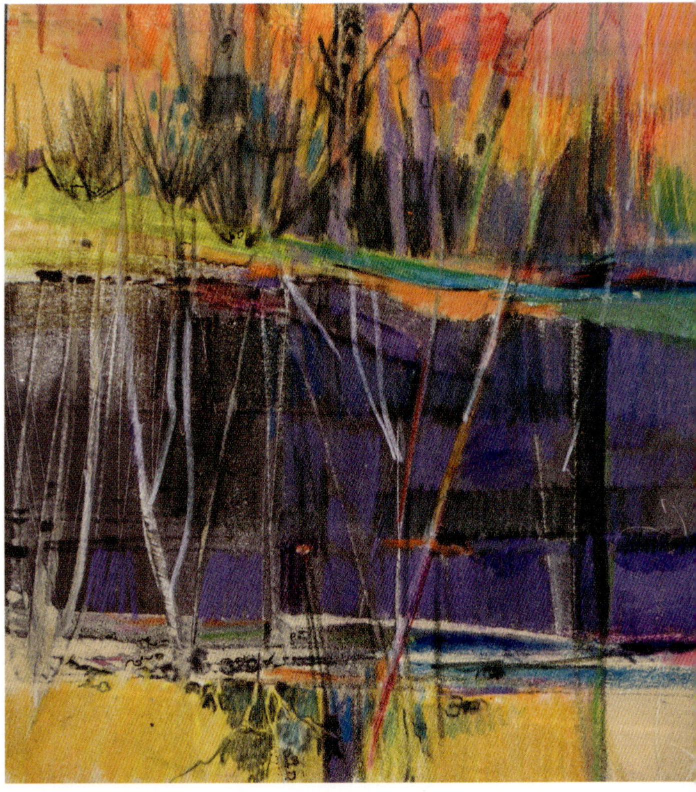

RIVERBANK ONE / 8" × 8" (20CM × 20CM) / MONOTYPE UNDERPAINTING WITH COLOR PENCIL AND PASTEL ADDED ON RIVES BFK PAPER

By using different colors, and by breaking the large shapes into smaller pieces, I was able to create two entirely different feeling landscapes from the same base print.

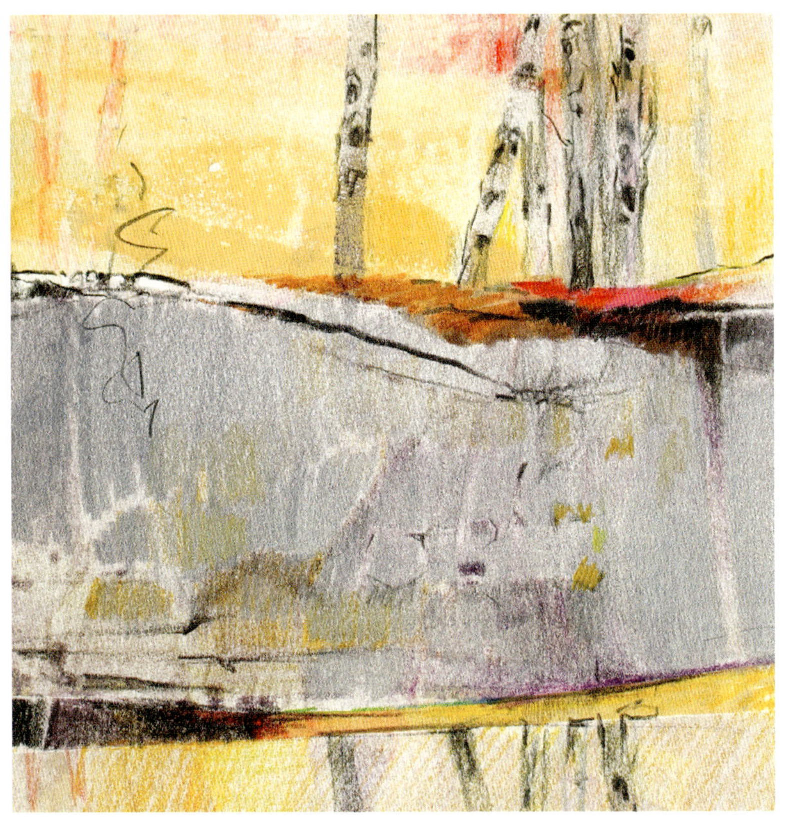

RIVERBANK TWO / 8" × 8" (20CM × 20CM) / MONOTYPE UNDERPAINTING WITH COLOR PENCIL AND PASTEL ADDED ON RIVES BFK PAPER

This image has a wintery feel because of the colors I used and the focus on tree shapes rather than vegetation.

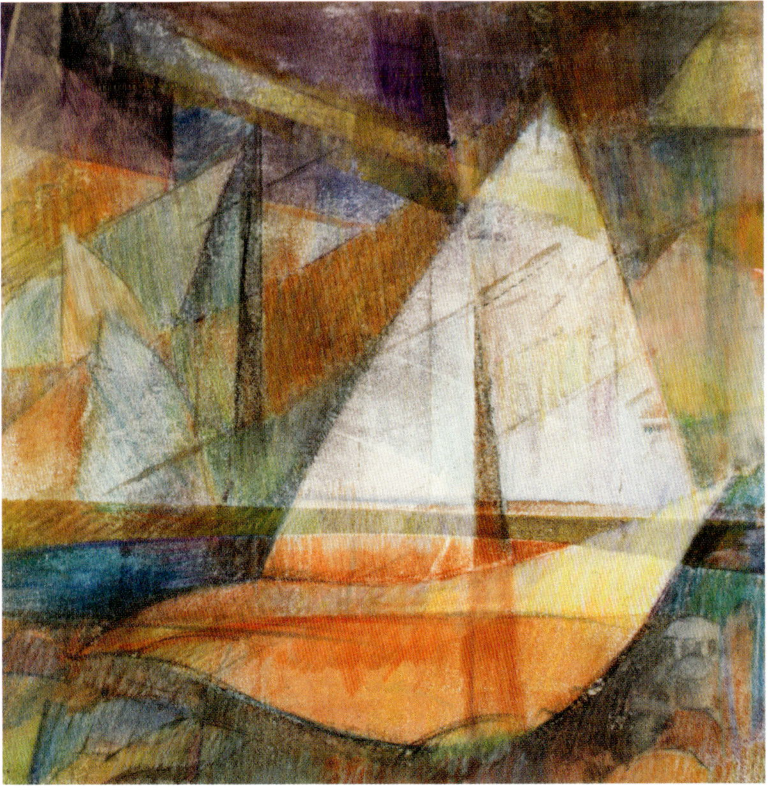

SAILBOAT / 8" × 8" / MONOTYPE UNDERPAINTING WITH COLOR PENCIL AND PASTEL ADDED ON RIVES BFK PAPER

When I rotated the image 180 degrees, it evoked a completely different feeling of space and subject. Sometimes simply rotating a ground can set the imagination off to discover new possibilities within an image.

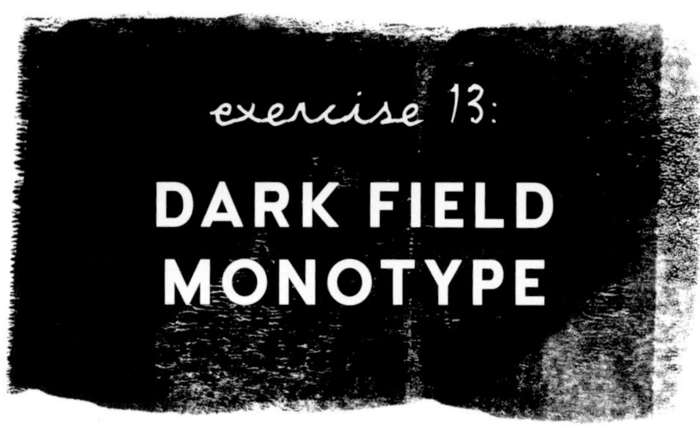

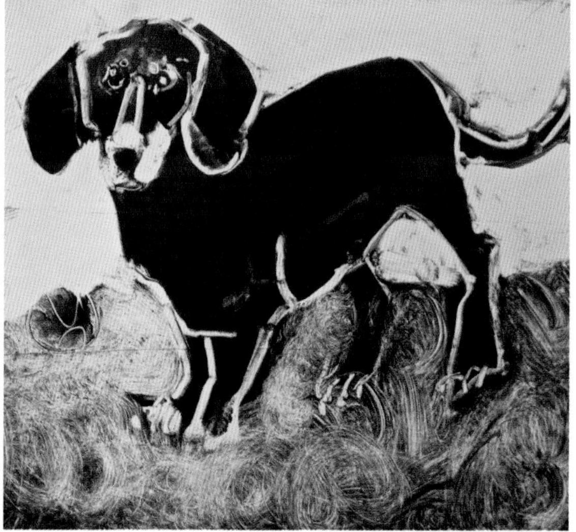

HANNIBAL / 8" × 10" (20CM × 25CM) / DARK FIELD
MONOTYPE ON STONEHENGE PAPER.

MATERIALS

- Akua black Intaglio ink and glass surface to roll out
  the ink

- brayer

- palette knife

- assorted tools for removing ink, such as cotton
  swabs, baby wipes, credit card, etc.

- plastic plate approximately 9" × 12" (23CM × 30CM)
  (a piece of 1/16" [1MM] Plexiglas works well)

- Stonehenge paper or smooth drawing paper for
  printing image onto, cut 11" × 15" (28CM × 38CM)

- liquid dish soap for clean up

- reference photo of your choice

- masking tape

- spoon

DIRECTIONS

STEP 1

Put a 1" (25MM) border of masking tape on your plate
to keep the edges clean and straight.

STEP 2

Brayer on an even deposit of black ink onto your plate
surface to cover it entirely. Hold the plate up to a light
to check ink coverage. The ink should appear solid but
not so thick that it is messy.

STEP 3

Make your image by drawing on the plate, then
remove ink with cotton swabs, baby wipes and other
tools. (Baby wipes dissolve the ink.) Working on a
lightbox or near a window enables you to see better.
Check your work by holding it up to the light.

STEP 4

When you are satisfied with the image, remove the
tape from the plate, and clean off any areas that need
it. Secure your plate with masking tape so the surface
is flat and smooth. The ink side should face up.

STEP 5

Carefully position your drawing paper on top of your
plate, laying it down gently. Hinge the paper at the top.

STEP 6

Rub the back of the paper with the back of a spoon to
transfer the image onto the paper (if you don't have
access to a press). Use small, circular movements with
solid pressure to rub each area, working top to bottom, left
to right. Lift the paper occasionally to check your work.

CRITIQUE

- How did it feel to draw in this reverse manner?

- How much variety do you have in your lines and in
  the size of your shapes?

- Did you leave more dark than light or vice versa?

- Could you see ways to improve the composition by
  eliminating or adding ink in certain areas?

TAKEAWAY

The dark field monotype is an excellent way to
explore value, line and texture.

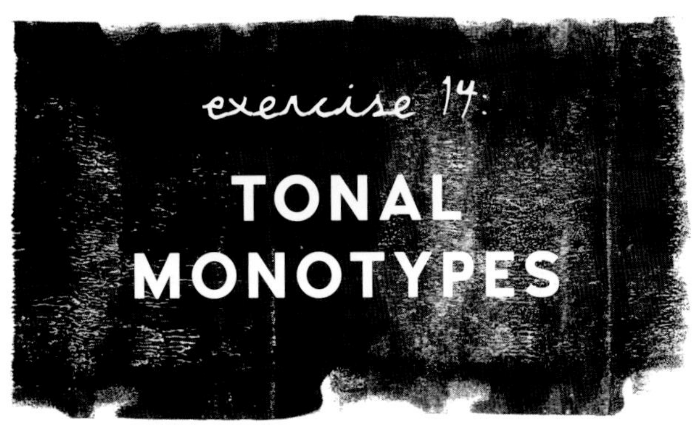

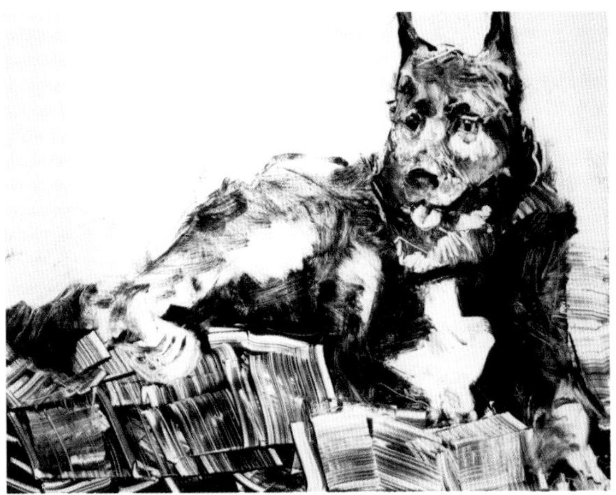

TIMBER / 8" × 10" (20CM × 25CM) / DARK FIELD MONOTYPE WITH AKUA BLENDING MEDIUM ADDED TO INK ON STONEHENGE PAPER

MATERIALS

- same materials as in exercise 13
- Akua blending medium
- assorted brushes
- small bowl
- pencil

DIRECTIONS

STEP 1

Tape the plate around the edges and ink the entire surface of your plate.

STEP 2

Draw your image with pencil on the plate. Remove areas of ink by wiping away with a baby wipe.

STEP 3

Place a few drops of the Akua blending medium into a small bowl. The blending medium makes the Intaglio ink thinner and more transparent. Mix a small amount of ink with the blending medium on your brush to get lighter values. (Avoid puddling the ink when using the blending medium. Puddles will spread when you print the image.)

STEP 4

When finished with your drawing/painting, remove the tape, clean the edges, and print.

CRITIQUE

- Compare this image to the monotype in the previous exercise. How do the midtones you added with the blending medium add to the overall quality of the image?

- Can you see ways to improve your composition by increasing or decreasing the amount of dark or light areas?

- Notice the variety of edges, textures, line quality and values you are able to achieve!

TAKEAWAY

Like the charcoal underpainting, the tonal monotype is both a subtractive and additive approach, in which you develop big shapes of dark and light, then add pastel and ink to create midtones.

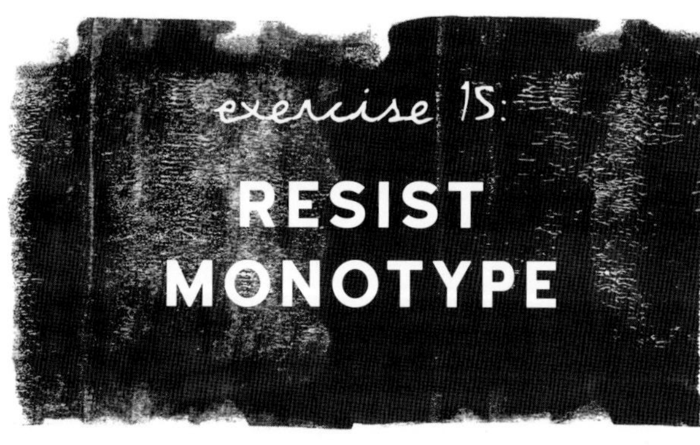

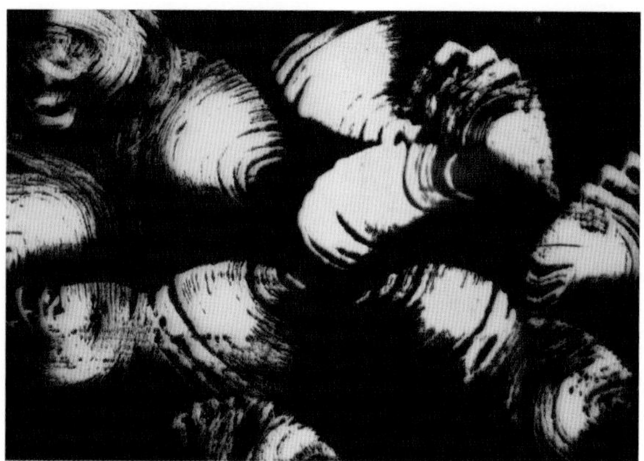

SHELLS / 4" × 6" (10CM × 15CM) / MONOTYPE ON PAPER

I used a fan brush dipped in blending medium to "paint" the marks you see here. I then rolled over the entire plate with a brayer charged with Akua ink. The blending medium resists the Intaglio ink, revealing the brushstrokes.

DIRECTIONS

STEP 1

Start with a clean, dry plastic plate and tape the plate to be slightly less wide than the brayer you have. Dip the fan brush into the blending medium and make marks on the plate to create a pattern.

STEP 2

Charge your brayer with Intaglio ink and roll over the plate. Notice how the Intaglio ink resists the blending medium.

STEP 3

Consider adding other marks to the plate to add variation. Then print your plate.

CRITIQUE

- Can you imagine ways to incorporate this resist approach in your image making?
- Consider other experiments to do using colored inks, masking techniques and stencils.

TAKEAWAY

Once you begin exploring monotypes, the possibilities are limitless.

MATERIALS

- black Akua Intaglio ink
- Akua blending medium
- wide brayer, 5"–6" (13CM–15CM)
- 9" × 12" (23CM × 30CM) plastic plate
- fan brush
- Stonehenge paper
- masking tape

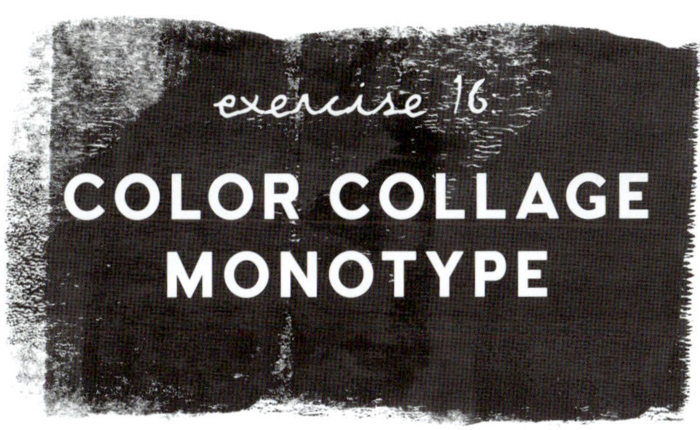

- leaves
- brayer and glass surface to roll out ink
- rubbing tool for printing image or press
- printmaking paper
- baby wipes or liquid dish soap for cleanup
- masking tape

DIRECTIONS

STEP 1
Put 2 strips of ink onto your glass plate—one straight from the jar and one mixed with some white to lighten it. Mix well with a palette knife on the glass.

STEP 2
Tape the edges of the plate, then roll one of the colored inks over the entire plate to create a solid color.

STEP 3
Ink up the leaves with the brayer using the lighter color ink, and place ink-side up onto the plate.

STEP 4
Remove the tape from the edges of the plate and print.

CRITIQUE

- How did the colored ink differ from the black ink?
- Was the overlay of leaves effective in creating a sense of space or depth in your printed image?
- How would you add pastel to this?

TAKEAWAY

These prints can be used as is for cards or as grounds for other imagery or poetry.

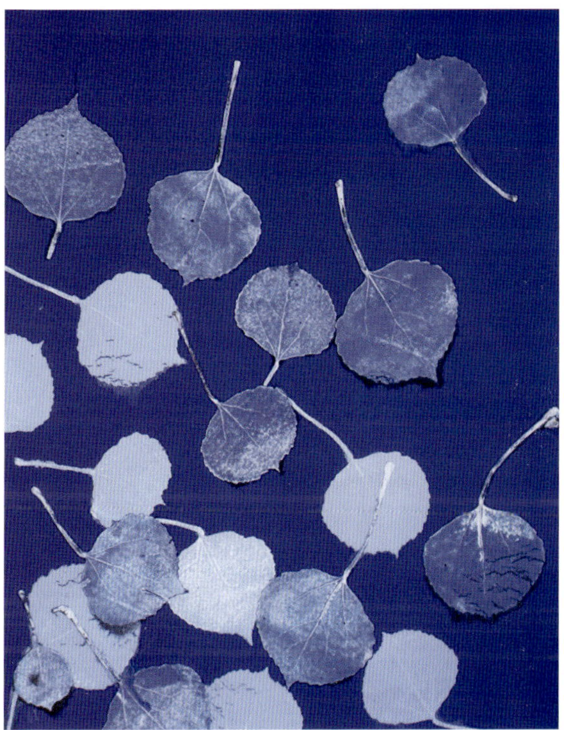

BLUE LEAVES / 10" × 8" (25CM × 20CM) / MONOTYPE ON DRAWING PAPER

MATERIALS

- palette knife
- 9" × 12" (23CM × 30CM) plastic plate
- 1 color of Akua Intaglio ink plus Titanium White Akua ink

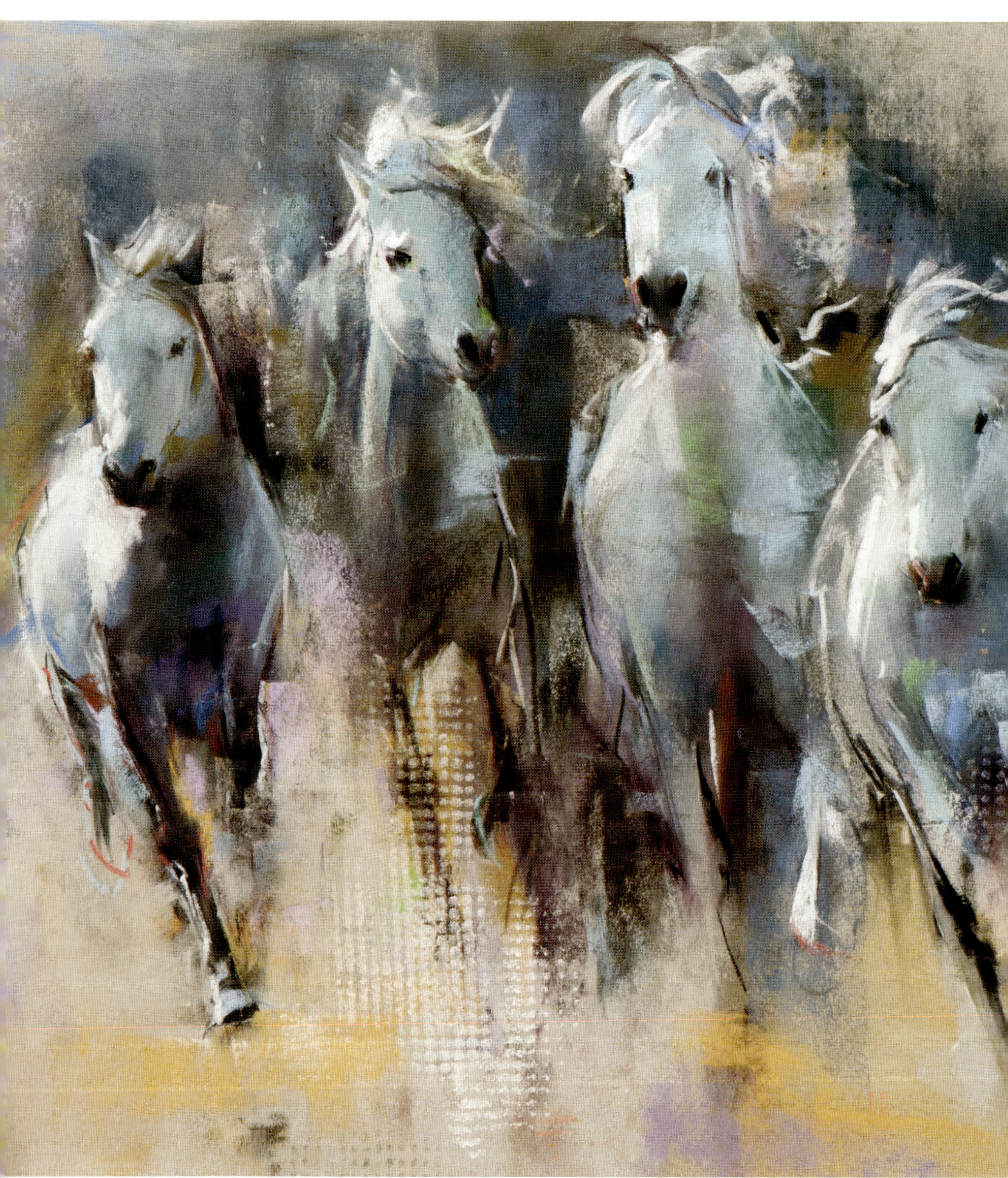

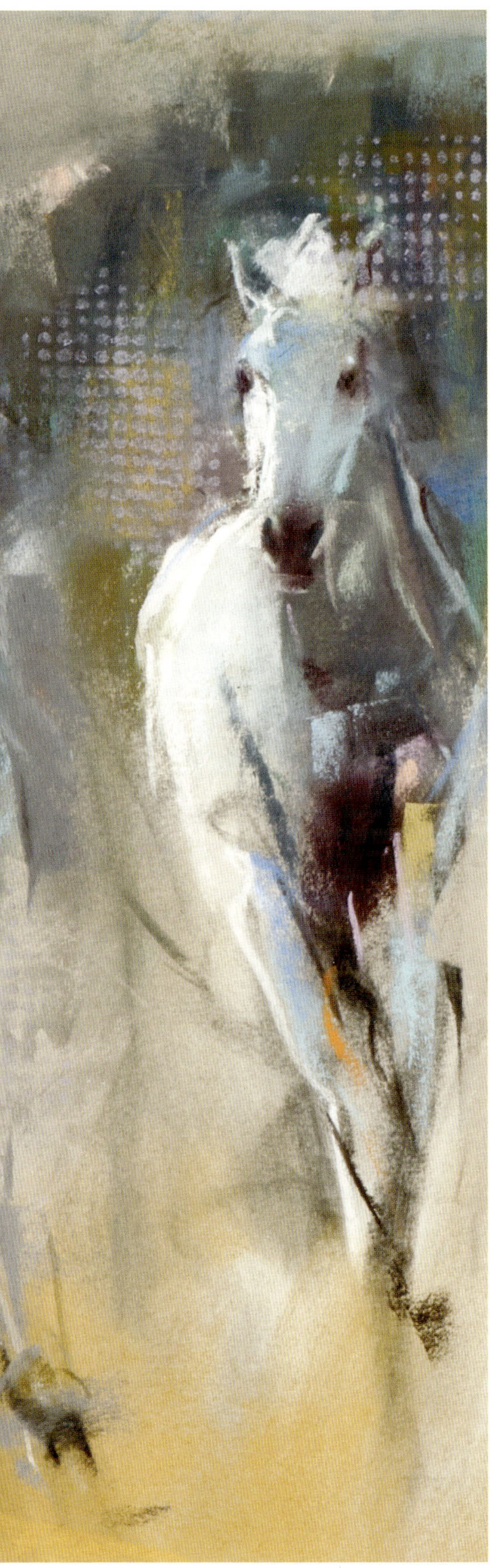

BRINGING PASTEL TO THE STAGE

In the previous chapters you were introduced to many techniques for creating dynamic marks, and you were introduced to new ways to think about the role of underpaintings, and you explored how to "set the stage" to let your imagination respond to the ground.

Chapter 5 presents and explores many ways of working with pastel on various grounds with other media. You'll see how the same pastel stick can be can used to obscure and erase, take on chameleon like roles, and even combine with oil and acrylic media to form matte or glossy paints. You'll also learn how to transfer pastel and charcoal drawings onto archival surfaces with the use of a press.

At the printmaking studio at which I studied, I was one of very few pastelists. When it came to drawing into a print, I would reach first for my pastels. I discovered that I could completely alter the mood and story of the image by building on the print as simply another kind of underpainting.

OPAL HERD / 22" × 30" (56CM × 76CM) / PASTEL ON RIVES BFK PAPER

This painting exemplifies the powerful expressiveness of the pastel medium.

POWERFUL OPACITY

Those of us who love pastels will agree that you can't have enough of them. No brand is perfect for everyone, and which brand of pastels best suits an artist often depends on the kind of art they make, the surface they prefer using and how they work. These are the ways I test a pastel that is new to me:

- I draw on my dry skin to see how creamy or soft it is.
- I dissolve its marks with a wet brush to see how moveable it is over different surfaces.

- I put it over sumi ink to see how opaque it is.
- I explore how it works for frottage with thin paper, and I try to use it in a pastel transfer.
- I see how it erases, how it smears with a "smoosher," and how a razor blade removes it.
- I see how it goes over and under other pastels and media.

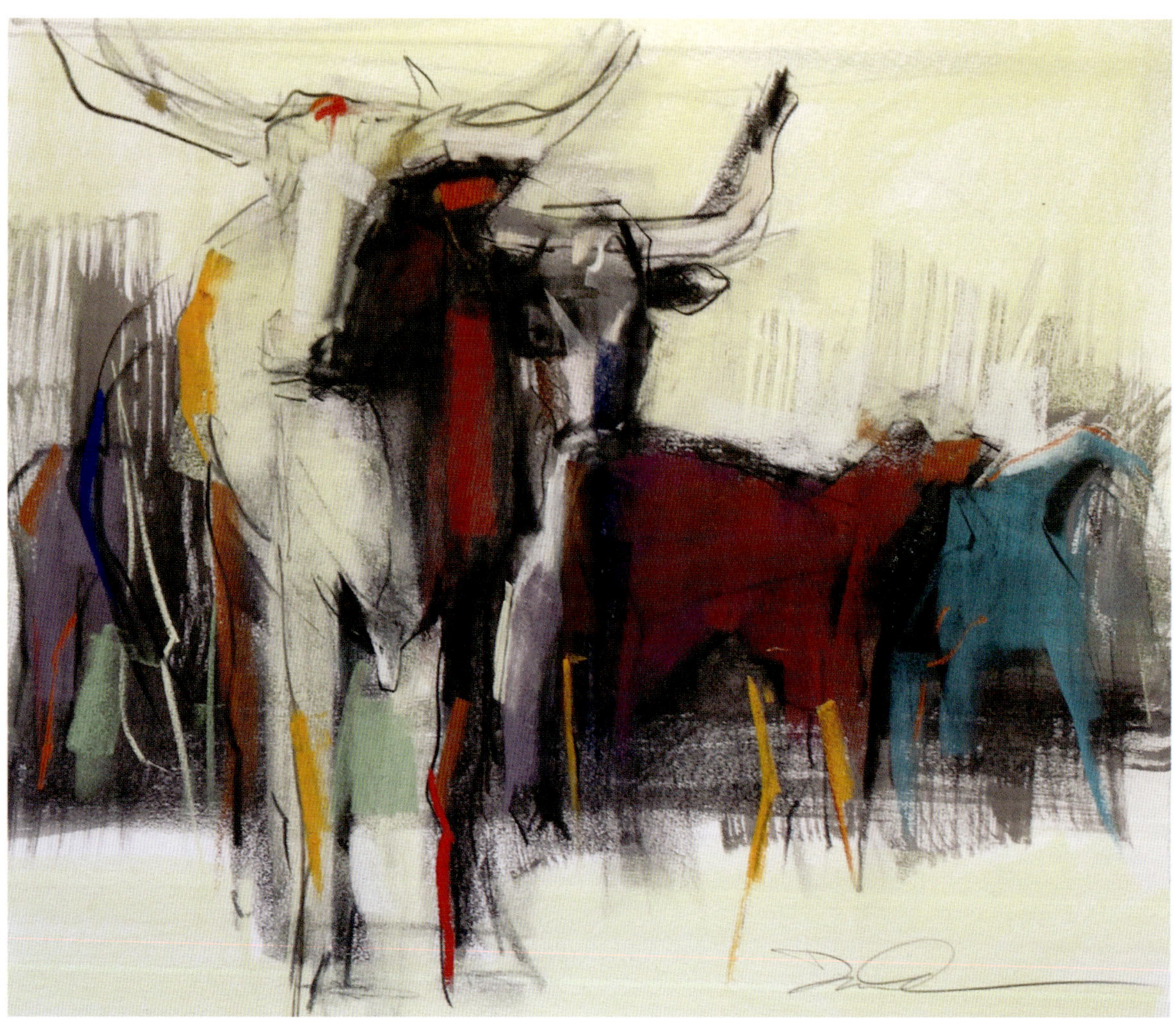

MOTHERHOOD / 18" × 20" (46CM × 51CM) / PASTEL AND SUMI INK ON RIVES BFK PAPER

In this painting I used pastel as solid, opaque color. The front cow is the "star," with the other figures acting as supporting actors. The shapes of the animals hold together and blend together as one solid unit.

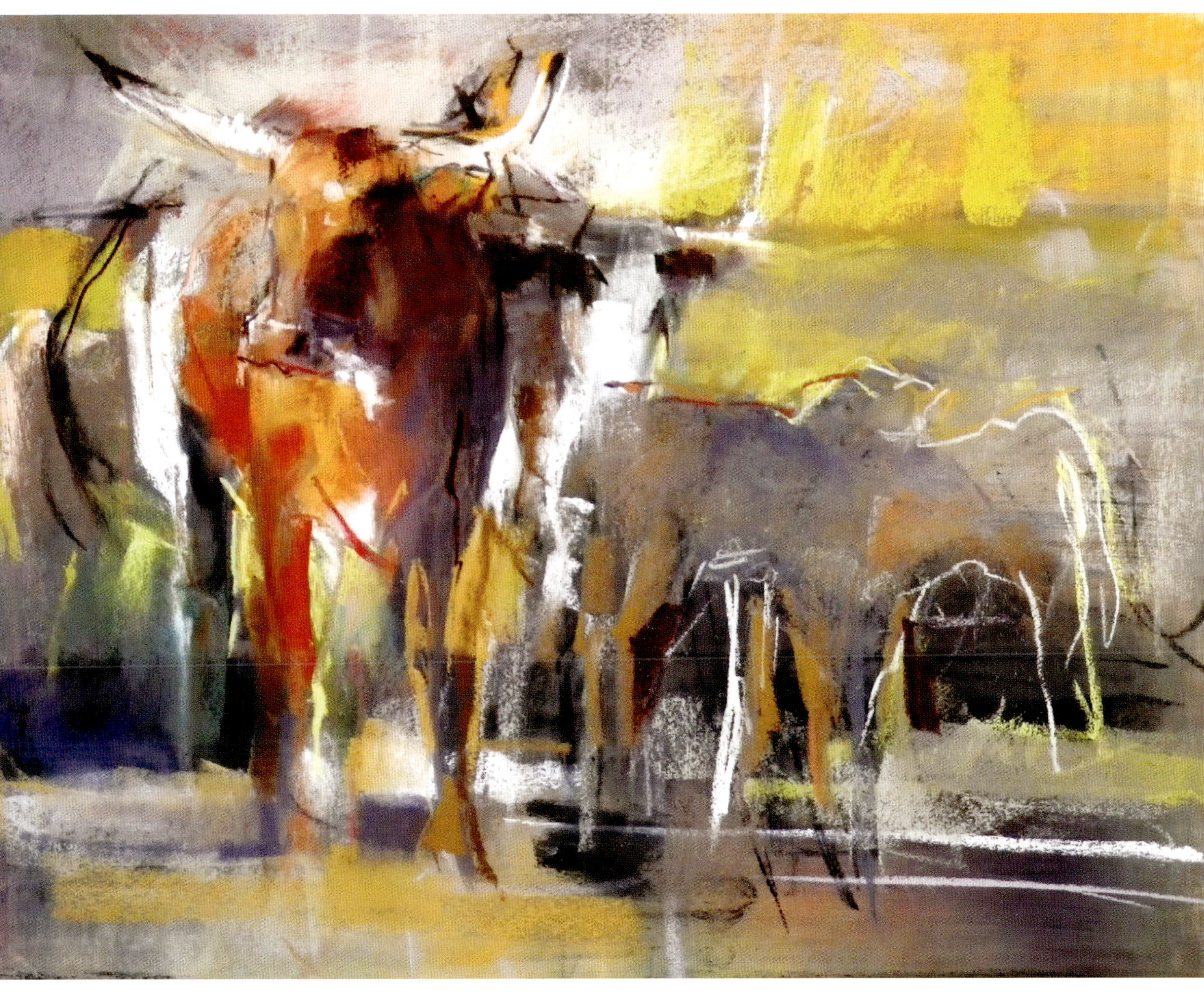

HOW NOW? / 18" × 22" (46CM × 56CM) / PASTEL AND SUMI INK ON RIVES BFK PAPER

The focus in this painting is also the front cow, but the way the animals are rendered is very different from *Motherhood*. Line, rather than shape, is used to describe the baby cows. They seem to float and be forming rather than solid and opaque as in the previous image.

EXPRESSIVE GESTURE

For many artists like myself, pastel and charcoal are interchangeable. They both combine tremendous expressive range with great immediacy. A stick of pastel can respond with the sensitivity of a Chinese brush or the crassness of a block of coal depending on the pressure, intention and twisting of your hand and wrist. The entire body of the pastel—tip, side and edges—can be used to create different marks. Pastel is the perfect medium to make bold and gestural marks, yet is still subtle enough to deposit whispers of color when used with the lightest pressure. Its opacity allows you to cover large areas with solid color in one big scrubbing motion, while its versatility lets you build transparent layers to create complex, faceted colors.

To explore the full range of expressive qualities of pastel, you need to remove all the wrappers and work on a really solid easel or wall. Some of the most beautiful marks I've ever seen were made by the late artist Rick Bartow. He taped his paper to a wall and stood at arm's length. With a pastel in his hand, he smashed his palm against the paper and tumbled the pastel the entire length as he drew his hand down the wall. That is an expressive gesture!

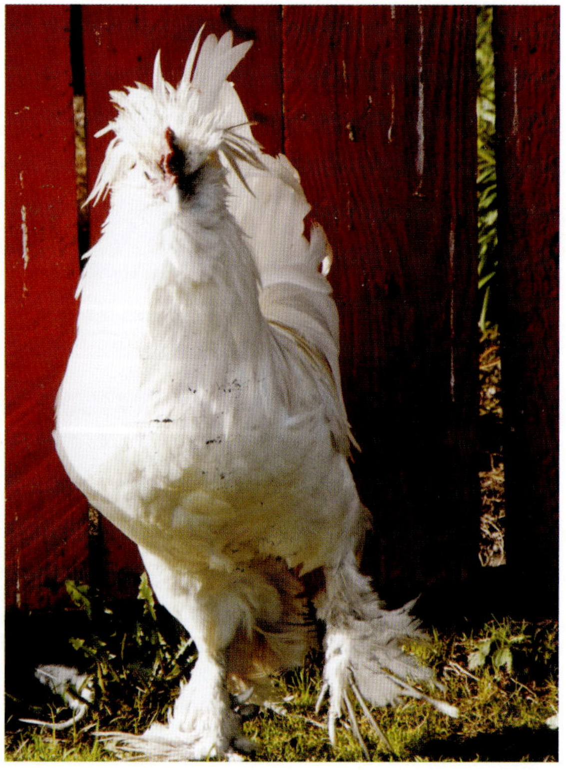

PHOTO REFERENCE
This rooster waltzed out from behind a building and begged me to photograph him as he posed. How could I refuse?

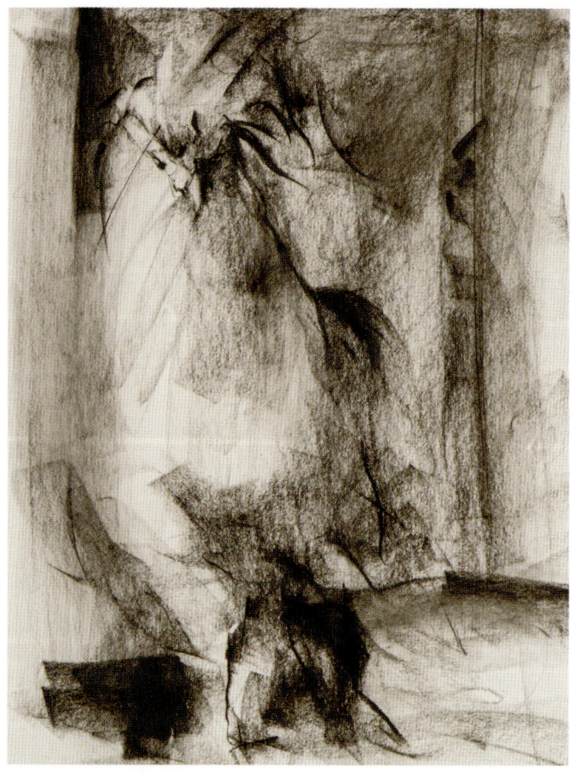

CHARCOAL SKETCH
I drew the rooster from the reference to familiarize myself with his proportions and the value distribution of the image.

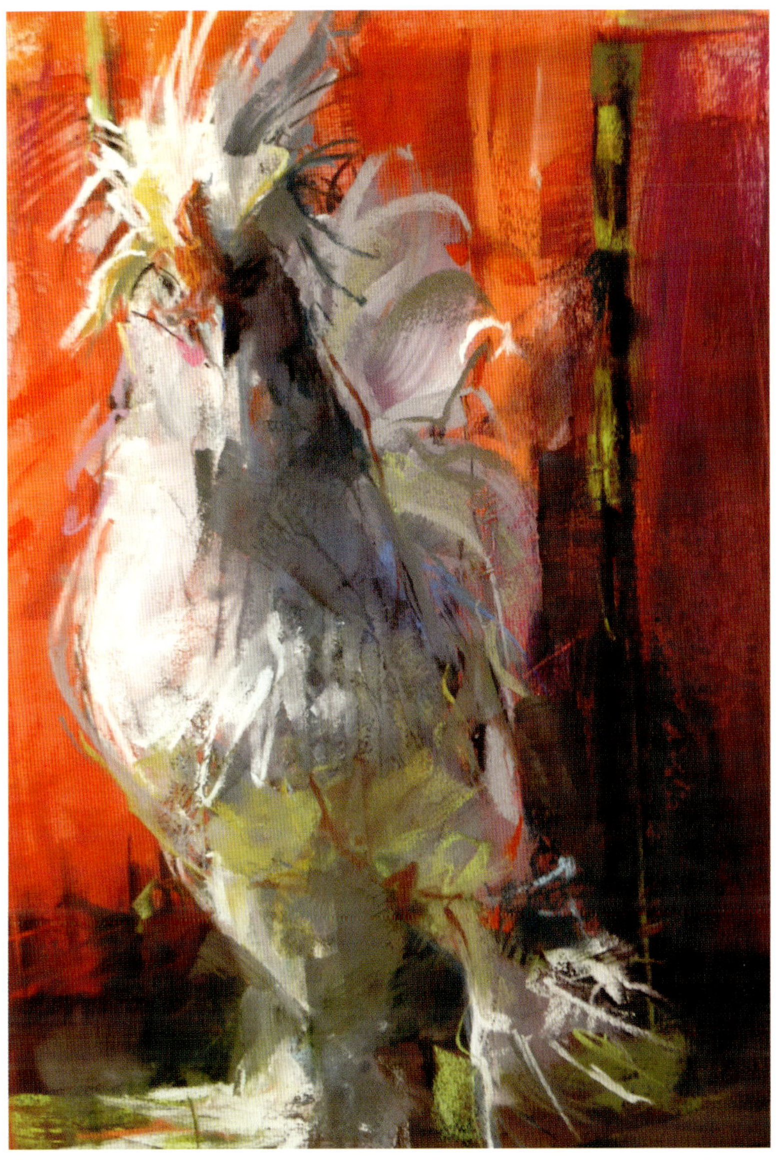

The ability of pastel to evoke temperament and character with the mere twist of a stroke is one of the most wonderful aspects of this medium. Those of us who love to draw gesturally will relate to the efficiency and immediacy of the pastel medium; it is as close to our fingertips as possible and responds to our energy instantaneously.

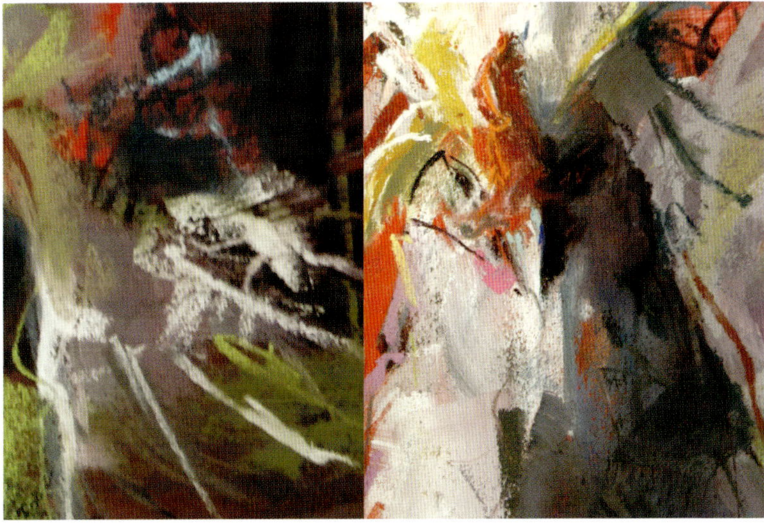

GESTURAL STROKES

These two images show the marks I made to create the shape of the gestural movement. Only a drawing tool like pastel or charcoal can express this kind of stroke.

PRINTING WITH PASTEL

There is a belief among fine artists that one should avoid painting or drawing on newsprint or nonarchival substrates. This belief is based on the fear (or hope) that you may create a masterpiece and not be able to sell it knowing that it will not last for 300 years. I want to let you know that if you do happen to create a masterpiece on a piece of newsprint, there is a safety net called counterprinting.

Take a quality photo of your masterpiece to have as documentation, and then find a press. The counterprint option is to use your original painting as your plate, much as you saw in chapter 4 with the paper plate monotype. The image will be flipped and a little bit lighter, but it will be beautiful! The result is often more luminous than the original, because it is only one pastel layer thick, which allows the paper to shine through. The other benefit of making a counterprint is that the original pastel will not shed any dust because it is so compressed. Remarkably, the original image will not lose intensity either!

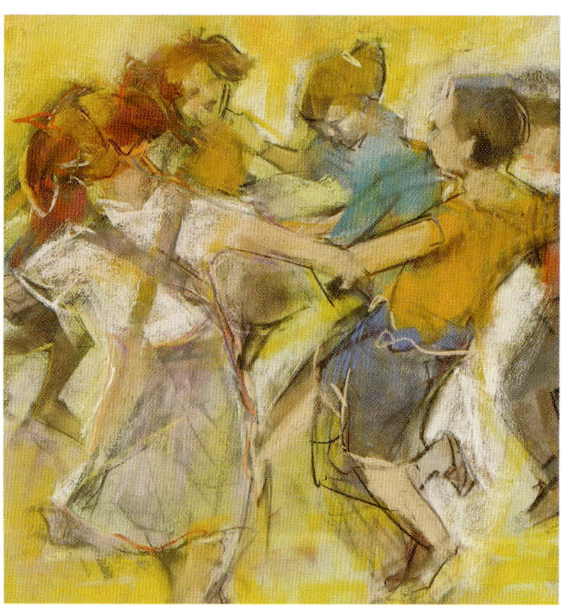

CIRCLE ROUND / 22" × 22" (56CM × 56CM) / PASTEL ON STONEHENGE PAPER

This is the original painting created exclusively with pastel. I used the painting as a plate from which to print.

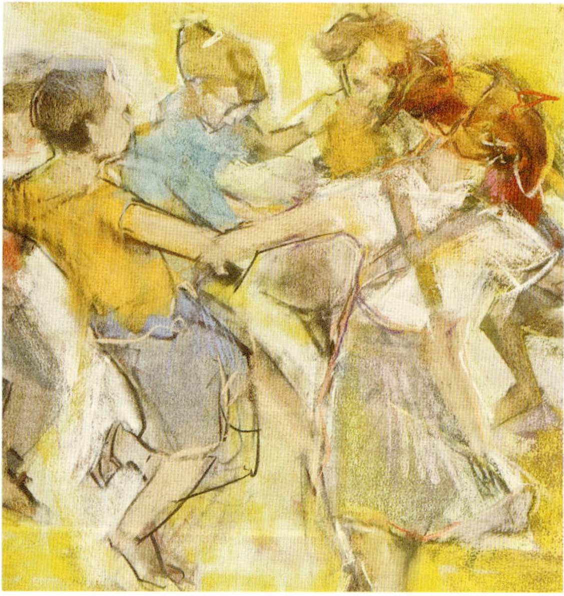

COUNTERPRINT OF *CIRCLE ROUND*

I took the original image of *Circle Round* and placed it pastel-side up on a press bed. I moistened another sheet of Stonehenge paper and carefully placed it on top of the original. When it goes through the press, the pastel "prints" onto the moistened paper. The image is flipped horizontally and is slightly lighter than the original but still luminous. The original image appears exactly the same as before it was printed. In fact, shedding of pastel dust will not be a problem because the image has been compressed under a ton of pressure.

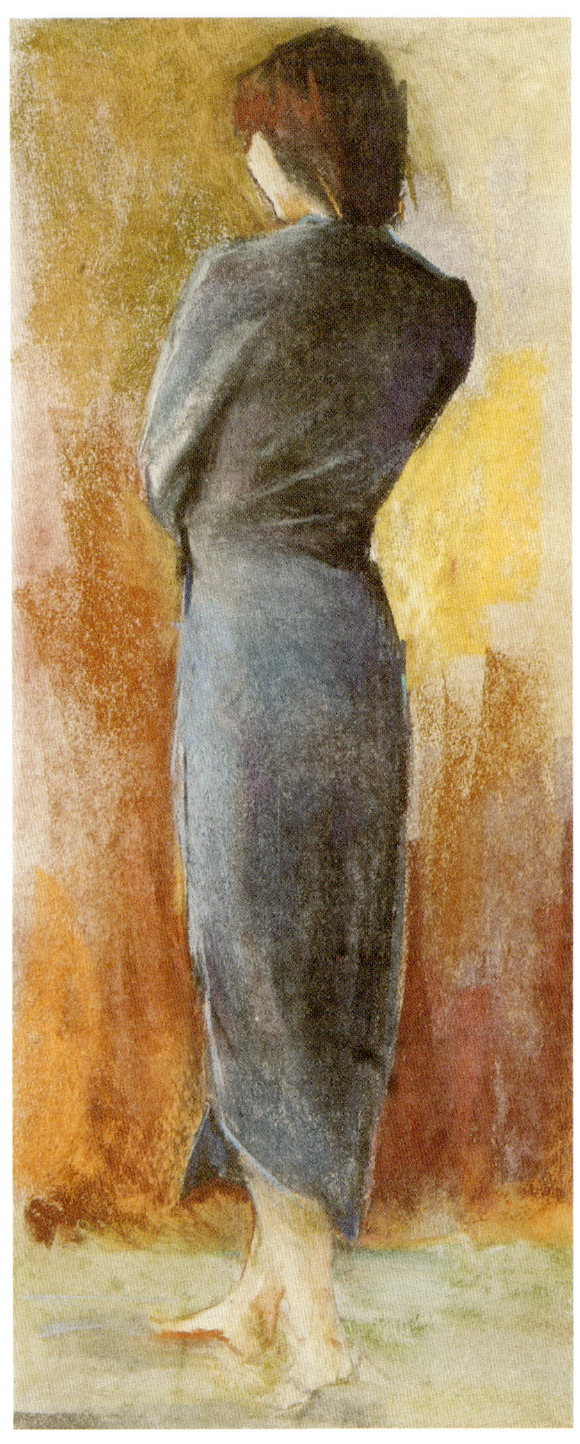 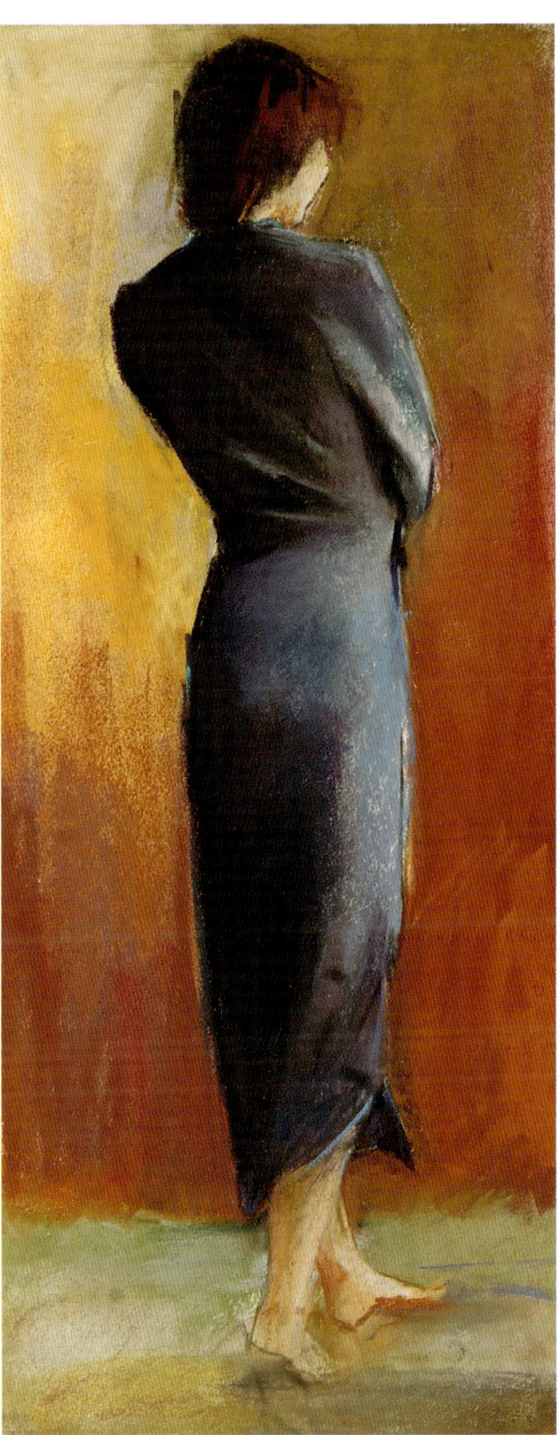

COUNTERPRINT OF *ROBE*

This is the counterprint of *Robe*. Notice that it is a mirror image of the original and a bit lighter, but luminous nonetheless. This process can be done with charcoal as well, and it is known to have been done by artists like Degas and Gauguin.

ROBE / 30" × 12" (76CM × 30CM) / PASTEL ON RIVES BFK PAPER

This is the original image I used as a plate to make a counterprint.

PASTEL AS PAINT

I think of pastel as simply pigment in a stick. Paints are essentially pigment in a carrier medium. Traditional printmaking involves using a slightly intimidating range of thick and thin inks, viscosity adjusting agents, transparent bases and other mysterious media. After playing with all these different printing media, it seemed only natural to just add linseed oil or acrylic medium to the pastel to make a brushable paint. As a matte medium, pastel blends effortlessly on images with paints and inks that have a similar finish. Pastel and paint can be seamlessly integrated so you can't tell where one medium begins and the other ends. When blended with glossy carriers, pastels can deliver new types of contrast in finish and texture according to the brushability and character of the carrier. Brushing water on pastel is a way of using this same idea to bring watercolor to the pastel stage.

CHIEF / 48" × 36" (122CM × 91CM) / PASTEL AND MIXED MEDIA ON BOARD WITH PUMICE GROUND

This painting was done primarily with pastel, using matte medium and clear gesso on a brush to move the pastel around like paint. The matte medium and the clear gesso both have a tooth that grabs pastel. Layers of pastel are added on top in places where I wanted to "draw" rather than paint. Because there was dry pastel on the surface, I framed this piece with glass and spacers.

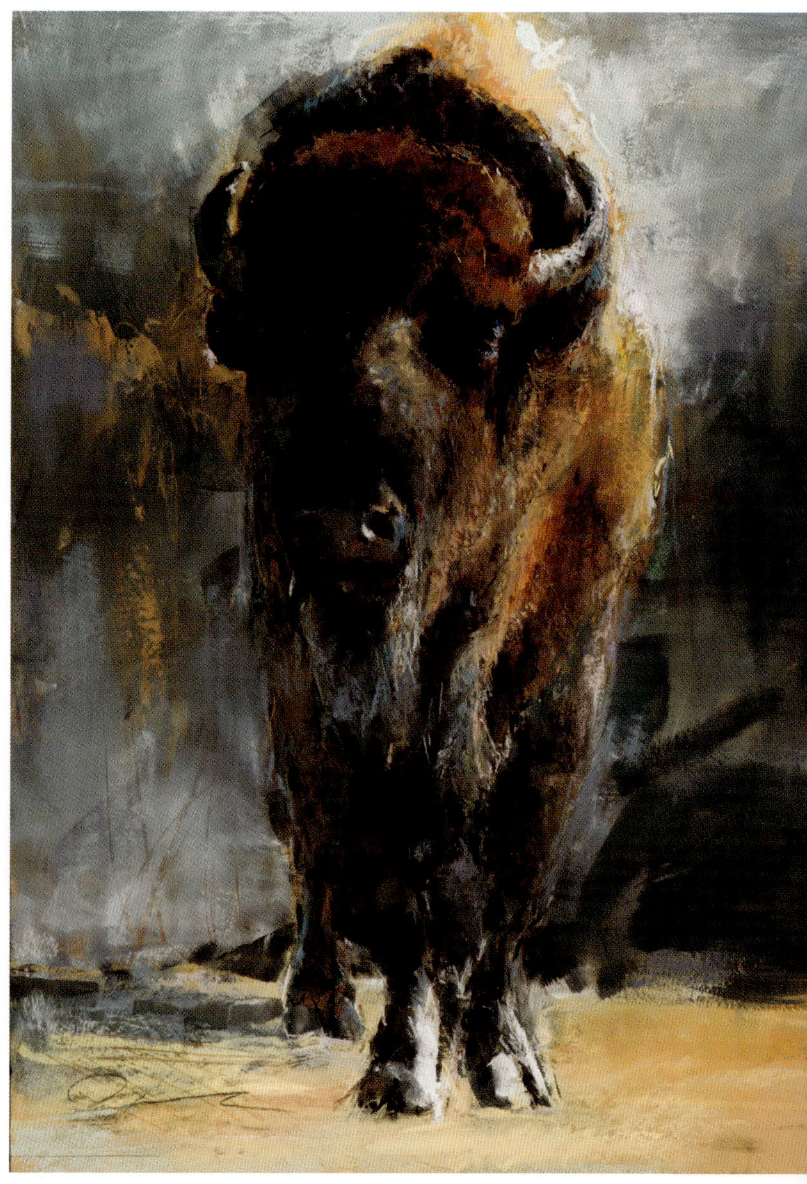

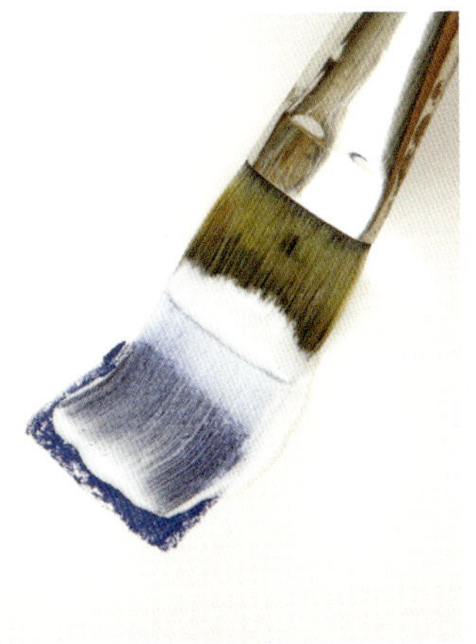

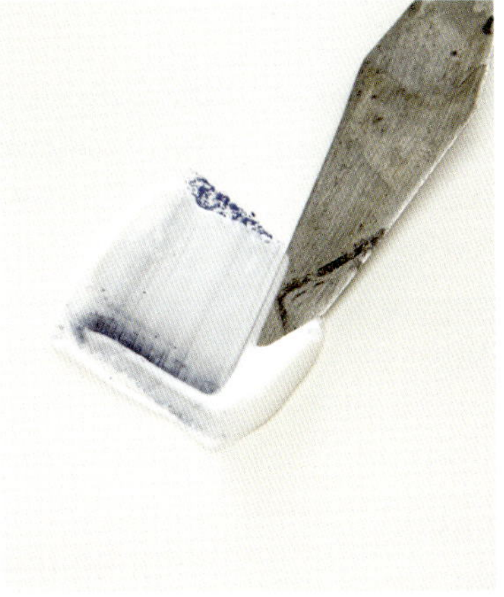

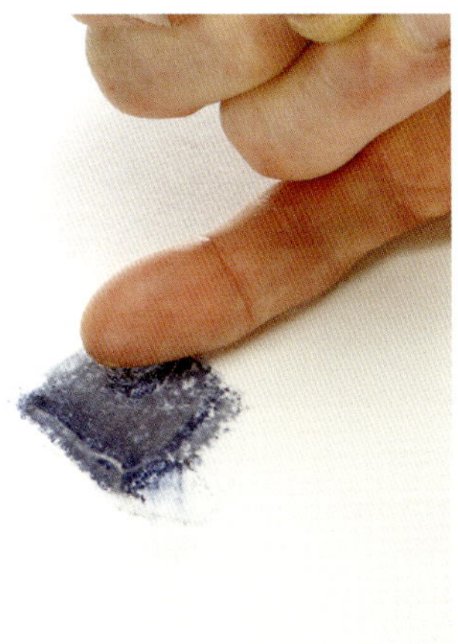

APPLYING MATTE MEDIUM WITH A BRUSH

When you want to move the pastel around like paint, apply matte medium with a brush.

APPLYING MATTE MEDIUM WITH A PALETTE KNIFE

When you don't want the pastel to smear, apply matte medium with a palette knife or spreader.

THE SURFACE IS SEALED

When the matte medium is completely dry, the pastel will not come off or shed.

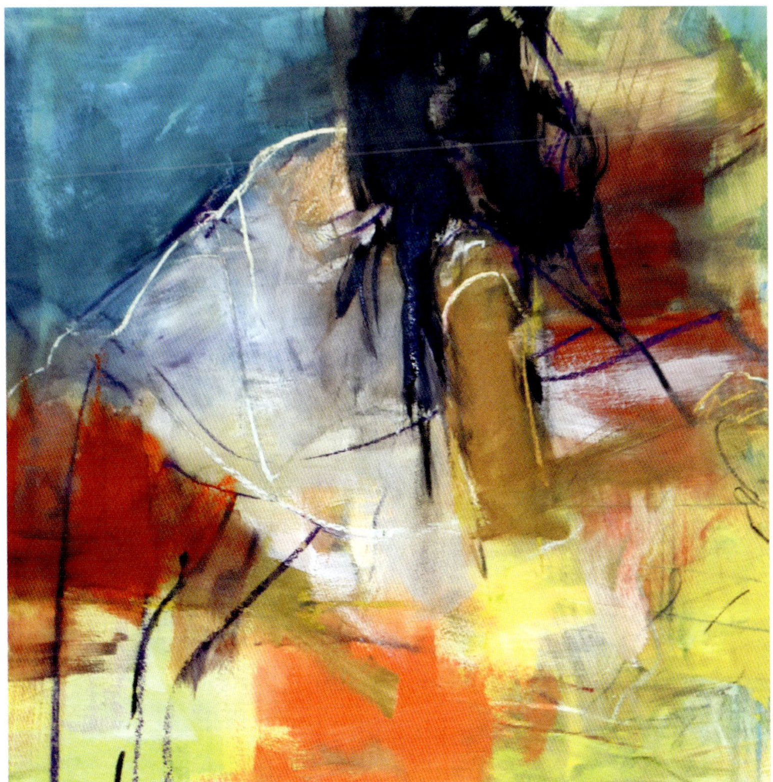

SHAWL / 24" × 24" (61CM × 61CM) / PASTEL, SUMI INK AND ACRYLIC ON GESSOED CANVAS

When I use pastel on canvas with other media I make sure that any dry material (like charcoal or pastel) is completely sealed with an archival matte spray varnish. It may take many thin layers to achieve this, but in the end, nothing will come off.

PASTEL AS CHAMELEON

A chameleon blends into the background by using two strategies. One is to match the color and texture of the environment in which it finds itself, and the other is to break up shapes so identifiable forms are lost. One of the most amazing qualities of pastels is the way it can be used in this same way in your images. Pastels can be used to break up flat masses of color with similar value but different hues. Bold marks can move across edges to disrupt forms. Blending with other carriers can create glossy contrasts that redirect the eye and invite visual exploration for your viewer. I'd like to encourage you to explore how pastel can hide and disguise elements in your composition. By camouflaging areas or shapes, you can begin to explore figure-ground reversal, which allows parts of an image to be both part of the ground and part of the figure simultaneously.

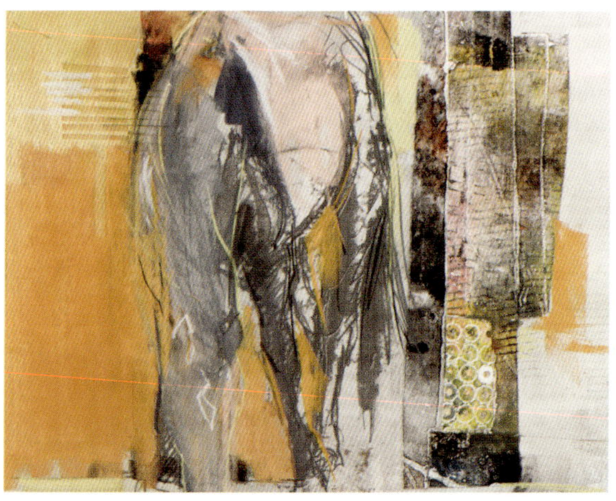

FOOD FOR THOUGHT / 22" × 26" (56CM × 66CM) / PASTEL OVER MONOTYPE AND TRACE MONOTYPE ON STONEHENGE PAPER

This image illustrates the idea of camouflaging an image. The viewer sees the figure and the ground simultaneously flip back and forth. One edge morphs into the background, then becomes part of the figure. Integrating materials to make them impersonate each other is another way to camouflage. I've used the pastel to the left of the horse's neck to cover the underpainting of monotype. Because pastel can mix with so many other mediums, it is easy to hide edges and transition between mediums. Once you get the hang of it, breaking up patterns and hiding edges becomes like a game.

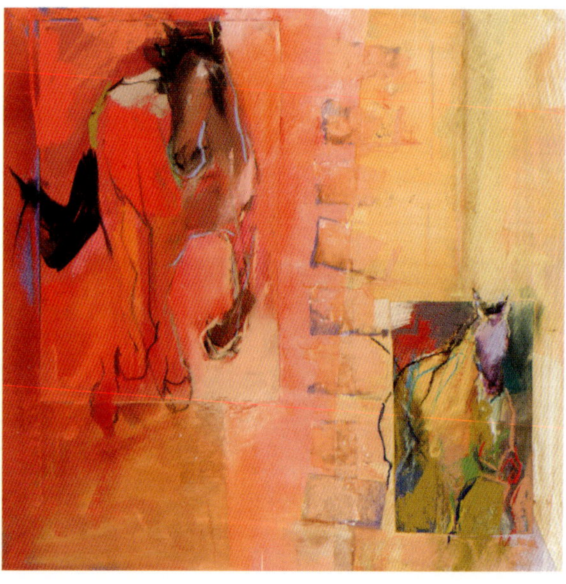

RED / 19" × 19" (48CM × 48CM) / COLLAGE OF PAPER PAINTED WITH INK, GOUACHE AND PASTEL ONTO MONOTYPE

This image is a collage pasted on top of a monotype. I extended the drawing over the edges of the collaged paper onto the monotype surface to make it appear as if the image is part of the monotype.

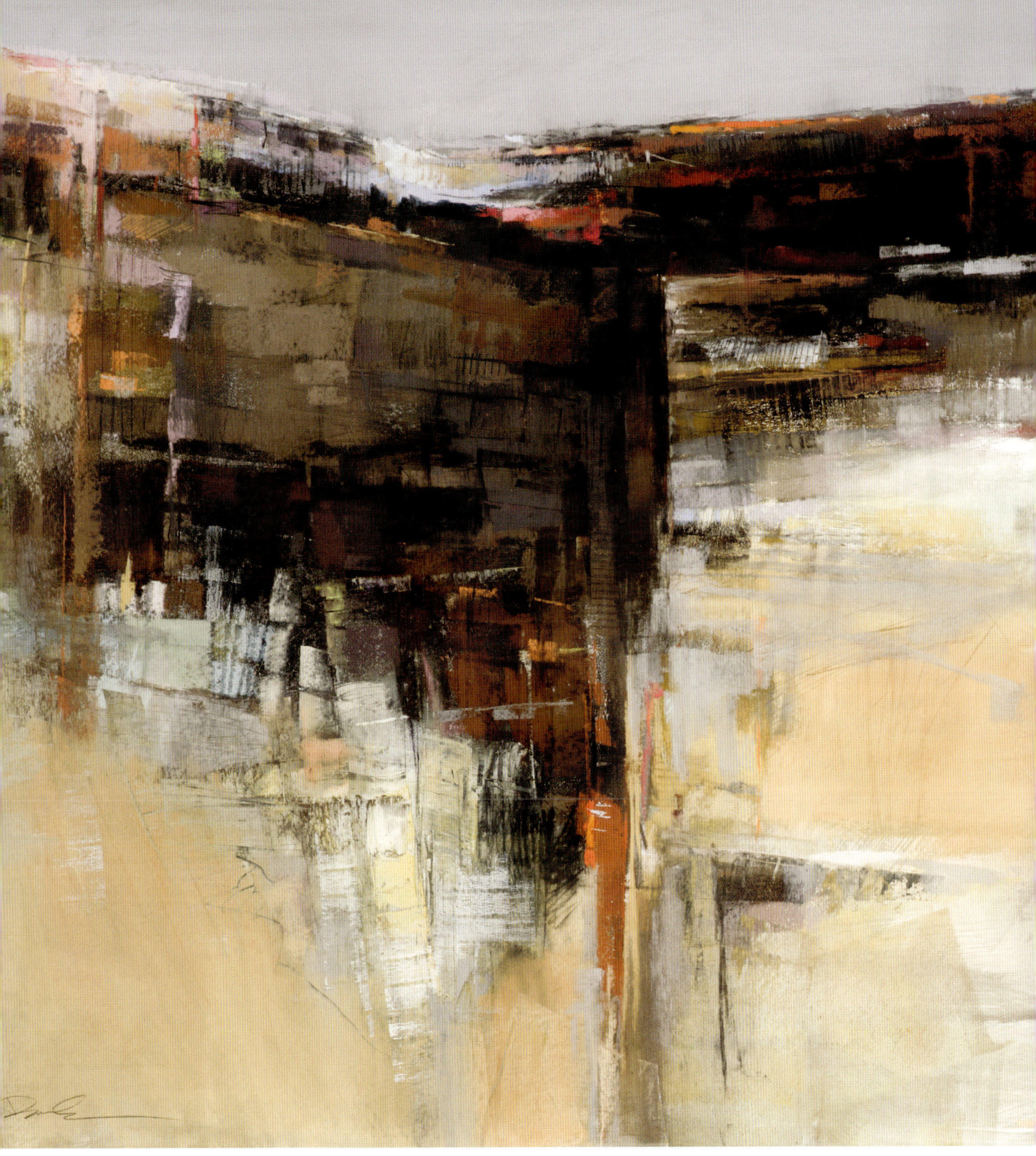

DEEP GORGE / 30" × 30" (76CM × 76CM) / PASTEL AND MIXED MEDIA ON RIVES BFK PAPER

This image grew out of a small section of another painting. The landscape I live in is layered volcanic rock, which is always shifting and crumbling. The shadows and colors change constantly as clouds move around the sky, and I wanted to capture the feeling of a landscape in flux with this image.

I drew with a brayer and oil paint and layered pastel "blocks" over the top make each piece of the cliff. In this way the physical process of painting imitates the nature I was describing.

MIXED MEDIA AND PASTEL

Sometimes artists become limited by a fear of failing or by following "rules" that aren't really rules. When I first began printmaking, I was overwhelmed by the change in tools and materials, and was humbled into feeling like a very messy beginner. Edward Degas experimented widely with pastel, monotypes and mixed media. He explored the same image over and over to see how it could be colored, edited and composed. Whenever I found myself wonder "what if . . ." I gave myself permission to be like Degas, and try it.

I learned that because pastel is simply pigment in stick form, virtually any other medium can be added to liquefy it. Used dry, it can be layered, scraped, rubbed or erased. Pastel is dust, however, and while dust sticks to everything, nothing sticks to dust. That is the only rule I use. Printmaking informed my pastel work with new mark making tools and layering approaches. Combining new mediums and tools with pastel seemed perfectly natural as I questioned more about what the difference between drawing and painting meant to me.

CROWN OF GOLD / 16" × 16" (41CM × 41CM) / COLOR MONOTYPE WITH PASTEL ON RIVES BFK PAPER

This image was painted with Akua Intaglio inks on paper, then printed with a press onto another piece of paper to create a monotype. I added pastel to the monotype in places where I wanted to enhance or sharpen edges. Pastel can be used on the press during the printing process or added to images afterwards.

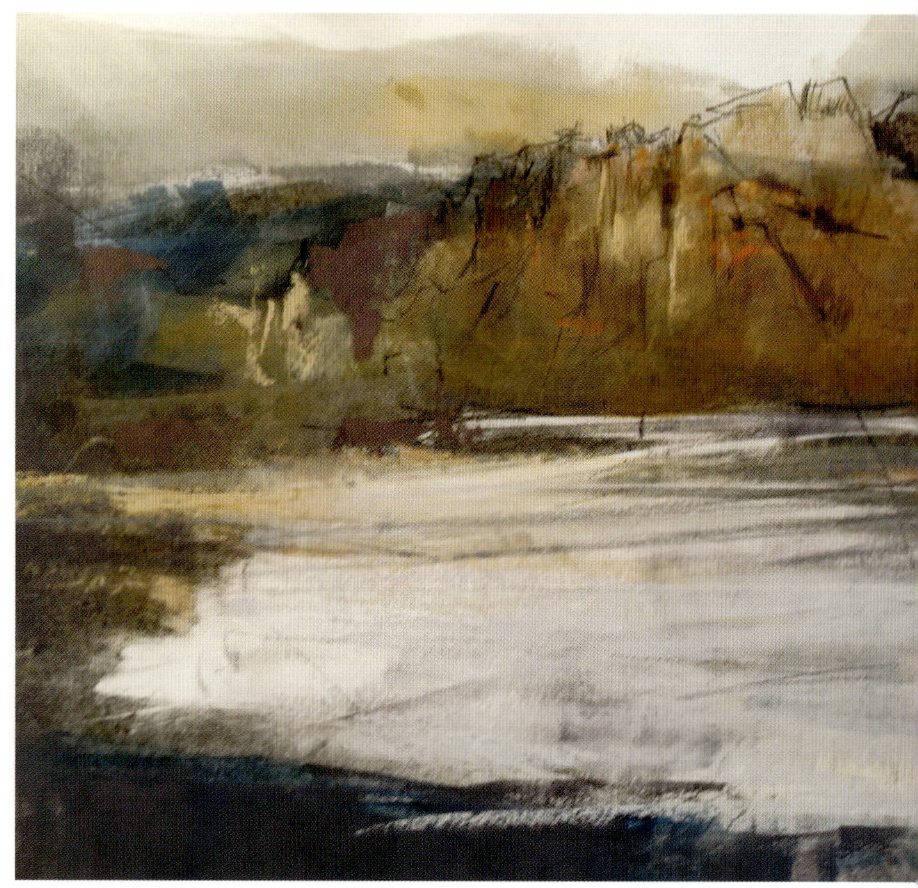

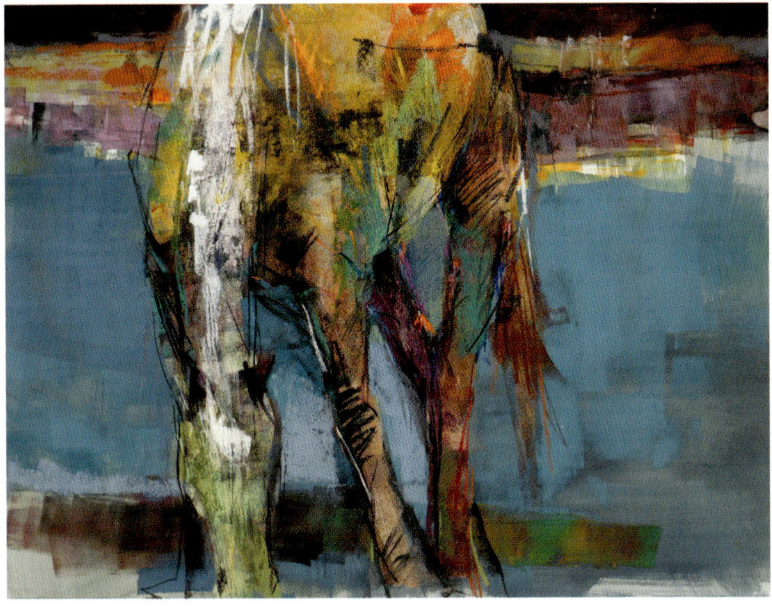

GRAZING THE BLUES / 22" × 30" (56CM × 76CM) / MIXED MEDIA AND PASTEL ON STONEHENGE PAPER

There is a relationship between the land and the horse, its colors and texture, that move in and out of each other seamlessly. The process used to make the image reflects the intention I had, which was to show how the horse lives in harmony with its environment.

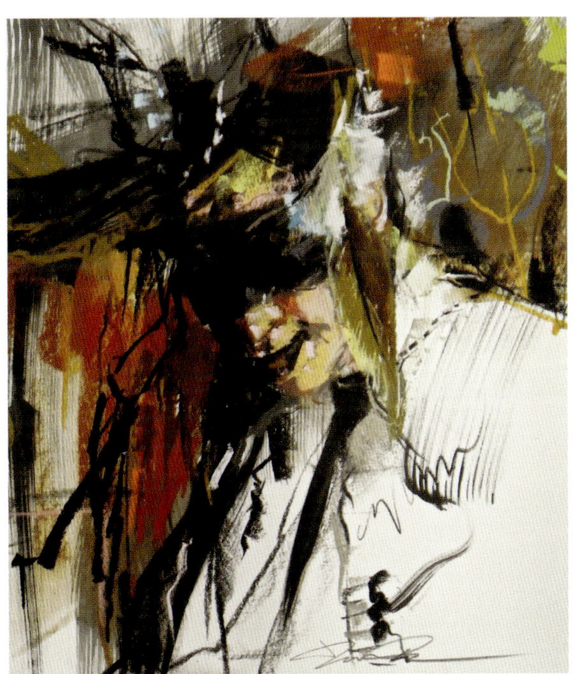

LOST IN THE DANCE / 20" × 18" (51CM × 46CM) / PASTEL, WATERCOLOR, ACRYLIC AND SUMI INK ON STONEHENGE PAPER

Pastel makes possible the combination of gestural drawing with painterly brushwork.

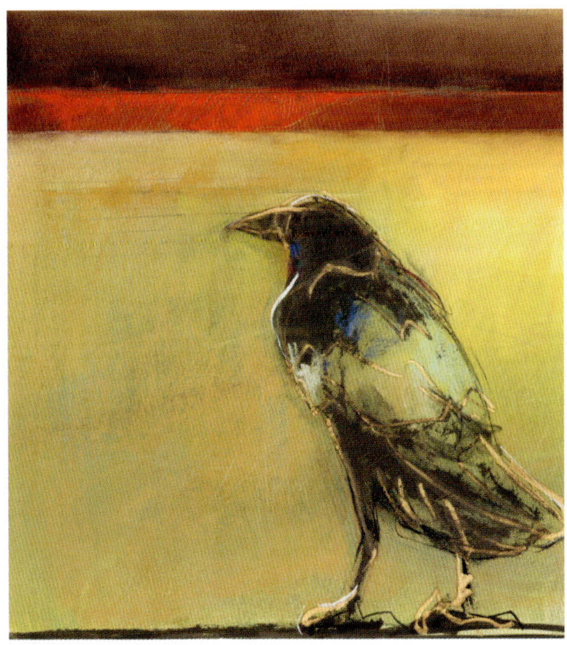

WAITING FOR A SIGN / 19" × 19" (48CM × 48CM) / PASTEL, OIL PASTEL AND SUMI INK ON RIVES BFK PAPER

The raven is a meaningful totem creature for me. The gold lines in this image are made with oil pastel drawn on top of the soft pastel.

MYSTERIOUS DARKS AND LUMINOUS LIGHTS

The crystalline nature of pastels gives the darkest darks and the lightest lights a liveliness and twinkle. Blending pastels with other media offers opportunities to enhance those qualities even more. I want to encourage you to think beyond the figure or the ground to the emotions you want to create. Think about the quality of the light you want to capture before you begin painting, and be mindful of maintaining that quality throughout the painting process. Like lighting a stage, you can create any mood or spatial quality you want to, from deep, dark and mysterious to expansive, luminous joy.

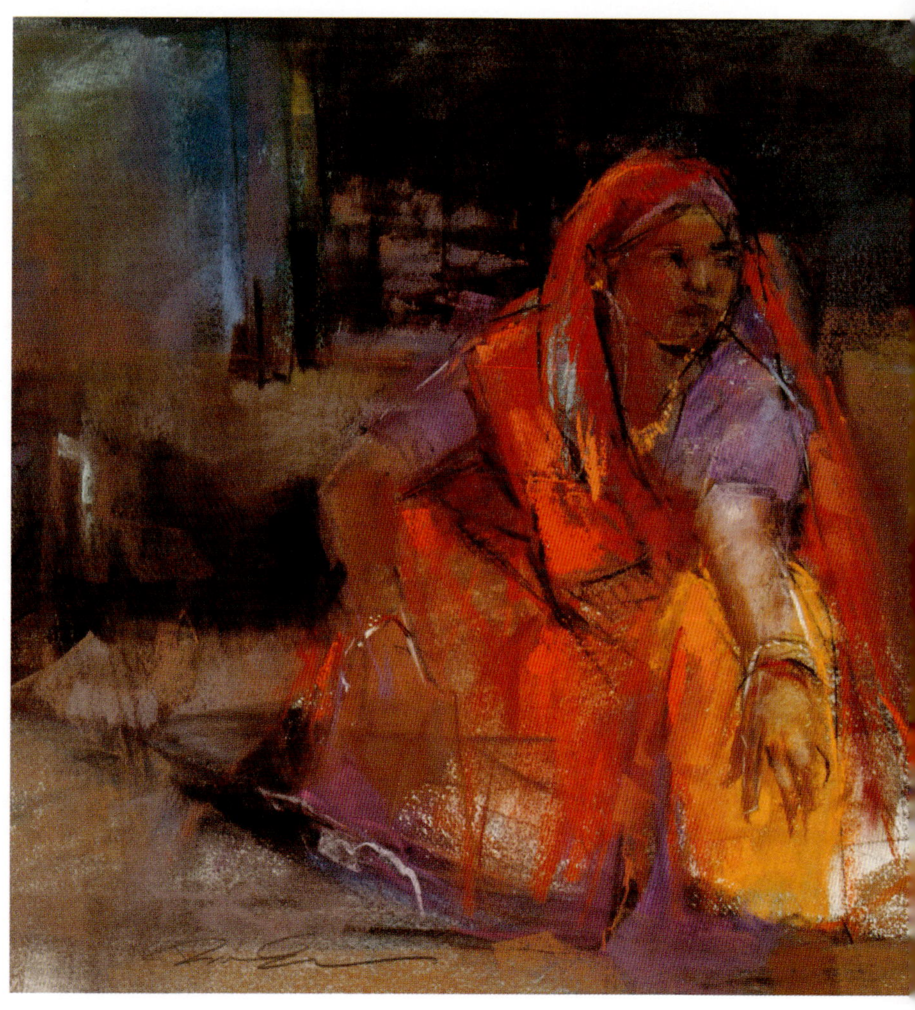

HIDDEN / 14" × 14" (36CM × 36CM) / PASTEL, WATERCOLOR AND SUMI INK ON STONEHENGE PAPER

I used sumi ink and dark values of watercolor to create a moody, dark underpainting for this image. Most of the figure blends in with the shadows, and only a few areas are described in full light. Like the image, the beauty of pastel is its ability to show depth even in darkness.

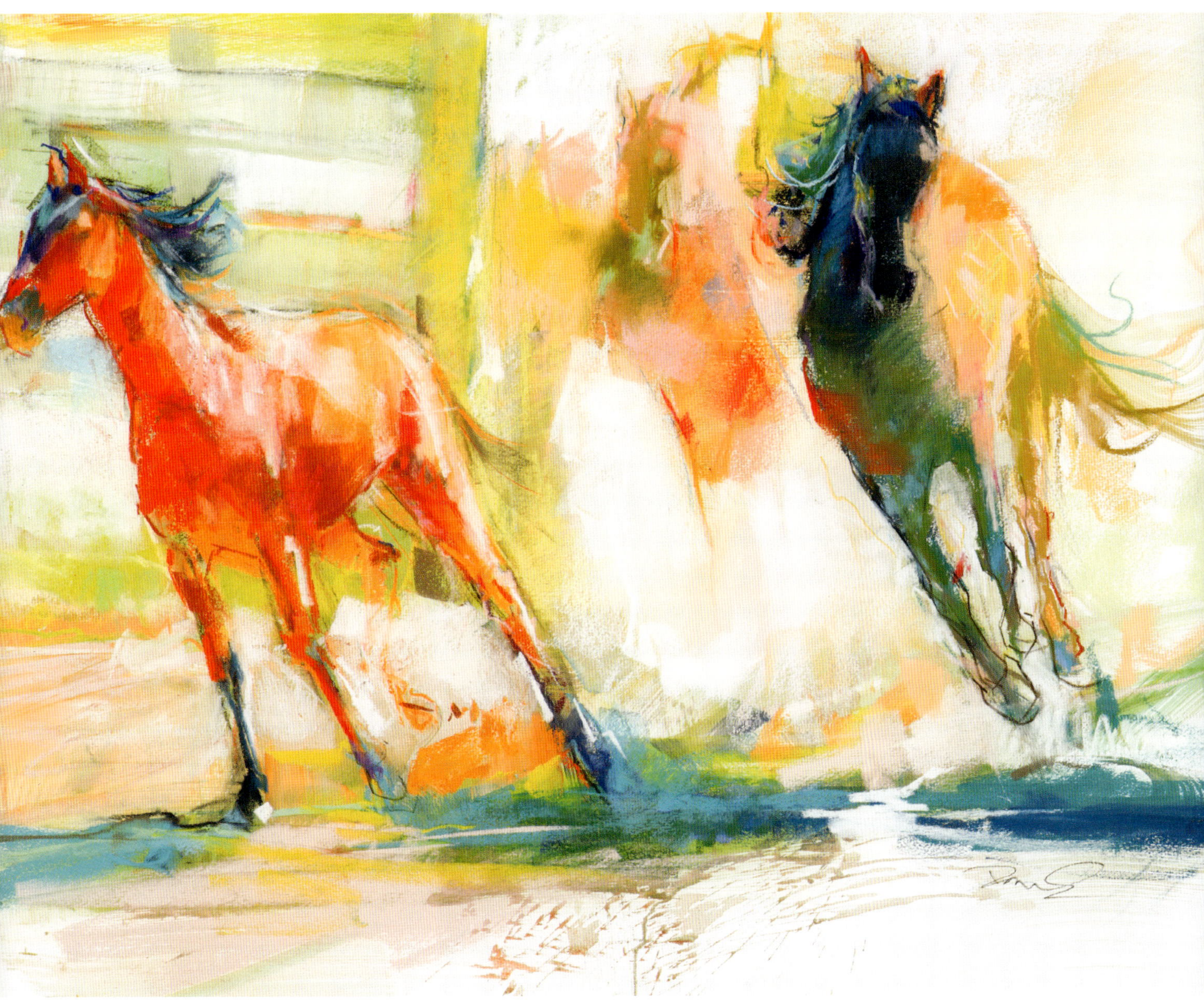

FREEDOM RUN / 22" × 30" (56CM × 76CM) / PASTEL AND WATERCOLOR ON STONEHENGE PAPER

I wanted to see how far I could push color, so the use of saturated complementary colors and a high-key background seemed like a good option. In contrast to the dark moodiness of *Hidden,* this image conveys the joyful mood of these horses as they break through the open gate and into the light. The use of analogous colors in this painting helps make the pastel glow from within.

MAKE AS MANY MISTAKES AS YOU CAN

I love when I feel like an explorer in my studio. "What will happen if …?" is a question I often ask myself. I try to notice the marks and textures that are happening as I work and be very present to changes that may be occurring. I'll explore a lot of possibilities and make lots of "mistakes" to discover what does or doesn't work. The truth is that if I'm not willing to take risks and try new things, I will be stuck repeating those techniques I know have worked in the past. The process of exploring means making loads of mistakes, and along the way I discover wonderful possibilities. This approach is inherently linked to my personal growth as an artist, and I hope you to find this process as freeing as I do.

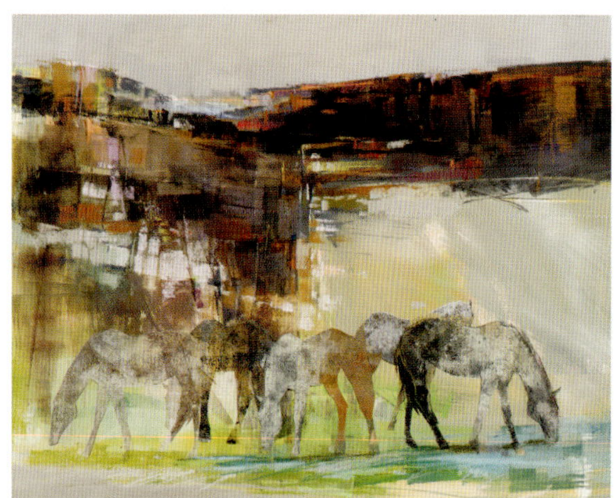

RIDGE LINE (BEFORE) / 22" × 30" (56CM × 76CM) / MIXED MEDIA AND PASTEL ON STONEHENGE PAPER

During the process of painting *Ridge Line* I had included these horses at the base of the cliff. I thought I would be very clever and imitate the cliff wall texture on the horses—as though they had been formed from it. After studying it for a while, I realized that I was trying to put everything into one image. I had to decide which was my focus—the horses, the water they were standing in, or the wall. In the end, the wall won out, and I eliminated the horses.

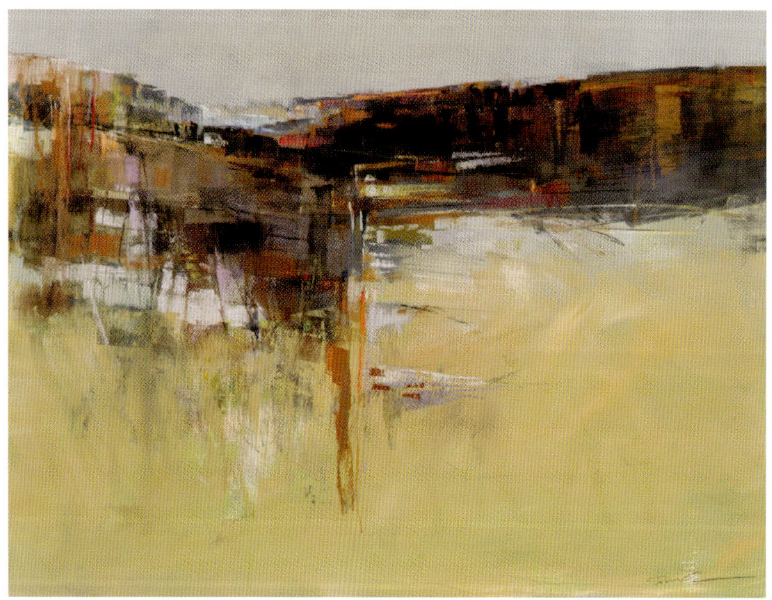

RIDGE LINE (AFTER) / 22" × 30" (56CM × 76CM) / MIXED MEDIA AND PASTEL ON STONEHENGE PAPER

This is the final version. Looking back, there may have been other options I could have chosen. What would you have done? The important thing to remember is that had I not taken a photograph of the image in process, I would not have anything to compare the final image to. Making mistakes is part of learning, but it is how we use those mistakes to keep learning that is even more important.

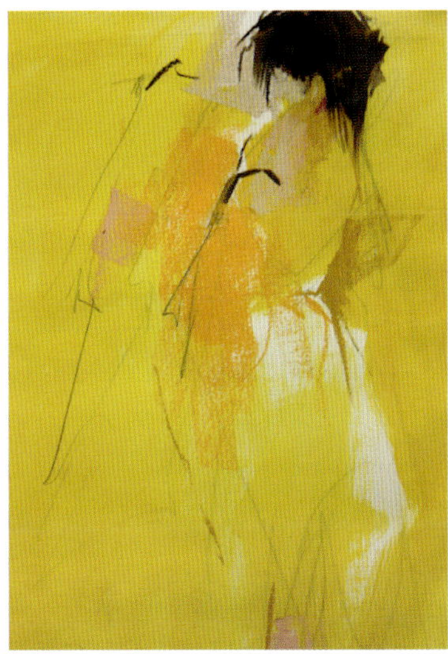

STEP 1

This is the first step in the process of creating this painting. There are big shapes, just a little line, a tiny bit of dark: I could have (and perhaps should have) stopped here.

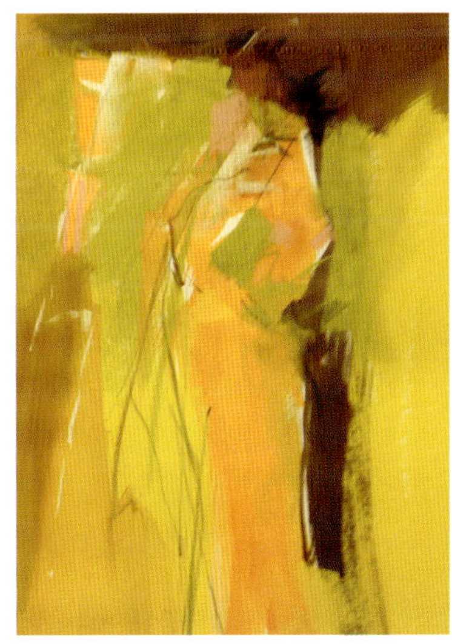

STEP 2

In this stage I added a dark value at the top, defined more edges, and broke big shapes into smaller ones. This is where the trouble begins.

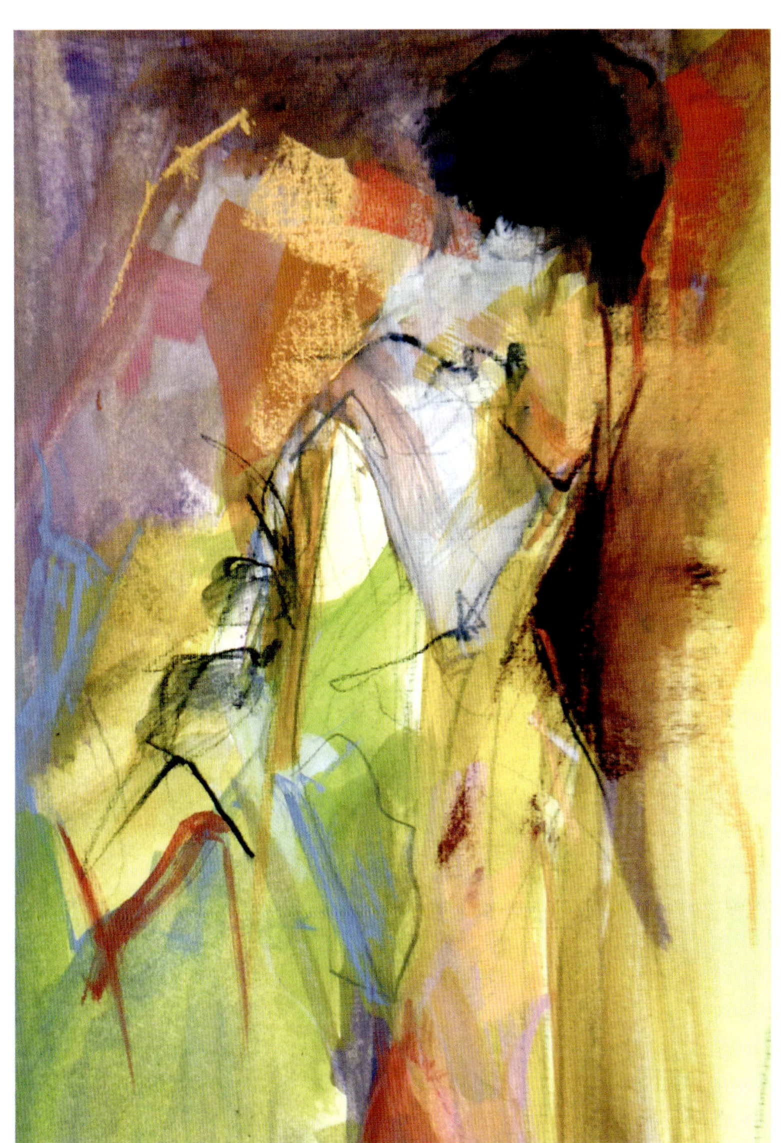

STEP 3

In this final stage I added lots of color and brought back the black hair. But I continued to break shapes into smaller pieces. I was confused as to what I was trying to convey, and it shows. Though the work is "pretty," it lacks the presence and simplicity that was strongest in step 1.

GEISHA / 24" × 18" (61CM × 46CM) / PASTEL ON STONEHENGE PAPER

PASTEL AS HERO

What do you do when an image doesn't have enough impact or punch? You can either scrap it and begin another painting, or summon our hero, the pastel, to save the day. Between the bolts of color and a huge spectrum of values, the pastel can take an image almost anywhere. Pastel can pull together disconnected forms, make darks and lights pop with contrast, or create energy and movement with the character of its marks. Is there anything a pastel can't do? I don't think so!

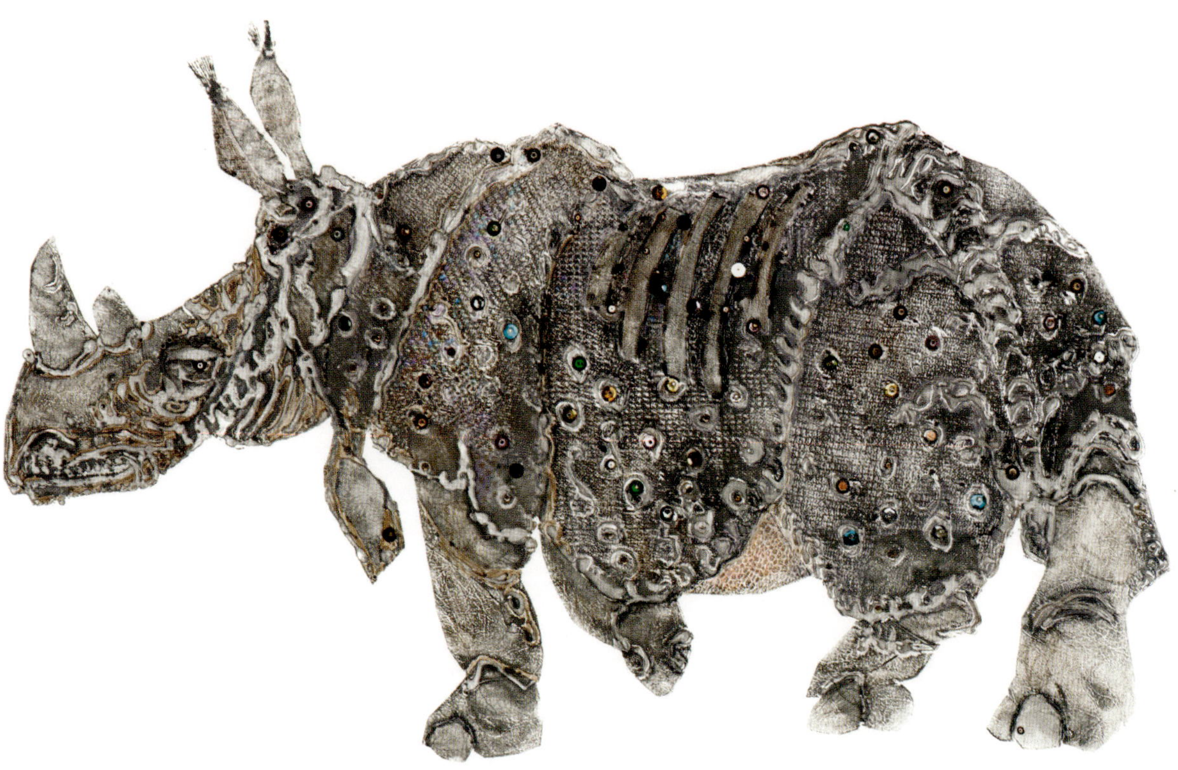

RHINESTONE RHINO / 30" × 44" (76CM × 112CM) / COLLOGRAPH WITH PASTEL ON RIVES BFK PAPER

With certain forms of printmaking, drawing onto a print after it has been printed is totally accepted. Collography (a form of embossing) encourages such drawing. The plate for the rhino is made of pool liner material, paper, burlap and hot glue. I inked it up with Akua Intaglio ink, ran it through the press, and printed onto moistened printmaking paper. The image was not as colorful as I'd hoped, but pastel came to the rescue! After enhancing the color with pastel, I embellished the surface with rhinestones and jewels.

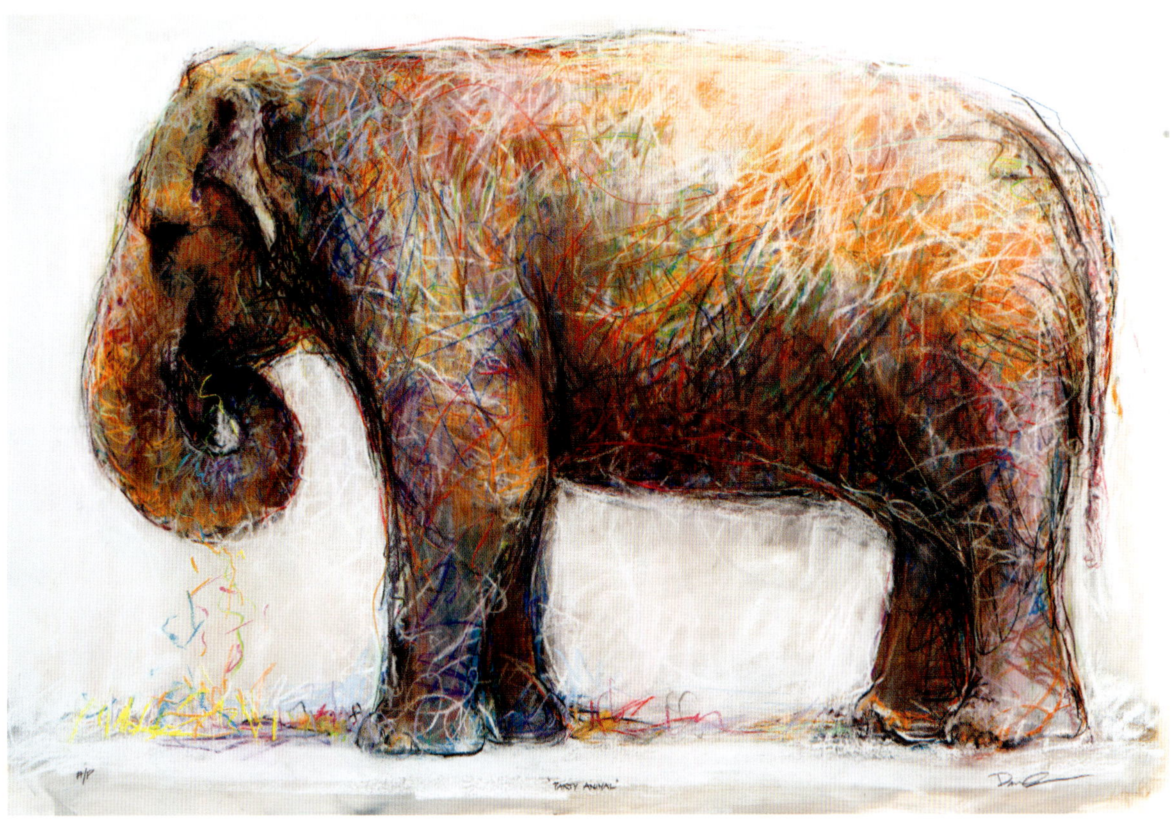

PARTY ANIMAL / 34" × 44" (86CM × 112CM) / DREMEL TOOL ENGRAVING INTO MASONITE PRINTED ON RIVES BFK PAPER WITH PASTEL ADDED

To make this enormous printing plate, I drew into a large piece of hardboard with a Dremel tool. The plate was inked by pushing the ink into the depressions of the carved image, then printed in a parking lot with a steam roller acting as the press. This elephant and the one below were pulled from the same plate, but were each drawn into with completely different results. Because the image was already there as a kind of underpainting, I could add pastel and mixed media however I wanted.

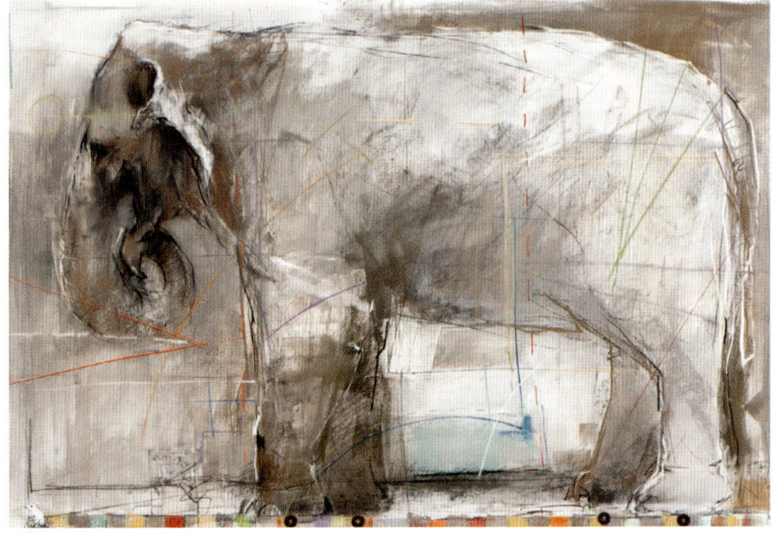

THE ELEPHANT'S NEW CLOTHES / 86" × 112" (56CM × 76CM) / DREMEL TOOL ENGRAVING INTO MASONITE PRINTED ON RIVES BFK PAPER WITH PASTEL ADDED

I drew into a second print of the same elephant using mixed media and pastel to tell a completely different story. By drawing into each print differently, unique images can evolve from the same plate.

NO FEAR!

In my workshops I treasure the students who come with no pastel experience. They have the opportunity to be true beginners. They have no expectation or judgement about what will happen as they pick up the pastel and begin exploring. They can revel in the beauty of the marks that appear and feel the joy of image-making. As we become more experienced with pastels (or any other media), we start to have expectations and judgements about what we "should" be doing. This is the doorway through which fear enters, and fear comes dressed in many forms. Fear of failure, fear of making mistakes, fear of looking bad and fear of wasting time and materials are possibilities. Will you choose to be a beginner again? Will each day be an opportunity to explore and play with pastels or printmaking with no judgement about where it takes you and what you produce? Can you revel in the experience as you use the elements and principles to guide your work toward completion?

David Bayles said in his book *Art & Fear*, "Your job as an artist is to push craft to it limits without being trapped by it. The trap is perfection. I believe that unless your work continually generates new and unresolved issues there is no reason for your next work to be any different from the last." If you really want to keep growing as an artist, you will take this to heart.

TWIN SOULS / 14" × 12" (36CM × 30CM) / SUMI INK AND PASTEL ON STONEHENGE PAPER

This whimsical image was part of an abstract horse series I did using sumi ink as underpainting. If there was any lack of commitment or trepidation about making a stroke, the sumi ink showed it tenfold!

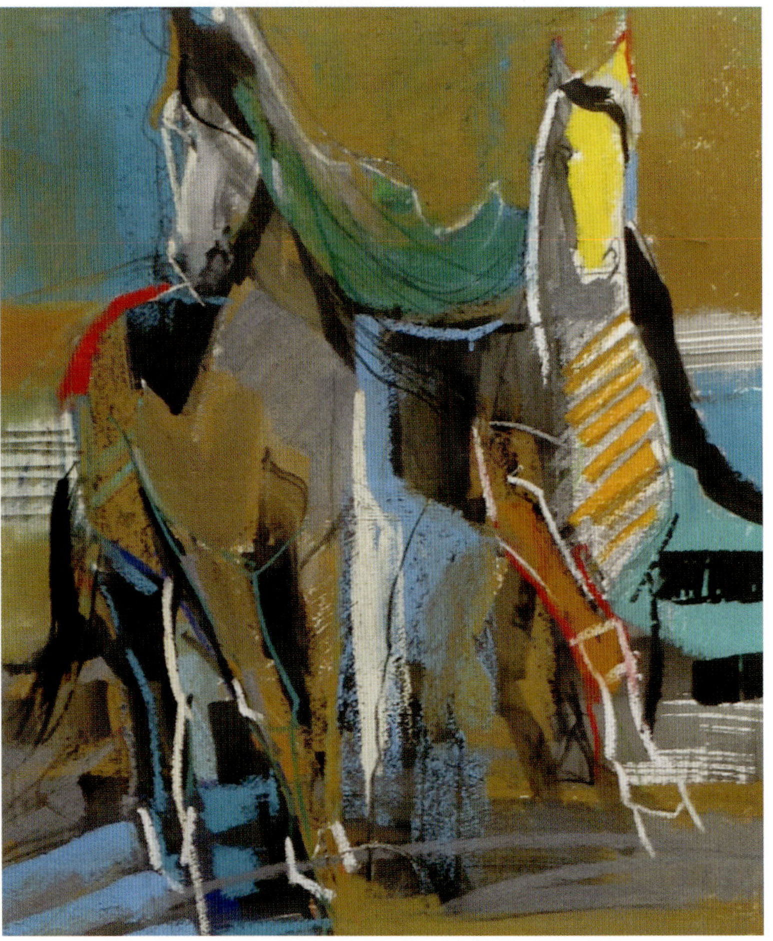

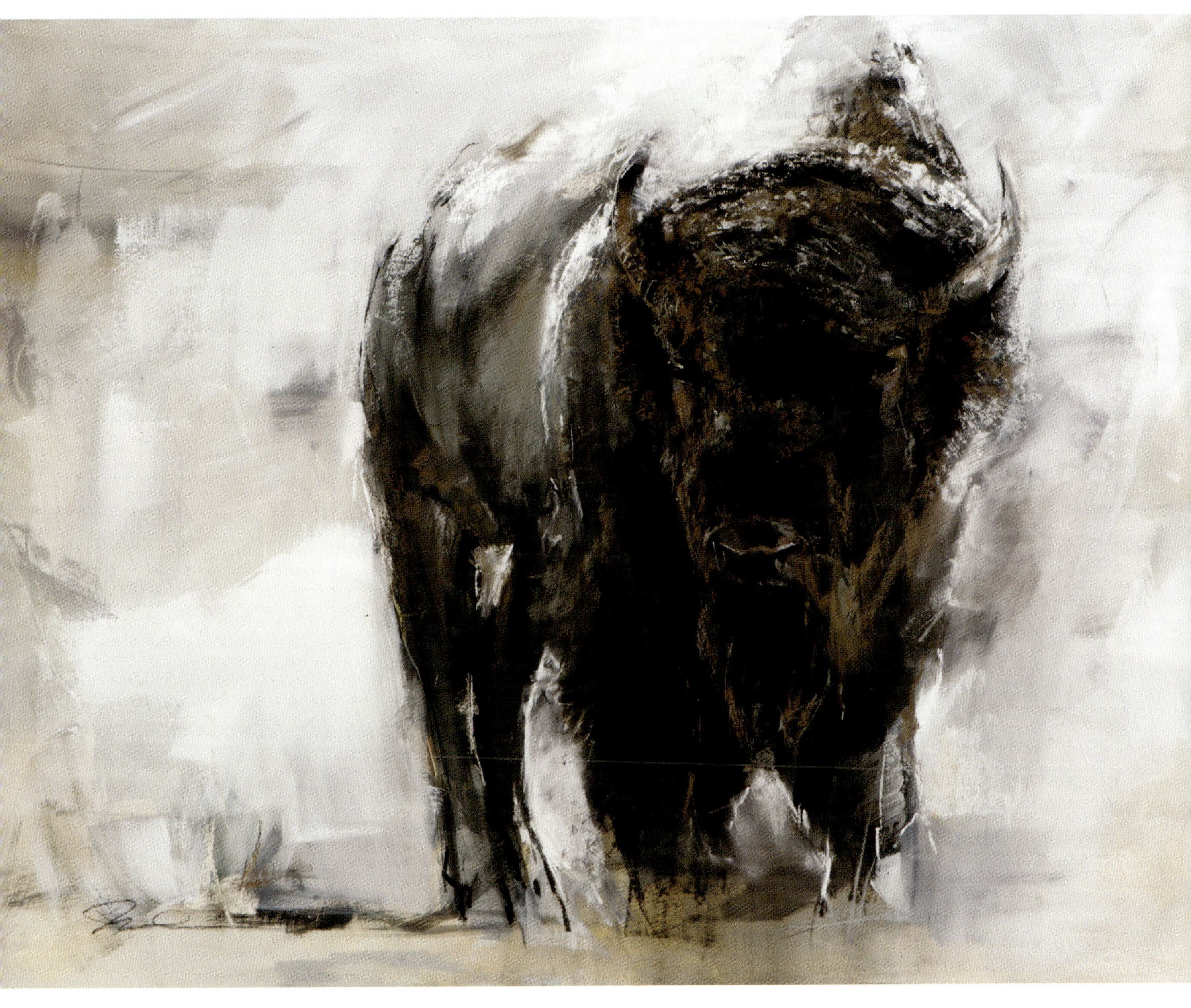

WINTER BISON / 36" × 48" (91CM × 122CM) / PASTEL AND MIXED MEDIA ON HARDBOARD WITH GESSO-PUMICE GROUND

Exemplifying "no fear," the look on this bison's face seems like a fitting image with which to end this chapter.

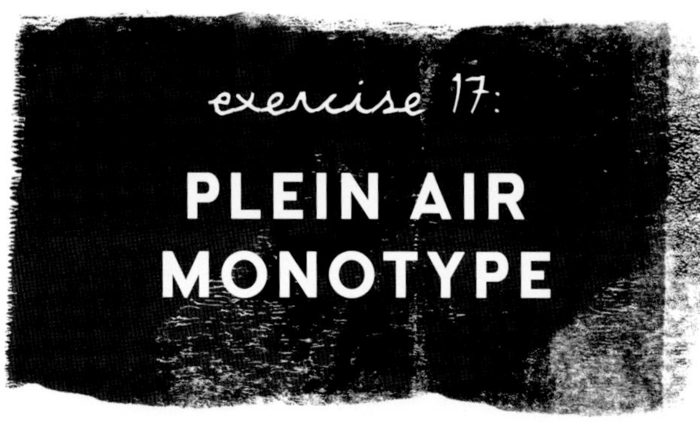

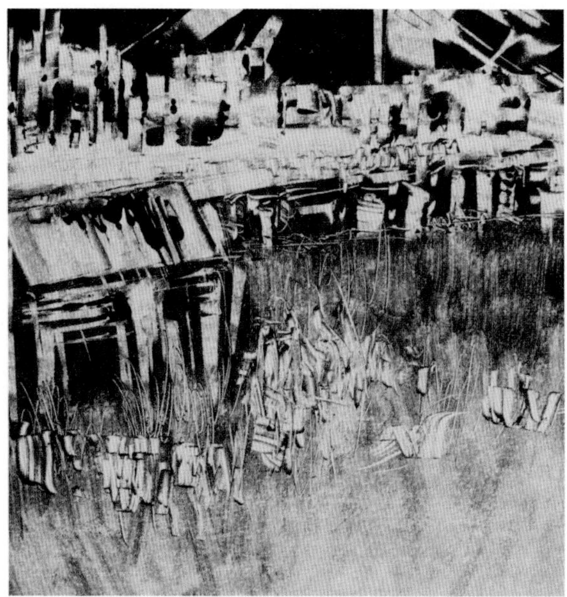

OLD SHED / 15" × 15" (38CM × 38CM) / MONOTYPE ON STONEHENGE PAPER BY DENALI BROOKE

MATERIALS

- brayer
- tools for removing ink (like stiff cardboard or credit card, baby wipes, scribing and wiping tools, dabbers and brushes, etc.)
- masking tape
- black Akua Intaglio ink
- plastic plates, 8" × 10" (20CM × 25CM)
- mat board pieces cut to 10" × 12" (25CM × 30CM) for taping plate onto
- paper or plastic plate for rolling out ink onto brayer
- smooth, flat surface, about 12" × 18" (30CM × 46CM), to work on
- paper to print on
- pin press or rubbing tool
- pastels

DIRECTIONS

NOTE: You may enjoy looking at the landscape monotypes of Edgar Degas before you begin this exercise.

STEP 1
Secure your plates to mat board with masking tape before you go on location.

STEP 2
On location, ink a plate with ink to create a dark field monotype ground.

STEP 3
Create your monotype.

STEP 4
Print on location or store your plates ink-side up in shallow storage boxes, and print later. Remember, the ink will not dry on plastic or glass.

STEP 5
Add pastel to the prints.

CRITIQUE

- How did the experience of creating a monotype on location compare with drawing or painting?
- Were you able to simplify the landscape with the monotype process?
- Did the process allow you to see differently?
- Can you imagine ways to incorporate grasses and elements from the environment into your work?

TAKEAWAY

Making monotypes on location heightens your awareness of shape and texture in the landscape.

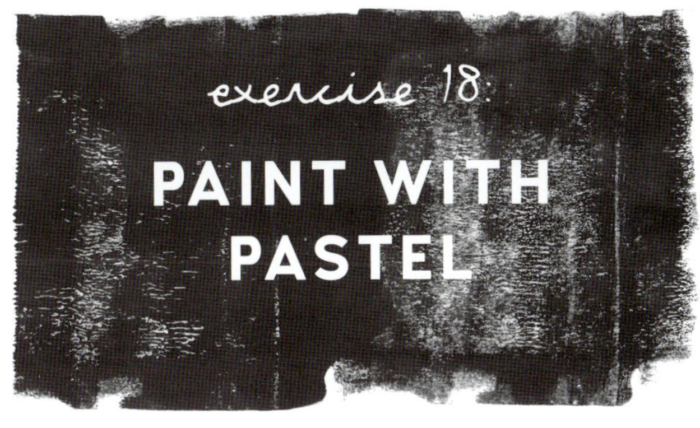

MATERIALS

- assorted pastel sticks and PanPastels
- pear or other subject
- 1" (25MM) flat brush
- water
- clear gesso or matte medium
- mixed-media drawing paper or Stonehenge paper

DIRECTIONS

STEP 1
Lightly pencil in a border for your image before you draw.

STEP 2
Draw your subject with a pastel.

STEP 3
Paint into the pastel with matte medium or clear gesso and a paintbrush. Let dry.

STEP 4
Add layers of pastel, separating each layer with a clear medium. Experiment with scratching through one layer to reveal the color in the layer below. Consider embossing texture or drawing with colored pencil.

CRITIQUE

- Adding brushwork into your pastel drawing expands the possibilities for layering and mark-making. Study your work to see how brushwork has altered your marks.

TAKEAWAY

There is very little distinction between drawing and painting.

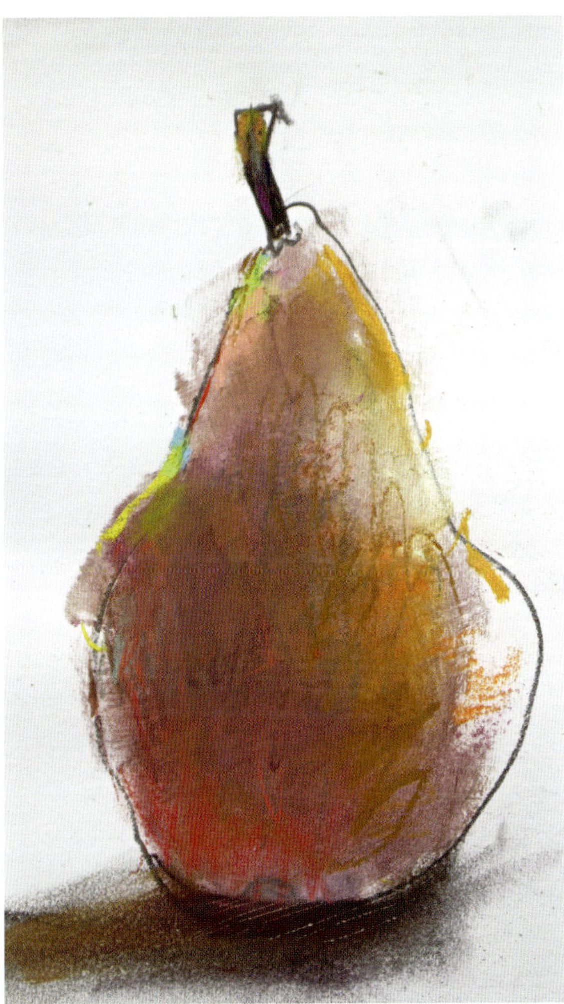

PEAR / 10" × 8" (25CM × 20CM) / PASTEL AND CLEAR GESSO ON DRAWING PAPER

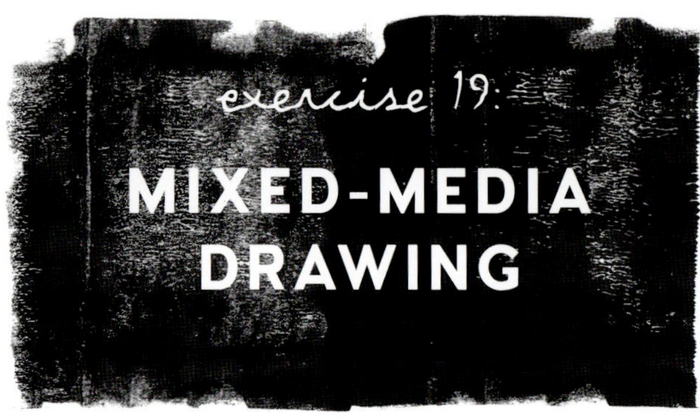

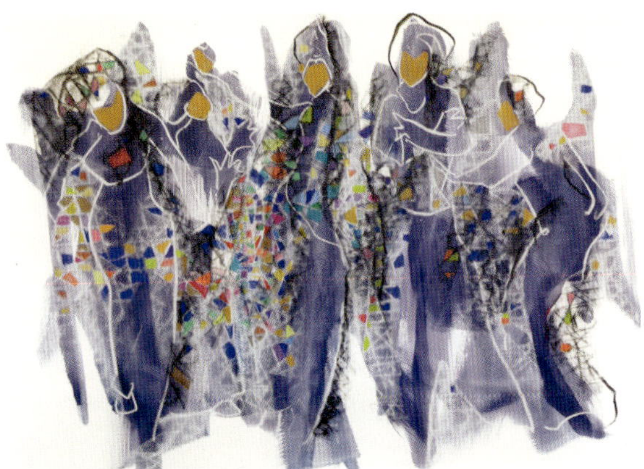

DANCING HER STORY / 22" × 30" (56CM × 76CM) / WATERCOLOR, COLOR PENCIL, PASTEL AND WHITE CRAYON ON RIVES BFK PAPER

MATERIALS

- watercolor
- wide brush
- white wax crayon
- PanPastels
- 4 sheets mixed media paper, about 10" × 12" (25cm × 30cm) or 12" × 16" (30cm × 41cm)
- stencil or texture material with holes
- colored pencils
- reference images of people dancing
- optional: sequins

DIRECTIONS

STEP 1

Put on some music that matches the mood of your reference photos.

STEP 2

Draw simplified contour lines of the figure with the white crayon. Avoid details. Put in only as few lines as you need, and be sure to press into the paper with the crayon to deposit the wax. You might consider using only straight lines, curvy lines or geometric shapes to make the figure. You are not trying to copy the photograph, but to get the gesture, so keep it simple.

STEP 3

Load your brush with watercolor and make one bold, expressive shape over most of the crayon lines. The wax should resist the watercolor. Let dry.

STEP 4

Place your stencil or texture with holes over the image and use a sponge applicator to apply PanPastel on top of the drawing to give it texture or pattern.

STEP 5

Add color pencil or glue sequins over the image if you wish, and then do three more.

CRITIQUE

Drawing with a white crayon on white paper is a kind of "blind" drawing that can help you be freer with your sketching. When you added the watercolor on top, were you pleasantly surprised with the way the lines looked? Could you let yourself enjoy the process without passing judgement? The more you let yourself play like this, the easier drawing will become. You might try this approach using the blind embossing technique presented in chapter 2. Instead of adding watercolor, you will add pastel with a flat applicator. Try it!

TAKEAWAY

Play is the key to learning.

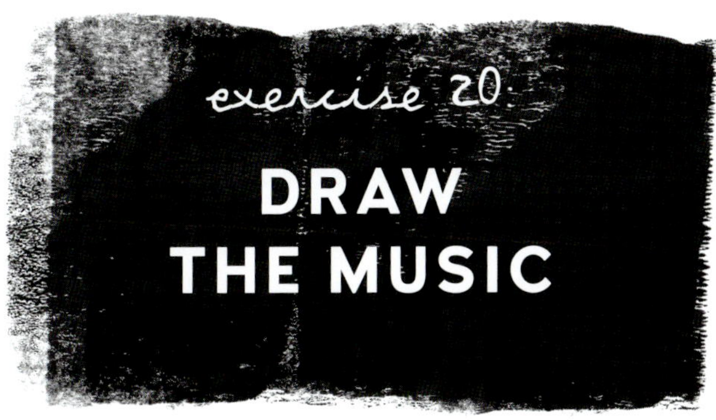

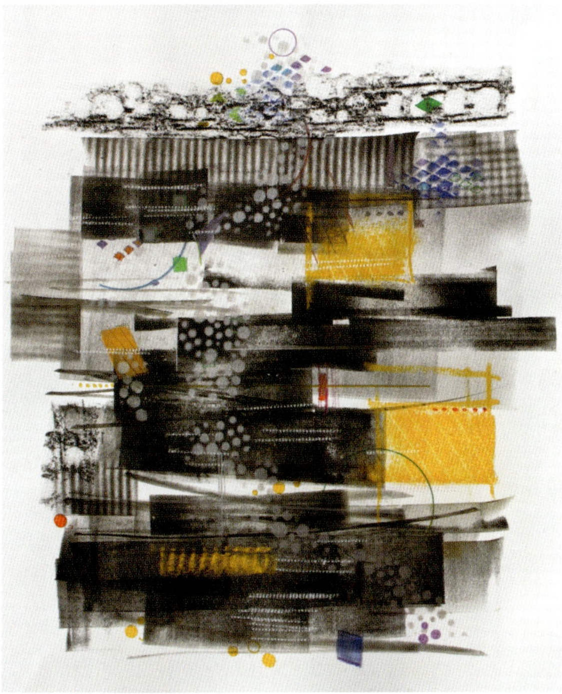

FUSION / 24" × 18" (61CM × 46CM) / OIL PAINT, PASTEL, CHARCOAL, COLOR PENCIL ON MIXED-MEDIA PAPER

MATERIALS

- black wax crayon for rubbing (no wrapper)
- 2"–3" (5CM–8CM) brayer and black water-miscible oil paint
- pastel sticks, PanPastels and applicator, color pencils
- lightweight drawing paper
- assortment of texture materials, stencils, etc.
- razor blade
- jazz or nonvocal music that has a beat you relate to

DIRECTIONS

STEP 1

Make sure you will be undisturbed for at least an hour. Stand at a table rather than at an easel.

STEP 2

Turn on the music. This drawing will be a visual interpretation of your emotional response to the music—the beat, rhythm, harmony and mood—without words, symbols or pictorial imagery.

STEP 3

Begin by rubbing textures from below the paper using the crayon (the frottage technique). Consider using textures that are varied in scale. This could relate to the texture of the music.

STEP 4

Add brayer marks and shapes, and offset textures with the brayer.

STEP 5

Create a layering of shapes that reflect the layers of sounds you hear in the music. Consider the pauses (white space of the page) as well as the notes. Add color with pastel and colored pencil.

STEP 6

Respond to the music's rhythm and beat until you feel your musical image is complete.

CRITIQUE

- What elements in the music did you respond to the most?
- How is it portrayed in the artwork?
- Is there a visual beat or unifying element in the piece?
- If you were to do a series of musical visions, what genre of music would you want to explore?

TAKEAWAY

Imagination is as far away as the next sound you hear.

chapter 6

TAKING FLIGHT

In chapter 5 you explored what is possible with the incredibly versatile medium of pastel. It is my intention that this exploration will make you ponder how else you might be able to use pastel in your creative process.

With this final chapter I encourage you to set aside time in your studio to explore and experiment with no intention of completing anything. Among your goals will be to make time to explore different mark-making techniques, take risks with surfaces and tools, and create more than one of the same image. Each sketch you make can offer new ideas and opportunities for future art-making. I believe that if you devote time to playing in your studio, your idea bank will grow faster than you can keep up with, and your art will take on a life of its own.

Like many artists I often feel the pressure to produce a finished product when I go into my studio. Once, a few years ago, I remember wishing that I could take my own workshop so I would have the time to play and experiment. What a crazy thought! Now I believe that my studio is a place I go to do the joyful work of being an artist. The production of art will take care of itself. Like an improv actor on a stage, I need just a line or a prompt to set the creative process in motion. This chapter is a collection of prompts to jumpstart both your work and your play in the studio.

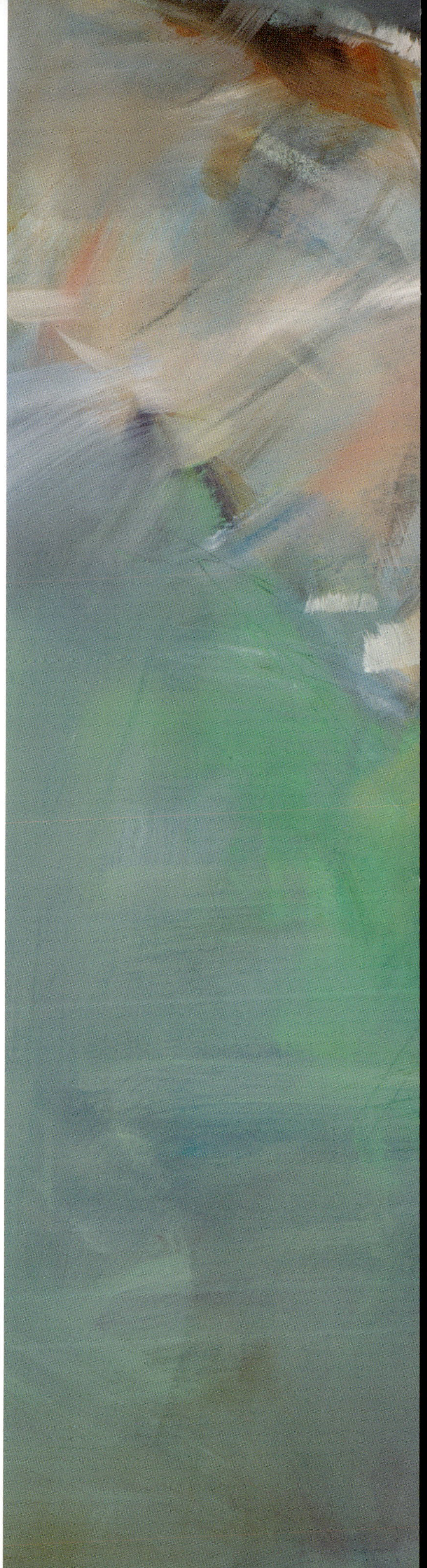

NIGHT OWL / 36" × 36" (91CM × 91CM) / PASTEL AND OIL ON CANVAS

This image shows a dynamic quality pastel can add to a painted surface.

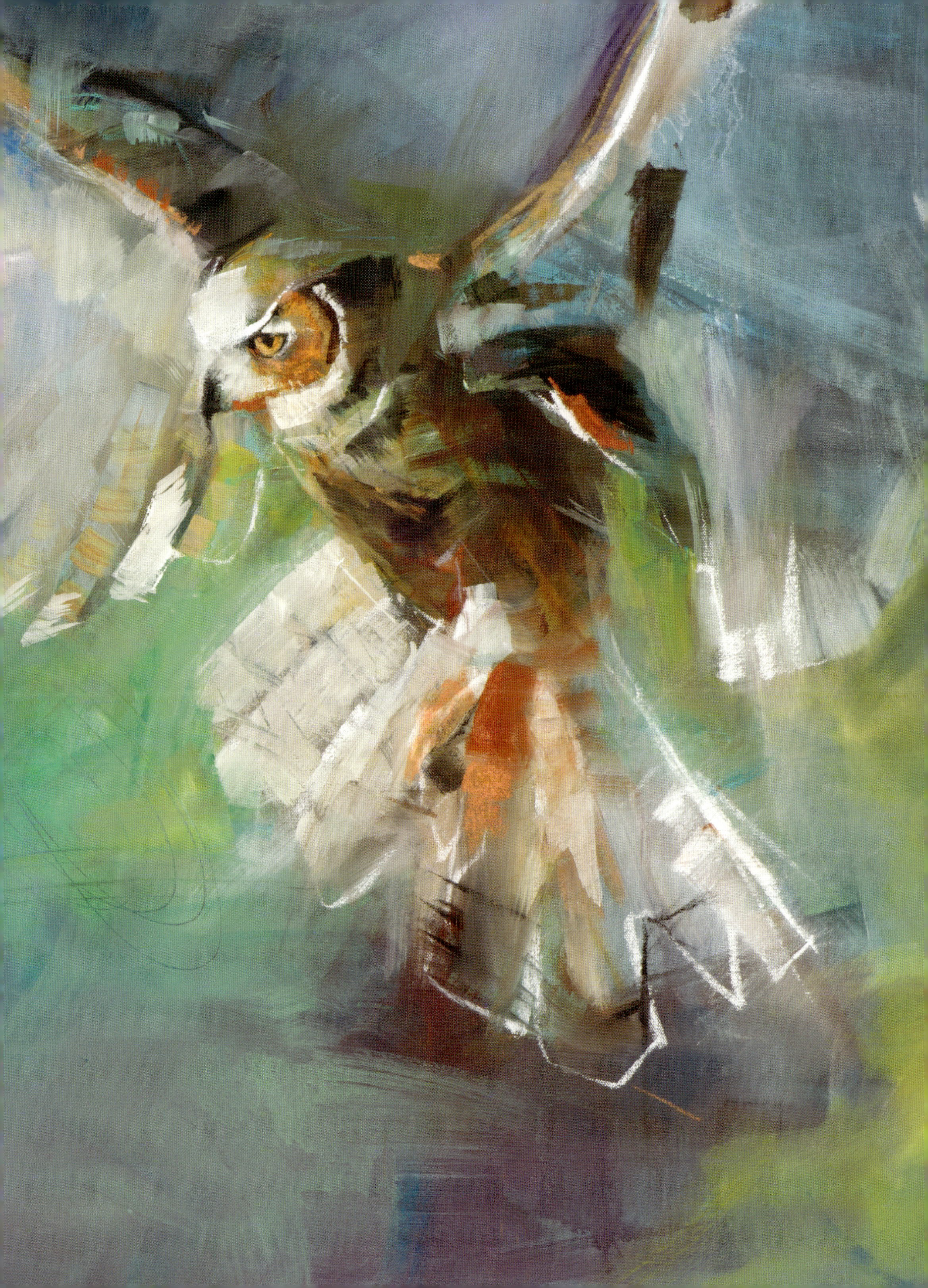

EXPLORE NEW WAYS OF DRAWING

Students of drawing are often limited by their exposure to drawing "methods." If challenged to produce fifty different versions of the same image, they might quickly exhaust their repertoire after ten or fifteen sketches. The drawings below demonstrate how the way you draw something alters the way you convey the impression of a subject. It is not a matter of describing more or less detail, but how you use the elements of line, shape, value, edges, texture, color and space that makes each person's art unique. Learning to draw never stops, and the artist is constantly on the lookout for new possibilities.

> ## THE SAME BUT DIFFERENT
>
> Notice how each of these four quick sketches of the subject conveys a completely different quality of mood and space. Instead of one sketch done in 20 minutes, try doing four 5-minute sketches!

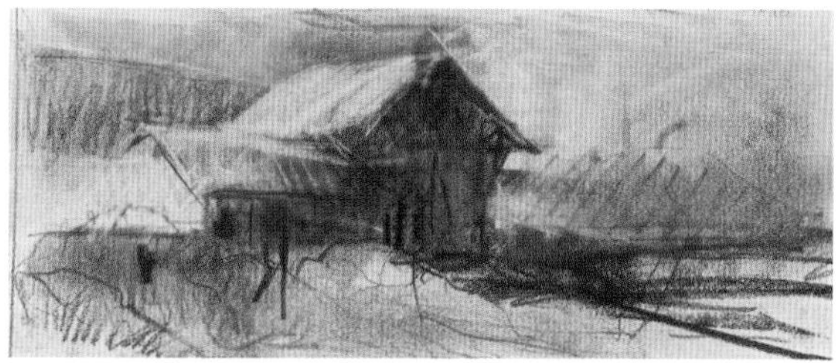

SKETCH 1

This drawing connects together dark values that convey a feeling of weight and heaviness. This image conveys deep space.

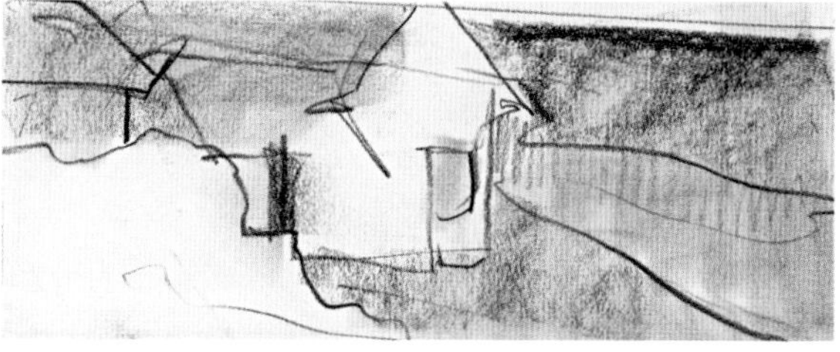

SKETCH 2

This drawing uses a loose line to enclose shapes and flat tone to set off the white space. As a result, the image conveys flattened space.

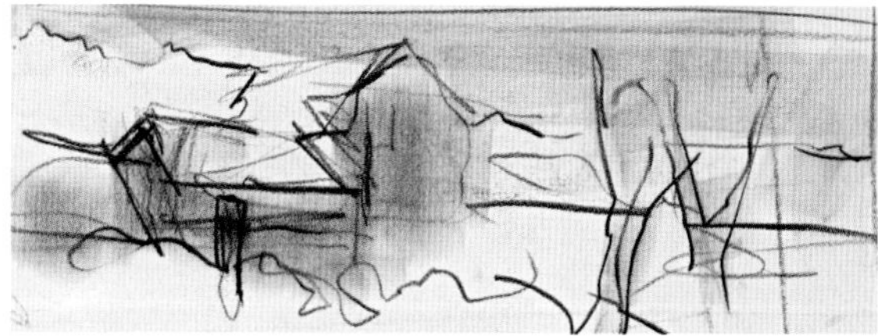

SKETCH 3

This drawing uses a gestural line with a little tone that conveys a kind of shorthand notation. The space is shallow but not completely flat.

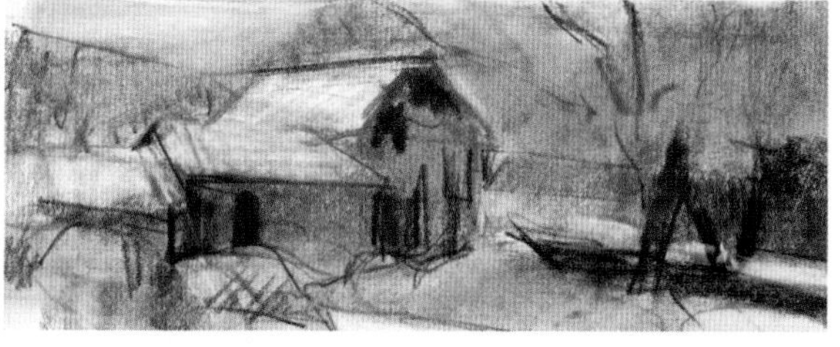

SKETCH 4

Because there is more dark than light in this image, the paths of light value seem to glow, changing the emphasis from the building to the roof. The image conveys deep space but a different mood than in sketch 1.

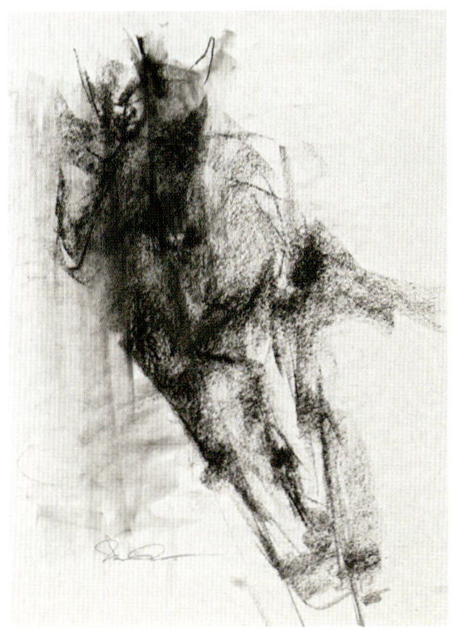

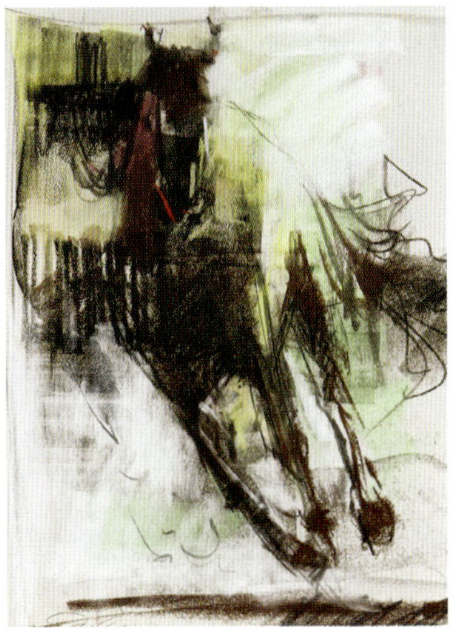

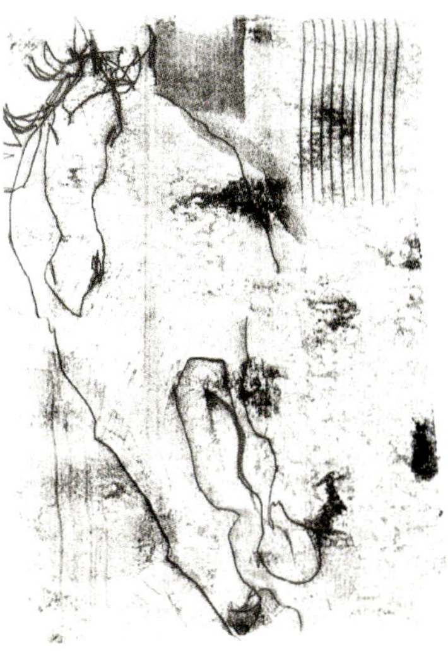

MASS GESTURE SKETCH

Use the side of the charcoal to quickly show form without line, using pressure and value to convey weight.

PASTEL AND BRAYER DRAWING

Create a background with brayer marks, and pull the image out of the background using as few colors as you can. Emphasize big shapes rather than details.

BLIND CONTOUR TRACE MONOTYPE

Set yourself up to do a trace monotype, but use a nonwriting tool like a knitting needle. Try not to peek until you are finished.

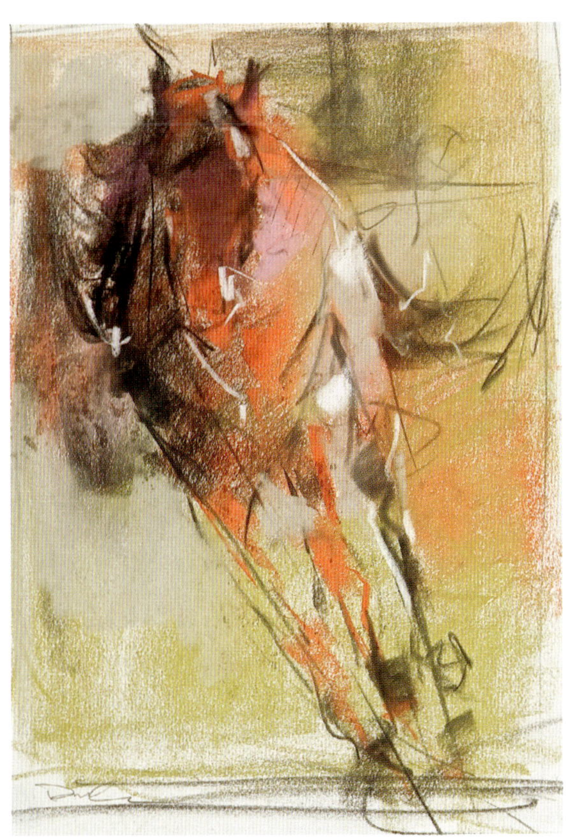

TIMER DRAWING

Using a timer can help you generate lots of quick sketches that have a simplicity and character to them that is hard to match. Each of these drawings took 10 minutes or less.

PASTEL AND MASS GESTURE SKETCH

Do a mass gesture drawing using just a few colors of pastel. Develop the background simultaneously with the figure.

THE FIVE FORMATS

The five formats are a tool to help you find unusual compositions. These formats are square, horizontal, vertical, strong horizontal and strong vertical. The point of this exercise is to draw one single subject or scene five times, each different from the others. You should not be merely "cropping" the photo five times, but redrawing. Each time you draw the image you will become more familiar and comfortable with it. I do these quick sketches to find new and different composition options. These sketches are more like footprint-sized sketches than tiny thumbnails because I want to have room to move my hand on the paper, and to feel the shape of the space. In footprint sketches, the midtones matter, as does the relationship between the negative and positive shapes. The brayer and General's Charcoal are both great tools for this exploration. It's the process of making a lot of images that don't work that will allow you to recognize when you've got one that does.

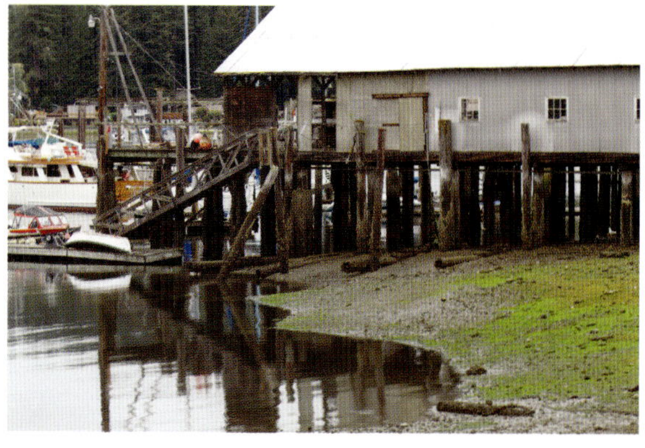

PHOTO REFERENCE

This is the photograph I took of the location that is shown in these composition sketches. Which of these seems to be most interesting to you? Choose your own photo to sketch with these formats, or use this one to explore other options. When you find one that works, do five more with different color options.

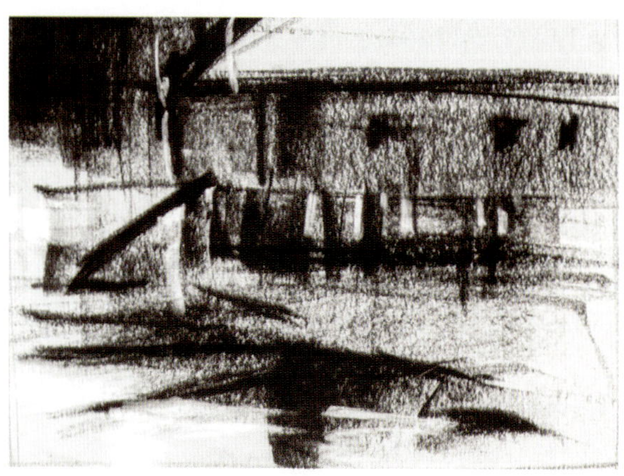

THE LANDSCAPE FORMAT

The actual size of the sketch should be a minimum of 6" × 8" (15CM × 20CM). Use charcoal. The ratio of height to width is 3:4.

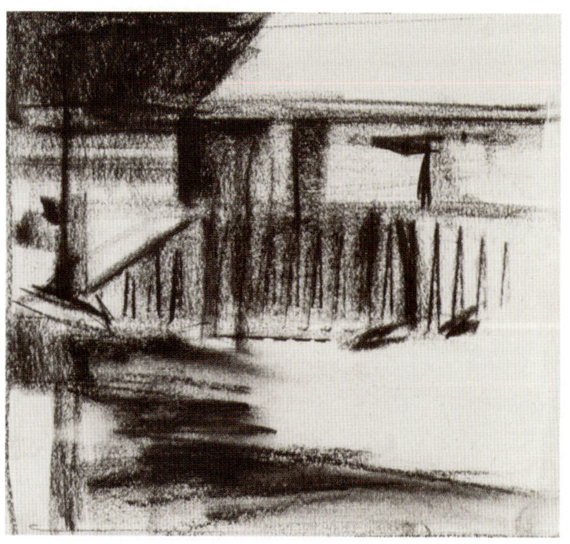

THE SQUARE FORMAT

The actual sketch should be a minimum of 6" × 6" (15CM × 15CM). Use charcoal. The ratio of height to width is 1:1.

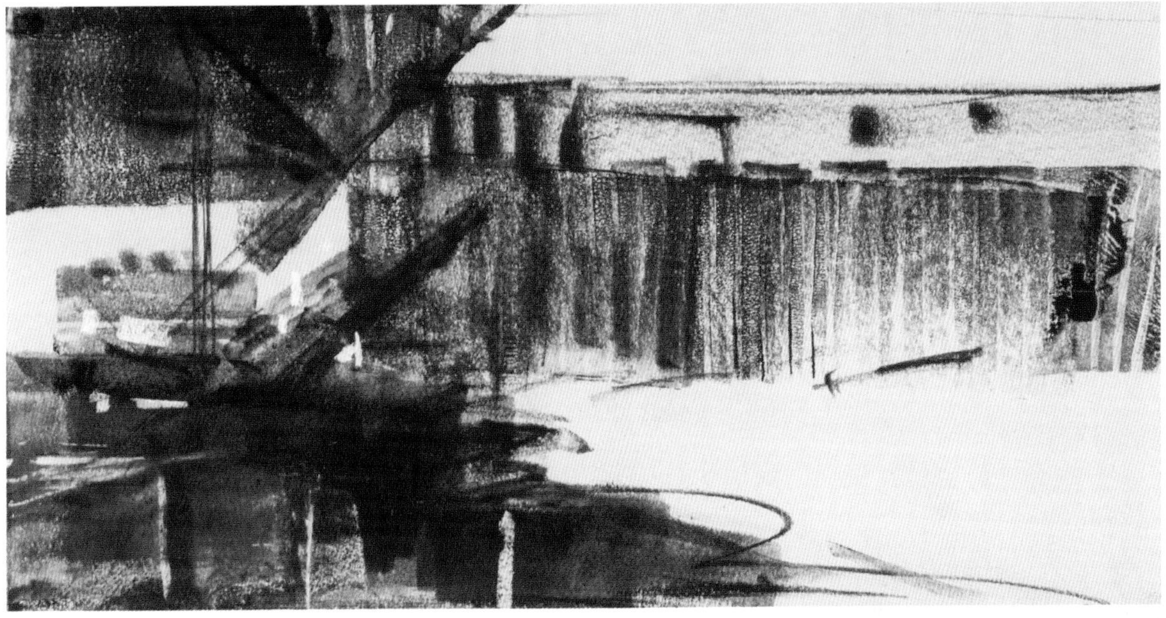

QUESTIONS FOR SELF-CRITIQUE

Compare each of the five formats by asking yourself the following questions:

- Which edges of the borders did you use? Did it change with each format?
- How do each of the formats create visual tension?
- In which format did you create the fewest negative shapes? The most?
- How does each format change the feeling of space?

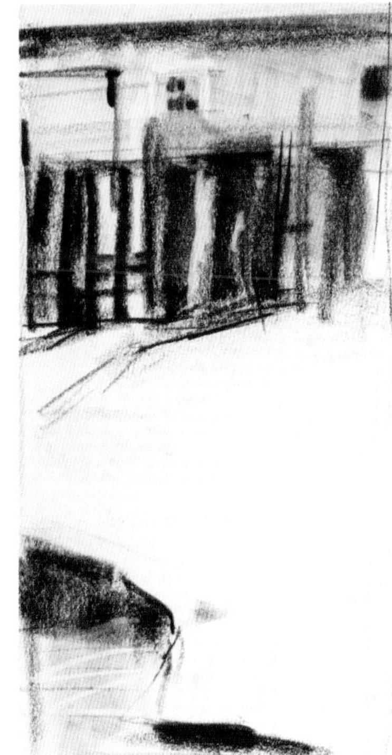

THE EXTREME PORTRAIT FORMAT

The actual size of the image should be a minimum of 12" × 6" (30CM × 15CM). Use charcoal. The ratio of height to width is 2:1.

THE EXTREME LANDSCAPE FORMAT

The actual size of the image should be a minimum of 6" × 12" (15CM × 30CM). Use charcoal. The ratio of height to width is 1:2.

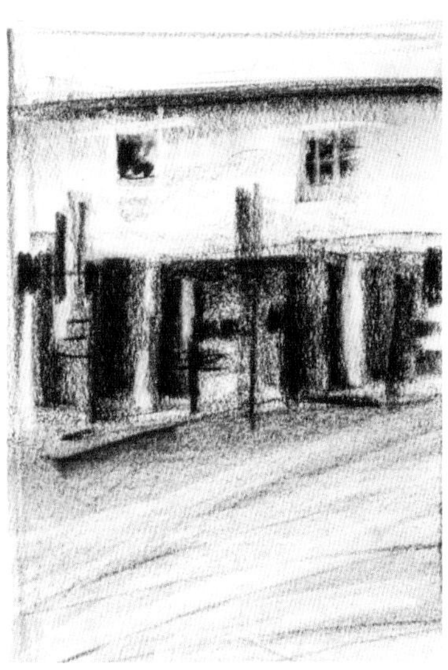

THE PORTRAIT FORMAT

The actual size of the image should be a minimum of 8" × 6" (20CM × 15CM). Use charcoal. The ratio of height to width is 4:3.

PAINTINGS WITHIN PAINTINGS

Nearly every good photographic reference has possibilities within it for more than one painting. Taking photo references is about gathering resources. Yet so often I see students taking photos that limit the possibilities for making more than one painting. When something attracts your attention, take photos of the subject with its environment. The environment can provide textures, shapes, lines and colors that may evolve into abstracted imagery that you can weave into the layers of your painting. You can find other painting possibilities within that image by cropping with the five formats and zooming in and out of the image. If you crop too closely to begin with, you won't have that information to weave into your imagery later.

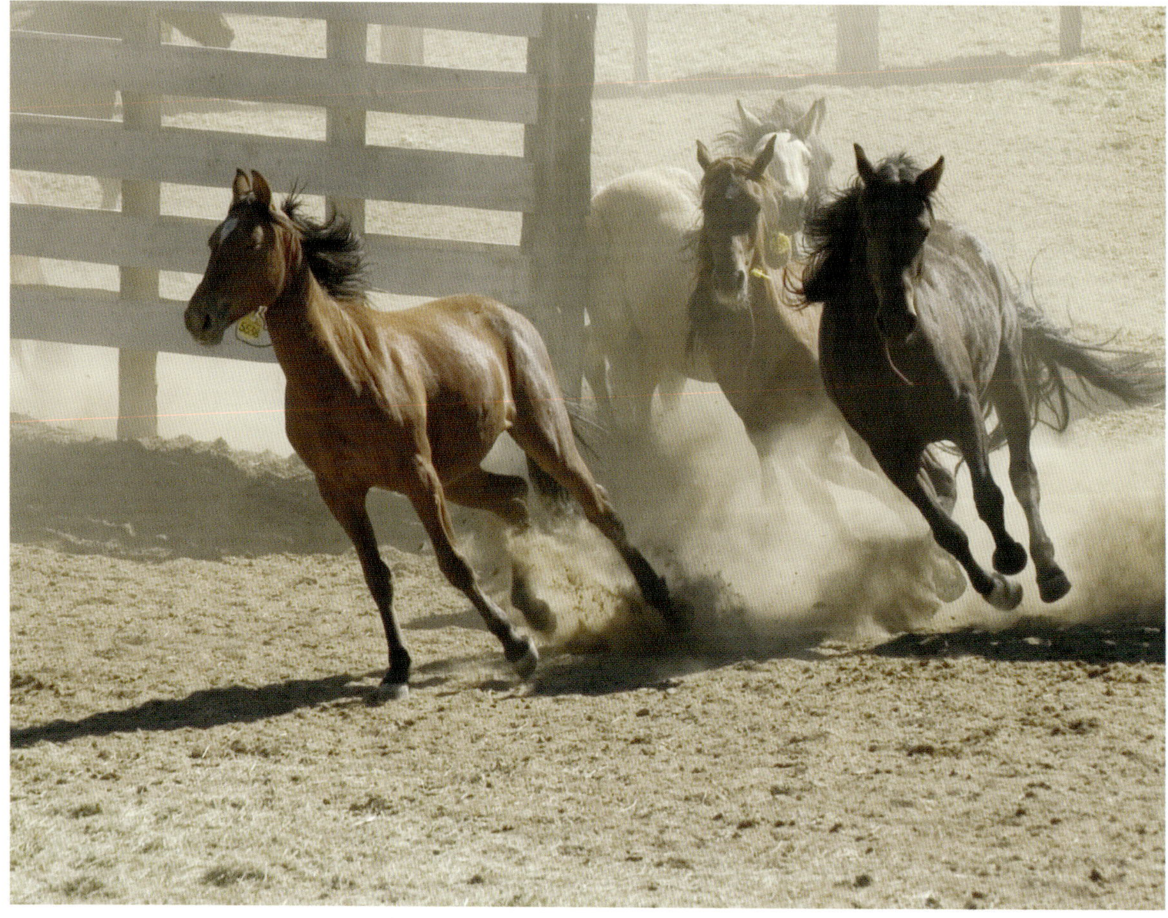

PHOTO REFERENCE
I took this photo at a round up of wild horses.

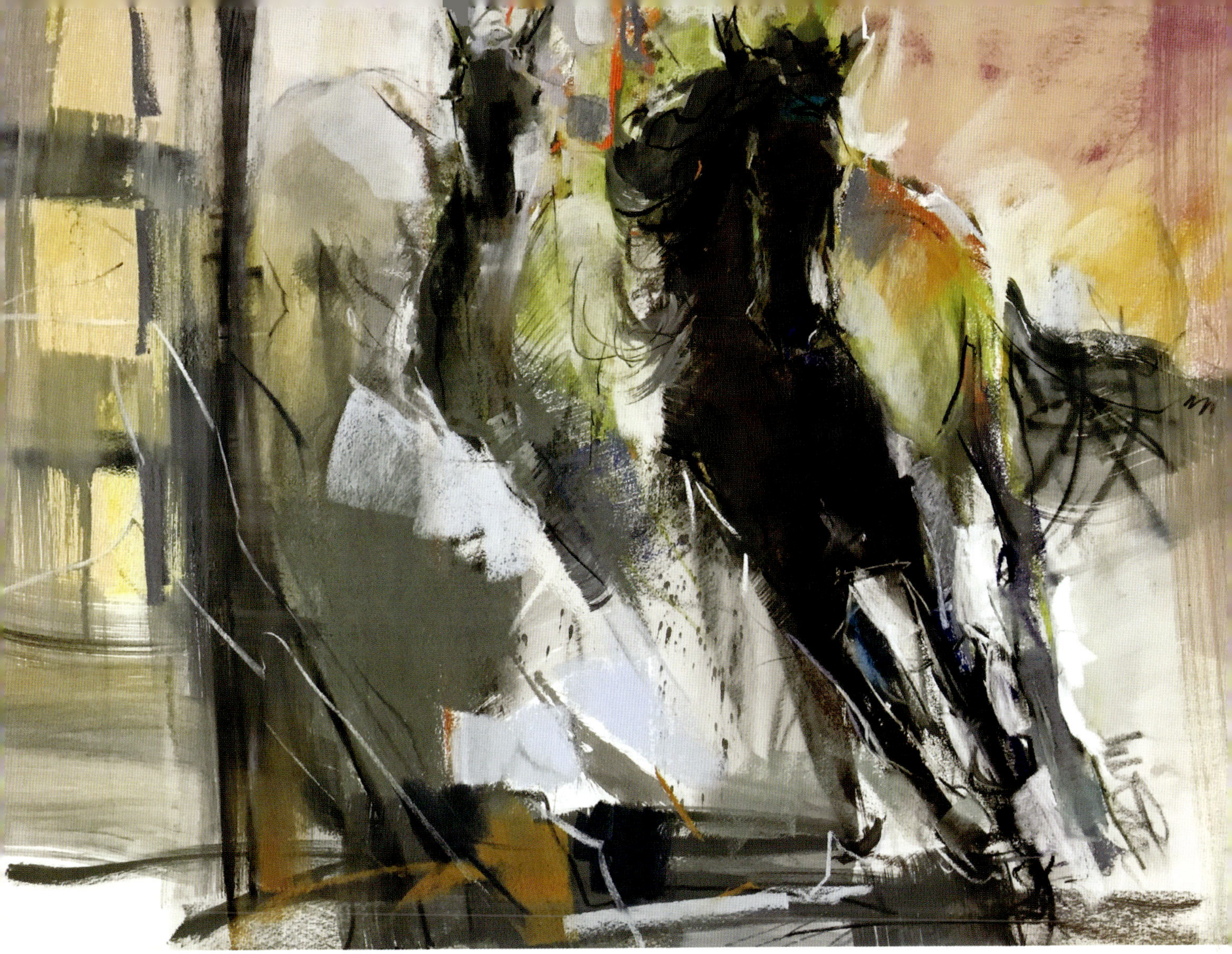

FIRST OUT THE GATE! / 22" × 30" (56CM × 76CM) / PASTEL AND MIXED MEDIA ON RIVES BFK PAPER

Notice how cropping in closely changes the energy of the piece and involves the viewer in a more immediate way. The abstract negative light blue shape to the left of the front horse is an echo of the shape of the front horse. This wasn't planned but was a result of responding to the shape of the dirt kicked up (rather than trying to depict the dirt itself).

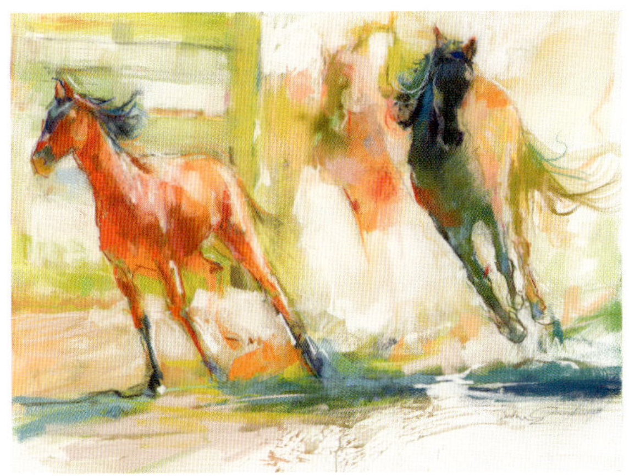

FREEDOM RUN / 22" × 30" (56CM × 76CM) / PASTEL AND WATERCOLOR ON STONEHENGE PAPER

Pulling back on the cropping creates an entirely different quality of space. There is more tension between the horses and a deeper feeling of space. The emphasis here is on the light around the horses rather than on the energy of the front horse.

LESS IS MORE

Students often tell me they have difficulty knowing when to stop painting or recognizing that their painting is finished and perfect as is. We've all struggled with this and at one time or another killed a painting with detail until the gestural feeling that made it special to begin with is gone. Students tell me they think the solution is to "loosen up." I suggest that if you start a painting with big shapes and hold onto those large shapes as long as possible, you can avoid the "too-many-mini-shapes massacre." Large shapes have power and energy—they dominate a space and make a statement. Smaller shapes should support the big shapes.

Small shapes are descriptive, and the smaller the shape, the more detail you are creating. If you go right to the tiny shapes too soon, you lose track of the big shapes and break up all that energy, like stabbing a hose with a knife. The power leaks away and you're left with a nongusher. We love paintings that gush (not leak) with power and movement!

In order to keep from focusing on the details too soon, keep in mind the hierarchy of information and the size of shapes you are making. You want the viewer to discover shapes within shapes and to enjoy the process of looking. Yes, the details need to be a part of the story, but not the whole story. Set a timer for 30 minutes for each piece you work on, and then take a photo of your work every 5 minutes. When you review the images, you will see when you started to "fuss," and when you should have stopped. Like the fish that got away, if you don't document your progress, you'll only imagine how great your painting could have been!

CRIMSON HOODOO / 10" × 8" (25CM × 20CM) / PASTEL AND SUMI INK ON RIVES BFK PAPER

Done on site, this was one of those little paintings that painted itself. I didn't try to copy what I was seeing; I just put down marks and shapes of color. It says everything there is to say with a minimum of detail.

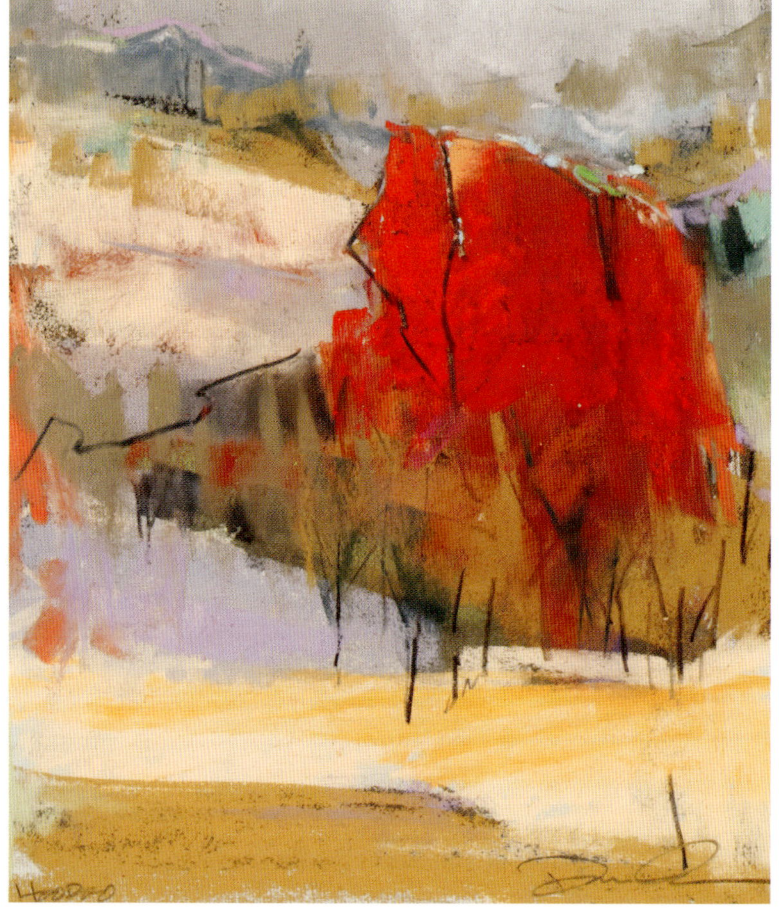

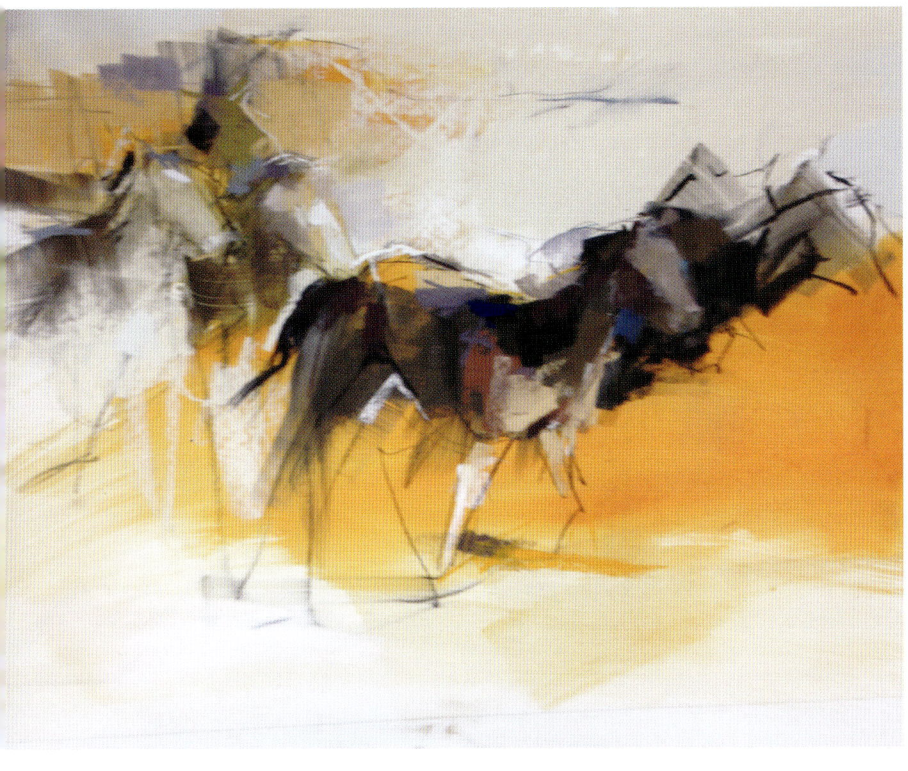

FALL IN THE CANYON / 24" × 36"
(61CM × 91CM) / CHARCOAL AND
PASTEL ON WALLIS PAPER

This painting says everything I want
to say. It captures the essence of
the horses and the canyon with no
detail whatsoever.

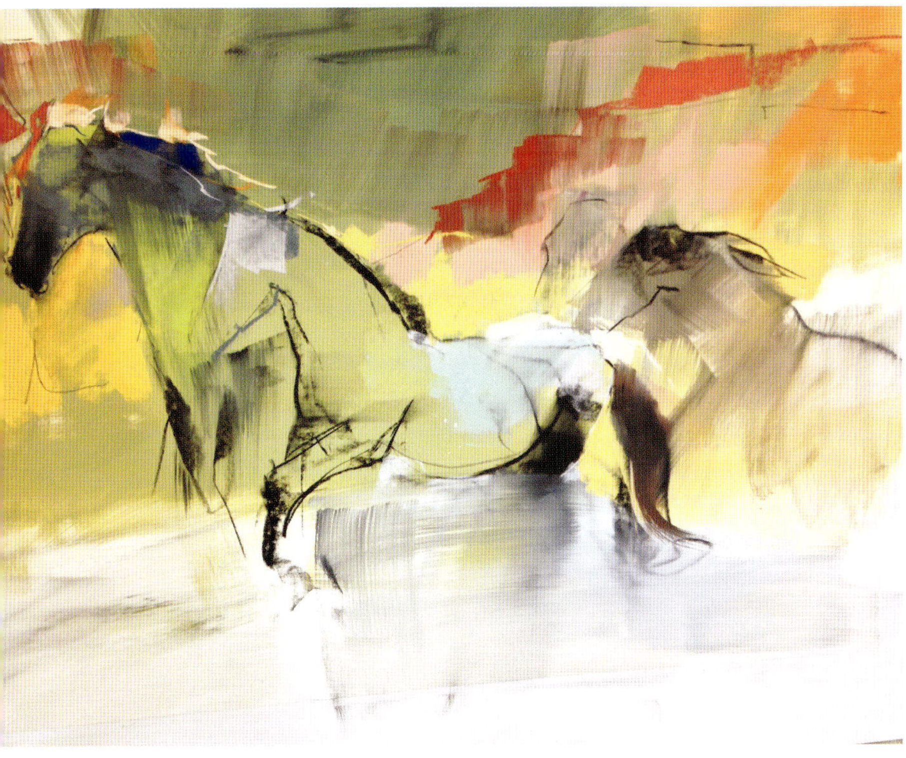

SPRING IN THE CANYON / 24" ×
36" (61CM × 91CM) / CHARCOAL AND
PASTEL ON WALLIS PAPER

I enjoy the energy in the calligraphic
black marks and the feeling of
openness and space that is implied
rather than described.

DOCUMENT YOUR PROCESS

I cannot overstress the value of documenting your work as you paint in the studio. As soon as you wonder what to do next, that is the time to pick up the camera and shoot.

When you document your process, you will have physical evidence of the steps you took to get you to your result. When you review your process, you may be surprised to see how many times along the way you could have stopped. This is such a helpful way to learn from yourself. It's the only way I know of to literally see the choices you've made and to see the possibilities you may not have noticed.

Very often we keep going because we don't know what to do or because we think we should put more time in. More often than not, the painting could have been "done" long ago; we just didn't recognize it. My philosophy is that it's better to stop early, and to stop often. As soon as I wonder if I should stop, I try to remember to ask myself how adding more of anything at that moment will make the piece better. I'll check in with the lists of elements and principles and take inventory. If colors cross forms, if lines move in and out of space in intriguing ways, and edges have beauty and variety, I can trust that it's a good time to stop—at least for a while!

STEP 1: PRINT MONOTYPE BACKGROUND

I began by creating a monotype of the pond floor using Akua Intaglio inks on Stonehendge paper. I will want to keep the textures of the monotype visible throughout the painting process, and documenting the image as I go will be a good way to check myself.

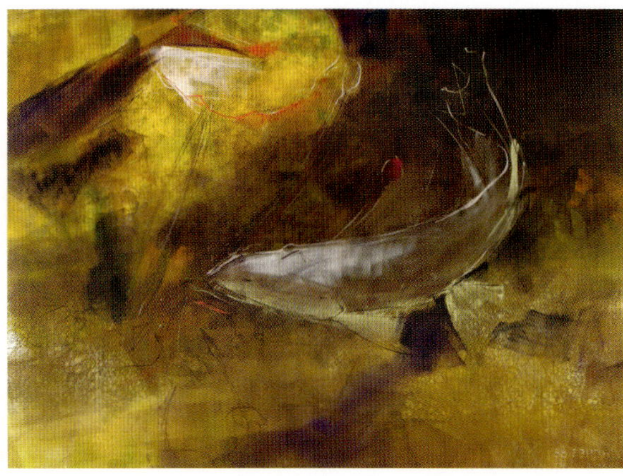

STEP 2: ESTABLISH SUBJECT PLACEMENT

Very light touches of pastel lines were added to "pull" the fish out of the background and establish placement. Note how the fish looks almost transparent at this point. Though it's difficult to stop to take a photograph, it's fun to be able to see how the image developed.

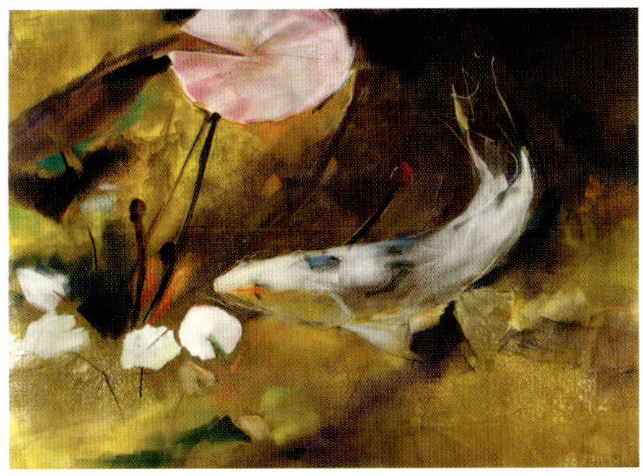 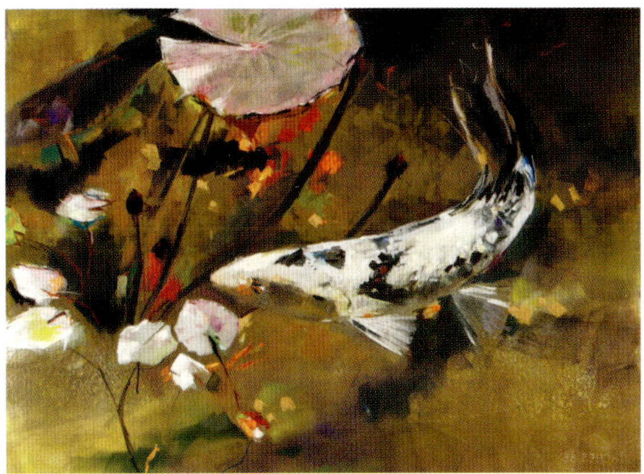

STEP 3: PRINT MONOTYPE BACKGROUND

I added more pastel color and took another photo. When I'm working on a painting it's almost impossible to see objectively. Looking at a small image in a photograph is almost like looking at someone else's painting, which keeps my ego out of it. I see here that the fish appears soft and murky, and that it could use some edge sharpening and a little more definition.

STEP 4: ESTABLISH SUBJECT PLACEMENT

This is the final after darkening shadows, muting the lily pad, sharpening some edges, and adding a few color notes. Having documented the process along the way allows me to replay the evolution of the painting, and helps me see where I might have stopped earlier in places. What do you think?

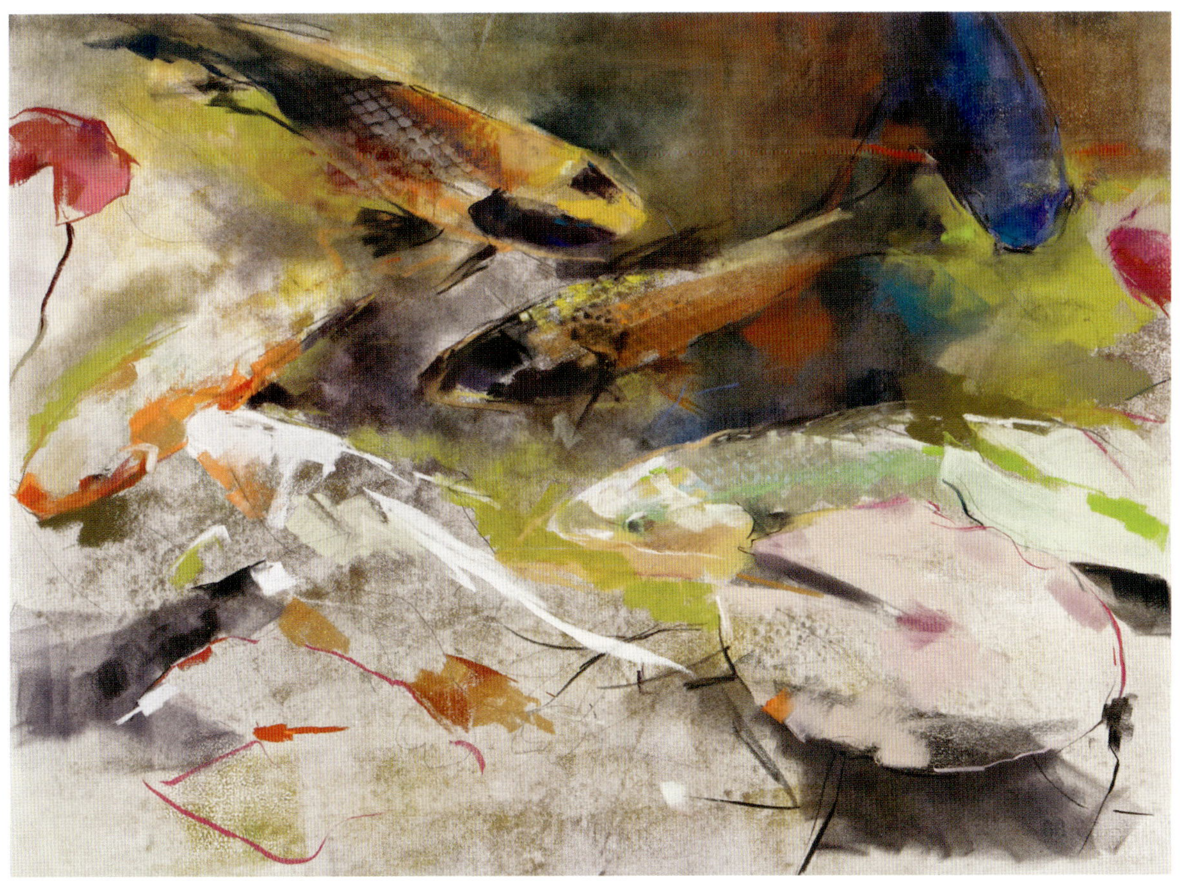

KOI / 22" × 30" (56CM × 76CM) / PASTEL MONOTYPE ON STONEHENGE PAPER

PUSH VALUE AROUND

To start this series of drawings I removed the distraction of color by converting a reference photo to black and white. I drew the image five times in a horizontal format, rearranging the grouping of value shapes each time. As you can see, sometimes there is much more light than dark, sometimes vice versa. This process pushes me to make new design decisions based on shape and value each time. I am not constrained by the values in the photo, which only shows the lighting at the moment the photo was taken. My choices have everything to do with which areas I wish to push back and which I choose to pull forward. Imagine you have a magic wand that rearranges the light and shadow on the reference. This approach can help you become more confident in your design and composition skills and may open your mind to new possibilities.

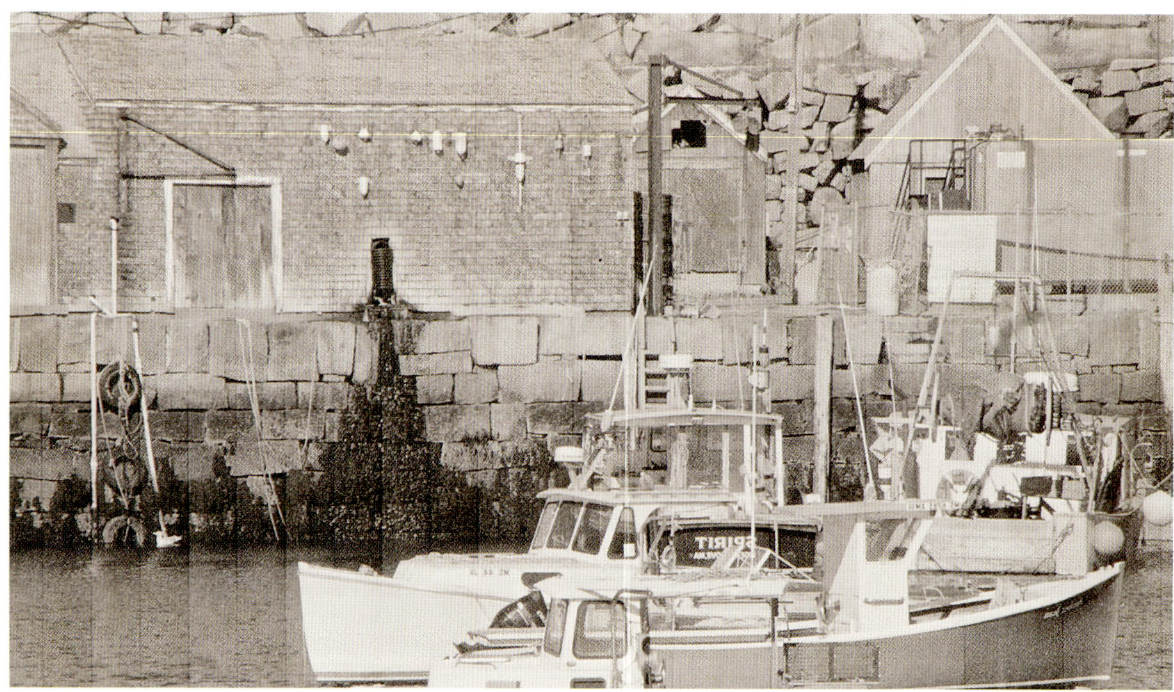

PHOTO REFERENCE
Near Halibut Point in Gloucester, Massachusetts.

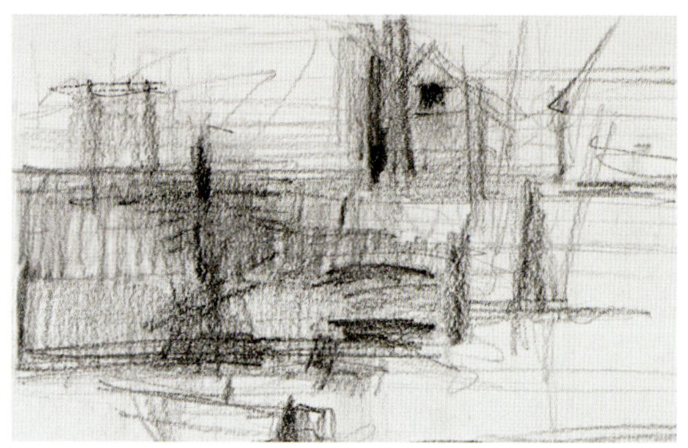

SKETCH 1
(6" × 9" [15CM × 23CM] graphite on paper)
Working from the photo reference, I used an ebony pencil to sketch the image with line and tone. As I developed the sketch, I paid special attention to the positive and negative shapes and the proportion of light to dark.

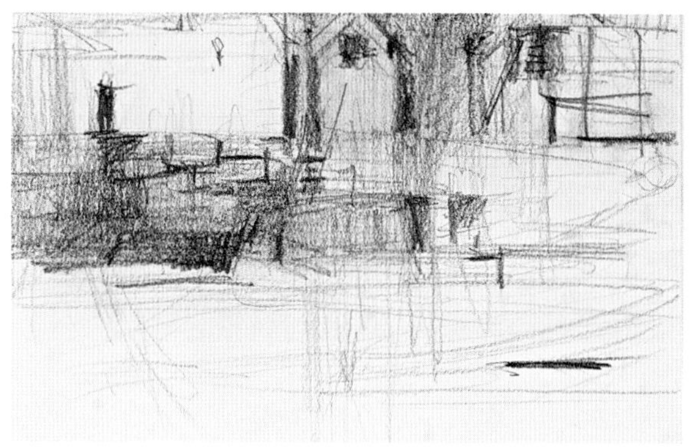

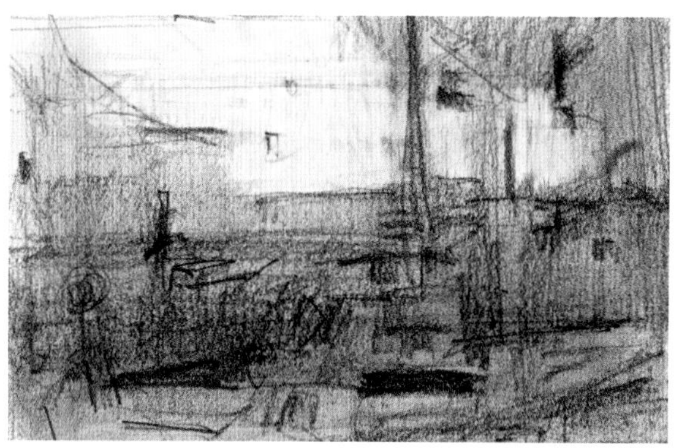

SKETCH 2

(6" × 9" [15CM × 23CM] graphite on paper)
I used the same ebony pencil but deliberately
changed the value distribution within the image. I
reconfigured shapes with value and put detail and
line in different places than in sketch 1. The boat in
the foreground almost disappears in this sketch.

SKETCH 3

(6" × 9" [15CM × 23CM] graphite on paper)
I darkened the image, changing the distribution of
values from more light to mostly dark. In so doing, I
created a totally different feel and emphasized the
white background shape.

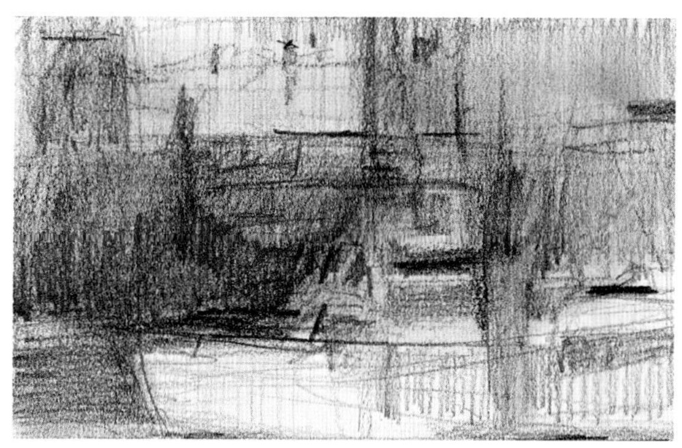

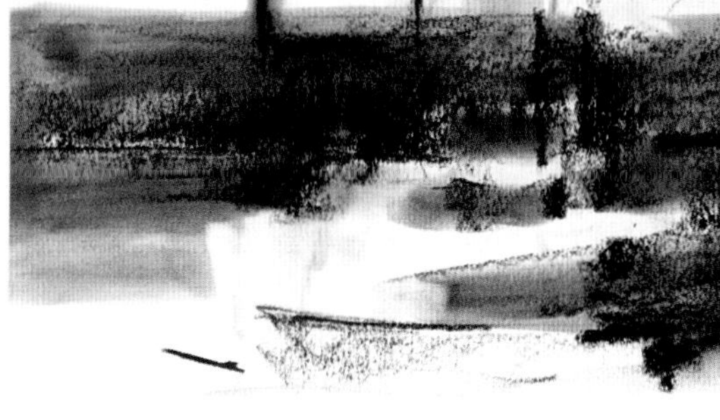

SKETCH 4

(6" × 9" [15CM × 23CM] graphite on paper)
Here I kept more dark than light but brought the boat
back into the foreground with light.

SKETCH 5

(6" × 9" [15CM × 23CM] charcoal on paper)
I changed from graphite to charcoal and was pleased
with the abstract beauty of this image. Because of the
contrast of value and the texture that can be created
with charcoal, I felt that the entire series brought me
to this one image. In other words, I could not have
made this image if I hadn't done all the ones before it.

SKETCH, SKETCH AND SKETCH SOME MORE

Do as many short sketches as you can
in order to get to the unexpected one
that you can't even imagine!

EDIT WITH HIGH CONTRAST

This series illustrates a process that I go through often in the studio. I select an image, do a quick value sketch and then photograph it. Even if the sketch appears dull, I convert the image to black and white and then boost the contrast. This often makes the structure of the image much more interesting and suggests design options I might not have thought of. When you push the contrast, light, thin lines that are used to separate forms become invisible, unnecessary details are eliminated, and dark shapes are allowed to merge together. Middle tones go either to the dark side or to the light end of the value scale. The relationship between positive and negative shapes becomes much more clear, and it is easier to see which elements are working harder than others.

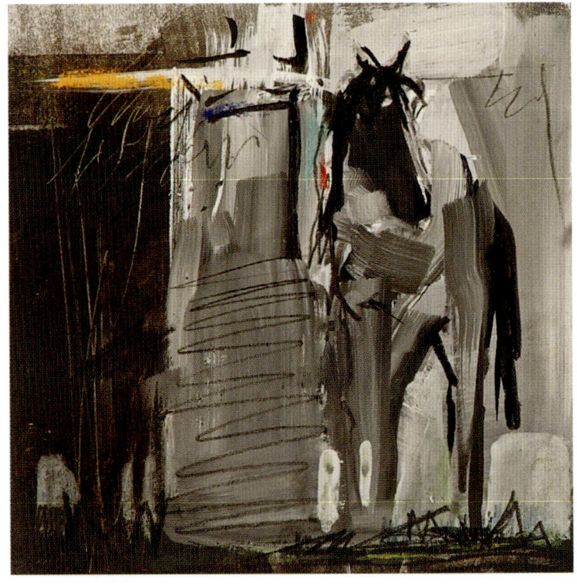

MIXED-MEDIA SKETCH

This is the 6" × 6" [15CM × 15CM] sketch I did from the Mustang reference. I used gouache, sumi ink and pastel.

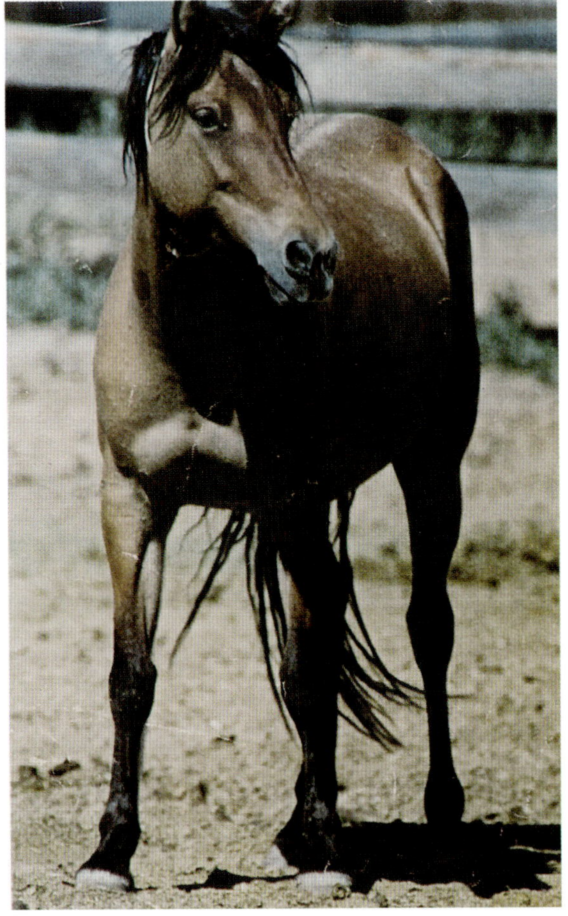

PHOTO REFERENCE

Mustang at the Wild Horse Corral in Burns, Oregon.

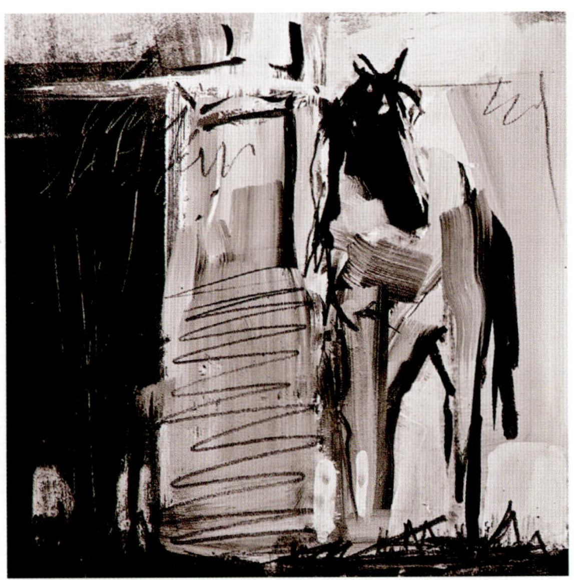

ENHANCE THE CONTRAST

By changing the distribution of values in PhotoShop, I can see that the image needs more contrast.

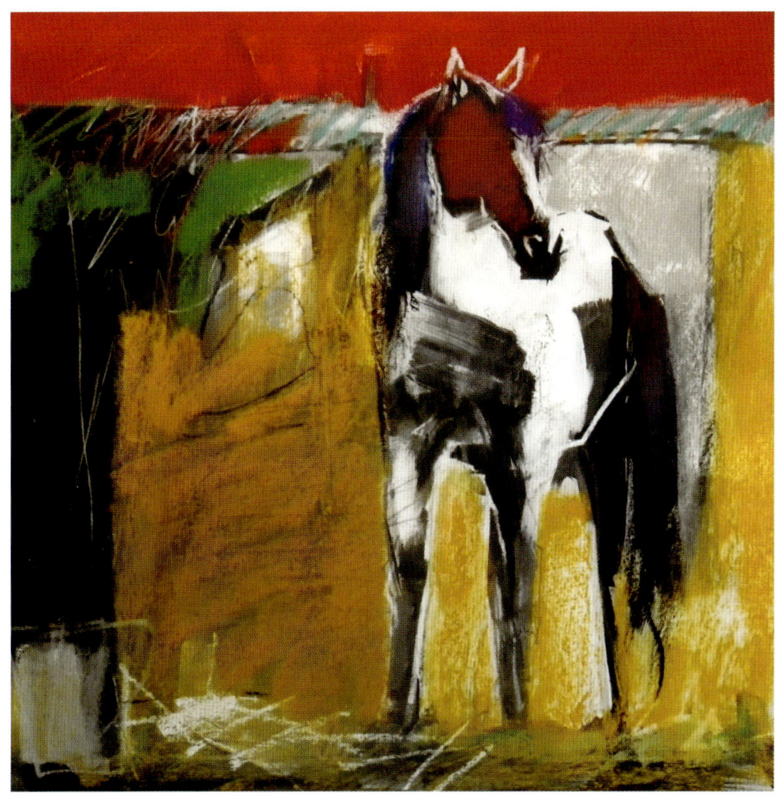

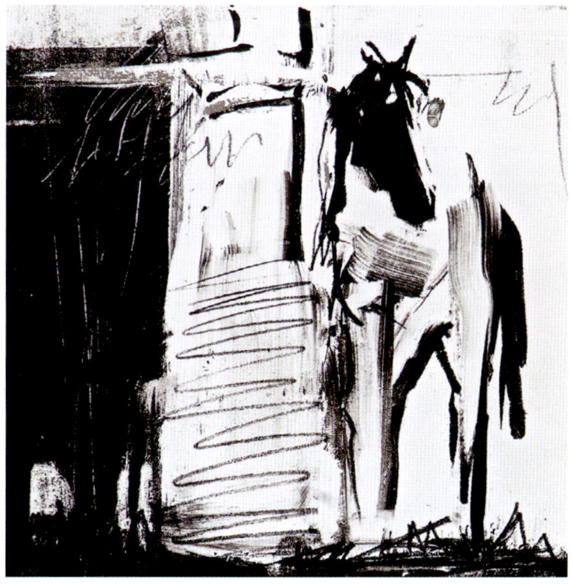

INVERT THE VALUES

What was white becomes black and vice versa. It is often a pleasant surprise to see the inversion, which offers yet another way to interpret the same image.

PUSH THE CONTRAST FURTHER

When the middle tones are eliminated, the guts of the image really show up. Minus unnecessary detail, all that is left is shape and line, the essence of the image.

CREATE MULTIPLES

A good way to explore color is to make multiple copies of a black-and-white sketch on which you can try out different color combinations. The easiest way to do this is to photocopy a line drawing. (I'd suggest making at least ten copies on card stock.) Because you don't have to redraw the image each time, you are free to explore color with whatever medium you choose. I find that watercolor, color pencil and gouache are easy to transport and provide different qualities of transparency and opacity. These little sketches are like seeds for much larger paintings later on.

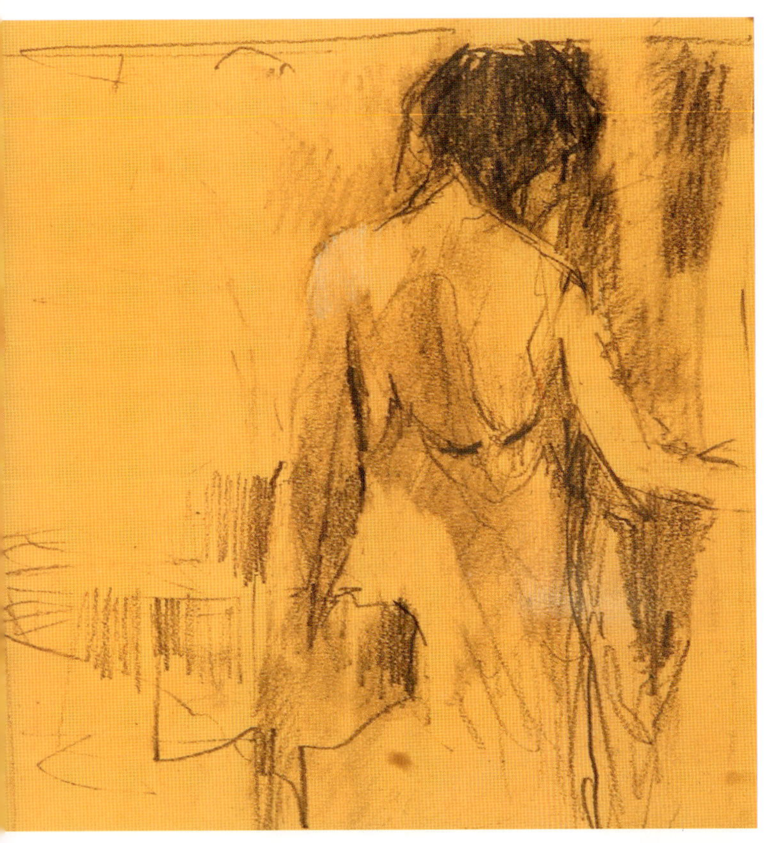

ORIGINAL SKETCH, 12" × 12" (30CM × 30CM), ON ORANGE PAPER
This is the original sketch I did from the photograph with ebony pencil.

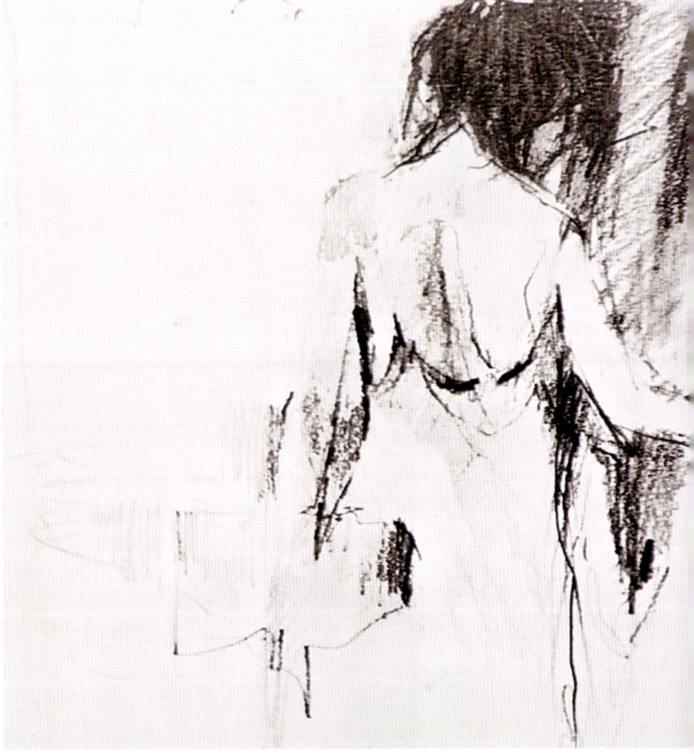

HIGH-CONTRAST PHOTO OF THE DRAWING
I photographed the drawing and skewed the contrast to eliminate light lines. I then photocopied the image onto cardstock in black and white so I can add color to the image without having to redraw it each time. Normally I make about a dozen copies.

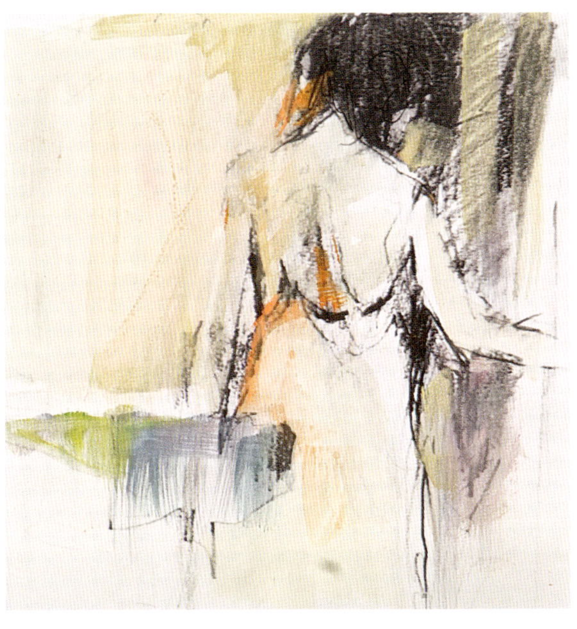 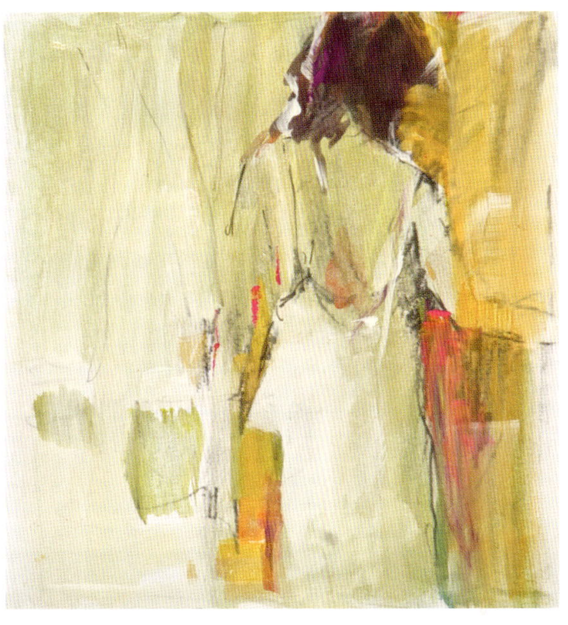

VERSION 1 OF BLACK AND WHITE PHOTOCOPY WITH COLOR ADDED

I painted this one with gouache and watercolor to try out different color combinations

VERSION 2 OF BLACK-AND-WHITE PHOTOCOPY WITH COLOR ADDED

Other color combinations using gouache and watercolor.

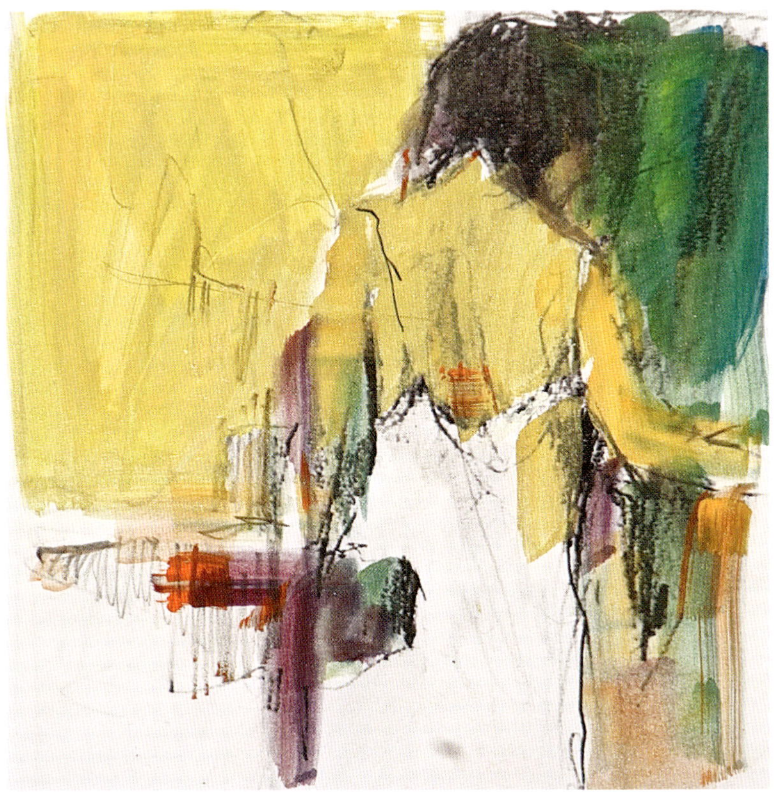

VERSION 3 OF BLACK-AND-WHITE PHOTOCOPY WITH COLOR ADDED

Final color combination using gouache and watercolor.

CONFRONT COLOR

For the longest time I painted with pastel on either white or lightly toned substrates. One day, I tried doing pencil sketches on bright orange cardstock and discovered how much fun it was. I bought other bright colors from the hobby store's scrapbooking department to do more sketches and was amazed at how dramatically my color choices were affected by each paper color. I would never have thought to use some of the colors that ended up inspiring me the most.

Up until then I had been using monotypes as abstract grounds but had never really considered using the ink to create a simple solid color. That was a game changer! This discovery pushed me outside of my comfort zone, and it can do the same for you. In fact, I encourage you create grounds in colors you actively dislike if you wish to grow. So much of my process is about confronting what I'm afraid of, and color was no exception.

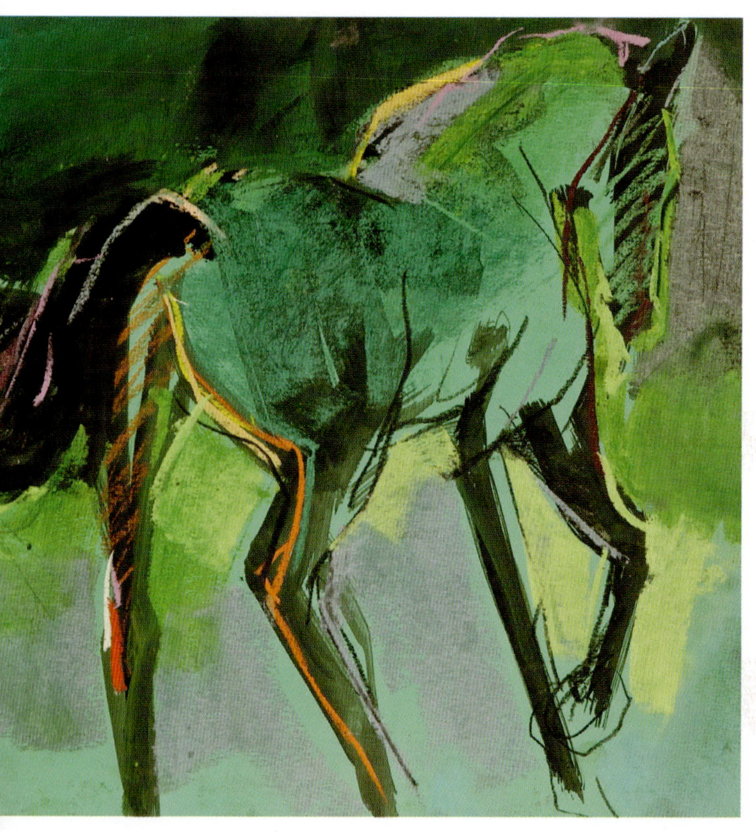

UNTITLED / 12" × 12" (30CM × 30CM) / PASTEL AND CLEAR GESSO ON GREEN PAPER

Using colorful scrapbooking paper from the hobby store is an inexpensive way to push your color vocabulary. It forces you to respond to the image based on color alone. Isolating the element of color in this way will surprise you, no matter what level of experience you have. It will also force you to use colors from your pastel box that you've never even thought of using!

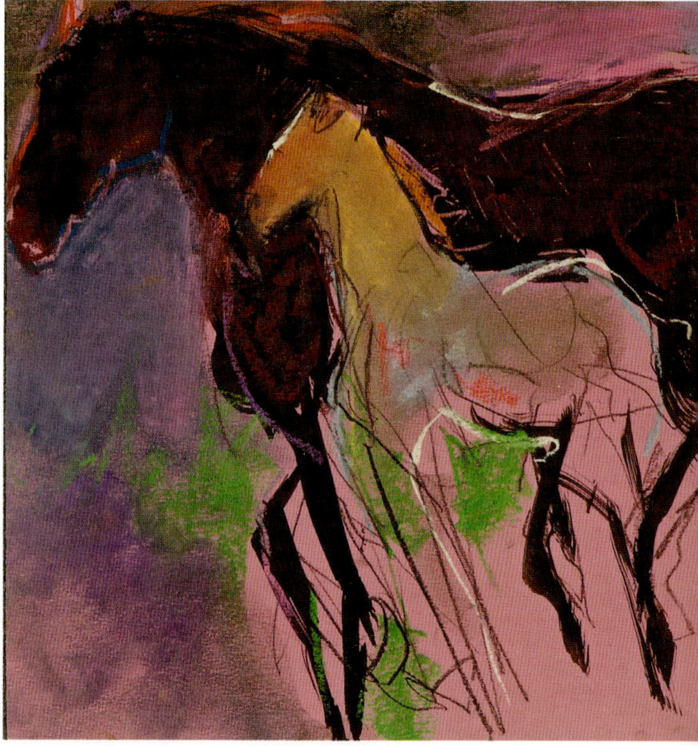

UNTITLED / 12" × 12" (30CM × 30CM) / PASTEL AND CLEAR GESSO ON MAGENTA PAPER

Using a brush with clear gesso helped me blend pastel into the paper and achieve subtle color changes. It was also very helpful to find a pastel the same color as the paper; this pastel became a "magic eraser" color that made errors disappear and brought unity to the image.

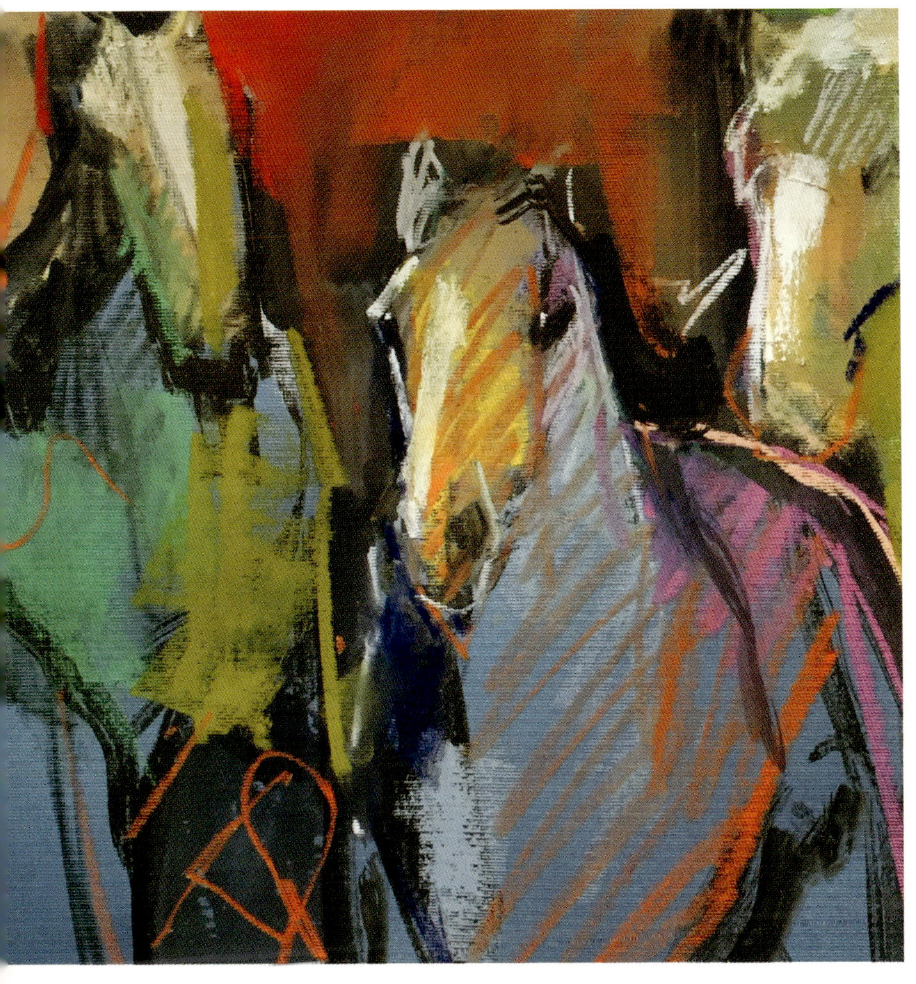

UNTITLED / 12" × 12" (30CM × 30CM) / PASTEL AND CLEAR GESSO ON ORANGE PAPER

You will expand your color choices and explore how complementary colors can make an image really pop if you draw on unusual color surfaces. Edgar Degas was a champion of using strong color papers for his grounds.

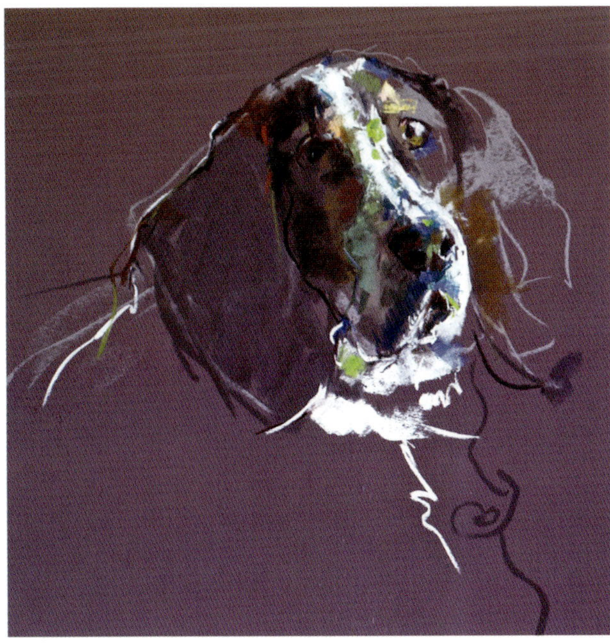

BASSETT / 17" × 17" (43CM × 43CM) / PASTEL ON MONOTYPE COLOR GROUND ON STONEHENGE PAPER

The darker the paper, the more light colors will show up. It is helpful to apply color gradually to a dark surface, starting with darker values.

PLAY WITH PIXELS

Technology is a wonderful tool, and I used it in every step of the way as I developed the content I have shared in this book. Digital technology allows you to photograph your work in progress, convert the images to black and white, enhance or suppress the contrast, skew the color way out of whack, and combine images together. It's exciting to instantly see options you hadn't even considered by altering any or all of the elements, and I wholeheartedly support this use of technology. That said, for me art is fundamentally a tactile, kinesthetic and emotional experience. I need to feel the pastel and smell the ink as I create a visual story or scene. My body physically moves and dances at the easel as I build the layers. A successful image is a physical record of my creative journey and the discoveries I made along the way. I encourage you to use technology as a tool, but not to be a slave to it.

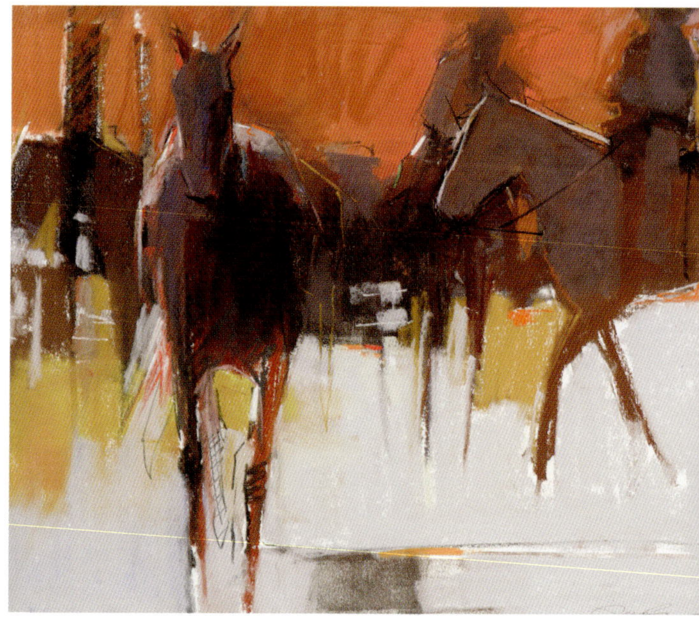

END OF DAY / 19" × 19" (48CM × 48CM) / PASTEL OVER OIL ON STONEHENGE PAPER

This is the way the painting looked when it was finished.

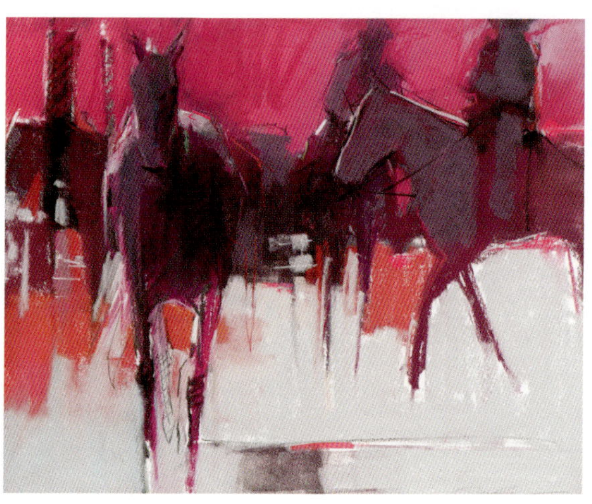

OPTION 1

I intensified the saturation and moved the color temperature to be a cooler pink.

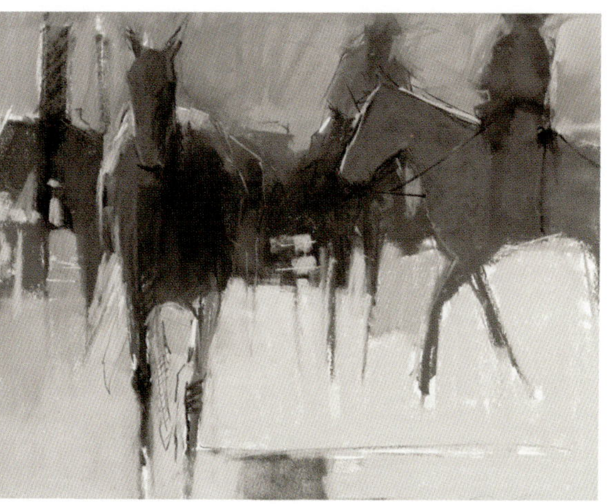

OPTION 2

I desaturated the image completely, making a black-and-white version.

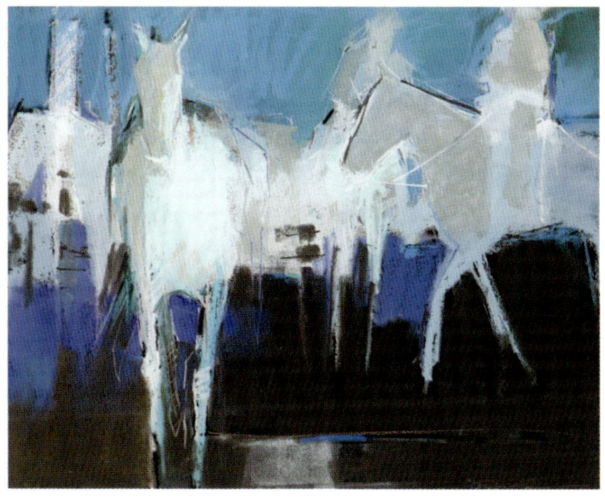

OPTION 3

I inverted the image and imposed monochromatic color on the image.

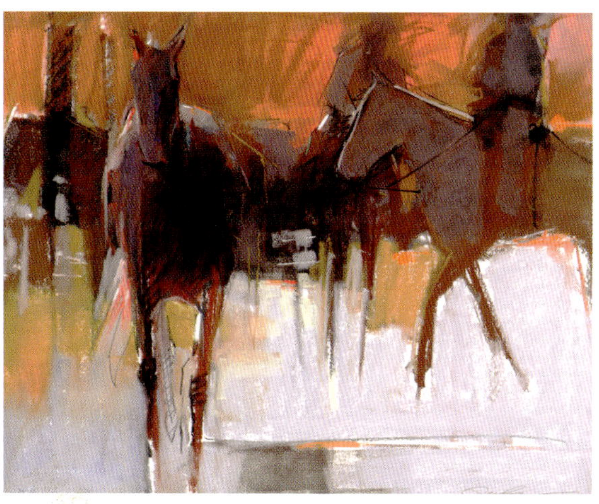

OPTION 4

The saturation of the original colors is intensified.

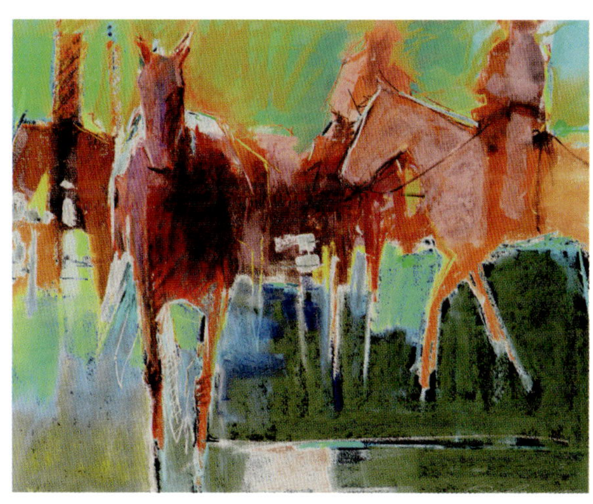

OPTION 5

Complementary colors are introduced.

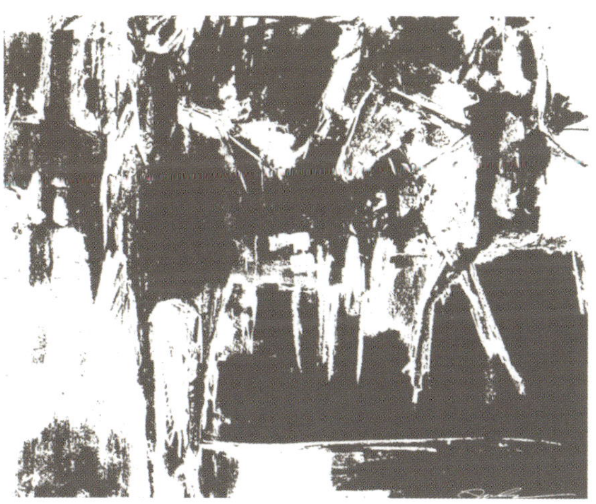

OPTION 6

A high-contrast image reveals new options for connecting shapes and values.

TECHNOLOGY IS A TOOL

The goal is to use technology as a tool to jolt our imagination, not to copy it.

BACK TO THE BEGINNING

For many years my husband and I practiced the martial art of Aikido. Often, we practiced the same technique hundreds of times in a single class. We tried to give our full attention to each effort, but we all know how easy it can be to lose focus during repetitive practice. This training carried over to my art and helped me realize that if I want to master something, I have to put in the time and give my attention to the experience and not the result. Only when you look back years later can you see where you were and realize how far you've come.

Going back to the basics is where I started at the beginning of this book, and it is where I return to at the end of each day in the studio. Even if nothing produced that day was worth saving, I ask myself what I learned about art, and I know that with each answer I have taken one small step along the path.

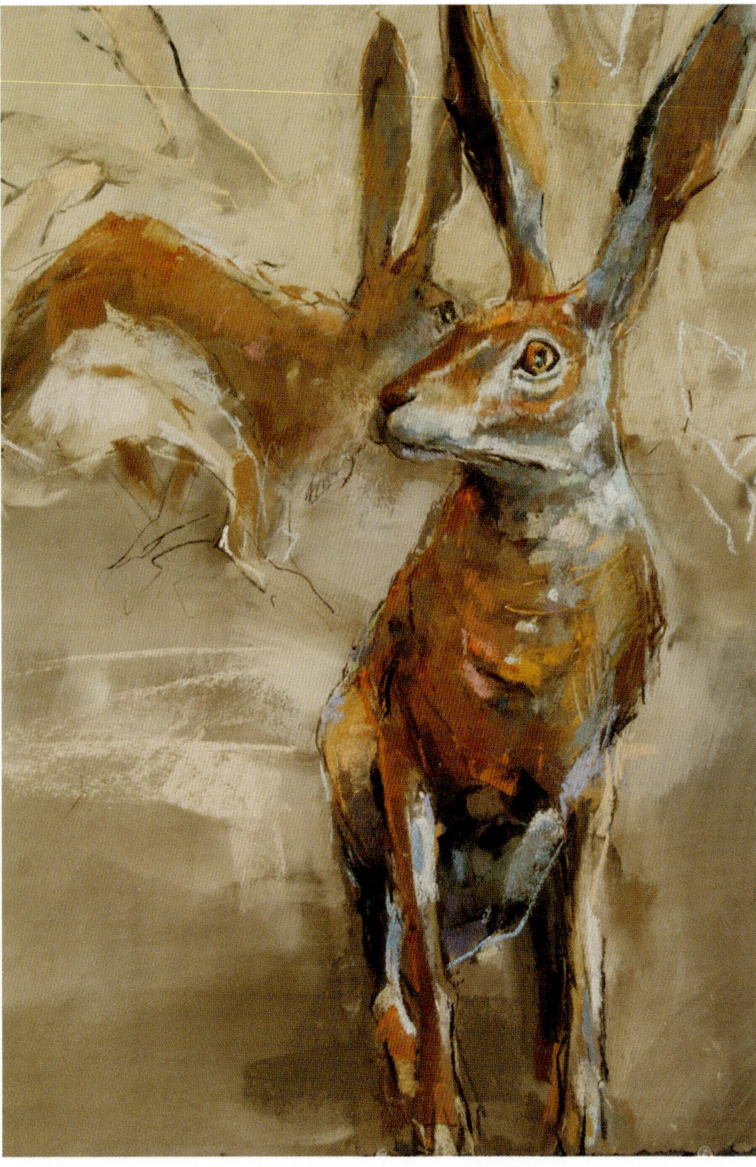

WHAT'S UP? / 76" × 71" (30CM × 30CM) / PASTEL ON RIVES BFK PAPER WITH GESSO-PUMICE GROUND

THE RABBIT STORY

When I first arrived in Oregon, I became an artist in residence in the local public school system. I designed art classes for kindergarten through high school and taught up to seven sessions a day. I taught the same topic to every age level. By the end of five years, I learned that if I could teach a kindergartner, I could teach anyone. The kindergarten kids became my teachers. They showed me how to enjoy painting and drawing and reminded me how to make the process come alive!

One day I brought rabbits along with some clay and pastels into a kindergarten class. The children observed and played with the rabbits as we talked about their shapes and sculpted them with fistfuls of clay. Then we set out to draw a picture of the rabbits with pastel. I sat down next to one child who asked for some help. When I looked to my right I saw a beautiful image of a large, colorful rabbit on the grass, a sky full of clouds behind it, and flowers blooming in front of it. I smiled thinking how wonderful it was, as I returned my attention to the child to my left. When I looked back to my right a minute later, the wonderful image of the rabbit had been obliterated. The little girl proudly held her chalk covered hands in front of her face, and smiled a huge, toothless smile. I stifled the urge to say NO and asked instead, "What happened?" She replied excitedly as she shrugged her shoulders, "He had to go!" She was totally involved in her story and the process and not at all attached to the product. I wish for you this same level of joy and engagement with your art.

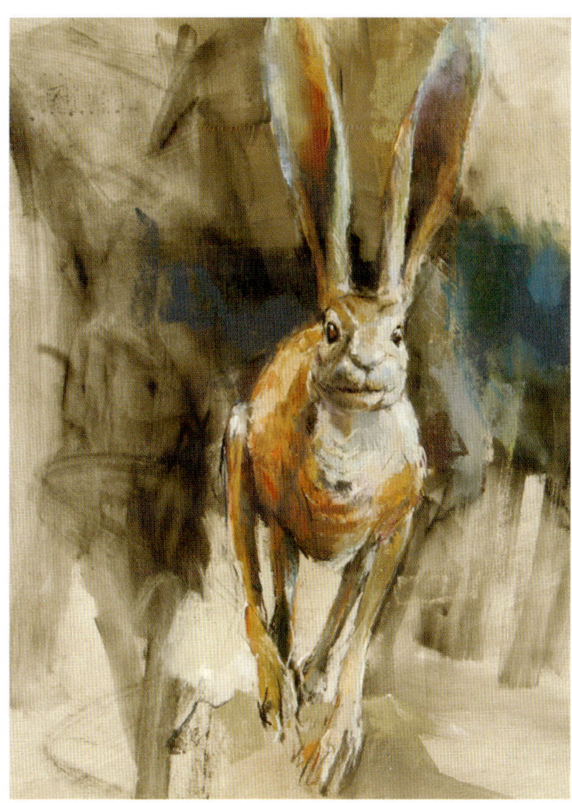

DARN RABBIT! / 30" × 28" (76CM × 71CM) / PASTEL ON RIVES BFK PAPER WITH GESSO-PUMICE GROUND

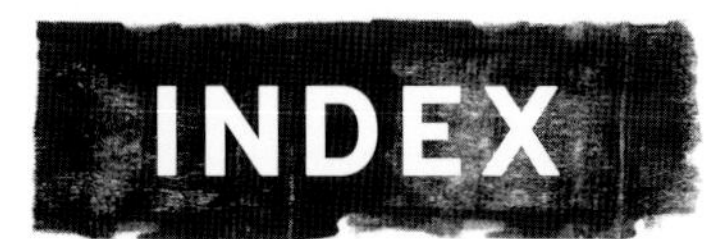

INDEX

ABOUT THE AUTHOR

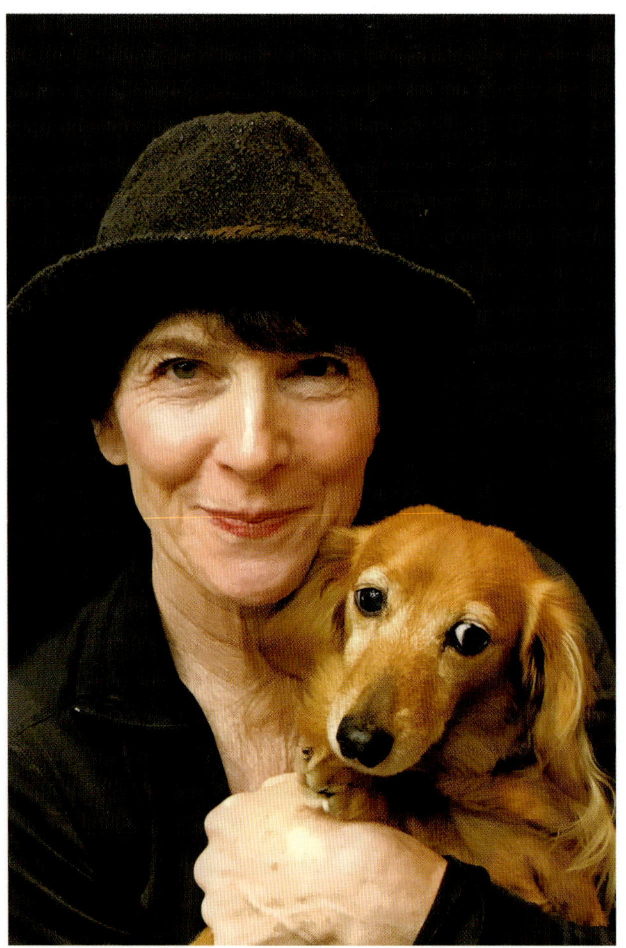

Dawn Emerson is an artist whose mission is to keep evolving and growing her art with a beginner's mind. Coming from an initial background in book design, she has explored other areas of art including graphic design, drawing, sculpture, printmaking, calligraphy and Chinese brush painting on her way to pastels and monotypes. Her bold use of color and facility with mixed media is present throughout her work. When her subject is animals and horses Dawn expresses a unique quality of energy, movement and emotion. She has received numerous awards for her pastels and mixed-media artwork and has been featured in several North Light books and publications. Dawn has been a signature member of the Pastel Society of America since 1997 and serves regularly as a judge and workshop instructor. When working with artists and students she seeks to inspire them, regardless of levels and ages, to look at the world of art in a way that is accessible and freeing. Her paintings are included in many private collections around the country. Dawn is represented by the Mockingbird Gallery in the beautiful high desert plateau of central Oregon, where she lives with her husband, Bruce, and an always changing collection of animals.

Visit **dawnemerson.com** for more.

Acknowledgments

I want to thank those teachers I've met in my life who have challenged me to do better than I thought I could: Iseri Sensei and Mulligan Sensei, from the days before I saw myself as an artist, to my art mentors Alex Powers, Skip Lawrence and Pat Clark, who taught me to think about drawing and imagery in a whole new way. I owe a special thanks to all the students I've had who have been my guides, my guinea pigs and my greatest inspiration. I thank the editors and designers at F+W who took this project on, and Gary Alvis for providing photo equipment and his expertise. Finally, I'd like to thank my family and friends for their encouragement and patience while I wrote.

Dedication

This book is dedicated to my amazing husband Bruce who knows me all too well but loves me anyway, to my generous friend Denali who kept us laughing, and to Lena, who snoozed peacefully through it all.

North Light Books
An imprint of Penguin Random House LLC
penguinrandomhouse.com

Printed in China
10   9   8   7

ISBN 978-1-4403-5046-7

Edited by Kristy Conlin
Designed by Jamie DeAnne
Photographs by Christine Polomsky